Psychological Interventions In Early Psychosis

Psychological Interventions in Early Psychosis

A TREATMENT HANDBOOK

Edited by

JOHN F.M. GLEESON AND PATRICK D. McGORRY

The University of Melbourne, Australia

John Wiley & Sons, Ltd

Other Wiley Editorial Offices

John Wiley & Sons Inc., 111 River Street, Hoboken, NJ 07030, USA

Jossey-Bass, 989 Market Street, San Francisco, CA 94103-1741, USA

Wiley-VCH Verlag GmbH, Boschstr. 12, D-69469 Weinheim, Germany

John Wiley & Sons Australia Ltd, 33 Park Road, Milton, Queensland 4064, Australia

John Wiley & Sons (Asia) Pte Ltd, 2 Clementi Loop #02-01, Jin Xing Distripark, Singapore 129809

John Wiley & Sons Canada Ltd, 22 Worcester Road, Etobicoke, Ontario, Canada M9W 1L1

Wiley also publishes its books in a variety of electronic formats. Some content that appears in print may not be available in electronic books.

Library of Congress Cataloging-in-Publication Data

Psychological interventions in early psychosis : a treatment handbook /
edited by John F.M. Gleeson and Patrick D. McGorry
    p.   cm.
Includes bibliographical references and index.
    ISBN 0-470-84434-5 (cloth)—ISBN 0-470-84436-1 (paper : alk. paper)
    1. Psychoses—Treatment.   2. Cognitive therapy.   I. McGorry, Patrick D.
    II. Gleeson, John.
RC512 .P7365   2003
616.89′14—dc22   2003022091

British Library Cataloguing in Publication Data

A catalogue record for this book is available from the British Library

ISBN 0-470-84434-5 (hbk)
ISBN 0-470-84436-1 (pbk)

Contents

About the Editors   vii
Contributors   ix
Foreword   xiii
Preface   xv

1 An Overview of the Background and Scope for Psychological Interventions
   in Early Psychosis   1
   Patrick D. McGorry

2 Changing PACE: Psychological Interventions in the Prepsychotic Phase   23
   Lisa J. Phillips and Shona M. Francey

3 Cognitive-Behavioural Therapy for Acute and Recent-Onset Psychosis   41
   Ron Siddle and Gillian Haddock

4 Psychological Intervention in Recovery from Early Psychosis:
   Cognitively Oriented Psychotherapy   63
   Lisa Henry

5 The Dynamics of Acute Psychosis and the Role of Dynamic Psychotherapy   81
   Johan Cullberg and Jan-Olav Johannessen

6 Working with Families in the Early Stages of Psychosis   99
   Jean Addington and Peter Burnett

7 A Group Psychotherapeutic Intervention During Recovery From
   First-Episode Psychosis   117
   Ashok K. Malla, Terry S. McLean and Ross M.G. Norman

8 Cannabis and Psychosis: A Psychological Intervention   137
   Kathryn Elkins, Mark Hinton and Jane Edwards

9 The First Psychotic Relapse: Understanding the Risks, and the
   Opportunities for Prevention   157
   John F.M. Gleeson

10 Suicide Prevention in Early Psychosis   175
   Paddy Power

11 Psychological Treatment of Persistent Positive Symptoms in Young People
   with First-Episode Psychosis   191
   Jane Edwards, Darryl Wade, Tanya Herrmann-Doig and Donna Gee

12 Cognitive Therapy and Emotional Dysfunction in Early Psychosis 209
   Max Birchwood, Zaffer Iqbal, Chris Jackson and Kate Hardy

**13 Principles and Strategies for Developing Psychosocial Treatments
   for Negative Symptoms in Early Course Psychosis** 229
   Paul R. Falzer, David A. Stayner and Larry Davidson

14 Making Sense of Psychotic Experience and Working Towards Recovery 245
   Rufus May

15 Psychological Therapies: Implementation in Early Intervention Services 261
   Gráinne Fadden, Max Birchwood, Chris Jackson and Karen Barton

Index 281

About the Editors

John F.M. Gleeson is currently Associate Professor in the Department of Psychology, The University of Melbourne and the Northwestern Mental Health Program (a program of Melbourne Health). His major research interests include secondary prevention in psychotic disorders, and he is currently the Chief Investigator of a randomized trial at EPPIC, examining the effectiveness of a multi-modal relapse prevention intervention. He was previously Acting Director of Clinical Programs and Senior Psychologist at ORYGEN Youth Health, which incorporates the EPPIC Program. He has previously held a range of senior clinical and teaching roles at EPPIC since 1994. In 1998 he developed a Graduate Diploma in Young People's Mental Health, and has lectured extensively, nationally and internationally, on psychosocial treatments in first-episode psychosis.

Patrick D. McGorry is currently Professor/Director of ORYGEN Youth Health, which is linked to The University of Melbourne and the Northwestern Mental Health Program in Melbourne, Australia. He has contributed significantly to research in the area of early psychosis over the past 16 years. Over that time he has played an integral role in the development of service structures and treatments specifically targeting the needs of young people with emerging or first-episode psychosis. More recently there has been a broadening of his focus to cover the full spectrum of mental disorders in young people. In the last 2 years he has published over 50 journal articles and chapters in many well-respected international journals such as the *American Journal of Psychiatry*, *Schizophrenia Research* and *Archives of General Psychiatry*. He is currently the President of the International Early Psychosis Association and an Executive Board Member of the International Society for the Psychological Treatments of the Schizophrenias and other Related Psychoses. He is also a member of the Organizing Committee of the World Psychiatric Association Section on Schizophrenia, the Advisory Board of UCLA Center for the Assessment and Prevention of Prodromal States (CAPPS) and a member of the Editorial Board of *Schizophrenia Research*.

Contributors

Dr Jean Addington, Associate Professor, Department of Psychiatry, University of Toronto, Center for Addiction and Mental Health, 250 College Street, Toronto, Ontario M5T 1R8, Canada

Karen Barton, Assistant Psychologist, Birmingham Early Intervention Service, Harry Watton House, 97 Church Lane, Aston, Birmingham B6 5UG, UK

Professor Max Birchwood, Director, Early Intervention Service and Director of Research and Development, Northern Birmingham Mental Health Trust and School of Psychology University of Birmingham, Harry Watton House, 97 Church Lane, Aston, Birmingham B6 5UG, UK

Dr Peter Burnett, Medical Director, ORYGEN Youth Health, Parkville Centre, Locked Bag 10/35 Poplar Road, Parkville, Victoria 3052, Australia

Professor Johan Cullberg, Professor of Psychiatry, Stockholm Center of Public Health, PO Box 17533, Stockholm, Sweden

Dr Larry Davidson, Associate Professor of Psychiatry and Director, Program for Recovery and Community Health, Yale University School of Medicine and Institution for Social and Policy Studies, Yale Program for Recovery and Community Health, Erector Square, Bldg #6W, Suite #1C, 319 Peck Street, New Haven, CT 06513, USA

Jane Edwards, Deputy Clinical Director, ORYGEN Youth Health, Parkville Centre, Locked Bag 10/35 Poplar Road, Parkville, Victoria 3052, Australia

Kathryn Elkins, ORYGEN Youth Health and Department of Psychiatry, The University of Melbourne, Parkville Centre, Locked Bag 10/35 Poplar Road, Parkville, Victoria 3052, Australia

Dr Gráinne Fadden, Consultant Clinical Psychologist, MERIDEN Programme, SBMHT, Academic Unit, 71 Fentham Road, Erdington, Birmingham B23 6AL, UK

Dr Paul R. Falzer, Clinical Assistant Professor of Psychiatry, Program for Recovery and Community Health, Yale University School of Medicine and Institution for Social and Policy Studies, Yale Program for Recovery and Community Health, Erector Square, Bldg. #6W, Suite #1C, 319 Peck Street, New Haven, CT 06513, USA

Dr Shona M. Francey, Coordinator/Psychologist, PACE Clinic, ORYGEN Youth Health and Department of Psychiatry, The University of Melbourne, Parkville Centre, Locked Bag 10/35 Poplar Road, Parkville, Victoria 3052, Australia

Donna Gee, Research Therapist, ORYGEN Youth Health, Parkville Centre, Locked Bag 10/35 Poplar Road, Parkville, Victoria 3052, Australia

Dr John F.M. Gleeson, Associate Professor, Department of Psychology, The University of Melbourne and the Northwestern Mental Health Program, Parkville Centre, Locked Bag 10/35 Poplar Road, Parkville, Victoria 3052, Australia

Dr Gillian Haddock, Reader in Clinical Psychology, University of Manchester, Tameside General Hospital, Fountain Street, Ashton-u-Lyne OL6 9RW, UK

Kate Hardy, Assistant Psychologist, South West Yorkshire Mental Health NHS Trust, Early Intervention Project, Ravensleigh Cottage, 28a Oxford Road, Dewsbury, UK

Lisa Henry, Research Fellow and Clinical Psychologist, ORYGEN Youth Health and Department of Psychiatry, The University of Melbourne, Parkville Centre, Locked Bag 10/35 Poplar Road, Parkville, Victoria 3052, Australia

Tanya Herrmann-Doig, c/o Chris Mackey & Associates, Clinical Psychology Services, 28 Villamanta St, Geelong West, Victoria, Australia

Mark Hinton, Consultant Clinical Psychologist, Early Intervention Services, Camden and Islington Mental Health and Social Care Trust, St Pancras Hospital, 4 St Pancras Way, London NW1 0PE, UK

Dr Zaffer Iqbal, Senior Clinical Research Fellow, University of Birmingham and Leeds Mental Health Teaching NHS Trust, CPPP Services, 17 Blenheim Terrace, Leeds LS2 9HN, UK

Dr Chris Jackson, Early Intervention Service, 97 Church Lane, Aston, Birmingham B6 5UG, UK

Professor Jan-Olav Johannessen, Chief Psychiatrist, Rogaland Psychiatric Hospital, Postboks 1163, 4095 Stavanger, Norway

Professor Ashok K. Malla, Professor of Psychiatry, University of Western Ontario, PEPP–London Health Sciences Centre, 375 South Street, London, Ontario N6A 5G6, Canada

Dr Rufus May, Clinical Psychologist, Bradford Assertive Outreach Team, Bradford District Community Trust, 48 Ash Grove, Bradford BD7, UK

Terry S. McLean, Clinical and Education Leader, PEPP–London Health Sciences Centre, WMCH building, 392 South Street, London, Ontario N6A 4G5, Canada

Professor Patrick D. McGorry, Director, ORYGEN Youth Health (incorporating EPPIC), Department of Psychiatry, The University of Melbourne, Parkville Centre, Locked Bag 10/35 Poplar Road, Parkville, Victoria 3052, Australia

Ross M.G. Norman, Departments of Psychiatry and Epidemiology and Biostatistics, University of Western Ontario, London Health Sciences Centre, 392 South Street, London, Ontario N6A 4GS, Canada

Lisa J. Phillips, Coordinator/Psychologist, PACE Clinic, ORYGEN Youth Health and Department of Psychiatry, The University of Melbourne, Parkville Centre, Locked Bag 10/35 Poplar Road, Parkville, Victoria 3052, Australia

Dr Paddy Power, Lead Consultant Psychiatrist & Honorary Senior Lecturer, Lambeth Early Onset (LEO) Service, South London and Maudsley NHS Trust, 108 Landor Road, London SW9 9NT, UK

Dr Ron Siddle, Consultant Grade Cognitive Behaviour Therapist, Manchester Mental Health and Social Care Trust, Department of Clinical Psychology, North Manchester General Hospital, Delaunays Road, Crumpsall, Manchester M8 5RB, UK

David A. Stayner, Clinical Assistant Professor of Psychiatry, Yale University School of Medicine and Director of Program Development, Yale Program for Recovery and Community Health, Erector Square, Bldg. #6W, Suite #1C, 319 Peck Street, New Haven, CT 06513, USA

Darryl Wade, Clinical Psychologist, ORYGEN Youth Health, Parkville Centre, Locked Bag 10/35 Poplar Road, Parkville, Victoria 3052, Australia

Foreword

From its origins in Melbourne over a decade ago, the idea of creating specialized services for early intervention in psychosis has grown to encircle the globe. It is an idea that has been actualized in the creation of new service configurations, new psychotherapies and psychotherapeutic perspectives, and a new and growing body of knowledge to inform clinical care. The idea that new onset psychosis and even pre-illness onset prodromal states might best be managed in specialized settings and by specially trained teams may in time rank along with the deconstruction of the asylum as a major turning point in our thinking about the management of serious mental illness. How has this new therapeutic movement taken hold so quickly? What are its essential elements?

Two critical observations derived from longitudinal research set the stage for the current focus on early psychosis. First was the observation that in all societies where investigators looked, substantial time (12 to 18 months) typically elapsed between the onset of psychotic symptoms and the time a person found their way to a clinician who could institute appropriate treatment. Furthermore, many studies seemed to indicate that patients with the longest *duration of untreated psychosis* responded more slowly and less completely once treatment was begun.

Second, modern first-episode psychosis studies established the fact that once patients with a first psychotic episode were identified and treated, most had a rapid and robust initial treatment response. Among the most demoralizing findings, however, was the additional observation that given available treatments and treatment systems, within a year or two the vast majority of patients went on to suffer a relapse. After the first relapse, once again, most or nearly all went on to have one or more subsequent relapses. With each turn of this cycle, the quickness and completeness of treatment response was truncated leaving clinicians treating these individuals feeling powerless to turn back the tide of what could sometimes seem like an inexorable march towards chronicity. Based on watching far too many young persons transformed over the span of a few years into 'chronic patients', some hypothesized that repeated or prolonged periods of psychosis itself heralded a deteriorative neurobiological process that proceeded irreversibly in only one direction. While research has not, on balance, upheld a 'biological toxicity' hypothesis of prolonged psychosis, it is clear that by whatever mechanism, prolonged and repeated episodes inflict suffering and dismantle lives.

Together, duration of untreated psychosis and first episode studies point to an inescapable conclusion: our health systems fail to get patients with a first episode of psychosis into treatment and in most instances fail to prevent recurrences and deterioration. It is from the imperative to do better that early psychosis research and service development derive their momentum.

As this volume makes clear, psychosocial interventions are at the center of the array of services that must be developed to create a comprehensive system of care for persons who have suffered a first episode of psychosis. The treatment approaches described are both *illness phase-specific*, for example focusing on the pre-psychotic phase, first episode, and first-relapse and *individual problem-specific*, addressing problems such as co-occurring substance abuse, suicidality, negative symptoms and treatment-resistance. Common elements of these approaches include a focus on relationship-building and engagement, the flexible adaptation of techniques to meet individual needs and preferences, the mobilization of families as allies in the treatment effort, and the integration of person-oriented approaches with current biological understanding of psychosis. Unlike earlier generations of psychological therapies that rested on endorsement from authorities, the approaches outlined here have been developed within a framework of evaluation research and evidence-based practice. While the data are not all in yet, over the next several years we can look forward to the results of rigorous evaluations or randomized trials to further clarify the utility of these approaches and guide their refinement and dissemination.

This volume describes work in progress. As a status report from those on the leading edge of creating and evaluating specialized early psychosis programs, it represents the best current thinking regarding treatments and treatment systems for young people balanced on the edge of catastrophe. From theory to practice to evaluation and reformulation of practice it may be a blueprint for saving lives.

Wayne S. Fenton, M.D.
Bethesda, Maryland

Preface

Every clinician knows that the human relationship with the person diagnosed with a psychotic disorder and particularly schizophrenia is the cornerstone of effective therapy and the foundation for recovery. This was one of the major tenets of an earlier generation of psychotherapeutic effort in schizophrenia and related psychoses but had drifted out of focus during the 1980s with the rise of an excessively narrow biological psychiatry and the decline of the traditional psychoanalytic approach. The lack of a blueprint or body of knowledge and skills for working with psychotic patients meant that many of their most salient needs were ignored. Fortunately this situation is changing for the better.

Since the publication of Carlo Perris' eclectic and seminal text in 1989, *Cognitive Therapy with Schizophrenic Patients*, there has been a steady growth in the application and evaluation of cognitive, cognitive-behavioural, and integrated need-adapted psychodynamic treatments for schizophrenia and psychosis. Over the past 5 years these developments have been reflected in the publication of a number of treatment handbooks for the clinician based in the mental health setting. The majority of these treatment handbooks have presented the innovative cognitive-behavioural methods of UK-based clinical and experimental psychologists, and have reflected their contributions to the treatment of psychotic symptoms and relapse prevention. The principal aim of these texts has been to add to the repertoire of trained cognitive-behavioural therapists in their work with patients with established (and often treatment-resistant) forms of psychotic disorders. Somewhat less attention has been paid to the earlier application of psychological interventions for first-episode patients whose clinical, personal and broader developmental needs often differ from patients with longer-term illnesses.

In parallel with this psychological renaissance, international interest in intensive early intervention in psychosis has grown exponentially. This paradigm shift is reflected in major research growth in early psychosis and a raft of service and policy reforms that have extended throughout Europe, Scandinavia, Canada, the USA, Australia and the Asia-Pacific region, in addition to the establishment of the International Early Psychosis Association, and the publication of several texts with a focus on early psychosis. The International Society for the Psychological Treatments of the Schizophrenias and Other Psychoses similarly has expanded and given unequivocal support for the early use of psychological interventions in psychotic illness and for early intervention itself. Given these developments at the international and local service system level, we were motivated to bring together the range of psychological treatments for early psychosis. This text aims to equip clinicians to address the psychological needs of first-episode patients across specific early stages of treatment.

Psychological Interventions in Early Psychosis is envisaged as a practical treatment handbook for the clinician with previous training in a range of psychotherapies, and for the postgraduate student undertaking training. The text is organized according to phases of illness commencing with the prepsychotic *at-risk* phase and extending to protracted recovery from psychotic symptoms. In addition, the collection of contributions includes cognitive and cognitive-behavioural interventions which have not previously been described in available psychosis-related texts—namely suicide prevention and treatment of comorbid cannabis abuse.

The introductory chapter, by Patrick McGorry, outlines the imperative for psychological intervention in early psychosis to be integrated with biological treatments—an argument that is placed within the historical context of psychotherapies for schizophrenia. Chapter 2 outlines the preventive rationale for cognitive therapy with patients presenting with features of 'at-risk mental state' for the development of acute psychosis. The clinical implications from research undertaken at PACE (a research-based clinic in Melbourne for young people at heightened risk for psychosis) are detailed, an approach that has been taken up enthusiastically in the UK EDIE project. Chapter 3, contributed by Ron Siddle and Gillian Haddock, introduces the reader to the clinical lessons from the SoCRATES study in the UK, with a detailed description of psychological interventions for the acute phase of early psychosis.

The phases of cognitively orientated therapy for early psychosis (COPE), which was developed at EPPIC as a short-term focal therapy, is described by Lisa Henry in Chapter 4. The intervention aims to ameliorate the risk of the 'self' being overwhelmed by the stigma of diagnosis and the impact of entry into treatment, and to treat secondary morbidity. Our Scandinavian colleagues, Johan Cullberg and Jan-Olav Johannessen, are ideally placed to outline, as they do in Chapter 5, the place of brief, adapted psychodynamic therapies in the early stages of recovery from the acute episode. Chapter 6 outlines the specific needs of the family members of first-episode patients in dealing with the uncertainty, grief and trauma surrounding the experience in caring for the young person. The approach, described by Jean Addington and Peter Burnett, details family work undertaken at EPPIC, in Melbourne, Australia, and Calgary, Canada. A second key Canadian contribution is included in Chapter 7, by Ashok Malla, Terry McClean, and Ross Norman, in which the opportunities for recovery from acute psychosis, which can be provided within the group context, are expertly explored.

Chapter 8 introduces the reader to a treatment strategy recently trialled at EPPIC for comorbid cannabis abuse—a significant variable in relapse and prolonged recovery following the initial episode. Kathryn Elkins, Mark Hinton and Jane Edwards outline the scope of the problem and describe specific clinical interventions with illustrative case vignettes. Chapter 9 by John Gleeson focuses upon the first psychotic relapse. Starting from a critical understanding of the construct of relapse as applied to the first-episode group, the chapter provides guidelines for understanding and formulating the risk for psychotic relapse. The prime interventions for relapse prevention are included, with reference to two contrasting case vignettes.

Although others have described the importance of understanding demoralization following a first episode of psychosis, Chapter 10 by Paddy Power introduces the reader to a manualized cognitive-behavioural therapy (CBT) intervention for first-episode patients with suicidal ideation. The chapter reviews the data pertaining to the huge but understudied issue of suicide and self-harm in the psychotic population, before describing the 'LifeSPAN' intervention which was evaluated within a randomized-controlled trial of CBT at EPPIC.

Chapter 11, contributed by Jane Edwards, Darryl Wade, Tanya Herrmann-Doig and Donna Gee, describes CBT for 'prolonged recovery' from the first episode. The ramifications of delayed recovery from positive psychotic symptoms after the first episode are outlined, together with the rationale for individual symptom-based CBT interventions for this patient group. Drawing upon the EPPIC 'STOPP' (Systematic Treatment of Persistent

Psychosis) model, interventions for hallucinations and delusions are detailed with illustrative case material. In Chapter 12, Max Birchwood, Zaffer Iqbal, Chris Jackson and Kate Hardy argue cogently for an increased focus upon interventions for emotional distress associated with psychosis in both research trials and in clinical practice. Chapter 13 addresses the difficult area of negative symptoms—a much neglected issue in psychological literature for early psychosis. While the use of low-dose antipsychotic medications and in particular atypical agents has reduced the extent and severity of this clinical syndrome, it remains a tenacious clinical challenge. Paul Falzer, David Stayner and Larry Davidson review the relevant literature on negative symptoms and posit five principles, derived from research and clinical experience, for working with first-episode patients with negative symptoms.

The subjective experience of psychosis and principles from the recovery model are integrated in Chapter 14, contributed by Rufus May, who brings a unique dual perspective from his experience as both consumer and clinical psychologist. This is essential reading for all clinicians and consumers.

Finally, Chapter 15 attempts to answer the frequently asked question: 'How can services undertake highly specialized psychosocial interventions in a contemporary mental health setting with limited resources and high caseloads?' While acknowledging these apparently formidable constraints, this chapter highlights some of the strategies successfully adopted within the West Midlands Region in the UK via a range of comprehensive training programmes. Their experience is mirrored around the world in an increasing number of settings.

We hope that this handbook will stimulate clinicians and researchers alike to continue to innovate and evaluate novel interventions for first-episode patients and their families, with the aim of improving outcomes. We would like to thank all our colleagues for their generous efforts in contributing to this work. In addition, we would like to acknowledge all of the consumers and their families who contributed to these ideas and applications. Finally, thank-you to our own families for enduring our preoccupation with this project, and special thanks to Theresa Cheng for her tireless and essential administrative efforts in preparing this manuscript.

John Gleeson and Patrick McGorry
Parkville, Australia
August 2003

1 An Overview of the Background and Scope for Psychological Interventions in Early Psychosis

PATRICK D. McGORRY

ORYGEN Youth Health and Department of Psychiatry, The University of Melbourne, Australia

In recent years there has been a renaissance of interest in psychological interventions in psychosis. This revival has been catalysed by a number of forces, notably a welcome growth in therapeutic optimism, the advent of novel drug therapies, the reform and community embedding of mental health services, the rise of consumerism in mental health care and the steady extension of cognitive therapies across the full spectrum of psychiatric disorder with an accompanying evidence base. Naturally, people experiencing early psychosis are in a particularly good position to benefit from effective forms of psychological intervention. They have many currently unmet psychological needs, extensive comorbidity, and at this phase of illness the task of recovery is challenging but potentially more achievable. While drug therapies are essential for the vast majority of people with psychotic disorder, optimal recovery in a psychological and functional sense is rarely achieved without skilled psychological assistance. This chapter reviews the origins and vicissitudes of the psychological approach to psychosis during past eras and the basis for future evolution and extension with a particular focus on early psychosis.

HISTORY

The modern origins of psychological interventions in psychosis can be traced back to the French Revolution and the emergence of so-called moral treatment in the late eighteenth and early nineteenth centuries. Pinel in France, and the York Retreat and later John Conolly in England were the pioneers of this change in approach (Jones, 1983). The harsh custodial methods used to respond to madness began to be leavened by a more humane approach which reflected the more liberal thinking of the period. Some patients began to be cared for in smaller facilities characterized by a lack of physical restraint, greater freedom and humane attitudes, and early forms of behavioural management. However, whatever the symbolic significance of such models, they failed to generalize or prosper, and were largely swept aside by the growth of the asylums during the latter half of the nineteenth century and first half of the twentieth.

Psychological Interventions in Early Psychosis
Edited by J.F.M. Gleeson and P.D. McGorry. © 2004 John Wiley & Sons, Ltd.

Psychological treatments for schizophrenia and other psychoses were almost totally neglected during much of this period for two reasons. Firstly, psychoses, particularly schizophrenia, were seen as severe and degenerative neuropsychiatric diseases for which there was no effective treatment. The Kraepelinian model meant that a diagnosis of, in particular, schizophrenia or dementia praecox created profound therapeutic nihilism—an effect which largely persists to this day, despite the subsequent development of effective treatments and demonstration that the course is not in fact one of deterioration (Harrison et al., 2001). Ironically, Kraepelin personally believed that a supportive psychotherapeutic approach was often helpful to the patient (Nagel, 1991). Custodial care was the only practical option during much of the asylum era, and although it was originally inspired partly by humanitarian ideals, it resulted in reality in much suffering and iatrogenic harm. Secondly, despite the rise of new psychological treatments within the psychoanalytic paradigm, people with psychoses, again especially schizophrenia, were initially believed to be unable to benefit from such treatments. Freud in particular stated that such patients were unable to form a relationship—especially a transferential one—with the therapist, and hence could not be treated with psychoanalysis. According to Federn (1952), Freud regarded patients with schizophrenic-type psychotic disorders as a 'nuisance to psychoanalysis'.

The Neo-Freudians however, specifically the interpersonal school led by Harry Stack Sullivan, began to seriously question this view from the 1920s. They regarded the organic disease model for schizophrenia to be a mistaken concept, believing that the syndrome was largely an adaptational problem based on earlier experiences and, perhaps, some constitutional predisposition. Having much more faith in the patient's capacity to relate, they developed a new type of psychotherapy aimed at a mutual doctor–patient understanding of the patient's development and of the unconscious conflicts that created the symptoms. Sullivan, who quite rightly perceived the person with schizophrenia as 'much more simply human than otherwise' (Sullivan, 1947), not only developed a theory of schizophrenia which attempted to explain the disorder on an interpersonal basis, but his modified form of psychoanalytic psychotherapy was more reality oriented, active and flexible (Sullivan, 1947). He was also acutely aware of the possibilities for prevention and early intervention in schizophrenia and wrote some seminal papers on this topic (Sullivan, 1927). His successors, notably Frieda Fromm-Reichmann at Chestnut Lodge, extended his work greatly even as biological treatments were emerging. Fromm-Reichmann also projected an optimistic approach to the patient which resonates well with the thinking of the current early psychosis paradigm:

> I am thinking especially of the diagnosis of schizophrenia as being connected in the minds of many lay people and unfortunately also in the judgement of many psychiatrists with the connotation of psychotherapeutic inaccessibility. They believe that only shock treatments and psychosurgery can help to relieve the suffering of these patients, even though they realise that this may be accomplished at the expense of the emotional integrity and further development of the patients' personalities. The diagnosis "schizophrenia" given by a psychiatrist of my school of psychiatric thinking is coupled with the knowledge that he and the patient are heading for hard work, but it is by no means offered in the spirit of prognostic discouragement. (Fromm-Reichmann, 1960, p. 61)

In many settings, prior to the advent of antipsychotic medication, psychoanalysis became the treatment of choice for schizophrenia. In many parts of the world, particularly in the USA for a time, psychoses were regarded as disorders with a psychological basis rather than neuropsychiatric diseases. Despite this, however, even in the heyday of psychoanalytic treatment, most patients were institutionalized with no access to these time-consuming and arcane interventions. During the 1940s many were exposed to the widespread use of electro-convulsive therapy (ECT) and psychosurgery. While Arieti (1974) evolved the interpersonal approach further, presciently moving it in a cognitive direction and integrating it with bi-ological therapies, the times were changing. The discovery of antipsychotic medication in the early 1950s, the associated slow decline of the asylum model, and the rise of biolog-ical psychiatry, ultimately changed the landscape of treatment for people with psychotic disorders. The perspective slowly changed from psychological reductionism to biological reductionism. The rationale and technique enabling clinicians to work psychologically with patients evaporated, resulting in greatly reduced therapeutic contact with patients who, de-spite being more psychologically accessible due to effective antipsychotic therapy, became increasingly ignored as human beings. For many the excessive doses of only partially ef-fective medicines did indeed relieve suffering, but only 'at the expense of the emotional integrity and further development of the patients' personalities'. They often led impover-ished lonely lives in community settings, graduating to a new state of neglect. This trend has continued inexorably until the present day, and while it has affected psychiatry as a whole, it has particularly affected psychotic disorders. Very few patients with psychotic illness cur-rently receive modern evidence-based psychosocial interventions (Jablensky et al., 1999). The specially adapted forms of psychoanalytic psychotherapy gradually became discredited in the treatment of schizophrenia, partly because they were based on a reductionistic and speculative theoretical stance, but mainly because it had proved difficult to find evidence for their efficacy either as a sole treatment or even as an adjunct to drug therapy (Gunderson et al., 1984; Malmberg & Fenton, 2003; May, 1968). While this view was later challenged (Gottdiener & Haslam, 2003), during the 1980s it became clear that psychoses were asso-ciated with a range of central nervous system (CNS) abnormalities that more definitively supported a disease model. The zeitgeist crystallized around this model, and schizophrenia was now seen exclusively as a disorder of the CNS structure and function. Only in the past decade, catalysed by the seminal work of Carlo Perris (1989), has there been some rebalancing and there is at last the potential to go beyond both forms of reductionism and move towards true integration of biological and psychosocial treatments in psychosis.

EARLY PSYCHOSIS: A NEW PARADIGM IN MENTAL HEALTH

Over the past decade, a growing sense of optimism about the prospects for better out-comes for schizophrenia and related psychoses has created substantial reform, and there is momentum in clinical practice in many countries to develop early intervention strategies. Clinicians and policy makers are enthusiastic about reform based on the early intervention idea because of the sound logic behind it, the unacceptably poor access and quality of care previously available to young people with early psychosis, and the increasing evidence that better outcomes can be achieved.

The growth of this paradigm is more broadly based than the earlier, unsuccessful psy-chotherapeutic endeavours. Some of the current optimism has flowed from the development of a new generation of antipsychotic medications with greater efficacy and fewer toxic side-effects, but a second major factor has been the belated recognition that a special focus on the early phases of illness could result in a substantial reduction in morbidity and better quality of life for patients and their families. This is not a new idea, having been formulated during the preneuroleptic era by Sullivan in particular, and others subsequently (Meares, 1959; Sullivan, 1927). However, due initially to a lack of effective treatment and subsequently to tenacious therapeutic nihilism, it remained dormant for decades. A revival of interest has come from several origins. From the psychotherapeutic perspective, Ugelstad (1979) proposed a secondary prevention effort focusing on intensive supportive psychotherapeutic intervention for first-episode schizophrenia in Scandinavia. Recognising that young first-onset patients were at maximum risk for poorer outcomes, and that the incidence of such cases was relatively small in any given catchment or sector, he outlined a practical way of focusing psychological expertise on the needs of such patients, who presented at a manageable rate for clinical services. This model gave rise to the Nordic Investigation of Psychotherapeutically-orientated treatment for new Schizophrenia (NIPS) project, an ambitious undertaking, the results of which were unfortunately inconclusive (Alanen et al., 1994). Interest in early intervention gradually re-emerged within mainstream psychiatry during the 1980s as a result of some key research studies (Crow et al., 1986; Falloon, 1992; Lieberman, Matthews & Kirch, 1992), and grew exponentially during the 1990s (Birchwood, Fowler & Jackson, 2000; Edwards & McGorry, 2002; McGorry & Jackson, 1999). This revival and its sustainability will depend on a stable recognition of the need for an integrative biopsychosocial approach to aetiology and treatment.

The first-episode research focus rapidly revealed the special clinical needs of young people at this phase of illness, the iatrogenic effects of standard care and an encouraging range of secondary preventive opportunities. This was especially clear when the clinical care of the first-episode and recent onset patients was streamed separately from chronic patients, something that is still difficult to engineer (McGorry & Yung, 2003). The key failures in care are: prolonged delays in accessing effective treatment, which consequently usually occurs in the context of a severe behavioural crisis; crude and typically traumatic and alienating initial treatment strategies; and subsequent poor continuity of care and engagement of the patient with treatment. Young people have to demonstrate severe risk to themselves or others to gain access, and a relapsing and chronically disabling pattern of illness to qualify for assured ongoing care. These features are still highly prevalent in most systems of mental health care, and even in developed countries with reasonable levels of spending in mental health (Garety & Rigg, 2001).

The increasing devolution of mental health care into community settings has provided further momentum, as has a genuine renaissance in biological and psychological treatments for psychosis. An exponential growth in interest in neuroscientific research in schizophrenia has injected further optimism into the field with a new generation of clinician-researchers coming to the fore. Several countries have developed national mental health strategies or frameworks that catalyse and guide major reform and mandate a preventive mindset and linked reform. Around the world an increasingly large number of groups have established clinical programmes and research initiatives focusing on early psychosis and it now constitutes a growth point in clinical care as well as research (Edwards & McGorry, 2002). This blend of science and sociology has the potential to lead to a sea change in the way these illnesses are conceived and managed.

While primary prevention is still out of reach, secondary prevention or 'early intervention' is an excellent interim option. This includes early detection of new cases, shortening delays in effective treatment, optimal and sustained treatment in the early 'critical period' of the first few years of illness, and may eventually include the capacity to identify a proportion of cases in the prepsychotic period. Reducing the impact and burden of psychotic disorders in society as a whole is an achievable and important objective. It may also be possible to reduce the prevalence by shortening the duration of illness by delaying onset, reducing the period of time spent living with the symptoms and disability, or accelerating recovery. However, none of this has yet occurred despite the development of highly effective treatments, because we have failed to translate recent advances to the real world in a timely manner. Even with existing knowledge, substantial reductions in prevalence and improved quality of life are possible for patients provided that societies are prepared to mandate and pay for it (Andrews et al., in press). Early intervention, with its promise of more efficient treatment through a proactive and enhanced focus on the early phases of illness, is an additional prevalence reduction strategy which is now available to be more seriously tested and, if found cost-effective (Carr et al., 2003; Mihalopoulos, McGorry & Carter, 1999), to be widely implemented. At least two randomized-controlled trials are in progress evaluating models of this type.

A FRAMEWORK FOR CLINICAL INTERVENTIONS IN EARLY PSYCHOSIS

The pattern and style of intervention in early psychosis differs from that required in later stages of these disorders. A staging approach is used here to summarize the key elements currently believed to be appropriate. Knowledge and evidence are accumulating steadily and the range and sequence of interventions is expected to evolve further. A fundamental principle is that careful integration of drug and psychosocial interventions is always essential.

Prepsychotic or Prodromal Phase

In most patients a prolonged period of symptoms and increasing disability, commonly termed the 'prodrome', occurs before the onset of severe and persistent positive psychotic symptoms sufficient to allow the diagnosis of schizophrenia or first-episode psychosis (Agerbo et al., 2003; Häfner et al., 1995). Such psychosocial damage is usually extremely difficult to reverse. Recently it has also been shown that active neurobiological change may occur during this period (Pantelis et al., 2003). The prepsychotic phase is an active focus of research (McGorry et al., 2002) and this is leading to better understanding of the process of onset as well as the treatment needs and options. It is already clear that psychological interventions are likely to benefit patients at this phase and may have preventive or ameliorative effects on the onset process. The following points reflect an acceptable clinical approach to such patients at the present time.

- The possibility of psychotic disorder should be considered in any young person who is becoming more socially withdrawn, performing more poorly for a sustained period of time at school or at work, behaving in an unusual manner, or becoming more distressed or agitated yet unable to explain why.
- Subthreshold psychotic features combined with the onset of disability (Yung et al., 2003) indicate very high risk. The young person and the family should be actively engaged in assessment and regular monitoring of mental state and safety. This should be carried out in a home, primary care or non-psychiatric setting if possible, to reduce stigma.

- Concurrent syndromes such as depression and substance abuse, and problem areas such as interpersonal, vocational and family stress, should be appropriately managed.
- Information about the level of risk of progression to psychosis should be carefully provided, conveying a sense of therapeutic optimism. It should emphasize that current problems can be alleviated, that progression to psychosis is not inevitable, and if psychosis or schizophrenia does occur then effective and well-tolerated treatments are readily available. Engagement at this early stage will help to reduce any subsequent delay in accessing treatment for first-episode psychosis and hence shorten the duration of untreated psychosis.
- The use of antipsychotic medication during the prodrome is the subject of current research (Bechdolf, Wagner & Hambrecht, 2002; Cornblatt et al., 2002; McGlashan et al., 2003; McGorry et al., 2002; Miller et al., 2003; Woods et al., in press). At present, it should be reserved for patients who are clearly and persistently psychotic.

First-Episode Psychosis (FEP)

Two key issues in FEP are the *timing* of intervention (and thus the duration of untreated psychosis (DUP), (McGlashan, 1999)) and its *quality* (the sustained provision of comprehensive phase-specific treatment) (Birchwood, 2000; Edwards & McGorry, 2002; McGorry & Jackson, 1999; National Collaboration Centre for Mental Health, 2002; National Service Framework, 1999; Zipursky & Schulz, 2002).

There are often prolonged delays in initiating effective treatment for first-episode psychosis. Prolonged DUP is associated with poorer response and outcome (Harrigan, McGorry & Krstev, 2003; McGlashan, 1999; Norman & Malla, 2001). Early identification of people in the earliest phases of psychotic disorders combined with optimal treatment is very likely to reduce the burden of disease while it is active (Malla & Norman, 2002). Any improvements in long-term outcome should be seen as a bonus, rather than as a prerequisite for improving clinical standards during early illness (Lieberman & Fenton, 2000).

FEP tends to be more responsive to treatment than subsequent episodes and later phases of illness, but it can be more demanding because of the range of clinical issues to be addressed. Syndromes, and hence diagnoses, tend to be unstable and may evolve over time. The umbrella term 'psychosis' allows this syndromal flux and comorbidity to be accommodated, and treatment commenced for all prominent syndromes, before a stable diagnosis such as schizophrenia or bipolar disorder needs to be applied. Whether or not core 'schizophrenia' can be securely diagnosed or not is not crucial for effective treatment in first-episode psychosis. Treatment-relevant syndromes are positive psychosis, mania, depression, substance abuse and the negative syndrome. Some of the main principles of treatment of FEP are as follows.

- Strategies to improve access to treatment for FEP include better mental health literacy, more informed primary care, and greater responsiveness of public and private psychiatry to possible cases. Community-wide education systems should be developed to improve understanding of how psychotic disorders emerge in a hitherto healthy person and how to seek and obtain effective advice, treatment and support (Johannessen et al., 2001; Larsen et al., 2001). Above all, a high index of suspicion and a low threshold for expert assessment should be set for FEP.

- Entry and retention within specialist mental health services is often based on a reactive crisis-oriented model in which individuals must reach a threshold of behavioural disturbance, risk, disability or chronicity. This resource-poor model creates unnecessary trauma, demoralization and therapeutic nihilism in patients, families and clinicians. Instead, services should aim for proactive retention of most patients throughout the first 3–5 years of illness, combining developmental (youth) and phase-specific perspectives (Edwards & McGorry, 2002; National Service Framework, 1999).
- Initial treatment should be provided in an outpatient or home setting if possible (Fitzgerald & Kulkarni, 1998). Such an approach can minimize trauma, disruption and anxiety for the patient and family who are usually poorly informed about mental illness and have fears and prejudices about inpatient psychiatric care. Inpatient care is required if there is a significant risk of self-harm or aggression, if the level of support in the community is insufficient, or if the crisis is too great for the family to manage, even with home-based support.
- Inpatient care should be provided in the least restrictive environment. Optimal inpatient units should ideally be streamed by phase of illness and developmental stage, be relatively small in size, and be adequately staffed so that 1 : 1 nursing of highly distressed, suicidal or agitated young people is possible without locking sections of the unit or secluding the patient, unless this is absolutely necessary. The use of traditional psychiatric 'intensive care', a pragmatic intervention which lacks a solid evidence base, is especially traumatic for these patients (McGorry et al., 1991; Meyer et al., 1999; Shaw, McFarlane & Bookless, 1997). Where streaming is not possible, a special section may be created in a general acute unit for young recent-onset patients.
- Pharmacological treatments should be introduced with great care in medication-naïve patients; they should do the least harm while aiming for the maximum benefit. Appropriate strategies include graded introduction, with careful explanation, of low-dose antipsychotic medication (Emsley, 1999; Merlo et al., 2002; Remington, Kapur & Zipursky, 1998) plus antimanic or antidepressant medication where indicated. Skilled nursing care, a safe and supportive environment, and regular and liberal doses of benzodiazepines are essential to relieve distress, insomnia and behavioural disturbances secondary to psychosis, while antipsychotic medication takes effect.
- The first-line use of atypical antipsychotic medication is recommended on the basis of better tolerability and reduced risk of tardive dyskinesia. In the longer term, the risk–benefit ratio may change for some patients, for example if weight gain or sexual side-effects associated with the atypical agents develop. Typical antipsychotic medications may then be one of the options considered (Geddes et al., 2000; Kapur & Remington, 2000; National Collaborating Centre for Mental Health, 2002).
- Of particular relevance here is the principle that psychosocial interventions, especially cognitive-behavioural therapy (CBT), are important components of early treatment, providing a humane basis for continuing care, preventing and resolving secondary consequences of the illness, and promoting recovery (Lewis et al., 2002). During the recovery phase CBT may also be helpful for preserving a stable sense of self, in maintaining self-esteem, for comorbid substance use, mood and anxiety disorders and improving treatment adherence (Jackson et al., 1998).
- Families and, whenever possible and appropriate, other members of the person's social network should be actively supported and progressively educated about the nature of the

problem, the treatment and the expected outcomes. If there are frequent relapses or slow early recovery, a more intensive and prolonged supportive intervention for families is required (Gleeson et al., 1999; Zhang et al., 1994).

- If recovery is slow and remission does not occur despite sustained adherence to two antipsychotic medications (at least one of which is an atypical medication) for 6 weeks each, early use of clozapine and intensive CBT should be seriously considered (Edwards et al., 2002b; National Collaborating Centre for Mental Health, 2002).
- Early use of clozapine should also be considered if suicide risk is prominent or persistent (Meltzer et al., 2003).

Recovery and Relapse: Treating Schizophrenia and Related Psychoses in the Critical Period

Relapses are common during the first 5 years after a first-episode psychosis (Robinson et al., 1999), a phase which has been termed the 'critical period' (Birchwood, Fowler & Jackson, 2000; Birchwood & Macmillan, 1993). Young people naturally find it difficult to accept the lifestyle change of taking daily medication, especially if they have substantially recovered. Poor adherence often contributes to one or more relapses which are risky, disruptive and may confer an increased chance of treatment resistance. Secondary consequences, such as worsening substance abuse, vocational failure, family stress and homelessness, are common during this phase, as the social fabric of the young person's life is put under severe strain.

It is essential that high-quality and intensive biopsychosocial care is provided continuously and assertively during this critical period. In practice, however, patients are rapidly discharged to primary care and must experience acute relapse, a suicide attempt or manifest severe disability and collateral psychosocial damage before further specialist care is provided, often in a reactive 'too little, too late' manner. Services currently tend to disengage at precisely the time when they are most needed and could be of most value. Typically they only become re-involved during increasingly brief acute episodes of care, superimposed on a low base of so-called 'shared care'. This minimalist model is highly inappropriate for the needs of patients during this stormy critical period of illness. Key features of clinical care during this phase are as follows:

- A solid therapeutic relationship and a staged approach to psychosocial intervention is essential (Hogarty et al., 1997a, 1997b). Good adherence to antipsychotic medication and specific psychosocial interventions, particularly family interventions, can reduce the risk of relapse (Pilling et al., 2002a; Schooler et al., 1997). A significant advantage of an atypical antipsychotic over a typical agent in the prevention of relapse has recently been demonstrated (Czernansky, Mahmoud & Brenner, 2002) though it remains unclear whether this is due to better efficacy, better tolerability and hence increased adherence, or both. Poorly engaged and frequently relapsing patients benefit most from intensive case management or assertive community treatment (ACT) models of care (Marshall & Lockwood, 2003). Comorbid substance abuse commonly contributes to relapse, and interventions based on CBT and motivational interviewing are now being developed and show early promise, although this is likely to remain a challenging issue (Barrowclough et al., 2001). Clozapine and CBT are indicated for emergent treatment resistance (Pilling et al., 2002a).

- In fully remitted patients, antipsychotic medication should be continued for at least 12 months and then an attempt may be made to withdraw the medication over a period of at least several weeks. Close follow-up should be continued with specialist review for a further period of at least 12 months, and any relapse rapidly identified and treated.
- At least 10–20% of patients fail to fully remit after a trial of two antipsychotic medications. They should be considered as manifesting 'treatment resistance', which means that more active biopsychosocial intervention is urgently required.
- Even in fully remitted patients, a range of psychological, family and vocational issues need to be addressed. Comorbidity, especially substance abuse, depression, post-traumatic stress disorder and social anxiety, is common and should be actively identified and treated.
- Every patient has the right to a safe, secure and agreeable home environment.
- Family support and intervention should be consistently provided during this phase (Lenior et al., 2002).
- Suicide risk must be actively monitored and addressed (Meltzer et al., 2003; Power et al., 2003).
- Vocational recovery interventions should be offered when a stable clinical state has been achieved (Drake et al., 1999; Lehman et al., 2002).
- Most patients should remain principally within specialist mental health care throughout the early years of illness, rather than be discharged to primary care on improvement of acute symptoms. Optimal treatment in this phase is complex, relying heavily on good adherence to medication and an array of psychosocial interventions, which depend on a cohesive team approach. True 'shared care' arrangements, which include primary care clinicians and are driven by clinical rather than cost imperatives, should be actively developed.

WHY PSYCHOLOGICAL TREATMENTS ARE NECESSARY IN EARLY PSYCHOSIS

Modern low-dose drug therapies, while not effective in all cases, are clearly the cornerstone for recovery in early psychosis. Why, therefore, are psychological treatments necessary? In fact drug therapies, while necessary, are not sufficient for full recovery in most patients. More specifically psychological and psychosocial interventions have a role for the following reasons:

To develop a therapeutic alliance

This is a difficult task in this age group and in the face of the obstacles thrown up by the disorder itself. A range of engagement strategies can be utilized (Othmer & Othmer, 1994; Power & McGorry, 1999), however the developmental stage of most patients, combined with the impact of the illness upon relatedness and social cognition, creates special difficulties. Furthermore, a subgroup of patients have experienced developmental neglect or abuse and have even more serious problems with trust and engagement. Most systems of psychiatric care fail to prioritize continuity of care, and even when a stable trusting therapeutic relationship is established it frequently cannot be maintained. If these barriers can be overcome and a good therapeutic alliance established and maintained, then a passport to recovery and better outcomes and quality of life can be achieved (Frank & Gunderson, 1990).

To provide emotional support in the face of disturbing subjective experiences and stigma

This is a central yet under-appreciated task for psychosocial interventions. The impact of psychotic and related psychopathological experiences is typically disturbing and over-whelming, and patients need accurate empathy for this as well as emotional support and practical help with coping strategies in the early phase of treatment. The experiences can produce trauma (McGorry et al., 1991; Meyer et al., 1999; Shaw, McFarlane & Bookless, 1997) and often the therapeutic environment can add to this rather than alleviate it. The stigma-laden 'recovery' environment represents a further risk factor to patients as they struggle to adjust and recover. Active supportive psychotherapy with strong emotional sup-port is essential in the early stages of treatment for psychosis, though it can be difficult to provide this in a setting where engagement with the patient is undermined by a range of conflicting factors.

To promote understanding of psychosis, active participation in treatment, and adherence to medication

Accepting the need for continuing medication represents a major change in mindset and lifestyle for young people who have developed a psychotic disorder. Despite this there has been very little application of compliance-aiding strategies from other fields of medicine to psychiatry or the exploration of novel strategies. There has been one study in more established schizophrenia that has demonstrated improved compliance (Kemp et al., 1998) but this has not yet been replicated in early psychosis. A range of psychological, motivational and educative strategies are likely to be necessary as well as increasing maturity and personal experience of the persistence of the illness. Psychological interventions will be essential to translate efficacious treatments into real world benefits for patients.

To specifically target individual symptom complexes, comorbidities and maladaptive schemas

Later in the recovery process, there is a role for modified CBT in tackling specific symptom complexes and also longer term maladaptive schemas undermining self-esteem. Positive psychotic symptoms, depression, social anxiety, substance abuse and even negative symp-toms are obvious targets for such an approach. Cognitive analytic therapy (see below) may well have a place in addressing longer term and premorbid issues. There has been substantial progress in recent years in developing and evaluating these forms of intervention, many of which are described in this book.

To reduce treatment resistance

While most patients with a first episode of psychosis achieve an initial remission from at least the more florid positive symptoms, the subset of around 10–20% who fail to do so are at serious risk of chronic illness. In addition to clozapine, there is strong face validity and some evidence that CBT will help to improve the degree and quality of remission (Edwards et al., 2002b).

To enhance coping and adaptation

Once again recognition of the degree of difficulty in surviving and adjusting to this typically overwhelming crisis and challenge is the key. The illness and its treatment occur during a phase of life in which not only are coping capacities and personal identity still immature, but parental attachment and peer relationships are also in flux and more tenuous. The development of COPE therapy (Jackson et al., 1996, 1998) was focused on these aspects of recovery.

To improve cognitive functioning

Cognitive impairment has been recognized as another dimension that is critically important to functional recovery. Psychological interventions aimed at enhancing cognitive functioning have been developed in recent years with variable success (Pilling et al., 2002a, 2002b; Wykes & van der Gaaz, 2001) but have not yet been systematically applied in early psychosis.

To improve interpersonal relationships that may have been a problem in any case as a result of risk factors independent to the psychosis, and may have worsened or been disrupted by the effects of illness

Here the framework of cognitive analytic therapy or CAT (Ryle & Kerr, 2002) may be particularly useful as a generic intervention which aims to improve distress and interpersonal functioning. The capacity for individual formulation and a strongly collaborative approach based on mutually agreed issues is particularly appealing for this age group and should help with engagement. The CAT model is being adapted for several more severe forms of mental disorder, including borderline personality disorder (Ryle, 1997) and, currently, psychotic disorders (Ryle & Kerr, 2002).

To provide support and assistance to family members

Family interventions are the most strongly evidence-based of all the psychosocial interventions in psychotic disorders. The needs of family members in early psychosis are not only intense but also phase specific; however, they have not yet been adequately addressed in research or routine clinical practice. Crisis intervention, emotional support, stigma management and education are obvious strategies. This is another vital focus for psychological interventions in the future.

To promote vocational recovery

Vocational rehabilitation has proved to be promising as an intervention even in late phases of disorder in very disabled patients (Drake et al., 1999; Lehman et al., 2002). There is an obvious opportunity to develop more preventively oriented vocational interventions during early psychosis to enable young people to resume their vocational trajectories as soon as possible in the recovery process and to limit the secondary collateral damage wrought by the illness. This will require quite a different approach and has the potential to result in major cost-effectiveness advantages since such interventions are likely to be much more effective earlier in the course of illness. Better quality of life, less poverty and marginalization for patients, and a reduction in the massive indirect costs of the illness are probable benefits. This should be a priority area.

To reduce the risk of suicide and aggression

Suicide is the main cause of premature mortality in schizophrenia and other psychotic disorders (Power et al., 2003). Typically this occurs during the early years of illness when the disorder is at its most virulent and the adaptational task is most overwhelming for patients and families. Clinical services generally are tenuously involved with many patients during this phase, and though there is a crucial need for highly assertive treatment, they have not offered proactive psychological interventions designed to reduce demoralization and suicide risk. There is preliminary evidence that such a focus may be helpful for the subgroup at especially high risk (Power et al., 2003). Antidepressants are similarly underutilized in schizophrenia, and clozapine, which has been shown recently to reduce suicide risk in schizophrenia (Meltzer et al., 2003), is withheld from many patients until much later in the course of their illness.

Similarly, although aggression is a frequent clinical problem—particularly during the acute phase of illness for a subset of patients—there have been very few studies of how psychological interventions could improve this situation. The adolescent and young adult period, especially in males, is the peak phase of life for offending behaviour (Rutter & Smith, 1995), yet there has been little study of, or preventive intervention for, 'comorbid' psychosis and offending behaviour.

To prevent relapse

The early years of illness, especially the first 2–5 years post-entry to treatment, are the peak period for experiencing a relapse of the disorder (Birchwood & Spencer, 2001; Gleeson, 2001; Linszen et al., 1994; Robinson et al., 1999). While medication adherence is the most powerful factor reducing the risk of relapse, psychosocial interventions also have much to offer and warrant greater research and clinical interest.

To reduce harm from comorbid substance use

While comorbid substance use is a common clinical problem in early psychosis, there is little evidence that intervention is effective. Barrowclough et al. (2001) show some benefit in more established illness, however studies of intervention with early psychosis patients are still in progress (Edwards et al., 2002a; Kavanagh et al., 2002).

To reduce the risk of transition to psychosis from prodromal or 'ultra high risk'

Psychological interventions to reduce symptoms and risk of transition in prodromal or ultra high-risk states are being actively developed and evaluated (Morrison et al., 2002; Phillips et al., 2002). Such approaches are likely to be very appealing if effective.

KEY PRINCIPLES FOR PSYCHOLOGICAL INTERVENTION IN EARLY PSYCHOSIS

Psychological interventions in early psychosis should be developed and delivered according to several general principles:

- Psychological interventions should be based on clinically testable theories in individuals and groups of patients.
- Psychological interventions should be highly compatible with biological models of vulnerability and of disorder.
- Psychological interventions should be pragmatic in terms of length and depth of intervention.
- Psychological interventions should be offered as part of a multi-modal treatment approach.
- Given the extensive and variable needs of patients and families, a broad range of interventions should be available.
- Interventions should be sequenced according to phase of illness, because the pattern of needs and, hence, opportunity for psychological intervention varies according to phase.

The latter two principles will be briefly elaborated.

The Optimal Range of Psychological Intervention

Schizophrenia is an illness that happens to a person with a unique psychological makeup.
(Gabbard, 1994)

While the foundation for all interventions and for recovery is a healthy and stable relationship with the patient, a range of approaches is necessary to achieve this and to move beyond it. Many young people will find it very difficult to develop such a trusting relationship with a clinician because of their developmental stage, their previous experience of relationships with older people, a lack of experience and comfort with health and mental health services, and the disorganizing effects of the illness. Knowledge and training in a range of approaches is indispensable to the clinician. Crisis intervention, psychodynamic knowledge, cognitive-behavioural techniques, coping enhancement strategies, communication and educational strategies and group and family intervention skills are all part of the required repertoire. The use of these techniques and approaches should be directly linked to a careful assessment of needs and perceived needs of the patient and his or her family members at any given point in time. These needs evolve with time and the phases of the illness, and are affected by the response of the underlying disorder to drug therapies. The notion of a hierarchy of needs and capacities of the patient is helpful. The most urgent items—such as finding food, shelter, emotional support and a stable and secure environment—must be dealt with first (EPPIC, 2001). Unless these needs are met, the task of addressing other key needs, even central ones such as medication adherence, will be undermined (Hogarty et al., 1997a). Even when the basic human needs are less stark, working alongside the patient in an advocacy and case management mode to tackle real-life problems demonstrates a commitment to the patient and family which builds trust and opens the door to more ambitious recovery goals. This sort of trust is vital if there is to be a chance of overcoming stigma, denial, tendencies to act out destructively, especially via substance abuse and an understandable failure to cope. An active therapeutic role which should move beyond the confines of office-based intervention can be provided without raising expectations too high or risking 'over-involvement' if the therapist is confident, energetic, well-trained and supervised. In most settings, the much greater risk is one of under-involvement and low expectations which harm the patient and increase the risk of demoralization.

How far one can go in moving on to address other internal and interpersonal problems in the person's life depends on the resources and capacities of the patient. For most patients, a return to pre-illness capacity and potential would be a successful outcome. For some others, taking a broader view of additional comorbidity and mental health needs may give the patient an opportunity to tackle other problems in his or her life. Psychodynamic understanding can be useful here provided it is mobilized within an active and antiregressive structure, such as has been developed in cognitive-analytic therapy. Elsewhere I have outlined a simple three-level model to grade the complexity of interventions in early psychosis (McGorry, 2000). Levels 1 and 2 include psychoeducation, crisis support, supportive psychotherapy, and relapse prevention strategies, and should be available to all patients. Level 3 includes CBT for early treatment resistance, suicide risk reduction and substance abuse, and should be offered to subgroups on a needs basis.

The Sequence and Phase-Oriented Delivery of Psychological Intervention

The range of skills referred to above need to be tailored to the phase of illness and influenced by the mental state and level of engagement of the patient. The key phases identified are the prepsychotic phase, the first episode of psychosis, the early recovery period (6 months) and the late recovery period (6 months to 5 years). During the prepsychotic phase it is possible to engage a subgroup of patients who are help-seekers and are at demonstrably increased risk of progressing to a fully fledged psychotic disorder (Phillips et al., 2002; Yung et al., 1996). Psychological interventions may reduce the risk of such progression and may delay or obviate the need for drug therapies, at least in some patients (McGorry et al., 2002; Morrison et al., 2002). The quality and content of such interventions differs from what is required at later stages of illness. Within the first psychotic episode, the sequence of interventions flows from the level of accessibility and engagement of the patient, which in turn depends on mental state, time with the service, and a range of factors intrinsic to the patient, the clinician and the context. The notion of graduating from one level to the next (Hogarty et al., 1997a, 1997b), as well as defining subgroups with special needs, are useful ways to focus specific strategies. Certain needs emerge at predictable time periods, e.g. treatment resistance, psychotic relapse and suicide risk, and hence should be addressed in a timely manner during the phases of recovery. Integration with drug therapies is fundamental and requires close cooperation and joint sessions with the psychiatrist and clinical case manager.

FUTURE

The revival of interest in psychological interventions in schizophrenia and psychotic disorders generally has particular relevance for patients with early psychosis. If these treatments do indeed have a part to play in the optimal recovery of patients with these disorders, then they are likely to be most effective if offered during the early stages. There are certainly many needs identifiable for which psychological interventions are appropriate and necessary and it seems clear that optimal recovery will not occur or will be more difficult to achieve in their absence. It is equally clear that the resources to create, evaluate, translate and fully mandate this element of treatment have not yet been mobilized in a sufficiently substantial way to meet this challenge. The scale of such an undertaking is similar to the international endeavour, which has underpinned the replacement of typical antipsychotic medications by the atypical agents over the past decade. Even this process is incomplete, despite the massive investment involved. The creation and implementation of evidence-based psychological interventions and a service system to support them will arguably require even greater investment and culture change in most countries.

Many fundamental questions remain unanswered. The timing, content, depth and dose of the currently available therapies has not been explored. Some of the logic and rigour of research designs from pharmacology need to be adapted and applied in psychotherapy research in early psychosis. These include 'dose-finding' studies, studies examining the optimal timing, combining and sequencing of treatments, matching of treatments to subgroups, integration of drug and psychological interventions in multicell designs as has occurred in depression, and cost-effectiveness studies of differing forms and combinations of intervention. The extent and quality of our evidence-base still leaves much to be desired.

One of the major challenges for psychotherapy research generally is to demonstrate the value of special technical content of any kind. Most of the benefit of psychological intervention inevitably flows from so-called 'non-specific' factors such as the therapeutic alliance, trust, hope, optimism and continuity of care. These elements need to be acknowledged and fully exploited in clinical practice, however there is a problem if we find it impossible to show that any additional focus or expertise contributes further benefit. Can CBT really reduce the impact of hallucinations and delusions? Can suicide risk be reduced in patients at high risk through specific technical interventions? Can we reduce the harm resulting from substance abuse? If this is not possible, then the current enthusiasm for psychological interventions will once again dissipate. One of the nails in the coffin of psychoanalytic psychotherapy in schizophrenia was the failure to demonstrate an advantage for insight-oriented psychotherapy over supportive psychotherapy (Gunderson et al., 1984), despite the fact that both forms of intervention were probably helpful to patients. The demise of the one accepted theroretical paradigm supporting psychological intervention in schizophrenia has justified serious personal neglect of patients. While the current situation for CBT in psychosis looks more promising for severe forms of psychosis (Sensky et al., 2000), the results of some research in early psychosis are not yet very compelling (Jackson et al., 1998; Lewis et al., 2002). Better research designs, multicentre studies and integrative designs are needed to clarify and demonstrate the role and complementary value of psychological interventions in early psychosis.

On the positive side, in recent years there has been a significant international effort to tackle these issues and develop a set of psychological and psychosocial interventions for patients and families with early psychosis. Some of this effort is reflected in the pages of this monograph and demonstrates that a beachhead has been established from which further refinement and a stronger evidence base can be constructed. Unlike previous foundations, this one seems to lack the fatal flaw of reductionism and is more securely built on bio-psychosocial principles. If this is so, it will not only survive but will benefit from and enhance future advances in drug therapies.

REFERENCES

Agerbo, E., Byrne, M., Eaton, W.W. & Mortensen, P.B. (2003). Schizophrenia, marital status, and employment: A forty-year study. *Schizophrenia Research*, **60**, 32.

Alanen, Y.O., Ugelstad, E., Armelius, B.A., Lethinen, K., Rosenbaum, B. & Sjöström, R. (Eds) (1994). *Early Treatment for Schizophrenic Patients. Scandinavian Therapeutic Approaches*. Oslo: Scandinavian University Press.

Andrews, G., Sanderson, K., Corry, J., Issakidis, C. & Lapsley, H. (in press). The cost effectiveness of current and optimal treatment for schizophrenia: Evidence based medicine is affordable. *British Journal of Psychiatry*.

Arieti, S. (1974). *Interpretation of Schizophrenia*. New York: Basic Books.

Barrowclough, C., Haddock, G., Tarrier, N., Lewis, S.W., Moring, J., O'Brien, R., Schofield, N. & McGovern, J. (2001). Randomized controlled trial of motivational interviewing, cognitive behavior therapy, and family intervention for patients with comorbid schizophrenia and substance use disorders. *American Journal of Psychiatry*, **158**, 1706–1713.

Bechdolf, A., Wagner, M. & Hambrecht, M. (2002). Psychological intervention in the prepsychotic phase: Preliminary results of a multicentre trial. *Acta Psychiatrica Scandinavica*, **106**, S413:41.

Birchwood, M. (2000). The critical period for early intervention. In M. Birchwood, D. Fowler & C. Jackson (Eds), *Early Intervention in Psychosis. A Guide to Concepts, Evidence and Interventions* (pp. 28–63). Chichester: John Wiley & Sons.

Birchwood, M. & Macmillan, F. (1993). Early intervention in schizophrenia. *Australian and New Zealand Journal of Psychiatry*, **27**, 374–378.

Birchwood, M. & Spencer, E. (2001). Early intervention in psychotic relapse. *Clinical Psychology Review*, **21**(8), 1211–1226.

Birchwood, M., Fowler, D. & Jackson, C. (Eds) (2000). *Early Intervention in Psychosis. A Guide to Concepts, Evidence and Interventions*. Chichester: John Wiley & Sons.

Carr, V.J., Neil, A.L., Halpin, S.A., Holmes, S. & Lewin, T.J. (2003). Costs of schizophrenia and other psychoses in urban Australia: Findings from the Low Prevalence (Psychotic) Disorders Study. *Australian and New Zealand Journal of Psychiatry*, **37**, 31–40.

Cornblatt, B., Lencz, T., Correll, C., Author, A. & Smith, C. (2002). Treating the prodrome: Naturalistic findings from the RAP Program. *Acta Psychiatrica Scandinavica*, **106**, S413: 44.

Crow, T.J., Macmillan, J.F., Johnson, A.L. & Johnstone, E.C. (1986). The Northwick Park study of first episodes of schizophrenia. II. A randomized controlled trial of prophylactic neuroleptic treatment. *British Journal of Psychiatry*, **148**, 120–127.

Czernansky, J.G., Mahmoud, R. & Brenner, R. (2002). A comparison of risperidone and haloperidol for the prevention of relapse in patients with schizophrenia. *New England Journal of Medicine*, **346**, 16–22.

Department of Health (1999). *National Service Framework for Mental Health Modern Standards and Service Models*. London: Department of Health.

Drake, R.E., McHugo, G.J., Bebout, R.R., Becker, D.R., Harris, M., Bond, G.R. & Quimby, E. (1999). A randomised controlled trial of supported employment for inner-city patients with severe mental illness. *Archives of General Psychiatry*, **56**, 627–633.

Edwards, J. & McGorry, P.D. (Eds) (2002). *Implementing Early Intervention in Psychosis: A Guide to Establishing Early Psychosis Services*. London: Dunitz.

Edwards, J., Hinton, M., Elkins, K. & Athanasopoulos, O. (2002a). Cannabis and first-episode psychosis: The CAP Project. In H. Graham, K. Mueser, M. Birchwood & A. Copello (Eds), *Substance Misuse in Psychosis: Approaches to Treatment and Service Delivery*. Chichester: Wiley.

Edwards, J., Maude, D., Herrmann-Doig, T., Wong, L., Cocks, J., Burnett, P., Bennett, C., Wade, D. & McGorry, P. (2002b). A service response to prolonged recovery in early psychosis. *Psychiatric Services*, **53**, 1067–1069.

Emsley, R.A. (1999). Risperidone in the treatment of first-episode psychotic patients: A double-blind multicenter study. Risperidone Working Group. *Schizophrenia Bulletin*, **25**, 721–729.

EPPIC (2001). *Case Management in Early Psychosis: a Handbook*. Melbourne: EPPIC.

Falloon, I.R.H, (1992). Early intervention for first episode of schizophrenia: A preliminary exploration. *Psychiatry*, **55**, 4–15.

Federn, P. (1952). *Ego Psychology and the Psychoses*. New York: Basic Books.

Fitzgerald, P. & Kulkarni, J. (1998). Home-oriented management program for people with early psychosis. *British Journal of Psychiatry*, **172** (Suppl. 33), 39–44.

Frank, A.F. & Gunderson, J.G. (1990). The role of the therapeutic alliance in the treatment of schizophrenia. Relationship to course and outcome. *Archives of General Psychiatry*, **47**, 228–236.

Fromm-Reichmann, F. (1960). *Principles of Intensive Psychotherapy*. Oxford, UK: University of Chicago Press.

Gabbard, G.O. (1994). *Psychodynamic Psychiatry in Clinical Practice*. Washington, DC: American Psychiatric Press.

Garety, P.A. & Rigg, A. (2001). Early psychosis in the inner city: A survey to inform service planning. *Social Psychiatry and Psychiatric Epidemiology*, **36**, 537–544.

Geddes, J., Freemantle, N., Harrison, P. & Bebbington, P. (2000). Atypical antipsychotics in the treatment of schizophrenia: Systematic overview and meta-regression analysis. *British Medical Journal*, **321** (7273), 1371–1376.

Gleeson, J.F. (2001). *Early signs and risk factors for relapse in early psychosis*. Unpublished PhD thesis, University of Melbourne, Australia.

Gleeson, J., Jackson, H.J., Stavely, H. & Burnett, P. (1999). Family intervention in early psychosis. In P.D. McGorry & H.J. Jackson (Eds), *The Recognition and Management of Early Psychosis. A Preventive Approach* (pp. 376–406). Cambridge, UK: Cambridge University Press.

Gottdiener, W.H. & Haslam, N. (2003). A critique of the methods and conclusions in the Patient Outcome Research Team (PORT) report on psychological treatments for schizophrenia. *Journal of the American Academy of Psychoanalysis and Dynamic Psychiatry*, **31** (1), 191–208.

Gunderson, J.G., Frank, A.F., Katz, H.M., Vannicelli, M.L., Frosch, J.P. & Knapp, P.H. (1984). Effects of psychotherapy in schizophrenia: II Comparative outcome of two forms of treatment. *Schizophrenia Bulletin*, **10**, 564–598.

Häfner, H., Maurer, K., Löffler, W., Bustamante, S., an der Heiden, W. & Nowotny, B. (1995). Onset and early course of schizophrenia. In H. Häfner & W.F. Gattaz (Eds), *Search for the Causes of Schizophrenia* (Vol. III; pp. 43–66). New York: Springer.

Harrigan, S.M., McGorry, P.D. & Krstev, H. (2003). Does treatment delay in first-episode psychosis really matter? *Psychological Medicine*, **33**, 97–110.

Harrison, G., Hopper, K., Craig, T., Laska, E., Siegel, C., Wanderling, J., Dube, K.C., Ganev, K., Giel, R., An der Heiden, W., Holmberg, S.K., Janca, A., Lee, P.W.H., León, C.A., Malhotra, S., Marsella, A.J., Nakane, Y., Sartorius, N., Shen, Y., Skoda, C. (Dec.), Thara, R., Tsirkin, S.J., Varma, V.K., Walsh, D. & Wiersma, D. (2001). Recovery from psychotic illness: A 15- and 25-year international follow-up study. *The British Journal of Psychiatry*, **178**, 506–517.

Hogarty, G., Greenwald, D., Ulrich, R.T., Kornblith, S., DiBarry, A., Cooley, S., Carter, M. & Flesher, S. (1997a). Three year trials of personal therapy among schizophrenic patients living with or independent of family. II: Effects on adjustment of patients. *American Journal of Psychiatry*, **154**, 1515–1524.

Hogarty, G., Kornblith, S., Greenwald, D., DiBarry, A., Cooley, S., Ulrich, R.T., Carter, M. & Flesher, S. (1997b). Three year trials of personal therapy among schizophrenic patients living with or independent of family. I: Description of study and effects on relapse rates. *American Journal of Psychiatry*, **154**, 1504–1514.

Jablensky, A., McGrath, J., Herrman, H., Castle, D., Gureje, O., Morgan, V. & Korten, A. (1999). *People Living with Psychotic Illness: An Australian Study 1997–98—An Overview*. Overview of the method and results of low prevalence (psychotic) disorders as part of the National Survey of Mental Health and Wellbeing. On behalf of Low Prevalence Disorders Study Group, Commonwealth Department of Health and Age Care, Canberra, Australia.

Jackson, H.J., McGorry, P.D., Edwards, J. & Hulbert, C. (1996). Cognitively orientated psychotherapy for early psychosis (COPE). In P. Cotton & H.J. Jackson (Eds), *Early Intervention and Prevention in Mental Health*. Melbourne: Academic Press.

Jackson, H.J., McGorry, P.D., Edwards, J., Hulbert, C., Henry, L., Francey, S., Maude, D., Cocks, J., Power, P., Harrigan, S. & Dudgeon, P. (1998). Cognitively-oriented psychotherapy for early psychosis (COPE). Preliminary results. *British Journal of Psychiatry*, **172** (Suppl. 33), 93–100.

Johannessen, J.O., McGlashan, T.H., Larsen, T.K., Horneland, M., Joa, I., Mardal, S., Kvebaek, R., Friis, S., Melle, I., Opjordsmoen, S., Simonsen, E., Ulrik, H. & Vaglum, P. (2001). Early detection strategies for untreated first-episode psychosis. *Schizophrenia Research*, **51**, 39–46.

Jones, W.L. (1983). *Ministering to Minds Diseased. A History of Psychiatric Treatment.* London: William Heinemann.

Kapur, S. & Remington, G. (2000). Atypical antipsychotics [comment]. *British Medical Journal*, **321** (7273), 1360–1361.

Kavanagh, D.J., Young, R., Saunders, J., Dawe, S. White, A. & Shockley, N. (2002). Management of substance use in early psychosis: A pilot study. *Acta Psychiatrica Scandinavica*, **106** (s413), 22.

Kemp, R., Kirov, G., Everitt, B., Hayward, P. & David, A. (1998). Randomised controlled trial of compliance therapy. 18-month follow-up. *British Journal of Psychiatry*, **172**, 413–419.

Larsen, T.K., McGlashan, T.H., Johannessen, J.O., Friis, S., Guldberg, C., Haahr, U., Horneland, M., Melle, I., Moe, L.C., Opjordsmoen, S., Simonsen, E. & Vaglum, P. (2001). Shortened duration of untreated first episode of psychosis: Changes in patient characteristics at treatment. *American Journal of Psychiatry*, **158**, 1917–1919.

Lehman, A.F., Goldberg, R., Dixon, L.B., McNary, S., Postrado, L., Hackman, A. & McDonnell, K. (2002). Improving employment outcomes for persons with severe mental illnesses. *Archives of General Psychiatry*, **59**, 165–172.

Lenior, M.E., Dingemans, P.M., Schene, A.H., Hart, A.A. & Linszen, D.H. (2002). The course of parental expressed emotion and psychotic episodes after family intervention in recent-onset schizophrenia. A longitudinal study. *Schizophrenia Research*, **57** (2–3), 183–190.

Lewis, S., Tarrier, N., Haddock, G., Bentall, R., Kinderman, P., Kingdon, D., Siddle, R., Drake, R., Everitt, J., Leadley, K., Benn, A., Grazebrook, K., Haley, C., Akhtar, S., Davies, L., Palmer, S., Faragher, B. & Dunn, G. (2002). Randomised controlled trial of cognitive-behaviour therapy in early schizophrenia: Acute phase outcomes. *British Journal of Psychiatry*, **181**, S91–S97.

Lieberman, J.A. & Fenton, W.S. (2000). Delayed detection of psychosis: Causes, consequences, and effect on public health. *American Journal of Psychiatry*, **157**, 1727–1730.

Lieberman, J.A., Matthews, A.M. & Kirch, D.G. (1992). First-episode psychosis: Part II. Editors' Introduction. *Schizophrenia Bulletin*, **18**, 349–350.

Linszen, D.H., Dingemans, P.M., Lenior, M.E., Nugter, M.A., Scholte, W.F. & Van der Does, A.J.W. (1994). Relapse criteria in schizophrenic disorders: Different perspectives. *Psychiatry Research*, **54**, 273–281.

Malla, A.K. & Norman, R.M.G. (2002). Early intervention in schizophrenia and related disorders: Advantages and pitfalls. *Current Opinion in Psychiatry*, **15**, 17–23.

Malmberg, L. & Fenton, M. (2003). Individual psychodynamic psychotherapy and psychoanalysis for schizophrenia and severe mental illness (Cochrane Review). *The Cochrane Library*, Issue 1. Oxford: Update Software.

Marshall, M. & Lockwood, A. (2003). Assertive community treatment for people with severe mental disorders (Cochrane Review). *The Cochrane Library*, Issue 1. Oxford: Update Software.

May, P.R.A. (1968). *Treatment of Schizophrenia: A Comparative Study of Five Treatment Methods.* New York: Science House.

McGlashan, T. (1999). Duration of untreated psychosis in first-episode schizophrenia: Marker or determinant of course? *Biological Psychiatry*, **46**, 899–907.

McGlashan, T.H., Zipursky, R.B., Perkins, D., Addington, J., Miller, T.J., Woods, S.W., Hawkins, K.A., Hoffman, R., Lindborg, S., Tohen, M. & Breier, A. (2003). The PRIME North America randomized double-blind clinical trial of olanzapine versus placebo in patients at risk of being prodromally symptomatic for psychosis. I. Study rationale and design. *Schizophrenia Research*, **61**, 7–18.

McGorry, P. (2000). Psychotherapy and recovery in early psychosis: A core clinical and research challenge. In B. Martindale, A. Bateman, M. Crowe & F. Margison (Eds), *Psychosis: Psychological Approaches and their Effectiveness* (pp. 266–292). London, UK: Gaskell/Royal College of Psychiatrists.

McGorry, P.D. & Jackson, H.J. (Eds) (1999). *The Recognition and Management of Early Psychosis: A Preventive Approach.* New York: Cambridge University Press.

McGorry, P. & Yung, A. (Eds) (2003). Early Psychosis Symposium. *Australian and New Zealand Journal of Psychiatry,* **37** (4), 393–436.

McGorry, P.D., Chanen, A., McCarthy, E., Van Riel, R., McKenzie, D. & Singh, B.S. (1991). Posttraumatic stress disorder following recent-onset psychosis: An unrecognised post-psychotic syndrome. *Journal of Nervous and Mental Disease,* **179**, 253–258.

McGorry, P.D., Yung, A.R., Phillips, L.J., Yuen, H.P., Francey, S., Cosgrave, E.M., Germano, D., Bravin, J., Adlard, S., McDonald, T., Blair, A. & Jackson, H. (2002). Randomized controlled trial of interventions designed to reduce the risk of progression to first episode psychosis in a clinical sample with subthreshold symptoms. *Archives of General Psychiatry,* **59**, 921–928.

Meares, A. (1959). The diagnosis of prepsychotic schizophrenia. *Lancet,* **i**, 55–59.

Meltzer, H.Y., Alphs, L., Green, A.I., Altamura, A.C., Anand, R., Bertoldi, A., Bourgeois, M., Chouinard, G., Islam, M.Z., Kane, J., Krishnan, R., Lindenmayer, J.P. & Potkin, S., for the InterSePT Study Group. (2003). Clozapine treatment for suicidality in schizophrenia: International Suicide Prevention Trial (InterSePT). *Archives of General Psychiatry,* **60**, 82–91.

Merlo, M.C.G., Hofer, H., Gekle, W., Berger, G., Ventura, J., Panhuber, I., Latour, G. & Marder, S.R. (2002). Risperidone, 2mg/day vs 4 mg/day, in first-episode, acutely psychotic patients: Treatment efficacy and effects on fine motor functioning. *Journal of Clinical Psychiatry,* **63**, 885–891.

Meyer, H., Taimimen, T., Vuori, T., Äijälä, Ä. & Helenius, H. (1999). Posttraumatic stress disorder symptoms related to psychosis and acute involuntary hospitalization in schizophrenic and delusional patients. *Journal of Nervous and Mental Disease,* **187**, 343–352.

Mihalopoulos, C., McGorry, P. & Carter, R. (1999). Is phase-specific, community-oriented treatment of early psychosis an economically viable method of improving outcome. *Acta Psychiatrica Scandinavica,* **100**, 47–55.

Miller, T.J., Zipursky, R.B., Perkins, D., Addington, J., Woods, S.W., Hawkins, K.A., Hoffman, R., Preda, A., Epstein, I., Addington, D., Lindborg, S., Marquez, E., Tohen, M., Breier, A. & McGlashan, T.H. (2003). The PRIME North America randomised double-blind clinical trial of olanzapine versus placebo in patients at risk of being prodromally symptomatic for psychosis II. Baseline characteristics of the 'prodromal' sample. *Schizophrenia Research,* **61**, 19–30.

Morrison, A.P., Bentall, R.P., French, P., Walford, L., Kilcommons, A., Knight, A., Kreutz, M. & Lewis, S.W. (2002). Randomised controlled trial of early detection and cognitive therapy for preventing transition to psychosis in high-risk individuals. Study design and interim analysis of transition rate and psychological risk factors. *British Journal of Psychiatry,* **181** (Suppl. 43), S78–S84.

Nagel, D.B. (1991). Psychotherapy of schizophrenia: 1900–1920. In J.G. Howells (Ed.), *The Concept of Schizophrenia: Historical Perspectives.* Washington, DC: American Psychiatric Press.

National Collaborating Centre for Mental Health (2002). *Schizophrenia: Core Interventions in the Treatment and Management of Schizophrenia in Primary and Secondary Care. Clinical Guideline 1.* London: National Institute for Clinical Excellence. Abba Litho Sales Ltd.

Norman, R.M.G. & Malla, A.K. (2001). Duration of untreated psychosis: A critical examination of the concept and its importance. *Psychological Medicine,* **31**, 381–400.

Othmer, E. & Othmer, S.C. (1994). *The Clinical Interview Using DSM-IV (Vol. 1): Fundamentals.* Washington, DC: American Psychiatric Press.

Pantelis, C., Velakoulis, D., McGorry, P.D., Wood, S.J., Suckling, J., Phillips, L.J., Yung, A.R., Bullmore, E.T., Brewer, W., Soulsby. B., Desmond, P. & McGuire, P.K. (2003). Neuroanatomical abnormalities in people who develop psychosis. *The Lancet,* **361** (25 January), 281–288.

Perris, C. (1989). *Cognitive Therapy with Schizophrenic Patients.* London: Guilford Press.

Phillips, L.J., Leicester, S.B., O'Dwyer, L.E., Francey, S.M., Koutsogiannis, J., Abdel-Baki, A., Kelly, D., Jones, S., Vay, C., Yung, A.R. & McGorry, P.D. (2002). The PACE Clinic: Identification and management of young people at 'ultra' high risk of psychosis. *Journal of Psychiatric Practice*, **8**, 255–269.

Pilling, S., Bebbington, P., Kuipers, E., Garety, P., Geddes, J., Orbach, G., Morgan, C. (2002a). Psychological treatments in schizophrenia: I. Meta-analysis of family intervention and cognitive behaviour therapy. *Psychological Medicine*, **32**, 763–782.

Pilling, S., Bebbington, P., Kuipers, E., Garety, P., Geddes, J., Martindale, B., Orbach, G. & Morgan, C. (2002b). Psychological treatments in schizophrenia: II. Meta-analysis of randomized controlled trials of social skills training and cognitive remediation. *Psychological Medicine*, **32**, 783–791.

Power, P. & McGorry, P.D. (1999). Initial assessment of first episode psychosis. In P.D. McGorry & H. Jackson (Eds), *The Recognition and Management of Early Psychosis: A Preventive Approach* (pp. 155–183). New York: Cambridge University Press.

Power, P., Bell, R., Mills, R., Herrmann-Doig, T., Davern, M., Henry, L., Yuen, H.P., Khademy-Deljo, A. & McGorry, P.D. (2003). Suicide prevention in first episode psychosis: The development of a randomised controlled trial of cognitive therapy for acutely suicidal patients with early psychosis. *Australian and New Zealand Journal of Psychiatry*, **37**, 414–420.

Remington, G., Kapur, S. & Zipursky, R.B. (1998). Pharmacotherapy of first-episode schizophrenia. *British Journal of Psychiatry*, **172** (Suppl. 33), 66–70.

Robinson, D.G., Woerner, M.G., Alvir, J., Ma, J., Bilder, R., Goldman, R., Geisler, S., Koreen, A., Sheitman, B., Chakos, M., Mayerhoff, D.L. & Lieberman, J.A. (1999). Predictors of relapse following response from a first episode of schizophrenia or schizoaffective disorder. *Archives of General Psychiatry*, **56**, 241–247.

Rutter, M. & Smith, D.J. (Eds) (1995). *Psychosocial Disorders in Young People: Time Trends and their Causes*. Chichester: John Wiley & Sons.

Ryle, A. (1997). *Cognitive Analytic Therapy and Borderline Personality Disorder: The Model and the Method*. Chichester: John Wiley & Sons.

Ryle, A. & Kerr, I.B. (2002). *Introducing Cognitive Analytic Therapy: Principles and Practice*. Chichester: John Wiley & Sons.

Schooler, N.J., Keith, S.J., Severe, J.B., Matthews, S.M., Bellack, A., Glick, I.D., Hargreaves, W.A., Kane, J.M., Ninan, P.T., Frances, A., Jacobs, M., Lieberman, J.A., Mance, R., Simpson, G.M. & Woerner, M.G. (1997). Relapse and rehospitalisation during maintenance treatment of schizophrenia. The effects of dose reduction and family treatment. *Archives of General Psychiatry*, **54**, 453–463.

Sensky, T., Turkington, D., Kingdon, D., Scott, J.L., Scott, J., Siddle, R., O'Carroll, M. & Barnes, T.R. (2000). A randomised-controlled trial of cognitive-behavioural therapy for persistent symptoms in schizophrenia resistant to medication. *Archives of General Psychiatry*, **57**, 165–172.

Shaw, K., McFarlane, A. & Bookless, C. (1997). The phenomenology of traumatic reactions to psychotic illness. *Journal of Nervous and Mental Disease*, **185**, 434–441.

Sullivan, H.S. (1927). The onset of schizophrenia. *American Journal of Psychiatry*, **6**, 105–134.

Sullivan, H. (1947). *Conceptions of Modern Psychiatry*. Washington, DC: Wm. Alanson White.

Ugelstad, E. (1979). Possibilities of organizing psychotherapeutically oriented treatment programs for schizophrenia within sectorized psychiatric services. In C. Mueller (Ed.), *Psychotherapy of Schizophrenia: Proceedings of the Sixth International Symposium on the Psychotherapy of Schizophrenia*. Amsterdam–Oxford: Excerpta Medica.

Woods, S.W., Breier, A., Zipursky, R.B., Perkins, D.O., Addington, J., Miller, T.J., Hawkins, K.A., Marquez, E., Lindborg, S.R., Tohen, M. & McGlashan, T.H. (in press). Randomized trial of olanzapine versus placebo in the symptomatic acute treatment of the schizophrenic prodrome. *Biological Psychiatry*.

Wykes, T. & van der Gaaz, M. (2001). Is it time to develop a new cognitive therapy for psychosis—cognitive remediation therapy (CRT)? *Clinical Psychology Review*, **21**, 1227–1256.

Yung, A.R., McGorry, P.D., McFarlane, C.A., Patton, G.C. & Rakkar, A. (1996). Monitoring and care of young people at incipient risk of psychosis. *Schizophrenia Bulletin*, **22**, 283–303.

Yung, A.R., Phillips, L.J., Yuen, H.P., Francey, S.M., McFarlane, C.A., Hallgren, M. & McGorry, P.D. (2003). Psychosis prediction: 12 month follow up of a high risk ('prodromal') group. *Schizophrenia Research*, **60**, 21–32.

Zhang, M., Wang, M., Li, J. & Phillips, M.R. (1994). Randomised-control trial of family intervention for 78 first-episode male schizophrenic patients: An 18-month study in Suzhou, Jiangsu. *British Journal of Psychiatry*, **156** (Suppl. 24), 96–102.

Zipursky, R.B. & Schulz, S.C. (Eds) (2002). *The Early Stages of Schizophrenia*. Washington, DC: American Psychiatric Publishing Inc.

2 Changing PACE: Psychological Interventions in the Prepsychotic Phase

LISA J. PHILLIPS AND SHONA M. FRANCEY
PACE Clinic, ORYGEN Youth Health and Department of Psychiatry, The University of Melbourne, Australia

INTRODUCTION

Psychological interventions during the acute and recovery phases of psychotic illnesses are emerging as effective in promoting recovery, in the development of effective coping strategies, and in enhancing the response to drug treatment (see, for example, Beck, 1952; Bentall, Haddock & Slade, 1994; Birchwood & Chadwick, 1997; Drury et al., 1996a; Hodel et al., 1998; Hogarty et al., 1991; Kingdon, Turkington & John, 1994; Kuipers et al., 1997; Lewis et al., 2001; Sensky et al., 2000). Psychological approaches to the management of hallucinations, delusional thinking, stress and anxiety, social skill deficits and cognitive deficits that occur as a consequence of psychosis have all been described (Perris & McGorry, 1998).

There is, therefore, a logical case for the application of psychological treatment approaches to the emergent phase of psychotic disorders. A diverse range of symptoms has been reported during the prepsychotic phase by young people identified as being at very high risk of psychosis (Yung & McGorry, 1996; Yung et al., 2003). These range from non-specific symptoms, such as depressed mood or sleep disturbance, to low-grade or attenuated forms of psychotic symptoms, such as delusional thinking and hallucinations. It is possible that treatment of these subthreshold symptoms will prevent, or at least delay, the progression of illness. Psychological approaches are likely to be key components of preventive interventions offered during the prepsychotic phase. It is possible that the application of psychological treatment approaches in this early phase of disorder might be more acceptable to clients and safer than drug treatments or might reduce or avoid the need for drug treatment.

This chapter outlines progress towards the development of a specific psychological treatment approach for young people identified as being at imminent or 'ultra high risk' (UHR) of developing a psychotic disorder. This approach has been developed and evaluated at the Personal Assessment and Crisis Evaluation (PACE) Clinic in Melbourne, Australia. The conceptual framework and guiding principles for the treatment are described and illustrative case examples are provided. It is expected that this approach will undergo significant refinement as the aetiology of psychosis is further clarified, and as the needs of young people during the onset phase become better understood. These refinements will undoubtedly also be informed by general developments in clinical psychology. It is hoped that the strategies

Psychological Interventions in Early Psychosis
Edited by J.F.M. Gleeson and P.D. McGorry. © 2004 John Wiley & Sons, Ltd.

and approaches described here will form a solid base upon which future developments will take shape.

Information regarding the criteria used to identify the UHR population can be obtained from the earlier publications of our group (McGorry, Yung & Phillips, 2001; Phillips, Yung & McGorry, 2000; Phillips et al., 2002; Yung et al., 2003). The criteria used to identify UHR clients were derived by combining established trait and state risk factors for psychosis with common phenomenology from the prodromal phase of psychotic disorders. According to PACE inclusion rules, the UHR subjects must meet inclusion criteria for at least one of the following groups: (a) *Attenuated Psychotic Symptoms Group*, who have experienced subthreshold, attenuated forms of positive psychotic symptoms during the past year; (b) *Brief Limited Intermittent Psychotic Symptoms Group (BLIPS)*, who have experienced episodes of frank psychotic symptoms that have not lasted longer than a week and have spontaneously abated; or (c) *Trait and State Risk Factor Group*, who have a first-degree relative with a psychotic disorder or have a schizotypal personality disorder in addition to a significant decrease in functioning during the previous year. They must all be aged between 14 and 30 years and cannot have experienced an acute psychotic episode of longer than 1 week, or received neuroleptic medication prior to referral to the PACE Clinic. Early work at PACE demonstrated that young people meeting intake criteria have a 40% chance of developing an acute psychotic episode in the 12 months after recruitment—even when they receive supportive therapy (Yung et al., 2003).

The PACE Clinic operates as a stand-alone clinical research unit within a larger psychiatric service for young people. Triage workers initially screen referrals to the Clinic over the telephone. If appropriate, a clinical interview is then conducted to assess presenting problems in depth and to determine if intake criteria are met. Those individuals who meet the criteria described above are then given the opportunity to participate in the research being conducted at PACE, which includes intervention studies as well as projects designed to enhance the understanding of the onset phase to acute psychosis and risk factors for psychosis. In an attempt to encourage young people to attend PACE, the clinical research programme is based within a large shopping complex that is well known and frequented by young people in the target age range. There is also a capacity for some outreach services, particularly during the early assessment and engagement phase. At present, psychologists conduct the psychological interventions, but other staff at PACE include psychiatrists, social workers and research staff.

The psychological treatment described in this chapter was included in the first randomized-controlled intervention trial at the PACE Clinic between 1996 and 1999. The treatment approach is primarily cognitive-behavioural in orientation following the success in other centres demonstrated with this approach in the treatment of people with both first-episode and established psychotic disorders (Drury et al., 1996a; Kuipers et al., 1997; Lewis et al., 2001; Sensky et al., 2000). Cognitive therapy with individuals experiencing psychotic illnesses involves exploring cognitive/reasoning biases and appraisals of the self and the illness. Cognitive models of psychosis propose that the core symptoms of psychosis are derived from basic disturbances in information processing, which result in perceptual abnormalities and disturbed experience of the self. Cognitive biases, inaccurate appraisals and core self-schema contribute further to unusual beliefs (Frith, 1992; Garety & Hemsley, 1994; Garety et al., 2001). Like all people, those at risk of psychosis attempt to make sense of their experiences in the light of their earlier development, and the meaning they attach to events will influence symptoms, emotional responses and behaviour. The aim of cognitively oriented therapy is to assist people to develop an understanding of the cognitive processes that influence their thoughts and emotions, and to develop more realistic and positive views of themselves.

The design and outcomes of the first PACE intervention study are outlined in detail elsewhere (McGorry et al., 2002). Briefly, results of this study demonstrated a reduced transition rate to acute psychosis in the 'Treatment' group, who received a combination of low-dose antipsychotic medication and cognitively oriented therapy over a 6-month treatment period, compared to the 'Control' group who received supportive therapy alone ($p = 0.026$). At follow-up (6 months after the cessation of treatment) this difference was no longer significant (McGorry et al., 2002). We have concluded that the provision of very low dose risperidone together with a specific cognitively oriented psychological treatment delayed the onset of acute psychosis in the UHR clients.

OVERVIEW

The underlying goal of the specific psychological treatment offered at the PACE Clinic to young people identified as being at ultra high risk of psychosis is to strengthen the individual's coping resources thereby reducing their vulnerability to developing further, or more severe, symptoms. This may ultimately avert the onset of an acute psychotic episode. The theoretical orientation and techniques are not exclusive to this therapy, but their integration and application to the UHR population are unique.

This therapy was designed to be provided on an individual basis but could potentially be adapted to suit a group treatment situation. In the first treatment study, the therapy was brief—approximately 15 sessions in total, offered weekly to fortnightly over a 6-month period. The frequency of sessions was flexibly negotiated and informed by the mental state of individual clients. Each session extended for approximately 45 minutes but was truncated if the client had difficulties focusing or concentrating or was not well-engaged in therapy.

Stress–Vulnerability Model of Psychosis

The stress–vulnerability model of psychosis informed our treatment approach. The stress–vulnerability model has provided a framework for psychological treatment across the lifetime course of the illness, ranging from first-episode psychosis to more long-standing illnesses (e.g., Drury, Birchwood & Cochrane 2000; Fowler, Garety & Kuipers, 1995; Haddock et al., 1998c, 1999; Jackson et al., 1998; Lewis et al., 2001; Sensky et al., 2000; Tarrier et al., 2000). These models incorporate both biological factors, which underpin the development of these disorders, and the role of psychological and social factors. In addition, we would assert that the stress–vulnerability interaction is also an important basis for cognitive approaches for emerging psychosis.

A common underlying assumption of all variants of the stress–vulnerability model is that ambient/environmental stressors (such as relationship issues, substance use, or lifestyle factors) are key precipitants to psychosis. This implies that the implementation of appropriate coping strategies may ameliorate the influence of vulnerability (Boeker, Brenner & Wuergler, 1989). As a result, strategies for managing stress and the individual's coping response form a core component of the treatment described in this chapter.

Treatment Modules

In addition to enhancing stress management techniques, this therapy was also designed to target specific symptoms experienced by individual clients. As indicated earlier, a wide range of symptoms are attributed to the onset phase of psychotic disorders and are described by UHR clients—psychotic symptoms, neurotic symptoms, substance use problems, family and relationship difficulties, self-esteem issues and so forth (Yung & McGorry, 1996; Yung et al., 2003). In order to respond flexibly to the variation in presenting symptoms and problems in the UHR group, the therapy was designed to incorporate a range of modules targeting different symptoms. Four modules were developed:

- Stress management
- Positive symptoms
- Negative symptoms/depression
- Other comorbidity.

These are described separately below. The assessment of the presenting problem(s) and the client's own perception of their functioning informed the selection of modules in individual cases.

Collaborative Approach

The overriding principle of this therapy is collaboration. Both the client and the therapist have a role in deciding which modules will be utilized, and the client is acknowledged as the 'expert' of his or her own situation. The therapist, who is expected to have a positive, supportive attitude toward the client, guides the therapy towards solutions to defined problem areas. The duration of the therapy is explicitly stated to the client at the outset, with the understanding that this is a short- to medium-term treatment, not prolonged psychotherapy. The therapy is designed to be relatively flexible to respond to changes in symptomatology or situation.

THE BASICS

Phases of Therapy

As with most brief psychotherapy approaches, the UHR psychological treatment can be separated into three distinct phases: *Assessment/Engagement*, *Treatment*, and *Termination*. The aims and a guideline of the length of each of these phases are summarized in Box 2.1.

The engagement phase is obviously crucial. It provides the opportunity for the patient to get to know the therapist (and vice versa) and allows the therapist the opportunity to set ground rules for the rest of the therapy process and to assess expectations of the client. It also enables the therapist to emphasize the collaborative nature of the therapy. It is important that the language used by the therapist, as well as the 'therapy tools', are understood by the client and are appropriate for their developmental level. Cognitive development and other processes, which may be affected by the symptoms and experiences that contribute to the UHR status of this specific client group, should also be carefully assessed. For instance, an individual who experiences brief and intermittent auditory hallucinations may have

Box 2.1. Phases of treatment, aims and duration
Assessment/Engagement
Aims: To conduct a thorough assessment of the issues the client brings to the therapy sessions resulting in a concise formulation that directs the therapy (includes a risk assessment, and crisis plan if required). A mutually trusting and positive working relationship is established between the therapist and client during this phase.
Duration: Approximately **2** sessions.
Therapy
Aims: To address the issues and goals derived from the assessment process via a range of interventions drawn from the treatment modules.
Duration: Approximately **9** sessions.
Termination
Aims: To conclude the therapy process with the client. Additional 'booster' sessions focusing on self-monitoring symptoms and recognizing when assistance might be advisable in the future are available if either the therapist or client thinks that they are required.
Duration: Approximately **4** sessions plus up to **3** 'booster' sessions.

occasional concentration difficulties. Similarly, an individual who experiences persistent perplexity associated with intermittent paranoid thoughts may suffer marked social anxiety.

Key strategies for promoting engagement beyond basic counselling skills are:

- offering practical help;
- working initially with the client's primary concerns and source of distress (Othmer & Othmer, 1994);
- flexibility with time and location of therapy (office based, school, client's home);
- provision of information and education about symptoms;
- working with family members, if appropriate, as well as the identified client;
- collaborative goal-setting.

Further discussion of the importance of the engagement phase in therapy, and strategies for assisting in enhancing engagement with clients experiencing psychotic symptoms, have been presented in other publications (Chadwick, Birchwood & Trower, 1996; Fowler, Garety & Kuipers, 1995; Jackson et al., 1998).

Case Management

The therapists who implemented this therapy were also responsible for the provision of regular case management for the UHR clients. This means that in addition to providing the therapy, the clinician working with the client also has to assist the client in dealing with more practical issues such as finding housing, arranging social security payments, enrolling in school, applying for employment and so forth. Obviously, if resources allow, a separate case manager can undertake these tasks. Combining case management with therapy can reduce the time available for specific therapeutic interventions, while attending to practical concerns can facilitate the initial engagement. Whatever the arrangement, it is essential that case management be provided in addition to the specific psychotherapy because neglecting difficulties in more fundamental aspects of daily living may impact on the efficacy of the therapy and increase the level of stress experienced by the client. Therefore, assistance with housing, financial arrangements, educational arrangements, employment, crisis management, where necessary, and liaison with other services (such as drug and alcohol, forensic, housing, and so forth) may need to occur prior to commencement of the therapy or during the course of treatment.

MODULES

Although this therapy comprises individual modules that target specific symptoms, it may not be appropriate to target one group of symptoms in isolation of other presenting difficulties, i.e., any individual therapy session may incorporate aspects of more than one module. As indicated previously, the therapy is designed to be individualized and responsive to presenting problems, age, general intelligence and motivation of the client, the formulation of the client's difficulties, and ability to complete homework tasks. Ongoing assessment and monitoring of the evolving needs of the client is essential to maintain relevancy and to allow flexible provision of the treatment components. The strategies described here are intended to be appropriately tailored to the individual needs of each client for the purposes of reducing the risk of psychosis. With the stress–vulnerability model in mind it was decided to provide the stress management module, including stress management techniques, to all participants. This module has the added advantage of providing an easily understood introduction to cognitive-behavioural principles, which sets the direction of future sessions.

Stress Management

The components of this module are drawn from traditional stress-management approaches including relaxation training, education about stress and coping, and more specific cognitive strategies (Bernstein & Borkovec, 1973; Clark, 1989; Clark, Salkovskis & Chalkley 1985; Liberman et al., 1975; Ost, 1987). Therapists may choose to be creative and adapt other strategies to the specific needs of each client. As well as being primarily cognitive-behavioural in orientation, these strategies educate the clients to recognize and monitor their own stress levels, to develop an understanding of precipitants to distress, to recognize associated physiological and behavioural correlates of stress, and to develop appropriate strategies for coping with stressful events.

Strategies include:

• Psychoeducation about the nature of stress and anxiety. This entails a detailed discussion of the physical, behavioural and cognitive signs of stress. The physiological reactions concomitant with 'flight and fight' responses are described to help in the process of distinguishing adaptive stress from unhealthy levels of stress. Personal signals of maladaptive levels of stress may also be identified.

- Stress monitoring: Diary use is encouraged to record varying stress levels over specific time periods and to identify precipitating events or situations, and consequences of anxiety or stress.
- Stress management techniques, such as relaxation, meditation, exercise, distraction are introduced.
- Maladaptive coping techniques are identified—for example, excessive substance use and/or excessive social withdrawal. The psychoeducation provided is aimed at reducing health damaging behaviours and promoting more adaptive responses to stress.
- Cognitions associated with subjective feelings of stress or heightened anxiety are identified through monitoring (which may include completion of an inventory of dysfunctional thoughts/irrational beliefs to identify maladaptive cognitions, such as the Dysfunctional Attitudes Scale) (Dyck, 1992; Weissman & Beck, 1978).
- Cognitive restructuring is introduced, which counters dysfunctional thoughts (e.g., negative self-talk, irrational ideas), with more positive coping statements (Meichenbaum, 1975), positive reframing, and challenging (Beck et al. 1979; Beck, Emery & Greenberg, 1985).
- Goal-setting and time management is introduced.
- Assertiveness training is provided.
- Problem-solving strategies are discussed.

Case example: Joan

Joan was a 19-year-old first-year university student who was referred to the service by a General Practitioner. She described a 4-month history of increasing levels of paranoid ideation coinciding with the commencement of university and moving out of home into a residential college. In addition, she reported occasional experiences of thought broadcasting—particularly during communal mealtimes at the college. As a result she had been avoiding meals and spending increasing amounts of time in her room.

Premorbidly, Joan described herself as a relatively shy and private person for whom the change to college and university life was a major one. She described increased stress since moving to college, particularly at social events. She worried that she was not fitting in with the other students, that she would be unable to handle the work requirements for her course, and that other students thought that she was unusual.

The potential relationship between stress and the emergence of her frightening psychotic symptoms was discussed and Joan was taught relaxation techniques. The thoughts underlying her anxiety, particularly in social situations, were explored and strategies for challenging these thoughts were devised. Self-talk and rehearsal techniques were found to be particularly useful. Additionally, a series of graded exposure exercises addressed her social anxiety. This ranged from spending half an hour one evening in the college library (a quiet area at the college) to eating dinner in the communal dining area with the other residents. Joan reported that her anxiety levels decreased substantially, as did the frequency and intensity of the suspiciousness and thought broadcasting. She was able to mix more on a social level within the college setting where she felt more settled.

Positive Symptoms

The treatment approaches incorporated within this module are primarily drawn from cognitive approaches for managing positive symptoms (Drury, Birchwood & Cochrane, 2000; Drury et al., 1996b; Haddock et al., 1998b, 1998c; Lewis et al., 2001). This work has demonstrated that cognitive therapy is a useful adjunct to medication in the treatment of positive symptoms. The goal of this module is to enhance strategies for coping with positive symptoms when they occur, to recognize early warning signs of these symptoms, and to prevent their exacerbation through the implementation of preventive strategies. For example, the therapist might assess with the client the relationship between feeling distressed and anxious and the experience of their psychotic symptoms. They might then brainstorm ways to alleviate stress that might also prevent or alleviate the experience of the distressing voices or unusual thoughts. The client would be encouraged to trial these strategies away from the therapy situation and to report back at the next session on those strategies that were useful and those that were not. Positive symptoms experienced by UHR individuals are less intense and frequent than the experiences of individuals who have had an acute psychotic episode. This might assist in guiding the UHR client to recognise more easily thoughts or perceptual experiences that are unusual or out of the norm. Similarly, attenuated delusional thoughts might be more easily dismissed or challenged than more entrenched and long-standing thoughts.

Strategies include:

- Education about symptoms: Providing UHR clients with a general biopsychosocial account of the origins of 'unusual' or anomalous experiences is thought to be beneficial for clients, serving to 'normalize' their experiences as well as enhancing their motivation for treatment. Fowler, Garety and Kuipers (1995) suggested that psychoeducation about psychosis is most effective if it is tailored to individual clients, and this notion can be extended to the UHR group, although the therapist's language needs to be appropriately adjusted because these clients have not been diagnosed with a psychotic disorder. The use of the word 'psychosis' may not always be appropriate and depends on the level of anxiety of the client and their general cognitive level. Often it is more useful to use the language the clients use, such as 'scary thoughts' and to focus the discussion on coping with current symptoms rather than emphasizing potential negative outcomes. In many cases the clients already have fears that they may be developing a psychosis. It is often useful to acknowledge these fears but to emphasize to the clients that they are currently not psychotic but are certainly experiencing difficulties. The aims of the treatment should be emphasized—i.e., to assist the client to develop and implement strategies to cope better with symptoms, and hopefully to stop these symptoms occurring in the future. Further discussion might address possible causes of symptoms, relationship to family history, relationship with substance use, and so forth. A general discussion about the level of risk of developing an acute psychotic episode is often particularly pertinent for clients with a family history of psychosis, and can enhance the engagement process and strengthen commitment to treatment.
- Verbal challenge and reality testing of delusional thoughts and hallucinations. These techniques draw upon the cornerstones of cognitive therapy—the development of an individualized, multidimensional model of beliefs relating to delusional thinking or perceptual abnormalities (What do these experiences mean to the clients? What conclusions

have they drawn from these experiences? How do they explain them?). The validity of beliefs are examined by reviewing evidence supporting them, generating and empirically testing alternative interpretations. Further information and descriptions about these strategies can be found in a number of publications (see, for example, Chadwick & Birchwood, 1994; Chadwick, Birchwood & Trower, 1996; Drury et al., 1996a).

- Coping enhancement techniques such as distraction, withdrawal, eliminating maladaptive coping strategies, stress-reduction techniques (Fowler, Garety & Kuipers, 1995; Haddock et al., 1998a).
- Normalizing psychotic experiences, using strategies, outlined by Fowler, Garety and Kuipers (1995). This involves suggesting to clients that the symptoms they have experienced are not discontinuous from normality or unique to them, but are relatively common and manageable. This can serve to decrease some of the associated anxiety and self-stigma.
- Reality testing of hallucinations or delusional thinking (Kingdon, Turkington & John, 1994). In collaboration with the client, the therapist devises specific experiments to test the beliefs that the client holds.
- Self-monitoring of symptoms to enhance the client's understanding of the relationship of their symptoms to external events and emotional states. It is also important to stress to the patient the need to be alert for any worsening of symptoms, which could indicate the onset of acute psychosis. These strategies might be revisited towards the end of the therapy process.

As indicated above, because the positive psychotic symptoms experienced by the UHR clients are either of a subthreshold/attenuated form or short lived, it is hypothesized that these approaches may be particularly potent. Through socratic questioning, and other cognitive restructuring approaches, the therapist can assist the client to rebuild upon their base of residual insight. In most cases it is useful to develop an ABC model of the specific positive psychotic symptoms that are being targeted in treatment, as one would when targeting anxiety or mood symptoms with cognitive-behavioural strategies. In practice the therapist, in collaboration with the client, investigates potential precipitants to symptoms, such as idiosyncratic appraisals of interpersonal interactions that may progress to psychotic, or referential interpretations. It is also useful to develop a formulation around the client's experiences that can guide the therapy process. This may need to be reviewed frequently because symptoms may be rapidly evolving in this subgroup (Chadwick, Birchwood & Trower, 1996; Fowler, Garety & Kuipers, 1995).

Case example: Jamaal

Jamaal was a 23-year-old mechanic who reported that he occasionally believed that he knew what people were thinking and at times he believed he could foresee the future. These beliefs had arisen over the past year but had not been present continually over that period. Usually he was sceptical about the likelihood of possessing these skills but he reported a 2-day period when he was continuously overwhelmed by 'symbols' in his environment, indicative of impending doom for his family and friends. He attempted to cope by retreating to his bedroom. Jamaal was able to question his ability to predict the future, which meant that he was open to the prospect of 'testing' his predictive powers. His therapist discussed with him the likelihood that he did not possess these abilities, but together they had agreed that Jamaal was more likely to abandon these thoughts if he had evidence to support this conclusion. A trusting, open relationship with his therapist was essential to enable Jamaal to agree to the 'tests' and they were not proposed until well into the course of therapy. In the first test he made some predictions of future events involving his best friend. These predictions were audiotaped and played back to Jamaal the following week in his friend's presence. His friend reported that none of the events Jamaal had predicted transpired. In the second test of Jamaal's mind-reading ability, videotaped interviews were paused and Jamaal was asked to say what the interviewee would say next. Jamaal's failure to accurately predict what would be said led him to the conclusion that he could not predict the future.

Negative Symptoms/Depression

Negative symptoms of psychosis include low motivation, emotional apathy, slowness of thought and movement, underactivity, lack of drive, poverty of speech and social withdrawal. These symptoms are often difficult to distinguish from those of depression. However, emotional flatness as opposed to depressed mood may be a key distinguishing feature. Many of the *Basic symptoms*, as described by Huber and colleagues and Häfner and colleagues, also fit into this category (Gross, 1989; Gross, Huber & Klosterkötter, 1998; Häfner et al., 1992, 1995, 1998; Klosterkötter et al., 1996, 1997, 2001; Koehler & Sauer, 1984). 'Basic symptoms' are subjectively experienced deficits in thought, language, perception, motor skills and energy and are thought to develop during the prodromal phase of psychosis. In a German study, which followed up for 8 years individuals reporting these experiences, some basic symptoms were found to be predictive of psychosis (Klosterkötter et al., 2001).

Strauss (1989) suggested that negative symptoms are important for two reasons: they are a response to overwhelming psychological and social stressors and they have a significant impact on the future course of the disorder. Although Strauss was directly referring to the experiences of individuals with longer-standing illness, these considerations apply equally well to the UHR client group. Therefore, it was considered important to address negative symptoms in therapy—despite evidence that they are less amenable to treatment when compared to positive symptoms. This might not be the case with the UHR population, however, as it is assumed that negative symptoms are less firmly entrenched. Interventions aimed at reducing negative symptoms are based on cognitive-behavioural principles and closely resemble those developed for the therapy of depression, although depression and negative symptoms are thought to have different aetiologies.

Strategies in this module include: goal-setting (ensuring that an achievable goal is identified on the basis of the client's current functioning), scheduling and monitoring of mastery and pleasure activities, problem-solving, social skills training and cognitive restructuring of negative and self-defeating cognitions (Beck et al., 1979). Some authors also stress the importance of recognizing the protective function of negative symptoms in enabling clients to avoid potentially stressful social situations, which could exacerbate or precipitate the first presentation of positive symptoms. While recognizing that negative symptoms are perhaps the most frustrating for clinicians, Strauss emphasized that it is important to avoid increasing the level of stress experienced by clients by pushing too hard against 'protective withdrawal' (Strauss et al., 1989). It is recommended that small and gradually increasing activity levels and challenging tasks be encouraged. This should follow a careful assessment of the protective function played by the current level of symptoms and the client's understanding of the nature and cause of current difficulties (Strauss et al., 1987). It is also important to recognize that change of long-standing patterns of behaviour will usually occur slowly over extended periods of time.

Case example: Chen

Chen's brother had been treated for a psychotic disorder and her aunt had a history of a depressive disorder. Over the previous 3 months, Chen, who was 21 years of age, had been feeling distant from her family and friends and had been missing occasional days of work because she had not felt capable of performing her required tasks. She admitted to periods of extremely low mood and tearfulness and had recent fleeting thoughts of suicide, and had made some superficial cuts to her wrists. Chen associated these experiences with a recent relationship break-up and subsequent feelings of loneliness and hopelessness about the future. Chen said that apart from the depressive periods she felt no emotion, which was congruent with her flat affect and monotone speech. Initially she contributed very little information voluntarily and the therapist had to use numerous prompts to raise a response to questions.

Chen was encouraged to monitor her thoughts—particularly those associated with the periods of low mood. She was also encouraged to express how she felt through poetry which, until recently, had been a regular activity. Through these procedures, in combination with discussions within the therapy sessions, key themes underlying Chen's depression were elicited. These were primarily associated with poor self-image and negative thoughts about herself. Over time Chen was able to challenge these beliefs and to develop positive beliefs about herself, which was associated with her depression lifting.

Other Comorbidity

This module outlines cognitive-behavioural treatment strategies for more specific and severe anxiety and substance use symptoms experienced by UHR clients. This module builds on the foundation provided by the Stress Management module. The most frequent comorbid problems experienced by young people in the prepsychotic phase and UHR clients are social anxiety, generalized anxiety, panic disorder (or symptoms of panic attacks), obsessive-compulsive symptoms, post-traumatic symptoms, and substance use (Yung & McGorry, 1996; Yung et al., 2003).

Components of treatment

1. Psychoeducation about the role of the sympathetic nervous system and psychological, behavioural, affective, and cognitive correlates of symptoms is introduced. This may include discussions about the risk of worsening symptoms and the subsequent development of diagnosable substance use disorder (Clark, 1989).

2. An appropriate model to explain the development of the client's symptoms is constructed, informed by their life experiences, coping strategies, developmental level, ongoing stressors, available supports and so forth. This model can be used to orient clients to the goals of therapy and as a springboard for other strategies. It provides a wider perspective for clients to view their symptoms.
3. Feelings associated with anxiety are discussed—including the relationship between thoughts, feelings and action in relation to anxiety. Self-talk is also discussed (building on/reviewing work in the stress management module) (Clark, 1989; Meichenbaum, 1975).

More specific techniques depending on the client's needs and presenting problems might include:

1. Managing physiological symptoms of anxiety through relaxation, meditation and other stress management techniques (Bernstein & Borkovec; 1973; Ost, 1987).
2. Exposure techniques (both *in vivo* and imaginal) (Butler, 1989).
3. Behavioural strategies, such as thought stopping, distraction, activity scheduling.
4. Cognitive strategies—including stress-inoculation training and cognitive restructuring (Beck et al., 1979; Beck, Emery & Greenberg, 1985; Clark, 1989).

Substance Use

A thorough assessment of substance use should be conducted. This includes examination of triggers of use, changing patterns of use over time, perceived benefits and costs of use and an evaluation of motivation to address substance use. With careful assessment it may be revealed that other underlying conditions (such as depression, positive psychotic symptoms, anxiety) have been contributing to problematic substance use. This discovery may direct the course of therapy. Motivational interviewing, whereby the therapist assists clients to weigh up consequences for continued use and reduced use of substances with respect to personal goals, may be useful in determining how committed a client is to changing substance use, and may assist in this process of change (Miller & Rollnick, 1991). If substance use is seen as a response to stressors, assistance in the development of other coping strategies may assist in reducing substance use. One of the key roles for the therapist may be in providing clients with information about the substances they use and to encourage them to reduce associated harm.

Case example: Stephanie

Stephanie was a 15-year-old secondary school student whose mother had a long history of schizophrenia, including many long-stay admissions to hospital. As a result, Stephanie was raised primarily by her father. Five months previously, Stephanie had been an average student at school with many friends. She had been actively involved in the drama program, with ambitions to become an actor. However, over the preceding few months, Stephanie had become less motivated to attend school. She appeared disinterested in subjects that usually engaged her, and she was more interested in spending time on her own in her bedroom. She complained of poor sleep and lethargy. Stephanie's father reported a decrease in her appetite. Stephanie admitted to periods of lowered mood and a negative view of the world.

Together with her therapist, Stephanie was able to identify some recent events that may account for some of the recent change in her behaviour. This included being teased at school about her mother's illness and the unfashionable clothes she wore compared to other girls in her class. In addition, Stephanie was concerned that she may become unwell like her mother. These issues were discussed with the therapist and the school's assistance was sought in addressing the teasing.

Case example: Stuart

Stuart was a 28-year-old unemployed man. He had a 10-year history of almost daily marijuana use and intermittent use of amphetamines, ecstasy, various prescription medications, and, most recently, heroin. Stuart reported occasional experiences of auditory hallucinations and paranoia over the time he had been using substances, which had occurred while intoxicated and when unaffected by substances. These experiences had always only lasted hours to days. Two weeks ago, however, he developed the belief that his friends wanted to kill him as part of a larger conspiracy involving an organization that was attempting to monitor him. Stuart said that his belief in this was strongest when he had been smoking marijuana. He was somewhat able to question the reality of these thoughts.

Stuart's therapist discussed with him the possibility that his substance use may be impacting on his experiences. Using motivational interviewing techniques (Miller & Rollnick, 1991) and providing Stuart with information about the impact his drug use was likely to be having on his body and the restrictions it has made on his life—particularly with respect to employment and relationships—the therapist was able to assist Stuart to arrive at the decision to reduce his substance use. The basic message that his substance use was likely to have contributed to his unusual and distressing thoughts was repeated regularly over the course of therapy. The therapist recruited the assistance of other organizations to arrange training for Stuart with a view to future employment. Over time his experience of the unusual thoughts about his friends and others diminished.

CONCLUSION

The psychological treatment outlined in this chapter represents the first attempt to develop a psychological treatment specifically aimed at assisting young people who are identified as being at 'ultra high risk' of developing a psychotic disorder. When combined with low-dose antipsychotic medication for 6 months, this treatment approach resulted in a lower rate of transition to psychosis compared to supportive therapy alone. This difference diminished over the following 6-month follow-up period, however (McGorry et al., 2002).

The strategies outlined in this chapter are not exclusive for the treatment of the ultra-high-risk population, nor are they exhaustive. Indeed, more recently the psychological treatment at PACE has been extended to incorporate a more comprehensive understanding of the developmental origins of psychological problems. The core underlying theoretical orientation continues to reflect cognitive-behavioural principles but the therapy has been broadened to allow a more extensive formulation—including personality factors—to be derived and addressed. Strategies from Cognitive Analytic Therapy have been applied with this aim (Ryle & Kerr, 2002). This extended model of psychological treatment is currently being assessed in a randomized trial and we anticipate producing a comprehensive manual incorporating other skills and approaches in the future. It is likely that other psychological strategies are also appropriate for individuals in this phase of illness, and we anticipate further innovations as the needs of this group continue to gain further attention in numerous studies internationally. Other centres have also begun developing psychological approaches to treating this client population and we await further information on their results (Bechdolf, Wagner & Hambrecht, 2002; Morrison et al., 2002).

ACKNOWLEDGEMENTS

The authors gratefully acknowledge the valued contributions of Steven Leicester, Elizabeth Cosgrave, Dominic Germano, Jenny Bravin, Henry Jackson, Alison Yung and Patrick McGorry in the development and evaluation of this treatment approach and this chapter. Thanks also to the clients and other staff of the PACE Clinic, and the sponsors and supporters of the PACE Clinic—particularly the National Health and Medical Research Council, Stanley Foundation and Janssen-Cilag Pharmaceuticals.

REFERENCES

Bechdolf, A., Wagner, M. & Hambrecht, M. (2002). Psychological intervention in the pre-psychotic phase: Preliminary results of a multicentre trial. *Acta Psychiatrica Scandinavica*, **106**, 41.

Beck, A.T. (1952). Successful outpatient psychotherapy of a chronic schizophrenic with a delusion based on borrowed guilt. *Psychiatry*, **15**, 305–312.

Beck, A.T., Emery, G. & Greenberg, R. (1985). *Anxiety Disorders and Phobias: A Cognitive Perspective*. New York: Basic Books.

Beck, A.T., Rush, A.J., Shaw, B.F. & Emery, G. (1979). *Cognitive Therapy of Depression*. New York: Guilford Press.

Bentall, R.P., Haddock, G. & Slade, P.D. (1994). Cognitive behavior therapy for persistent auditory hallucinations: From theory to therapy. *Behavior Therapy*, **25**, 51–66.

Bernstein, D.A. & Borkovec, T.D. (1973). *Progressive Relaxation Training: A Manual for the Health Professionals*. Champaign, Ill.: Research Press.

Birchwood, M. & Chadwick, P. (1997). The omnipotence of voices: Testing the validity of a cognitive model. *Psychological Medicine*, **27**, 1345–1353.

Boeker, W., Brenner, H.D. & Wuergler, S. (1989). Vulnerability-linked deficiencies, psychopathology and coping behaviour of schizophrenics and their relatives. *British Journal of Psychiatry*, **155** (Suppl. 5), 128–135.

Butler, G. (1989). Phobic disorders. In K. Hawton, P.M Salkovskis, J. Kirk & D.M. Clark (Eds), *Cognitive Behavior Therapy for Psychiatric Problems: A Practical Guide* (pp. 97–128). Oxford: Oxford University Press.

Chadwick, P. & Birchwood, M. (1994). The omnipotence of voices: A cognitive approach to auditory hallucinations. *British Journal of Psychiatry*, **164**, 190–201.

Chadwick, P., Birchwood, M. & Trower, P. (1996). *Cognitive Therapy for Delusions, Voices and Paranoia*. Chichester: John Wiley & Sons.

Clark, D.M. (1989). Anxiety states: Panic and generalized anxiety. In K. Hawton, P.M. Salkovskis, J. Kirk & D.M. Clark (Eds), *Cognitive Behaviour Therapy for Psychiatric Problems: A Practical Guide* (pp. 52–96). Oxford: Oxford University Press.

Clark, D.M., Salkovskis, P.M. & Chalkley, A.J. (1985). Respiratory control as a treatment for panic attacks. *Journal of Behaviour Therapy and Experimental Psychology*, **16**, 23–30.

Drury, V., Birchwood, M. & Cochrane, R. (2000). Cognitive therapy and recovery from acute psychosis: A controlled trial, III. Five-year follow-up. *British Journal of Psychiatry*, **177**, 8–14.

Drury, V., Birchwood, M., Cochrane, R. & Macmillan, F. (1996a). Cognitive therapy and recovery from acute psychosis: A controlled trial, I. Impact on psychotic symptoms. *British Journal of Psychiatry*, **169**, 593–601.

Drury, V., Birchwood, M., Cochrane, R. & Macmillan, F. (1996b). Cognitive therapy and recovery from acute psychosis: A controlled trial, II. Impact on recovery time. *British Journal of Psychiatry*, **169**, 602–607.

Dyck, M.J. (1992). Subscales of the Dysfunctional Attitudes Scale. *British Journal of Clinical Psychology*, **31**, 333–335.

Fowler, D., Garety, P. & Kuipers, E. (1995). *Cognitive Behaviour Therapy for Psychosis: Theory and Practice*. Chichester: John Wiley & Sons.

Frith, C.D. (1992). *The Cognitive Neuropsychology of Schizophrenia*. Hove: Lawrence Erlbaum.

Garety, P.A. & Hemsley, D.R. (1994). *Delusions: Investigations into the Psychology of Delusional Reasoning*. Oxford: Oxford University Press.

Garety, P.A., Kuipers, E., Fowler, D., Freeman, D. & Bebbington, P.E. (2001). A cognitive model of the positive symptoms of psychosis. *Psychological Medicine*, **31**, 189–195.

Gross, G. (1989). The 'basic' symptoms of schizophrenia. *British Journal of Psychiatry*, **155** (Suppl. 7), 21–25.

Gross, G., Huber, G. & Klosterkötter, J. (1998). The early phase of schizophrenia and prediction of outcome. *International Clinical Psychopharmacology*, **13** (Suppl. 1), S13–S21.

Haddock, G., Morrison, A.P., Hopkins, R., Lewis, S. & Tarrier, N. (1998a). Individual cognitive-behavioral interventions in early psychosis. *British Journal of Psychiatry*, **172** (Suppl. 33), 101–106.

Haddock, G., Slade, P.D., Bentall, R.P., Reid, D. & Faragher, E.B. (1998b). A comparison of the long-term effectiveness of distraction and focusing in the treatment of auditory hallucinations. *British Journal of Medical Psychology*, **71**, 339–349.

Haddock, G., Tarrier, N., Spaulding, W., Yusupoff, L., Kinney, C. & McCarthy, E. (1998c). Individual cognitive-behavior therapy in the treatment of hallucinations and delusions: A review. *Clinical Psychology Review*, **18**, 821–838.

Haddock, G., Tarrier, N., Morrison, A.P., Hopkins, R., Drake, R. & Lewis, S. (1999). A pilot study evaluating the effectiveness of individual inpatient cognitive-behavioural therapy in early psychosis. *Social Psychiatry and Psychiatric Epidemiology*, **34**, 254–258.

Häfner, H., Maurer, W., Löffler, W., Bustamante, S., an der Heiden, W. & Nowotny, B. (1995). Onset and early course of schizophrenia. In H. Häfner & W.F. Gattaz (Eds), *Search for the Causes of Schizophrenia* (Vol. III; pp. 43–66). New York: Springer.

Häfner, H., Maurer, K., Loffler, W., an der Heiden, W., Munk-Jorgensen, P., Hambrecht, M. & Riecher-Rössler, A. (1998). The ABC Schizophrenia Study: A preliminary overview of the results. *Social Psychiatry and Psychiatric Epidemiology*, **33**, 380–386.

Häfner, H., Riecher-Rössler, A., Hambrecht, M., Maurer, K., Meissner, S., Schmidtke, A., Fätkenhauser, B., Löffler, W. & van der Heiden, W. (1992). IRAOS: An instrument for the assessment of onset and early course of schizophrenia. *Schizophrenia Bulletin*, **6**, 209–223.

Hodel, B., Brenner, H.D., Merlo, M.C.G. & Teuber, J.F. (1998). Emotional management therapy in early psychosis. *British Journal of Psychiatry*, **172** (Suppl. 33), 128–133.

Hogarty, G.E., Anderson, C.M., Reiss, D.J., Kornblith, S.J., Greenwald, W.P., Ulrich, R.F. & Carter, M. (1991). Family psychoeduction, social skills training and maintenance chemotherapy in the aftercare treatment of schizophrenia. *Archives of General Psychiatry*, **48**, 340–347.

Jackson, H.J., McGorry, P.D., Edwards, J., Hulbert, C., Henry, L., Francey, S., Maude, D., Cocks, J., Power, P., Harrigan, S. & Dudgeon, P. (1998). Cognitively-oriented psychotherapy for early psychosis (COPE). Preliminary results. *British Journal of Psychiatry*, **172** (Suppl. 33), 93–100.

Kingdon, D., Turkington, D. & John, C. (1994). Cognitive behaviour therapy of schizophrenia: The amenability of delusions and hallucinations to reasoning. *British Journal of Psychiatry*, **164**, 581–587.

Klosterkötter, J., Ebel, H., Schultze-Lutter, F. & Steinmeyer, E.M. (1996). Diagnostic validity of basic symptoms. *European Archives of Psychiatry and Clinical Neuroscience*, **246**, 147–154.

Klosterkötter, J., Gross, G., Wieneke, A., Steinmeyer, E.M. & Schultze-Lutter, F. (1997). Evaluation of the 'Bonn Scale for the Assessment of Basic Symptoms- BSABS' as an instrument for the assessment of schizophrenia proneness: A review of recent findings. *Neurology, Psychiatry and Brain Research*, **5**, 137–150.

Klosterkötter, J., Hellmich, M., Steinmeyer, E.M. & Schultze-Lutter, F. (2001). Diagnosing schizophrenia in the initial prodromal phase. *Archives of General Psychiatry*, **58**, 158–164.

Koehler, K. & Sauer, H. (1984). Huber's basic symptoms: Another approach to negative psychopathology in schizophrenia. *Comprehensive Psychiatry*, **25**, 174–182.

Kuipers, E., Garety, P., Fowler, D.F., Dunn, G., Bebbington, P., Freeman, D. & Hadley, C. (1997). London–East Anglia randomised controlled trial of cognitive-behavioural therapy for psychosis. *British Journal of Psychiatry*, **171**, 319–327.

Lewis, S.W., Tarrier, N., Haddock, G., Bentall, R., Kinderman, P., Kingdon, D. & Drake, R.J. (2001). A randomised controlled trial of cognitive behavior therapy in early schizophrenia. *Schizophrenia Research*, **49** (Suppl. 1–2), 263.

Liberman, R.P., King, I., De Risi, W.J. & McCann, M. (1975). *Personal Effectiveness*. Champaign, Ill.: Research Press.

McGorry, P.D., Yung, A.R. & Phillips, L.J. (2001). 'Closing in': What features predict the onset of first episode psychosis within a high risk group? In R.B Zipursky & S.C. Schulz (Eds), *The Early Stages of Schizophrenia* (pp. 3–32). Washington, DC: American Psychiatric Press.

McGorry, P.D., Yung, A.R., Phillips, L.J., Yuen, H.P., Francey, S., Cosgrave, E.M., Germano D., Bravin, J., Adlard, S., McDonald, A., Blair, A. & Jackson, H.J. (2002). A randomized controlled trial of interventions designed to reduce the risk of progression to first episode psychosis in a clinical sample with subthreshold symptoms. *Archives of General Psychiatry*, **59**, 921–928.

Meichenbaum, D.H. (1975). Self-instructional methods. In F.H. Kanfer & A.P. Goldstein (Eds), *Helping People Change: A Textbook of Methods* (pp. 357–391). New York: Pergamon.

Miller, W.R. & Rollnick, S. (1991). *Motivational Interviewing: Preparing People to Change Addictive Behaviour*. New York: Guilford Press.

Morrison, A.P., Bentall, R.P., French, P., Walford, L., Kilcommons, A., Knight, A., Kreutz, M. & Lewis, S.W. (2002). Randomised controlled trial of early detection and cognitive therapy for preventing transition to psychosis in high-risk individuals. Study design and interim analysis of transition rate and psychological risk factors. *British Journal of Psychiatry*, **181** (Suppl. 43), S78–S84.

Ost, L.G. (1987). Applied relaxation: Description of a coping technique and review of controlled studies. *Behaviour Research and Therapy*, **25**, 397–410.

Othmer, E. & Othmer, S.C. (1994). *The Clinical Interview Using DSM-IV (Vol. 1): Fundamentals*. Washington, DC: American Psychiatric Press.

Perris, C. & McGorry, P.D. (1998). *Cognitive Psychotherapy of Psychotic and Personality Disorders: Handbook of Theory and Practice*. Chichester: John Wiley & Sons.

Phillips, L.J., Yung, A.R. & McGorry, P.D. (2000). Identification of young people at risk of psychosis: Validation of the personal assessment and crisis evaluation clinic intake criteria. *Australian and New Zealand Journal of Psychiatry*, **34** (Suppl.), S161–S163.

Phillips, L.J., Leicester, S.B., O'Dwyer, L.E., Francey, S.M., Koutsogiannis, J., Abdel-Baki, A., Kelly, D., Jones, S., Vay, C., Yung, A.R. & McGorry, P.D. (2002). The PACE Clinic: Identification and management of young people at 'ultra' high risk of psychosis. *Journal of Psychiatric Practice*, **8**, 255–269.

Ryle, A. & Kerr, I.B. (2002). *Introducing Cognitive Analytic Therapy: Principles and Practice*. Chichester: John Wiley & Sons.

Sensky, T., Turkington, D., Kingdon, D., Scott, J.L., Scott, J., Siddle, R., O'Carroll, M. & Barnes, T.R. (2000). A randomised controlled trial of cognitive-behavioural therapy for persistent symptoms in schizophrenia resistant to medication. *Archives of General Psychiatry*, **57**, 165–172.

Strauss, J.S. (1989). Subjective experience of schizophrenia: Toward a new dynamic psychiatry, II. *Schizophrenia Bulletin*, **15**, 179–187.

Strauss, J.S., Harding, C.M., Hafez, H. & Lieberman, P. (1987). The role of the patient in recovery from psychosis. In J.S. Strauss, W. Boker & H.D. Brenner (Eds), *Psychosocial Treatment of Schizophrenia: Multidimensional Concepts, Psychological, Family and Self-help Perspectives* (pp. 160–166). Toronto: Hans Huber.

Strauss, J., Rakfeldt, J., Harding, C.M. & Lieberman, P. (1989). Psychological and social aspects of negative symptoms. *British Journal of Psychiatry*, **155** (Suppl. 7), 128–132.

Tarrier, N., Kinney, C., McCarthy, E., Humphreys, L., Wittowski, A. & Morris, J. (2000). Two-year follow-up of cognitive behavioural therapy and supportive counselling in the treatment of persistent symptoms in chronic schizophrenia. *Journal of Consulting and Clinical Psychology*, **68**, 917–922.

Weissman, A. & Beck, A.T. (1978). *Development and validation of the Dysfunctional Attitudes Scale: A preliminary investigation*. Paper presented at the Annual Meeting of the American Education Research Association, Toronto, Canada.

Yung, A.R. & McGorry, P.D. (1996). The prodromal phase of first-episode psychosis: Past and current conceptualizations. *Schizophrenia Bulletin*, **22**, 353–370.

Yung, A.R., Phillips, L.J., Yuen, H.P., McGorry, P.D., Francey, S.M. & McFarlane, C.A. (2003). Psychosis prediction: 12 month follow-up of a high risk ('prodromal') group. *Schizophrenia Research*, **60**, 21–32.

3 Cognitive-Behavioural Therapy for Acute and Recent-Onset Psychosis

RON SIDDLE

Manchester Mental Health and Social Care Trust, UK

GILLIAN HADDOCK

University of Manchester, Tameside General Hospital, UK

INTRODUCTION

A number of recent randomized-controlled trials have indicated that cognitive-behavioural therapy (CBT) can be effective at reducing the severity of psychotic symptoms in patients with chronic and treatment-resistant psychosis (see Rector & Beck, 2001, for a review). CBT has usually focused on reducing the severity and impact of persistent hallucinations and delusions. Approaches have varied slightly in the type of CBT evaluated in these trials; however, they are generally time-limited, collaborative approaches that emphasize improvements in functioning and reducing distress rather than symptom removal or cure. Secondary disabilities associated with a long-term history of psychosis have also been addressed in these approaches, for example, low self-esteem, poor social functioning and stigma. Despite these findings in relation to chronic, treatment-resistant psychosis, there has been relatively little evaluation of the efficacy of this type of CBT with recent-onset and acute psychosis.

One rare exception was conducted by Drury and colleagues (1996). Forty acutely ill psychotic patients were randomly allocated to either an intensive CBT programme or a control programme of activities. The CBT group received individual CBT, family sessions and a group-based intervention focused on reducing stigma and increasing social support. This group had shorter inpatient stays and significantly more of these patients made a full recovery compared to the control group. Significant benefits in terms of perceived control over the illness and improvements in specific symptoms were found for the CBT group over a 5-year follow-up period (Drury, Birchwood & Cochrane, 2000). However, the study had a number of methodological problems that suggest that the findings should be treated with caution. For example, raters and clinical teams were not blind to the patients' treatment group. In addition, the design of the study did not allow any conclusions to be drawn regarding the relative contribution of the three elements of the CBT condition to the overall treatment outcome.

Subsequently, Jackson and colleagues (1998) developed a cognitive treatment approach that focused on facilitating the adjustment of the person and reducing secondary morbidity in

Psychological Interventions in Early Psychosis
Edited by J.F.M. Gleeson and P.D. McGorry. © 2004 John Wiley & Sons, Ltd.

first-episode psychosis (Cognitively Oriented Psychotherapy for Early Psychosis; COPE). Although outcome findings from a randomized-controlled evaluation of COPE have not yet been published, preliminary findings from a pilot study with 80 patients indicated that COPE was a promising approach, particularly in terms of differences in treatment takers and refusers on a sealing over/integration measure. This suggests that those who had received treatment were significantly more likely to have integrated their experiences than those who had refused (Jackson et al., 2001). However, there were no other significant differences between treatment takers, refusers or those who were not offered COPE on any symptom or other illness-related measures over a 1-year follow-up period.

Following the Drury study and other studies involving symptom-focused CBT in treatment-resistant schizophrenia, a pilot study was designed to assess the effectiveness of individual CBT alone in acute, recent-onset patients (Haddock et al., 1999b). This study failed to show significant benefits of CBT over supportive counselling, although significant benefits were demonstrated over the treatment period for both approaches. However, there were non-significant advantages for CBT, suggesting that statistical power was insufficient to demonstrate that individual CBT was an effective treatment over and above other types of psychological support.

THE SoCRATES STUDY

Based upon Haddock et al.'s (1999b) pilot study, the SoCRATES study* (Lewis et al., 2002) examined 318 inpatients or acutely ill day-patients, comparing CBT against supportive counselling and treatment as usual. Patients in the study were either having their first or second episode of psychosis (if the episode was within 2 years of their first). Patients were randomly allocated to one of three treatment conditions. These were: CBT plus treatment as usual; supportive counselling plus treatment as usual (SC); and treatment as usual alone. Therapy was delivered over 15–20 hours in a 5-week therapy envelope that was followed up by four booster sessions. End of treatment and 18-month follow-up data showed that all groups had a significant improvement on the main symptom outcome measure (Positive and Negative Syndrome Schedule Scores: PANSS; Kay, Opler & Lindenmayer, 1989) and those receiving a psychological intervention recovered more quickly than those who received treatment as usual. However, there were no overall significant differences in the outcome of patients who received CBT compared with supportive counselling. Nevertheless, when individual symptom outcomes were examined, those patients experiencing hallucinations fared better with CBT compared to SC. Although these early findings need further analysis in terms of the relative benefits of the various treatments, the overall findings suggest that psychological treatments during the acute and recent-onset phase are beneficial and, specifically, that CBT may be particularly helpful for hallucinations. Given these trends, a descriptive account of the CBT approach developed during the SoCRATES trial, and how it can be implemented, is worthy of dissemination. This is outlined here, with particular emphasis placed upon how the approach differs from that adopted with patients with chronic psychosis.

Treatment Approaches

Although the treatment was modified to meet the needs of the acute, first-episode group, the overall treatment method was guided by the Manchester approach to CBT for psychosis

---

* The authors would like to thank other members of the SoCRATES group in the development of the ideas within this chapter.

DEVELOPMENT

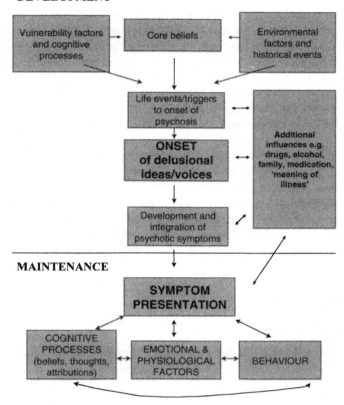

Figure 3.1. The Manchester Model of CBT
Source: From G. Haddock and R. Siddle (2003). Overcoming roadblocks in the cognitive-behavioral therapy of psychosis. In R. Leahy (Ed.) *Roadblocks in Cognitive-Behavioral Therapy: Transforming Challenges into Opportunities for Change.* Reproduced by permission of The Guilford Press

which was developed initially for the treatment of chronic treatment-resistant psychosis. Figure 3.1 illustrates the clinical formulation that underpinned this approach.

As can be seen in Figure 3.1, there is an assumption that biological and environmental factors interact to produce a specific vulnerability for the development of psychotic symptoms. The development of these symptoms is then mediated by a variety of factors, including illicit drug use and familial factors. Problematic symptoms, associated with distress, impaired functioning, and concern by carers, will usually result in an initial presentation to services, although studies have highlighted that delays in receiving effective treatment are common after the initial onset of acute psychosis. The initial presentation and encounter with psychiatric services sometimes acts as an additional moderating influence on the symptoms by activating self-stigmatizing cognitions relating to the meaning of illness and the role of treatment. In addition, biochemical management of the illness will impact on the initial severity. In other words, the symptoms will be determined by an interaction of cognitive, behavioural, physiological and environmental factors. CBT for psychosis is underpinned by the assumption that these various maintaining factors can be modified, regardless of the aetiology of the symptoms, using specific cognitive-behavioural techniques. This model guided the interventions for the recent-onset, acute patients in the SoCRATES study, with some modifications to meet the specific needs of this patient group. For example, the majority were inpatients recently admitted to acute psychiatric wards. In order to be included in the trial, patients had to be experiencing significant psychotic symptoms (scoring 4 or more on the PANSS subscales for hallucinations or delusions). Therefore, all patients recruited into the trial were experiencing either an acute exacerbation of a recently diagnosed illness or their first psychotic episode. Because patients were early in the course of their treatment, they were not usually considered to be treatment resistant, although some had not responded fully to medical and nursing treatment and were difficult to engage. This group of patients was also relatively young (mean age was 27 years), with a number of age-related developmental and familial issues. Many resided with their family of origin and had only recently left school or were still in the early stages of work, career, or college courses. Problems related to drug and alcohol abuse were common and they were poorly informed about mental illness. Finally, a significant number of patients in the trial had not previously been exposed to the terms 'schizophrenia' or 'psychosis' and no patients had previously been prescribed neuroleptics. Many patients (38%) were involuntarily detained under the Mental Health Act or were otherwise under pressure from their clinical teams to remain in hospital. These factors meant that a standard CBT for psychosis intervention that involved 1-hour weekly sessions over a period of 4 to 6 months in an outpatient clinic was not appropriate for this group.

Treatment Modifications

The modifications and emphases in the treatment during the SoCRATES study are outlined below.

Location, length and timing of sessions

As the majority of patients were inpatients or spending most of the day in a day-hospital setting, sessions were usually offered in the ward or elsewhere within the hospital environment. However, if a patient requested sessions to take place in another setting, such as in his or her home or GP clinic, this was usually accommodated. In practice, the vast majority of sessions took place in the hospital during the inpatient stay. If the treatment was not completed at discharge, community sessions (often in the patient's home) were offered. As the average length of stay was 5 weeks, the majority of the treatment occurred during this period. The aim was to complete between 15 and 20 hours of therapy (roughly equivalent to that offered to chronic patients) over a 5-week therapy envelope, followed by booster sessions (anticipated to be in the community) at 2, 4, 8 and 12 weeks after the therapy envelope. Therefore, there was a total treatment phase of approximately 4 months, although the intervention was most intensive during the first month, with 2–3 sessions delivered weekly. This short, intensive treatment period has the advantage of coinciding with other acute treatments (e.g. inpatient care) when the psychosis was most severe. This provided a potential advantage for accessing key cognitions associated with the psychosis and for establishing factors that may have precipitated the onset. The maximum session duration was 1 hour, although session length was flexible because many patients were unable to tolerate sessions of this length. To compensate, some patients received more frequent but shorter sessions. The rationale for the intensive nature of the intervention was that the patients would be available for a significant course of therapy during their inpatient episode and would be struggling to integrate their onset of psychosis into their lives. An intensive intervention during this phase was expected to provide strategies that would assist patients to make sense of their problems, allow them to recover more quickly, develop ways to cope more effectively with their problems and to reduce the development of secondary disabilities associated with their illness.

In practice, the aim of 15–20 hours of therapy was not met for many of the patients. The median number of hours received was 8.6, over an average number of 16.1 sessions (Lewis et al., 2002). We found that some patients refused more than a certain number of sessions as there were so many other issues to contend with, including the commencement of biological treatments, high levels of distress and the fear of being intruded upon while in hospital. Whereas some patients welcomed the intensive and frequent nature of treatment, others were unwilling to take part in any but the briefest of chats.

An examination of the therapist's perception of the best degree of success achieved with the patients revealed that, in 8% of cases, engagement was considered by the therapist to be poor. On the other hand, 46% had a CBT intervention that directly targeted the patient's delusional ideation (Everitt et al., 1999). In all patients, attempts were made to formulate the case and to address delusional ideas or the beliefs associated with hallucinations.

Attendance or engagement in the follow-up booster sessions was similarly variable although these were considered by the therapists to be extremely important in facilitating generalization of gains made in therapy over time and to aid integration of the *staying-well plans* into the patient's lifestyle and environment.

Drugs and alcohol

Drug and alcohol misuse were common problems for a substantial proportion (45%) of patients in the study. For some, the substance misuse was a direct precursor to the inpatient admission and this settled quickly, once abstinent in the ward environment. Since the majority of wards were not locked, a minority would continue to use substances despite being involved in inpatient treatment. The substance misuse may have been directly responsible for the exacerbation or onset of symptoms. Alternatively, the admission may have resulted from some of the secondary distress or social problems that resulted from substance use. Although integrated CBT treatments for psychosis and substance misuse have only begun to be developed and evaluated with acute or recent-onset patients, the role of substance use in the formulation was highlighted by therapists where indicated. For example, where substance use had unequivocally precipitated the onset or exacerbation of symptoms, this was highlighted by therapists; cognitive-behavioural strategies were also offered to assist patients who were willing to address their substance misuse. This was usually in the form of psychoeducation and relapse-prevention strategies. Motivational interviewing (Miller & Rollnick, 1991) strategies were not exhaustively offered although a motivational style incorporating the principles of motivational interviewing was emphasized as being appropriate for patients who did not acknowledge their substance use to be problematic.

Detention and disagreements regarding treatment and diagnosis

Thirty-eight percent of the patients in the trial were detained for treatment under the Mental Health Act (Lewis et al., 2002). This sometimes posed an obstacle to therapeutic engagement because patients perceived therapists as complicit in their detention. A similar problem arose with some non-detained patients who debated their diagnosis, or the treatment they were receiving. On the other hand, the therapist in these cases was sometimes perceived as independent from the medical and nursing team, and as someone who could advocate for the patient. In these circumstances it was helpful for therapists to be clear about the nature and purpose of therapy and the limits of confidentiality in sessions in order to successfully engage patients. Patients were reassured that, apart from information regarding risk issues, only information that the therapist had discussed with them would be fed back to the clinical team, and that this would be done only with the permission of the patient. During the SoCRATES trial, minimal feedback was given to clinical teams, which was extremely valued by some patients who were keen to discuss issues separately from the clinical team that was responsible for detaining them. This strategy was outlined to the clinical teams before the site was included in the study. There was little objection to this constraint, probably because the risk issue was the exception to the rule and because full disclosure was offered after the study was completed. For other patients, integration of the CBT approach in the inpatient setting, by engaging all of the treatment team, may have bolstered the effectiveness of the intervention. For example, there were some occasions when the ward team unwittingly undermined the work carried out in therapy by teaching patients reductionistic biological models of causation, or by preventing therapists from gaining access to the patients 'because they were ill', e.g. experiencing hallucinations. Thorough feedback and a collaborative relationship between therapists and other staff can be essential in this regard. Outside of the controlled research context which aims to reduce the leakage of the experimental treatment strategies into treatment as usual, it would be advisable to involve the entire clinical team in all therapeutic dealings with patients.

Acute psychotic symptoms

Because recruitment of patients occurred within 10 days of admission, symptoms were extremely severe in some cases, which interfered with the engagement process. However, even in these cases partial engagement was possible. Those who did not wish to be seen usually made this clear at the outset and did not even enter a room with a therapist. Persistence, but not coercion, was an important part of the engagement strategy. Sometimes a therapist would initially make several less formal contacts with a patient as part of a strategy to try to engage him or her in more structured CBT sessions. For a minority of patients, this structure could not be achieved, even with persistence. This was commonly because the patients had severe thought disorder which prevented their engagement in a coherent and consistent dialogue. Even these patients received some kind of ongoing support which they valued. However, the degree to which the therapist could engage them in a collaborative CBT approach was limited. For example, disorganized thinking in some cases interfered with the therapist and patients reaching agreement on the principal problems because the patients prevaricated within or between sessions, or because of impaired concentration, or because the extreme distress of the patients did not allow a clear picture of their difficulties to be elucidated. Even where the therapist appeared to be struggling to engage a patient in a CBT approach, the principles of collaboration, focusing on key thoughts and cognitions, and acknowledging and linking these with the patient's distress, could be carried out to some degree.

Rapid resolution of symptoms and keeping well

A substantial proportion of patients will respond to medical and nursing treatment as usual without an additional psychological intervention, i.e. their symptoms may rapidly recede once medication is commenced. A proportion of these will never experience another psychotic episode, whereas others will experience relapses. As a result, a CBT intervention that is focused solely on symptom management is sometimes difficult to justify to patients who might be ambivalent about therapy. In cases where improvement is rapid, the emphasis of the intervention was on relapse prevention or so-called 'staying-well' strategies. This term was often more appropriate and better accepted by patients than the phrase 'relapse prevention'. The keeping-well strategy included a detailed cognitive-behavioural assessment of the key precipitants to the patient's initial psychotic episode. Once these factors were identified, the intervention focused upon integrating strategies that would reduce the likelihood of their recurrence, or upon strengthening the patient's capacity to manage the precipitating factors when they recurred.

Developmental and familial issues

Developmental and familial issues were particularly pertinent to this group of patients, because many still resided with their families and were going through significant developmental stages. For example, some patients experienced their initial episode during their first attempt at becoming independent from families, when starting college or commencing their first job. Although these issues did not influence the overall format of treatment, attention needed to be paid to these significant areas of the person's life. For example, the potential difficulties and challenges associated with returning to employment or college post-discharge from hospital were sometimes a focus of therapy. Issues relating to stigma and the shame of hospital admission when their peers had been coping well in similar situations, were common, especially when colleagues or friends had witnessed their decline into psychosis. Sometimes family members were keen to be involved in therapy, and although this was not offered in SoCRATES, there may be important clinical indicators for working with the family as well as the individual.

The remainder of this chapter offers a practical guide to the practice of CBT with early schizophrenia.

INTERVENTIONS

Overview of Therapy

The initial phase of therapy is aimed at engaging the person into accepting some form of treatment. The engagement phase is followed by attempts to shift attributions related to hallucinations and introduce doubt into delusional ideas, thereby altering the severity and course of the illness. The intensity of the intervention that can be achieved is quite varied. However, for most patients, a clear formulation can be developed and shared, with an emphasis upon the alteration of core schema or perhaps underlying assumptions related to symptoms, as well as treating psychotic phenomenology directly. In all patients, there should also be an attempt to develop a staying-well plan that is influenced by the intensity of the intervention that has been achieved during the course of therapy.

Engagement

Many people with early schizophrenia in contact with health professionals are terrified by their symptoms, which allows a critical engagement opportunity—the exception being

patients with grandiose or religious delusions who can be particularly difficult to engage because their symptoms are seldom associated with distress. However, even in the latter cases,
the experience of hospitalization may cause frustration. The following approaches/strategies
can be helpful when trying to engage people into therapy:

Warm manner

In engaging patients, it is helpful if the therapist can demonstrate a warm and engaging
manner to the patient who may be reluctant to disclose sensitive material to a stranger.
Emotionally neutral questions, for example demographic enquiries, can be helpful initially,
while avoiding topics that might increase the patient's anxiety. If the patient seems comfortable with this initial approach, the therapist can start to discuss areas of concern in more
detail.

Questioning

Tactical withdrawal from any particularly sensitive areas can be helpful in developing and
maintaining engagement. A willingness to disclose personal details, for example personal
reactions to TV programmes, can also help to minimize tension that often occurs when
therapists explore a sensitive topic before the patient is fully engaged in the process of
therapy. Introducing personal disclosure can also be helpful early in therapy because it
prepares the patient for the use of personal disclosure that might be used later in therapy to
normalize symptoms or to highlight thinking errors.

Don't challenge ideas, but attempt to clarify them

Because many newly admitted inpatients with schizophrenia are bewildered by their symptoms, they are often highly receptive to an informed mental health professional who is keen
to talk with them without challenging their ideas. Although many hospitals strive to offer
information, support and therapy for their patients, it is apparent in many wards that the
staff are overwhelmed with managing risk and safety. The collaborative empirical style of
a CBT assessment contrasts with this traditional approach and accounts for its acceptance
by many patients.

Problem list

The gathering of a patient-focused problem list is a useful strategy to help to engage a
patient into therapy. The problem list should ideally contain 2–3 main problems, which
are described in the patient's own words. Even where the patient is reluctant to contribute
problems to the list, it is usually possible to agree upon at least one issue, e.g. getting out
of hospital.

Session structure and explanation

The session structure and clear focus in CBT helps to engage people with early schizophrenia, because there is often a degree of confusion in newly admitted psychotic patients. By
setting a clear agenda a focus can be maintained. Keeping the sessions within the patient's
concentration span is an important principle and sessions with acutely psychotic patients
should rarely be longer than 40–50 minutes. Ensuring that the patient is not overwhelmed
while experiencing medication side-effects for perhaps the first time is important. Therapists
may need to select their session time carefully to avoid mid-afternoon drowsiness, as well
as the pressure for therapy rooms at busy times on the ward, such as during shift handover
or doctor's rounds.

Assessment

The problem list will usually guide the initial assessment, which will necessarily vary in its degree of structure early in therapy. However, where the problems or symptoms are complex or are particularly extensive, a semistructured comprehensive assessment can be helpful at an early stage to develop a broad overview of psychopathology. The Present State Examination (Wing, Cooper & Sartorius, 1974) or the modified Krawiecka, Goldberg and Vaughn Scale (Krawiecka, Goldberg & Vaughn, 1977; modified by Lancashire et al., 1997) can be usefully integrated into the assessment process during early sessions. In most cases, once some progress is made in engagement and exploring symptoms, it is usual for a more extensive cognitive-behavioural analysis of the problems to be completed. There is a range of tools that can be helpful to facilitate this second-stage assessment.

Symptom-specific tools
There are a range of symptom-specific tools that can be helpful in facilitating a multidimensional assessment of the factors associated with psychotic symptoms which aids formulation of the problem in cognitive-behavioural terms. The list below is not exhaustive but provides some examples that have been found to be helpful by the authors.

- The Psychotic Symptom Rating Scales (PSYRATS; Haddock et al., 1999a) are brief semistructured interviews that are easy and brief to administer, and are focused around 6 dimensions of delusions and 11 dimensions of auditory hallucinations. The dimensions include frequency, duration, content, distress associated with the symptom, perceived control over the symptom, and level of conviction associated with beliefs.
- The Antecedent and Coping Interview (Tarrier, 1992) is another semistructured interview designed to assist with a cognitive-behavioural assessment of the factors associated with the onset, maintenance and response to psychotic symptoms. It elicits cognitive, behavioural and affective responses to symptoms.
- The Beliefs About Voices Questionnaire (BAVQ; Chadwick & Birchwood, 1995) is a self-report measure that is designed to explore beliefs regarding the benevolence and malevolence of auditory hallucinations and the degree of engagement and resistance with the voices. This information can be helpful in formulating how the symptoms might be maintained.
- The Maudsley Assessment of Delusions Schedule (MADS; Wessely et al., 1993) is a semistructured interview that provides an extremely detailed assessment of delusional ideation including items relating to reactions to hypothetical contradiction and conviction. The instrument is helpful in facilitating a useful discussion about the evidence used by the patient to maintain his or her delusion as well as measuring the severity of the delusion itself.

Normalizing symptoms and education

Some attempt at normalizing symptoms (Kingdon & Turkington, 1994), together with the provision of accurate information, is also an important part of the early stages of assessment and therapy. Symptoms can be considered as if they are situated at a point along a continuum from normality. This strategy can help the patient to minimize self-stigmatization and help to instil the optimism that he or she can resume something of a normal life. Normalizing interventions can also help at the point in therapy when alternative explanations for a patient's psychotic phenomena are considered. The patient may be able to more easily reattribute symptoms to 'my brain is playing tricks, as discussed by my therapist that time, or maybe it is similar to what happened to those people the therapist told me about, in those experiments'. Normalizing should occur during the initial assessment and engagement phases.

Rectifying knowledge deficits
During assessments there may be a number of opportunities for providing education. Many patients lack good knowledge of mental health problems, so opportunities to rectify knowledge deficits should be taken wherever possible. Therapists should take their time in exploring these knowledge deficits and ensure that details have been understood and taken on board before moving on to the next topic. In early schizophrenia, topics that might arise include how sound travels (hallucinations), simple explanations of top-down cognitive processing (hallucinations), consent and surgical operations (transmitters), security service recruitment (persecutory delusions), discussion of the evidence relating to telepathy, as well as more general information about mental health or medication.

Formulating the case

A formulation is essentially a hypothesis about the nature of a psychological difficulty underlying the problems on the patient's problem list (Persons, 1989). The aim of a case formulation is to understand how the patient's problems are caused and maintained. Appropriate interventions targeting key beliefs can be carried out and problems in therapy can be anticipated and overcome. Therapists will inevitably posit hypotheses about the nature of the presenting problems, even from reading the medical notes or a referral letter. In early schizophrenia, developing the formulation can be a little easier than in the more chronic population, because there is less opportunity for the patient to incorporate delusional evidence into his or her understanding of events. Critical events at the time of the onset of symptoms are also likely to be more recent, and therefore memorable, in early schizophrenia.

Where there are concerns regarding risk, any beliefs that patients have that may influence this risk should be addressed first. These might include a belief that their family would be better off without them, or that an individual, e.g., a neighbour, is a disciple of the devil and should be killed. The next priority should be beliefs that jeopardize therapeutic engagement, such as beliefs about the efficacy of the therapy, or delusions regarding members of the clinical team. Next, the therapist can address other issues. These might be selected on the basis of the frequency of problematic behaviours or the severity of problems; alternatively, problems most easily overcome in therapy may be chosen as a strategy to build confidence in treatment. Furthermore, the decision should be guided by a patient's own problem list, the indications from the formulation, and feedback provided within supervision.

Formulations will usually be shared with the patient, although the degree to which this is done depends upon the patient and the level of engagement. For example, in grandiose patients it may be appropriate to share only parts of the formulation with them, e.g. discussing the difficulties experienced prior to admission as a consequence of acting upon suspicions regarding other people, while avoiding the more controversial hypotheses relating to the grandiose claims.

Case example: Alfred

Alfred was admitted against his wishes after attacking his neighbours because he thought they were paedophiles. He expressed a number of grandiose delusions about being a spy and working for a national security organization.

The therapist's formulation was discussed with his supervisor and it was agreed that a likely mechanism for this grandiosity was a belief that Alfred had not achieved as much in life as he had expected. The delusional ideas may have provided a sort of compensatory mechanism helping him to feel better about himself.

Rather than present Alfred with this hypothesis directly, it was decided to share with Alfred the notion that he was a high achiever who was frustrated because he had not done as much in life as he had expected. What was different was that Alfred had a tendency to discount the achievements that he had made.

The therapist's strategy was therefore to assist Alfred in being less reliant upon a grandiose delusion by encouraging him to appreciate his (true) contribution to the world. This formulation was acceptable to Alfred and he appreciated the invitation to audit his achievements in life. Alfred was able to work with the therapist on a plan to leave hospital and to remain at home. This was achieved when Alfred recognized that he had been sufficiently successful in life – subsequently, the issue of his neighbours being paedophiles was no longer of concern to him. Alfred had 'done enough, and it was someone else's problem now'.

Therapists may begin their formulation with a simple flow diagram; this can be added to as further information becomes available, until a reasonably complete picture is obtained. After the patient is engaged in therapy, he or she should usually be involved in the formulation. Beliefs and attributions can be examined and altered during the next phase of therapy.

Working with delusions and hallucinations

Before the therapist attempts to introduce doubt concerning delusional ideas, precautions should be taken to prevent alternative explanations from being rejected. This will usually require that the therapist has engaged with the patient, and established a good working relationship. Once this has been accomplished, the therapist should have spent some time normalizing the psychotic ideas as discussed above, so that the introduction of doubt for delusional ideas or hallucinations does not require the patient to admit that he or she may have been misguided. Key interventions for modifying the degree of conviction in relation to psychotic beliefs are peripheral questioning and reality testing using behavioural experiments.

Peripheral questioning

Peripheral questioning involves asking patients a number of questions, peripheral to the delusion, which guide them to examine the veracity of their beliefs. Examples of peripheral questions relating to a delusion that a microphone planted in a patient's chest was recording his or her interactions might include:

- Would such a device be very big?
- Would such a device require batteries?

- Would such a device show up on X-rays?
- Who would monitor such a device?
- How would it have got there?

The therapist aims to tread the narrow line between reinforcing and challenging the delusion. Each question is asked with a tone of concerned curiosity, as an invitation to investigate the phenomenon. Most patients appreciate this shared empiricism and seem more willing to relinquish their delusions, especially when the nexus between self-esteem and belief maintenance has been broken by previously normalizing their ideas. Patients can be helped to realize that mild paranoia is ubiquitous, and that even beliefs concerning minor conspiracies are common place. The answers to some of these peripheral questions will often reveal a clear need for additional education. Therapists exploring hallucinations with peripheral questions may often find themselves having to educate the patient once it is recognized that the patient lacks basic general knowledge. On the basis of the patient's comments in the SoCRATES study, it appears that surprisingly little education was given to newly diagnosed patients with schizophrenia within treatment as usual.

There are some patients who derive benefit writing down the evidence for their delusional ideas. Care must be taken to ensure that if cognitive diaries such as a dysfunctional thought record (DTR) are to be used, the patient is aware of the purpose of the recording, precisely what should be recorded, how the entries should be evaluated, and how potential problems in completing the diary are considered and overcome. A three-column diary can be used to allow the recording of the situation, the thoughts and perhaps the evidence supportive of the thought. The third column can be used to promote discussion about thinking errors and the quality of this evidence. Consideration of the evidence supporting or refuting a delusional idea can come from the diary, but is often best generated within sessions, at least initially, where it is possible to challenge, in a sensitive manner, the quality of the supporting evidence.

Consideration of evidence
When considering evidence for delusional ideas in sessions, it is important that engagement is not jeopardized. The therapist needs to be aware of how the patient is perceiving the questions and ought to be prepared to tactically withdraw if the patient appears to be excessively distressed by the line of questioning. If the therapist wished to explore with a patient the nature of evidence recorded in the diary, questions might include:

'Hmm yes, that *is* a possible explanation for what you have noticed. Do you think that this kind of evidence would convince a jury?'

or . . .

'Hmm yes that *is* possible. Do you think that everybody would think in this way?'

The style of questioning involves accepting that the patient's initial hypothesis might be correct, without colluding with that individual. Then, a question is asked which is intended to make the patient reconsider his or her conclusions. The first example encourages the patient to consider the quality of evidence—a concept that most people understand from watching TV courtroom dramas. The second question attempts to instil the notion that not all people think alike and that a number of people may draw alternative conclusions from the same facts. This might be useful in preparing the patient for consideration of an alternative belief.

Lists of evidence for the delusion versus the evidence against the delusion can sometimes be helpful, although this should be done collaboratively so that the therapist does not appear to have outsmarted the patient by dismissing all of the patient's list and suggesting a 'better list'. It is worth remembering that people with schizophrenia will often operate from a range of different rules regarding legitimate evidence. The therapist may wish to help the patient to gradually modify these idiosyncratic rules, while respecting the patient's opinions.

Helping the patient to consider alternative explanations
Encouraging consideration of alternative hypotheses to account for experiences can help to diminish the intensity of conviction in the original belief. It is helpful to encourage the patient to generate as many alternative explanations as possible. Once a list of alternatives is being developed (which may include a number of bizarre explanations), a tentative option can be offered such as a normalized explanation incorporating the notion of stress. In a patient with a belief that he was possessed by the Devil, the following list of possible explanations were developed after a number of sessions of assessment, normalizing, education and peripheral questioning:

- Devil possession (his original delusion)
- God talking to him (his alternative)
- Stress induced the brain to play tricks (joint effort after normalizing).

It can be helpful if the therapist initially postpones the rejection of any of the hypotheses, and encourages further consideration of each option as a homework assignment. After a period of pondering multiple options the non-delusional explanations can be revisited in later sessions when they are less likely to be impulsively rejected. It can also sometimes be helpful to suggest something provocative like:

'maybe it's something like aliens causing the voices'.

As a possibility, this option may not seem very plausible. However, as a strategy to encourage the wider consideration of causal explanations it does sometimes help when an option is tentatively suggested as a possibility and only when the option suggested does not coincide with the patient's actual delusional belief. Another reason for introducing a bizarre causal explanation is that the patient then has the opportunity to dismiss an explanation, and can subsequently be invited to evaluate the quality of the evidence.

In order to summarize the causal explanations, a table can be constructed. The therapist can then draw upon the information gained over the previous sessions to highlight salient evidence to guide the patient to the discovery that the original explanation (i.e. the patient's delusion or attribution for a hallucination) is not as valid as was previously thought. Questions that help to highlight salient evidence in relation to hallucinations include:

- Has the voice ever promised or threatened you with things that have not happened?
- Has the voice ever commented upon things that only you know that you are sensitive about, e.g. having big ears, etc.?
- Has the voice ever commented upon your intentions when you have never mentioned these to anyone else, e.g. when you are to go to the toilet, etc.?

- Has the voice ever been heard in some place when nobody knew you were there, e.g. while you were at the toilet in the psychology department?
- Has the voice ever been heard by anyone that you really trust?
- Did the voice show up on a tape-recording?

These questions relate to patients who have already established the answers to these and other similar questions which were asked during the peripheral questioning and the subsequent education. By careful selection of evidence, the therapist can help patients to realize that there are more likely explanations for their symptoms than previously considered. Reality testing will then usually take the form of behavioural experiments.

Behavioural experiments

Behavioural experiments offer a means of testing the details outlined in the formulation. The aim is to challenge a belief. They can be used to gather data to educate the patient and can be used to modify or practise coping strategies. Behavioural experiments need to be carefully planned and should relate to the session content. Ideally, the patient suggests an experiment and how to conduct it. The patient should also be asked to anticipate what might be learned from the experiment, and potential problems with the experiment should be anticipated and raised by the therapist. Problems will include the patient forgetting to do the experiment, selectively focusing upon some unhelpful aspect of the results, or untoward events which allow the patient to arrive at an unhelpful conclusion.

The tape-recording of CBT sessions, which should be standard practice where possible to aid supervision and as a therapy tool, can be utilized for behavioural experiments for people with hallucinations.

One experiment involved asking a patient, who was hearing voices during the CBT session, to predict if the voices would be audible on the therapy tape. The patient was invited to take the tape away to test the hypothesis. This was then followed up and explored in the next session.

The therapist asked another patient, who was receiving what he believed to be telepathic messages, to write down a simple image or word and send this image telepathically to the therapist. Once this had been attempted over a number of trials, the roles were reversed and the therapist drew simple pictures and 'sent' these to the patient by telepathy. Caution is required using this type of experiment because there are a number of simple predictable images to be avoided in case the patient should be reinforced in his belief that he has received a telepathic message. These include a flower, a car, a house, a cat, a heart, etc., which people will typically draw when asked to provide a simple picture.

Other experiments can involve the gathering of additional evidence to support the hypothesis that voices are internally generated. These might include a period of subvocalization, when the patient tries to sing or carry out some other vocal or subvocal activity when the voices are heard. Because not all patients would be expected to derive benefit from this intervention, it is preferable to suggest it as a trial which may help some people who hear voices. Evidence derived from the experiment may then be used later when evaluating or re-evaluating possible causes of the voices.

The use of coping strategies

Coping strategies for use with patients who are deluded or hallucinated can be taught or enhanced (Tarrier et al., 1990). Incorporating coping strategies into the session can be used as a way of engaging the patient, even if such strategies are not the main focus of an intervention.

Rational responding

Rational responses are often common-sense statements which the patient can (mentally) rehearse at times of difficulty. Rational responses are used to help the patient to control elevated anxiety levels during behavioural experiments. Rational responses can be very effective when recorded onto a cassette and played by the patient on a portable cassette player during stressful activities such as travelling on a bus, walking through a crowd, or whatever precipitates anxiety. Though the use of these coping strategies can lead to inadvertent avoidance of counter evidence, this remains a worthwhile risk in some cases. In some patients with schizophrenia, the anxiety is so great that the therapist may allow or even encourage the development of some safety behaviours as an interim strategy to facilitate compliance with therapy. Many patients, when they are engaged in therapy, find that they garner reassurance from a rational-response tape made by their therapist, in preference to a recording of their own voice.

A patient in the SoCRATES study who believed he was possessed by the Devil because he heard voices arising from his stomach asked for a therapist-recorded summary of the evidence and a number of rational responses to help him to undertake additional evidence gathering at the church where he anticipated there would be thunder and lightning in anger from God. As a religious person this was a frightening prospect and the rational responses allowed him to have the confidence to investigate the outcome when he entered the church. His rational responses included:

- The voices have been wrong in the past.
- I do not have the mark of the Devil (666).
- The priest has said I should go to church.
- God is a loving God.

By hearing a recording of these rational responses and some other facts that had been recorded on the 5-minute audiotape, the patient was less apprehensive about going into the church. The absence of signs from God that He was angry at the patient helped to provide additional evidence against his original Devil-possession explanation.

Rational responses can be written on a card, a newspaper or a scrap of paper. Some patients like to pretend they are looking at a crumpled shopping list when they are surreptitiously rehearsing rational responses in a difficult situation.

Additional examples of rational responses appreciated by patients include:

- There is no evidence that the neighbours are talking about me.
- I have coped with these voices in the past.
- I do not need to do what the voices tell me.
- If these voices really were so powerful they would have killed me by now.

Distraction

Distraction techniques, which can be helpful in some cases (Haddock, Bentall & Slade, 1993), can include mathematical exercises, e.g. counting backwards from 1000 by 7's, or counting objects such as lamp posts, or people wearing sandals. An alternative strategy is focusing upon other senses, e.g. noticing smells or sounds unrelated to delusional beliefs

(Haddock, Bentall & Slade, 1993). Although these coping strategies may only produce a slight improvement, they may be sufficient to challenge assumptions regarding the power of voices and to instil greater self-efficacy. If the patient believes that the voice is the voice of the Devil, then any benefits received from a simple strategy, such as subvocal singing, can progress to a reconsideration of the power and identity of the voice. It is important to expect that not all of these strategies will be helpful and some people will not derive benefit from any of them. Because of this, it is useful for the therapist to explain any coping strategies clearly and suggest the strategies as 'an experiment to determine if any of these interventions will be effective' and encourage the patient to give the interventions an appropriate evaluation. In practice, this means that the patient should rehearse the coping strategy for several days when things are 'not too bad' before evaluating it under duress.

Negative symptoms

At present there is little empirical evidence for efficacious psychological interventions for negative symptoms, beyond the Sensky et al. trial (2000) in which negative symptoms were reduced in both CBT and a befriending control intervention. It might, therefore, be concluded that simply befriending and engaging the patient will offer some help for negative symptoms. In the SoCRATES study, aside from the benefits obtained in befriending the patient during the engagement phase, negative symptoms were addressed using standard CBT techniques such as activity scheduling, focusing upon dysfunctional thoughts and graded task assignment, drawn from depression interventions (Beck et al., 1979) as well as the literature on schizophrenia and psychopathology, e.g. social skills training (Benton & Schroeder, 1990) and long- and short-term goal-setting.

In acute, recent-onset patients with schizophrenia exposed to antipsychotic medication for the first time, drowsiness and boredom may exacerbate negative symptoms. Accordingly, it can be helpful if the therapist takes great care to acknowledge the efforts required by the patient to get out of bed, and participate in therapy. Despite the apparent business of acute psychiatric hospitals, there is often very little for patients to actually do. Patients requiring close levels of observation are further restricted in their freedom to participate in purposeful activity. The CBT therapist working with these patients will need to liaise closely with other therapists and nursing staff on the ward to maximize the opportunity for pleasurable and rewarding experiences. Remaining aware of the impact of negative symptoms upon patient compliance and striving to prevent the patient's negative symptoms or the therapist's reaction to negative symptoms from disrupting the process of therapy, is helpful. In practice, this involves arranging sessions at appropriate times of the day to avoid early morning, mid-afternoon and mealtimes. Sessions may need to be shorter than usual and therapists need to be even more alert to the patient's attention drifting. Where motivation is lowered, it may be tempting for the patient with negative symptoms to avoid the demands of therapy altogether rather than persist with therapy and assertively ask for shortened sessions.

Working with core beliefs

In order to exert an enduring treatment effect, therapists may attempt to address more than specific delusional ideas or other presenting symptoms. Core beliefs or schema are often considered to be at the heart of a person's vulnerability to psychosis and are generally considered to predispose certain individuals to stress and distress (Perris & Skagerlind, 1994). In the SoCRATES trial, attempts were often made to address core beliefs even if we were unable to collaboratively work directly on them with all patients. The role of core beliefs might be included in a formulation and attempts were made to address core beliefs implicated in the patient's psychosis where appropriate.

Core or overarching beliefs include enduring beliefs that the person is bad or that people are generally untrustworthy. These types of beliefs are assumed to have developed in early life and have an effect upon the nature of a person's psychotic beliefs. CBT with core beliefs aims to address dysfunctional models of the self and the environment.

Core beliefs can be incorporated into the formulation using a number of approaches. It is possible for the therapist to make inferences regarding the core beliefs on the basis of the thought records, the content of the voices, and the critical events that were occurring when the illness began. A specific question, which can be discussed in supervision to help the therapist to hypothesize about the nature of these beliefs, is what would a person have to believe in order to act as this patient does? Useful prompts can include:

I am ...
Others are ...
The World is ...

By using these prompts it can be a little easier to speculate on the person's core beliefs. Commonly encountered core beliefs included, 'I am bad', 'Others are out to get me', 'I am special', 'the world is unfair'.

It may be necessary to explore the patient's early experience to try to establish the source of core beliefs and to demonstrate, perhaps by the use of education regarding the development of core beliefs or schema, personal disclosure and guided discovery—the notion of a continuum of beliefs ranging from the extreme to normality. However, therapists should not lose sight of the fact that the core beliefs may have some benefits for the patient and that he or she may be unlikely to wish to give the beliefs up altogether. Self-esteem work, such as that outlined by Fennel (1997), may often be indicated, especially in patients with grandiose delusions whose low self-esteem can often be unrecognized.

Imagery techniques can be helpful in trying to alter retrospective attributions of unpleasant events during childhood. Cognitive imagery can help patients to re-evaluate an abuse experience and perhaps help them to realize that they may not be such 'bad' people and that neglect by a mother can say more about the mother than it says about them.

The aim is to moderate core beliefs. It may be appropriate to try to help the patient to shift from 'I am bad' to 'I behave badly at times' or 'I am less than perfect, but not really too bad'. Comparisons with Adolf Hitler, and other extreme examples, can be used to help patients to realize that they are not so bad after all. Other core beliefs that arise frequently include beliefs that others will do them harm and beliefs that *all* things are predetermined, e.g. via God's master plan or some high-level conspiracy.

Behavioural experiments can be used to test out moderated rules, including testing the notion that rejection or criticism is not 'the end of the world'. An example experiment involved asking patients to consider doing something that was clearly ridiculous or unreasonable and would result in a refusal or rejection, e.g. giving away their house or all their money as a strategy to explore key beliefs. In the example, when the patients said they obviously would not give away their home or their money, it was discussed that the refusal that the therapist had just experienced would not necessarily result in major rejection or any other disasters. The therapist can use this type of example to persuade patients to experiment with other challenges to their core beliefs.

Staying well

The aim of the staying-well procedure is to facilitate generalization and to maintain the gains of therapy. Once therapists have made gains in therapy, consolidation is important by focusing upon relapse prevention or 'staying-well work'. This might involve identifying individual relapse signatures (Birchwood et al., 1989) and individualized risk periods, as well as developing strategies to minimize such issues.

For example, a patient seen in the SoCRATES study with a religious delusion experienced exacerbations in his symptoms every day at 3 p.m. because this was the time at which he believed Jesus Christ was crucified. Other patients will have more conventional periods of heightened risk, including work-related stress, death of relatives and other stressful life events.

The following example illustrates a key issue that arose in the SoCRATES study when a therapist (the first author) was discussing elevated risk periods with a young woman who was approaching the end of her course of therapy. The patient was happy to identify exams and unemployment as possible risk periods, however she was not comfortable discussing family stresses. She was encouraged by the therapist to consider how she would cope with stressors such as her parents' ill health in the future. She tearfully revealed that she had been worried for some time about how she would cope when her parents died, and this discussion helped her to acknowledge the mortality of her parents and to discuss strategies that might help her to deal with this in the future.

For patients in the SoCRATES study, an individualized staying-well pack was developed and introduced to the patient. This included written information that reinforced lessons learned from the sessions in addition to general advice such as avoiding street drugs, ensuring adequate sleep, etc., contact numbers, a list of the patient's early warning signs and a personalized action plan which addressed three goals:

• How to maintain gains
• What to do if one or two early warning signs appear
• What to do if these early warning signs persist or if a broader range of early signs emerge.

These plans may be recorded on a single sheet of paper or they may be extensive. For most patients, even if they do not ask, we suggest that they keep at least one session tape, or a rational response tape from their therapy session. This tape can be used as a revision aid to maintain and extend gains, or as a tool for use in a future crisis.

A degree of self-therapy is desirable, particularly in the well motivated. These self-therapy sessions might involve regular evaluation of problems, perhaps listening to tape extracts, and managing difficulties associated with implementing approaches worked on in therapy. Allowing or encouraging a responsible and understanding relative, or key worker, to help with this can serve to extend the benefits of the CBT long after termination of therapy. It is helpful to try to involve or notify all members of the clinical team, especially where the therapist believes they can reinforce gains made within the therapy. The dissemination of the personalized action plan, which is likely to include all of the people who might have a role in minimizing setbacks in the future, should be planned collaboratively with the patient.

Booster Sessions

Booster sessions are useful in phasing out the therapist's intervention while encouraging the patients to assume more responsibility to maintain their well-being. Some patients do not always follow staying-well plans, even though they were in agreement when the plans were established. Booster sessions can be used to help to practise problem-solving skills and encourage the use of the staying-well plans. Booster sessions can offer an opportunity for the therapist and patients to review the period since the end of therapy and to improve the understanding of setbacks or crises. Based upon this review, the action plans can be adjusted to enhance the possibility of adherence.

In scheduling booster sessions, a reasonable strategy would be to progressively increase the periods between sessions, beginning with fortnightly, then 3-weekly and monthly, before moving on to 3, 4 and 6-monthly intervals. These sessions may be only 15–20 minutes in duration but it would be wise to allow a full hour in case a fuller examination of a setback is required.

SUMMARY

The differences between working psychologically with treatment-resistant patients and those in the early stages of their illness relate to differences in the setting, patient characteristics, developmental circumstances, substance abuse and insight into the nature of the problem. Some of these can be overcome, though others remain obstacles to therapy. In the SoCRATES study we attempted to engage patients into therapy at an early stage of the illness. We have described some of the techniques and strategies in a course of CBT for patients with early schizophrenia.

REFERENCES

Barrowclough, C., Haddock, G., Tarrier, N., Lewis, S., Moring, J., O'Brien, R., Schofield, N. & McGovern, J. (2001). Randomised controlled trial of motivational interviewing, cognitive behavior therapy and family intervention for patients with comorbid schizophrenia and substance use disorders. *American Journal of Psychiatry*, **158**, 1706–1713.

Beck, A.T., Rush, A.J., Shaw, B.F. & Emery, G. (1979). *Cognitive Therapy of Depression* (1st edn.). Chichester: John Wiley & Sons.

Benton, M.K. & Schroeder, H.E. (1990). Social skills training with schizophrenics: A meta-analytic evaluation. *Journal of Consulting and Clinical Psychology*, **58**, 741–747.

Birchwood, M., Smith, J., Macmillan, F., Hogg, B., Prasad, R., Harvey, C. & Bering, S. (1989). Predicting relapse in schizophrenia: The development and implementation of an early signs monitoring system using patients and families as observers. *Psychological Medicine*, **19**, 649–656.

Chadwick, P.D.J. & Birchwood, M. (1995). The omnipotence of voices, II: The Beliefs about Voices Questionnaire. *British Journal of Psychology*, **165**, 773–776.

Drury, V., Birchwood, M. & Cochrane, R. (2000). Cognitive therapy and recovery from acute psychosis: A controlled trial, III. Five-year follow-up. *British Journal of Psychiatry*, **177**, 8–14.

Drury, V., Birchwood, M., Cochrane, R. & Macmillan, F. (1996). Cognitive therapy and recovery from acute psychosis: A controlled trial, II. Impact on recovery time. *British Journal of Psychiatry*, **169**, 602–607.

Everitt. J., Leadley, K., Grazebrook, K., Siddle, R., Benn, A. & the SoCRATES Group. (1999). *The Socrates study: The process of cognitive behavioural therapy for acute, early schizophrenia*. Poster presented at 3rd International Conference on Psychological Treatments for Schizophrenia, 23–24 September, 1999. Oxford, England.

Fennel, M. (1997). Low self–esteem: Cognitive perspective. *Behavioural and Cognitive Psychotherapy*, **25**, 1–25.

Haddock, G. & Siddle, R. (2003). Overcoming roadblocks in the cognitive behaviour therapy of psychosis. In R. Leahy (Ed.), *Roadblocks in Cognitive Behavioral Therapy: Transforming Challenges into Opportunities for Change*. New York: Guilford Press.

Haddock, G., Bentall, R.P. & Slade, P.D. (1993). Psychological treatment of chronic auditory hallucinations: Two case studies. *Behavioural and Cognitive Psychotherapy*, **21**, 335–346.

Haddock, G., McCarron, J., Tarrier, N. & Faragher, E.B. (1999a). Scales to measure dimensions of hallucinations and delusions: The psychotic symptom rating scales (PSYRATS). *Psychological Medicine*, **29**, 879–889.

Haddock, G., Tarrier, N., Morrison, T., Hopkins, R., Drake, R. & Lewis, S. (1999b). A pilot study evaluating the effectiveness of individual inpatient cognitive-behavioural therapy in early psychosis. *Social Psychiatry and Psychiatric Epidemiology*, **34**, 254–258.

Jackson, H., McGorry, P., Edwards, J., Hulbert, C., Henry, L., Francey, S., Maude, D., Cocks, J., Power, P., Harrigan, S. & Dudgeon, P. (1998). Cognitively oriented psychotherapy for early psychosis (COPE). *British Journal of Psychiatry*, **172** (Suppl. 33), 93–100.

Jackson, H., McGorry, P., Henry, L., Edwards, J., Hulbert, C., Harrigan, S., Dudgeon, P., Francey, S., Maude, D., Cocks, J. & Power, P. (2001). Cognitively oriented psychotherapy for early psychosis (COPE): A 1 year follow up. *British Journal of Clinical Psychology*, **40**, 57–70.

Kay, S.R., Opler, L.A. & Lindenmayer, J.P. (1989). The Positive and Negative Syndrome Scale (PANSS): Rationale and standardisation. *British Journal of Psychiatry*, **155** (Suppl. 7), 59–65.

Kingdon, D. & Turkington, D. (1994). *Cognitive Behavioural Therapy of Schizophrenia*. London: Guilford.

Krawiecka, M., Goldberg, D. & Vaughn, M. (1977). A standardised psychiatric assessment scale for chronic psychiatric patients. *Acta Psychiatrica Scandinavica*, **55**, 299–308.

Lancashire, S., Haddock, G., Tarrier, N., Baguley, I., Butterworth, C.A. & Brooker, C. (1997). Effects of training in psychosocial interventions for community psychiatric nurses in England. *Psychiatric Services*, **48**, 39–41.

Lewis, S., Tarrier, N., Haddock, G., Bentall, R.P., Kinderman, P., Kingdon, D., Siddle, R., Drake, R., Everitt, J., Leadley, K., Benn, A., Grazebrook, K., Haley, C., Akhtar, S., Davies, L., Palmer, S., Faragher, B. & Dunn, G. (2002). Randomised, controlled trial of cognitive-behaviour therapy in early schizophrenia: Acute phase outcomes. *British Journal of Psychiatry*, **181** (Suppl. 43), S91–S97.

Miller, W.R. & Rollnick, S. (1991). *Motivational Interviewing: Preparing People to Change Addictive Behaviours*. New York: Guilford.

Perris, C. & Skagerlind, L (1994). Cognitive behaviour therapy with schizophrenic patients. *Acta Psychiatrica Scandinavica*, **89** (Suppl. 382), 65–70.

Persons, J. (1989). *Cognitive Therapy in Practice: A Case Formulation Approach*. London: W.W. Norton & Co.

Rector, N. & Beck, A.T. (2001). Cognitive behavior therapy for schizophrenia: An empirical review. *Journal of Nervous and Mental Disease*, **189**, 278–287.

Sensky, T., Turkington, D., Kingdon, D., Scott. J., Siddle. R., O'Carroll, M., Scott, J.L. & Barnes, T.R.E. (2000). A randomised controlled trial of cognitive-behavioural therapy for persistent symptoms in schizophrenia resistant to medication. *Archives of General Psychiatry*, **57**, 165–172.

Tarrier, N. (1992). Management and modification of residual positive psychotic symptoms. In M.J. Birchwood & N. Tarrier (Eds), *Innovations in the Psychological Management of Schizophrenia: Assessment, Treatment and Services* (pp. 147–169). Chichester: John Wiley & Sons.

Tarrier, N., Harwood, S., Yusopoff, L., Beckett, R. & Baker, S. (1990). Coping Strategy Enhancement (CSE): A method of treating residual schizophrenic symptoms. *Behavioural Psychotherapy*, **18**, 283–293.

Wessely, S., Buchanan, A., Reed, A., Cutting, J., Everitt, B., Garety, P. & Taylor, P.J. (1993). Acting on delusions, I: Prevalence. *British Journal of Psychiatry*, **163**, 69–76.

Wing, J.K., Cooper, J.E. & Sartorius, N. (1974). *Measurement and Classification of Psychiatric Symptoms: An Instruction Manual for the PSE and Catego Programme*. Cambridge: Cambridge University Press.

4 Psychological Intervention in Recovery from Early Psychosis: Cognitively Oriented Psychotherapy

LISA HENRY

ORYGEN Youth Health and Department of Psychiatry, The University of Melbourne, Australia

INTRODUCTION

Since its 'discovery', schizophrenia—or, as it was previously termed, dementia praecox—has been associated with severity of symptoms and chronicity (Kraepelin, 1898, 1919). The concept of schizophrenia historically incorporated assumptions of a pervasive and persistent impairment in cognitive and behavioural functioning, which resulted in a chronic course and poor outcome for the individual (Kraepelin, 1919). This pessimistic view dominated research and clinical practice for many years. At the level of the individual, the prevailing assumption was that the person was completely subsumed by, and lost to, the illness. Therefore, 'once a schizophrenic, always a schizophrenic' (Davidson, 1992, p. 5). However, the previous 40 years has witnessed a slow shift from this viewpoint with the introduction of effective treatments such as neuroleptic medications and research methods evaluating treatment outcomes; and policy change as evidenced by the shift from institutional care alone to the introduction of community mental health services (Zubin, Magaziner & Steinhauer, 1983).

Findings from large cohort, longitudinal studies examining the long-term course of schizophrenia have challenged Kraepelin's view of poor outcome being inevitable in schizophrenia (Bleuler, 1978; Ciompi, 1976; Goldstein, Tsuang & Faraone, 1989; Harding et al., 1987; Huber et al., 1980; Ogawa et al., 1987). Although these studies used different methodologies, their outcome findings are strikingly similar. One-half to two-thirds showed either total recovery or a significant improvement at the point of follow-up. As Huber and colleagues (1980, p. 595) stated: 'Schizophrenia does not seem to be a disease of slow progressive deterioration. Even in the second and third decades of illness, there is still potential for full or partial recovery.'

The heterogeneity of outcome in schizophrenia and other psychotic disorders has challenged the traditional conceptual model of schizophrenia, which focused primarily on pathology and aetiology and minimized the individual's ability to cope and facilitate recovery (Davidson, 1992; Davidson & Strauss, 1992). The reality of recovery in schizophrenia has been a factor in the adoption of cognitive therapy as an important and feasible component

Psychological Interventions in Early Psychosis
Edited by J.F.M. Gleeson and P.D. McGorry. © 2004 John Wiley & Sons, Ltd.

in the treatment of patients experiencing psychosis (Perris & Skagerlind, 1994; Vallis, 1998).

Interestingly, over the previous 25 years the biopsychosocial model has emerged as the treatment ideology for many psychiatric services treating psychotic disorders. The psychological approaches have been well documented and include:

- psychoeducation (McGorry, 1995);
- family interventions (Barrowclough & Tarrier, 1992, 1994);
- relapse prevention (Birchwood, 1992);
- remediation of information process deficits (Green, 1993);
- management of hallucinations and delusions (Chadwick, Birchwood & Trower, 1996; Fowler, Garety & Kuipers, 1995; Tarrier, 1992);
- psychological impact of the psychotic disorder of the sense of self (Davidson, 1992; Davidson & Strauss, 1992; Henry et al., 2002; Jackson et al., 1996, 1998, 2001; Perris, 1989).

This chapter focuses upon the final domain. A psychological intervention is described which was developed to reduce the potentially traumatic impact of a psychotic disorder. This intervention is called Cognitively Oriented Psychotherapy for Early Psychosis (COPE). Information pertaining to the development of COPE and its conceptual base has been well documented by our research group (Jackson, Hulbert & Henry, 2000; Jackson et al., 1999; McGorry et al., 1998). COPE was developed and evaluated at the Early Psychosis Prevention and Intervention Centre (EPPIC) in Melbourne, Australia, from 1993 to 1996. During this time EPPIC offered a comprehensive clinical facility for first-episode psychosis, servicing a catchment area of approximately 850,000 persons in metropolitan Melbourne. Information regarding the rationale for the service development and description of the EPPIC model of treatment can be found in earlier publications (Edwards et al., 1994; McGorry et al., 1996). Findings from the 1-year follow-up study, which evaluated the early model of COPE, suggested that COPE impacted upon insight and attitudes towards treatment (Jackson et al., 2001). The findings from the randomized-controlled trial of COPE, where it was compared to standard clinical care at EPPIC, will be published in the near future.

This chapter describes aspects of the phase-oriented therapeutic approach of COPE. Particular reference will be made to assessment issues in first-episode psychosis, and the focus upon the 'adaptation of self'. Detailed descriptions of the secondary morbidity focus has been thoroughly outlined elsewhere (Jackson, Hulbert & Henry, 2000) and will not be reiterated here. Components of the intervention will be described with case vignettes to illustrate the techniques used in COPE. The chapter is designed as a guide to clinical care and to assist clinicians working with people experiencing their first episode of psychosis.

THE FIRST-EPISODE PSYCHOTIC EXPERIENCE

What is the *human experience* of the psychotic disorder called schizophrenia? What is the personal impact of psychosis? How does one cope with the illness? Is it possible to make sense of and understand the psychotic experience? These unanswered questions provided the impetus for our research group to develop, and later refine, the COPE therapeutic model. Psychosis is often, but not always, experienced as a personal disaster with a potentially damaging mix of secondary trauma and loss. The individual's self-esteem may be battered by the psychotic experience and by the self-stigma associated with becoming a psychiatric patient (McGorry et al., 1998). Furthermore, most psychotic disorders emerge during adolescence and young adulthood, threatening disruption of the person's developmental trajectory. There are a number of key developmental tasks facing the individual at this stage of life, such as identity formation, which may be profoundly affected by the onset of illness (Erikson, 1968). At a time when their peers are testing and achieving their independence, young people recovering from psychosis are being monitored and treated by a range of health professionals. Additionally the vocational or educational opportunities for adolescents may be either lost or delayed (Kessler et al., 1995). As a result of their illness the young person may have difficulties relating to and re-integrating with their peer group.

The experience of psychosis, the treatment process and the response from the post-psychotic environment are potentially traumatic experiences, which have the capacity to change a person's usual way of construing themselves, their environment and their future. In short, psychosis may potentially threaten the core self or identity of the adolescent or young adult. Therefore it might be argued that the time to strengthen a person's sense of self and self-efficacy is as soon as possible after the first presentation (Coursey, 1989; Jackson et al., 1996; McGorry, 1992, 1994, 1995). This may reduce the risk of suicide, and possibly prevent severe impairments, such as negative symptoms, or the entrenchment of secondary morbidity (Jackson, Hulbert & Henry, 2000).

The aims of COPE were to:

- impart a message of hopefulness;
- harness support for the individual to reduce engulfment;
- promote integration, adaptation and recovery.

The intervention aims were based on two principles: first, the realization that the needs of first-episode clients are not the same as those with established illnesses (Edwards & McGorry, 1998); second, the hypothesis of the so-called 'critical period' which comprises the initial 2–5 years of psychosis during which time treatment may exert maximal impact in reducing the severity of the illness and associated psychosocial deterioration (Birchwood, 2000; Birchwood & Macmillan, 1993; Birchwood, McGorry & Jackson, 1997).

THE THERAPY OVERVIEW

Consistent with other cognitive oriented psychotherapies, COPE is a focal therapeutic approach, which is carefully tailored to each individual, based upon the clinical formulation. COPE concentrates upon assessment, developing a therapeutic alliance, and treatment to enhance an adaptive recovery from psychosis and prevent secondary morbidity. The goals of COPE are as follows:

1. To assess and therefore understand the patient's explanation of his or her disorder and gain an appreciation of the patient's attitude towards psychosis in general. This involves identifying the person's current and, if possible, potential problems, along with a formulation of factors contributing to their cause and maintenance. These factors include strengths, weaknesses, coping style, resources available, and the patient's perspective for considering any problems.

2. To engage with the patient and develop a collaborative therapeutic relationship.
3. To promote a style of adaptive recovery from psychosis. This is achieved by focusing upon how the person is adjusting to the experience of psychosis, the possibility of an ongoing vulnerability or continuation of symptoms and the patient's self-perception. The therapist might offer a new model of the patient's experiences and judgements about psychosis. Depending upon the patient's willingness to consider alternative perspectives, the vulnerability–stress model is introduced as a helpful framework for understanding the illness. The overarching aim is to decrease distress and promote an adaptive response.
4. To prevent or manage secondary problems that have developed in the wake of the psychotic disorder, such as depression, anxiety, and associated stigma, which can influence self-esteem.

COPE is offered to patients on an individual basis towards the end of the acute phase of the psychotic disorder, when the patient's mental state has stabilized and the patient is more likely to be responsive and ready to engage in therapy. Therapy can also be introduced after a relapse has occurred when the person might be 'psychologically ready' for therapy. The therapy was short-term consisting of 20 to 30 sessions, each of approximately 45 minutes duration.

The following section describes the assessment and adaptation components of COPE. For the sake of clarity, they will be presented as discrete phases, although in practice the therapy allowed for fluid movement between phases according to the needs of the patients. For example, the therapist may offer practical assistance, which may enhance the therapeutic alliance and alert the therapist to the functioning of the person, which in turn provides assessment information.

ASSESSMENT

The following section describes the therapy assessment phase, including a discussion about the importance of developing a therapy agenda. Examples of techniques and strategies that have proved useful at this particular phase of therapy are outlined. The usual practice is for the therapist to spend the first three sessions assessing and engaging the patient. An agenda for therapy is then developed. This is an interactive process and provides a structure for therapy with the opportunity for review sessions. The formal assessment phase is completed within three therapy sessions.

Assessing the Psychological Issues in Recovery

The basis of the assessment procedure is to assess the person's understanding and explanation of his or her experiences, and his or her ideas about the consequences of a psychotic episode. The assessment includes and moves beyond the gathering of automatic thoughts and associated events, to reveal attributions and associated feelings concerning their situation and experience. Additionally, the therapist needs to ascertain the person's prior aspirations, hopes and goals, and the impact of the psychosis upon these issues. This will influence the approach and techniques used by the therapist in the adaptation phase of therapy.

The first session is an introductory session in which the patient is provided with a rationale for therapy and for the assessment process. The assessment aims to elicit specific information from the patient in order to reach a formulation, which guides the therapeutic approach. The therapist must be alert to:

- the current stage in the acute-recovery phase;
- the presence of positive, negative, depressive or manic symptoms;
- the presence of secondary and/or comorbid symptoms;
- the level of current cognitive impairment (attention, concentration and memory);
- the current adaptation style and explanatory model;
- the extent of trauma and loss;
- the degree and content of knowledge about psychosis;
- the personality structure;
- previous therapeutic contact;
- the sociocultural and religious context.

Box 4.1 outlines questions and prompts, which may assist the therapist in assessing these issues.

Box 4.1. The assessment

Explanatory model

- How does the patient explain his or her mental illness? What is his or her theory?
- What was the meaning of the psychosis for the patient?
- What does the patient understand his or her illness to be? What does the patient call it?
- Does the patient have control over it?
- Why did this happen to the patient? Why at this time in his or her life?

Psychoeducation

- How does the patient define psychosis? What does he or she think it is and where does it come from? Why does the patient think it happened to him or her?
- What knowledge does the patient have about mental illness?
- Was there a stressor that precipitated the patient's admission/psychotic episode? What was going on in the patient's life prior to the psychotic episode?
- What were the early warning signs?
- How can relapse be prevented?
- Where does the patient believe he or she is within the episode, i.e. acute, recovery?
- What does the patient anticipate the recovery to be like?

Adaptation identity

- How does the patient's perception of being psychotic impact upon his or her life and lifestyle?
- How is the patient's self-perception now?

- How does the patient think other people view him or her? Do people treat him or her differently or behave differently towards him or her now?
- What was the patient's perception of his or her future before becoming psychotic?
- What perception does the patient have now of his or her future? Has it changed? Why has it changed?
- Does the patient believe that he or she is well?
- Does the patient believe that he or she was ever unwell?
- How does the patient plan to stay well?
- What are his or her coping strategies?
- Does the patient believe he or she has some control over his or her psychosis?

Secondary morbidity

- Does the patient have times when he or she feels depressed or anxious?
- How does the patient react when this happens?
- How does the patient cope with negative mood states?
- What is the meaning of being depressed or anxious for the patient?
- How does the depression, anxiety, etc., interfere in the patient's life?

Trauma and loss

- Did the patient experience the psychosis as being traumatic?
- How does the patient cope with the impact of hospitalization/psychotic episode/relapse?
- Was there anything related to the psychosis, but not the psychosis itself, which was considered traumatic?
- Has the patient's social, domestic and professional situation changed after having been psychotic?
- Is there anything the patient avoids because it reminds him or her of being psychotic?

Personality issues

- How does the patient describe his or her personality?
- Does the patient think he or she is different now compared to how he or she was before becoming unwell?
- How do the patient's family and friends describe his or her personality?
- Does the patient exhibit dependent, avoidance, schizoid, histrionic or borderline personality traits?
- How does personality and intellectual level impact upon the patient's ability to cope?

Therapeutic contract

- What does the patient want from therapy?
- What is the patient's perception of the therapist's role?
- Has the patient seen a therapist before? If so, what were these experiences like?
- Does the patient understand the role of time-limited therapy?

In addition a thorough *developmental and personal history* needs to be gathered. This can be done using a standard intake assessment.

Strategies

The patient should be given a clear and personally relevant rationale for meeting with a therapist. The therapist should acknowledge and attempt to understand the possible trauma of the patient's recent experience of psychosis and its consequences, the impact of this experience and current difficulties.

Depending on the stage of recovery and cognitive ability, the patient can be asked to write a few paragraphs addressing the following questions:

- What was your experience of being in hospital?
- What was your experience of being unwell?
- Why do you think this happened to you at this point in your life?
- How has it affected you?
- Has it changed you, if so how?

This exercise can be attempted either at home or during the session. The patient can be encouraged to take time to reflect and ask family and friends for input. Answers to these questions are useful in assisting the therapist to formulate a picture of the person and in developing a working agenda for therapy.

Engaging and assessing an adolescent can be challenging. This may be due to a range of issues such as developmental stage, intellectual ability, personality traits or phase of illness (Drury, 2000). These may play a role in the difficulty some young patients may have in articulating a response to the type of questions asked during a COPE assessment. Fowler, Garety and Kuipers (1995) adapted the 'Colombo technique' into a strategy for information gathering. This technique is useful for gathering information throughout therapy. The therapist responds to the patient's limited responses with exaggerated naivety and perplexity in an effort to encourage the patient to elaborate. The therapist employs standard counselling techniques such as probing, clarification, specification, summarizing and steering in order to clarify the information the patient provides to the therapist.

Case example: The Colombo technique

During the assessment session with Hannah, aged 21 years, the therapist found it difficult to obtain a clear history of her psychotic illness or Hannah's understanding of the psychotic experience. The therapist thought Hannah was somewhat hostile and impatient when replying to the therapist's questions. The therapist decided to approach this situation with Hannah in the following manner: 'I understand that the last few months have been a very unsettling time for you and I imagine you have told and re-told your experience of it to many people, so I can understand your frustration with my questions. However, I can't quite get a clear picture of what you think about all this, such as, why did it happen now? I don't know about you but I would be keen to sort it out, or have you already come to an understanding?'

Determining the agenda for therapy

Before embarking upon establishing the therapy agenda, the therapist needs to be satisfied that:

- a thorough assessment has been completed, entailing:
  - a cognitively oriented assessment, which explores the impact of the psychotic episode upon the person
  - a thorough developmental and personal history;
- the patient is engaged in therapy and alert to the role of therapy:
  - the patient is attending therapy appointments as required
  - the rationale for therapy has been collaboratively explored and agreed upon
  - the patient's mental state is stable, i.e. positive psychotic symptoms have significantly improved;
- the therapist has developed an initial formulation which will direct the focus of therapy:
  - the therapist has an understanding of why the psychosis emerged at that particular time in the patient's life
  - the therapist has an understanding of the patient's explanation of why he or she became unwell.

The agenda sets down the rationale for therapy. At this point in therapy the following points should be reiterated to the patient: the role of the therapist; the length of therapy; the timing of the review sessions; and the recovery focus of the therapy.

Determining the therapy agenda is an interactive process between the patient and the therapist. The patient is asked about current problems and issues he or she would like to cover during the course of therapy. The therapist should also derive agenda items from the formulation and assessment. The agenda should reflect the focus of recovery in first-episode psychosis, but should also allow some flexibility to include specific problems experienced by the patient. For example, a therapy agenda could include:

- What is psychosis?
- What happened and why?
- Where am I in the episode? Am I over it?
- How will I get over what has happened to me?
- How will I avoid it happening again?
- Relapse prevention and early warning signs.
- How to cope and deal with stress.
- What will my future hold for me now?
- Social environment and the presence of stigma.

The structured agenda helps to demystify the therapeutic process. Being clear with the patient is important to counteract the highly confusing and disempowering experience of most people in the post-psychotic phase (Henry et al., 2002). The agenda can provide a containing framework and the therapist should avoid introducing topics 'out of the blue' for discussion. However, the therapist should also be mindful that the post-psychotic phase is a dynamic period of the illness, so flexibility in the agenda may be required. New issues may emerge during the course of therapy such as a deterioration or change in illness status.

Case example: An agenda for therapy

Jonathan was a 23-year old male with part-time employment as a computer operator with a data processing company. He lived at home with his parents and younger sister and had a group of close friends. Six months prior to receiving treatment,

Jonathan reported experiencing delusions of reference from the television and from the background music played at work. Jonathan also had a 3-year history of frequent marijuana use, approximately four times per week. However, in the preceding 2 months he had commenced using marijuana daily and was withdrawing from work in order to avoid hearing the messages from the music. His marijuana use and inactivity had been causing arguments at home between him and his parents.

A possible agenda for therapy for Jonathan might include:

- What was Jonathan's experience of psychosis?
  - Providing the facts.
  - Exploring Jonathan's explanation for why he became unwell.
  - Exploring his appraisal of psychosis and acting to prevent or reduce stigma and trauma.
- Reviewing his use of marijuana:
  - Costs and benefits of using marijuana.
  - Impact of marijuana on his mental state, relationships and motivation.
- Has psychosis impacted upon Jonathan's confidence and self-esteem?
- Work issues.
- Social network:
  - Getting in touch with friends.

Further details of the COPE assessment and techniques can be found in the COPE manual (Henry et al., 2002). Additionally, Fowler, Garety and Kuipers (1995) offer a thorough description of cognitive-behavioural assessment and engagement techniques for working with people experiencing psychotic disorders. Fowler (2000) also provided a comprehensive description of issues to consider when developing a psychological formulation of early psychosis.

ADAPTATION

The following section describes the adaptation phase of therapy, incorporating a discussion about the concept of adaptation. Examples of techniques and strategies that have proved useful at this particular phase of therapy are outlined.

Concept of Adaptation

COPE is distinguished from other cognitive-based therapies for psychosis by its focus upon promoting a healthy adaptation to the episode of psychosis. Consideration of the following questions, and those listed in Box 4.1 under the adaptation heading, will assist in clarifying the concept of adaptation:

- What does becoming psychotic mean for the person?
- How is the person adjusting to the reality of having had a psychotic episode?
- Does the psychotic episode impact upon the person's self-perception now?
- How does the perception of illness influence the person's vulnerability to relapse?

The focus of adaptation is to determine the impact of psychosis on the person's sense of self and the aims of this approach are to:

- assist the person in a search for meaning in the experience;
- promote a sense of mastery over the potentially disempowering experience;
- protect and enhance self-esteem, which may have been severely threatened or damaged by the onset of the disorder (Coursey, 1989; Davidson & Strauss, 1992; Strauss et al., 1987).

A person's ability to cope successfully with the psychosis positively correlates with that person's capacity to form and maintain a set of self-protective cognitive biases. Therefore examining the situation and learning to reappraise the psychotic experience may assist in the recovery process (Fowler, 2000; Jackson et al., 1996). The trauma model is useful in understanding some of the phenomena seen in early psychosis (McCann & Pearlman, 1990). Emergence of a psychotic disorder, entry into treatment and being labelled as mentally ill are generally (but not always) traumatic experiences. These experiences may have a major disruptive effect upon the cognitive schemas of the individual. Horowitz (1986) described 'person schemas' that involve enduring but slowly changing views of oneself and of others. Each individual may possess a repertoire of self-schemas, but when a traumatic event occurs an appropriate schema for integrating the event may not be available. This may partially account for how young people deal with being diagnosed as mentally ill for the first time. The challenge posed to enduring self-schemas by the trauma of psychosis may arouse anxiety, which is managed by potentially maladaptive coping responses, such as massive denial.

A cognitive intervention, which targets the cognitive biases arising from the experience of psychosis, is an important step in the reappraisal process. Successful intervention will assist the person in making a positive adaptation to the onset of the disorder, play an active role in management of it, and help to maintain the best possible quality of life.

The road to adapting to the onset of a psychotic disorder may be influenced by internal and external mediating factors. Internal factors may include the person's pre-existing level of functioning, and quality of productive and non-productive coping skills and resources. The latter include problem-solving abilities, attribution style, the underlying structure and stability of the person's self-concept, and the person's core beliefs/schemas. External factors, which could potentially affect the person's appraisal of the psychotic experience, include age of onset of psychosis, the rate of onset of the initial episode, comorbidity, family psychiatric history and the level and quality of social support. A thorough assessment of these variables is essential before commencing therapeutic work (refer to Jackson et al., 1996, 1998, for more detailed discussions of the concept of adaptation; additionally, Jackson & Iqbal, 2000, provided an examination of the factors that may affect the process of adjustment to psychosis).

Strategies for Promoting Adaptation

The therapeutic strategies for promoting adaptation target specific goals of adaptation. The three specific goals of adaptation are, firstly, to instil hope, followed by identity work which focuses on the impact of psychosis upon self and, thirdly, on coping enhancement. These goals, and the strategies used to address them, are not necessarily discrete components.

In practice one strategy may address more than one adaptation goal. However, for the purpose of clarity, the following section describes the three components of adaptation separately.

Adaptation Goal: Instilling Hope

Instilling hope involves encouraging the person to recognize and realize his or her potential. Psychoeducation is one effective method of creating hope about the experience and reducing distress and disability associated with psychosis (McGorry, 1995). Accurate and tailored information can provide the basic framework for the individual to understanding their otherwise puzzling experiences. It is important to be mindful that the person is attempting to compensate not only for the cognitive and emotional disruptions wrought by the trauma of the psychotic symptoms, but also for the assault on self-esteem, identity and the disruption to lifestyle. In other words, the person is grappling with the meaning and significance of their predicament, while in a highly compromised state.

The information provided should focus upon the individual's symptoms and problems. Additionally, core issues need to be considered, including diagnosis, the phases of illness, and exploring the impact of psychosis upon the person's sense of self.

It is usually helpful to present a model of the disorder which incorporates an account of aetiology (Fowler, 2000). The vulnerability–stress model (Strauss & Carpenter, 1981; Zubin & Spring, 1977) has become the dominant conceptual framework for understanding psychosis. The vulnerability–stress model (Zubin & Spring, 1977) challenged the assumption that psychosis represented a disease characterized by an inevitably deteriorating course of illness. It provided an impetus to focus upon maximizing adaptive functioning and relapse prevention during the recovery phase. Furthermore, it is a simple model, which encourages the person to adopt an active role in the management of his or her illness. The model encourages understanding and normalization of the psychotic experience through psychoeducation.

The vulnerability–stress approach can be used to challenge the catastrophic view of psychosis and the sense of unpredictability, i.e. the notion that psychosis can recur without warning. The model can be used to ameliorate hopelessness and helplessness by challenging distortions about psychosis. Vulnerability may also be presented as malleable in response to the processes of maturation and compensation. The familiarity of the vulnerability concept, applicable to a range of health problems including asthma, provides a further normalizing effect. Detailed and accurate discussion about vulnerability enables the therapist to avoid communicating the implicit assumption that the patient will inevitably experience a static, permanent illness, which requires life-long medication.

Case example: Vulnerability–stress

Ben was a 21-year-old man who was living with his girlfriend at his parent's home. His General Practitioner referred Ben to EPPIC for a psychiatric assessment and treatment. Ben described hearing persistent sounds and voices when alone approximately 4 months prior to referral. In the previous 2 months, Ben was convinced that he was being followed. He was uncertain who was following him but he said he believed he was safer at home. Ben was treated as an outpatient at EPPIC and his psychotic symptoms abated with neuroleptic medication and case management.

Ben was working in a storage warehouse for a year prior to the referral and was on sick leave at the commencement of therapy. Six months prior Ben's car was stolen from outside his workplace and was later found incinerated. Ben had spent considerable time and money working on the car and was distressed when it was stolen and found destroyed. He reported it to the police who interviewed his work colleagues and employers about the theft. Ben believed that his employer communicated to the police that Ben had destroyed his car to obtain the insurance money. The police had interviewed Ben, and the insurance company was showing some reluctance in forwarding compensation. Ben said that he reduced his social involvement when he started to become anxious at work in response to a concern that people believed he had destroyed his vehicle.

Ben's older brother was diagnosed with schizophrenia 5 years previously and he continued to have some difficulties with psychotic relapses and unemployment.

Ben reported to the therapist that he was feeling depressed. He described himself as usually a very active and happy person who had many friends and a good relationship with his girlfriend. However, he described recent negative thoughts about the world, which was affecting his relationships with friends and family and causing him to withdraw socially. At the time of assessment there was a marked lack of interest in his usual activities, and he was hesitant about returning to work. When prompted, Ben acknowledged fears that he may never be able to work again like his brother with schizophrenia.

The therapist helped to formulate a possible explanation for Ben's illness using the stress–vulnerability model as a framework. The therapist suggested that the stress Ben had experienced over the previous 6 months in relation to his stolen car had contributed to his current difficulties and that this drop in functioning, along with his family history of psychosis, increased his susceptibility to developing a psychotic illness.

Therapeutic intervention focused upon providing Ben with information about psychosis and examining his prodromal signs and symptoms. It also focused upon reducing his level of anxiety and his mild depression, in addition to restoring his normal level of functioning as much as possible using cognitive-behavioural techniques. These techniques required Ben to examine his views and feelings about himself and his situation, and acknowledge the circumstances which led to his social isolation. It was revealed that Ben had withdrawn from his friends due to his misconception that he was no longer welcome, which resulted in Ben becoming depressed and anxious.

Adaptation Goal: Identity

The identity component of adaptation involves understanding the person's appraisal of his or her illness and the impact this appraisal has upon the person's identity. In the aftermath of a psychotic episode the person may have a different view compared to before the psychotic episode, about who he is and his expectations for the future, i.e. he may now believe that he does not have the potential to do the things he previously planned to do, such as study or be independent. This resonates with the concept of possible selves (Markus & Nurius, 1986), which accounts for changes in the perception of self via an evolutionary process, influenced by a range of factors, such as the onset of mental illness. The following section describes techniques that are useful for exploring the impact of psychosis upon self-concept.

The time-line technique can be used to visually summarize a person's life history and to differentiate between illness-specific and non-illness issues. The technique involves drawing a time-line and inviting the person to describe his or her life, the nature of relationships, and his or her self-perception:

1. before becoming psychotic;
2. when acutely psychotic;
3. now;
4. in the future.

In response, the person may describe some positive and negative attributes at each of the four time points. This allows the person to distinguish between trait and state, thereby encouraging distance from his or her self-perception from the psychotic illness. This opportunity to consider themselves within the broader context of their full history and the multiple possibilities for their future reduces the risk of engulfment. If a person is reluctant to respond to this exercise, the therapist could suggest that family and friends should be asked to describe the person in relation to the four time points. If the person is shy or unable to participate, the therapist could also engage in this activity, by saying 'Currently I see you as a punctual person. Have you always been like this?'

Adaptation Goal: Coping Enhancement

An area for specific therapeutic work is the strengthening of general coping resources, specifically in relation to the challenge of the psychotic experience and diagnosis. Coping strategies are particularly useful in the early to mid phases of therapy, especially if the person responds initially to a behavioural approach.

The techniques are based on developing a shared understanding of the patient's usual repertoire of coping mechanisms, followed by focusing upon the ways in which the person has coped with psychosis and its aftermath.

The therapist should reinforce strengths by recognizing that the person has been through a difficult time and done well to date, while suggesting that there may be other adaptive ways of coping. The therapist could draw attention to the under-utilization of the person's own strengths, for example by taking stock of the person's personal assets such as:

• social, vocational and environmental supports;
• interpersonal and communication skills;
• personality style;
• insight.

New coping strategies can be developed through learning from the experiences of others. This can be achieved through referring to published information such as guidance books, psychoeducational material and first person accounts (EPPIC, 2000). The therapist may wish to encourage the patient to establish contact with peers, self-help groups, mentors or psychoeducational groups.

After expanding the behavioural coping repertoire, the next task is to emphasize the cognitive aspects of coping by challenging distorted thinking patterns, which maintain uncertainty and anxiety. As highlighted by Perris (1992, p. 140) the aim is to '.... help the patient in the discovery of dysfunctional schemata, or working models which have contributed in determining his/her feelings and in ruling his/her behaviour, and eventually correct them'.

A strategy for this involves the therapist challenging the person's views about events and his or her involvement in those events. Some people may misinterpret events and then judge themselves harshly in these circumstances. It is important to ascertain what the patient is thinking and then challenge the distorted ideas. The four-column technique (Beck et al., 1979) is a useful tool. However, as noted by Fowler, Garety and Kuipers (1995), considerable effort is required in identifying areas of emotional difficulty and dysfunctional assumptions about self and others when working with people with psychotic disorders. Strategies involve exploring a belief (where did it come from?) and planning methods to test the belief (where is the evidence to support the belief?).

Both the empty-chair and role-play techniques are useful when patients have difficulty coping in a particular situation because they feel anxious. For example, a person might be unable to speak to or visit a particular person. Using the empty-chair or role-play techniques, the person's fears can be confronted by rehearsing with the therapist what he or she would like to say. These techniques can be powerful as they provide the opportunity for the person to experience his or her misinterpretations of situations in a safe, non-judgemental environment, and enable the therapist to provide feedback immediately. The techniques can be helpful to overt discussions concerning the person's views about what others think about someone experiencing a psychotic episode, and then practising ways of discussing psychosis with others.

A complete description of the details and techniques of the COPE adaptation focus can be found in the COPE manual (Henry et al., 2002).

THE EVOLVING MODEL OF COPE

The Incorporation of COPE into Case Management

Although COPE was developed and evaluated within the EPPIC service, the EPPIC clinicians were initially naïve to the details of the therapy. The COPE therapists worked alongside yet independently from the EPPIC clinicians. Upon the completion of the COPE randomized-controlled trial, the COPE research group decided to integrate COPE into EPPIC clinical case management. The integration process occurred through weekly case presentation supervision groups, headed by the author over a 3-year period. Sixteen case managers working at EPPIC during that time participated in the supervision groups.

The brief of case management is broad (Edwards, Cocks & Bott, 1999; EPPIC, 2001) and the psychological adaptation of the patient to the psychotic illness is one of the many therapeutic tasks for the case manager. The clinicians moved between the four phases of COPE based upon the pertinent issues for the patient at that period of time. When treating people in the wake of a psychotic episode, demanding issues arise which require prompt resolution by both the case manager and patient, such as: housing relocation, family appointments, work or educational conundrums, medical reviews and deteriorating mental state. Therefore, components of the COPE model were introduced into case management practice when appropriate.

Supervision emphasized the COPE assessment as the backbone of the psychological work. Case managers often incorporated segments of the COPE assessment and associated strategies into their practice. For example, during a case management appointment, the clinician may be prompted to assess the patient's explanatory model of his or her psychotic illness. The clinician may observe that the patient is both pessimistic and overwhelmed by the psychotic experience and may incorporate strategies from the adaptation phase of COPE. These might include psychoeducation and a discussion concerning the vulnerability–stress model of psychosis, tailored to the patient's experience.

COPE and Further Therapy Trials

A clinical research team based at EPPIC, led by Professor Henry Jackson, is currently evaluating a second-generation manual-based psychological therapy for first-episode psychotic patients in the context of a randomized-controlled trial. The therapy incorporates the lessons learned from the COPE trial, with additional modifications. The four phases of COPE are included: the psychological assessment, engagement, adaptation and secondary morbidity components. Influenced by the SoCRATES approach (Lewis et al., 2002), the therapy also entails treating positive symptoms and attempts to engage the participants into the therapy during the acute phase at between 2 and 4 weeks after entry into the EPPIC service. Results are expected during 2004 and will constitute a replication of the initial COPE studies and the more recent SoCRATES trial (Lewis et al., 2002).

ACKNOWLEDGEMENTS

The development of the COPE therapy model was a collaborative project. I wish to acknowledge the central role and contributions of Jane Edwards, Henry Jackson, Carol Hulbert, Patrick McGorry, Shona Francey, Dana Maude, John Cocks and Paddy Power in the development of the COPE therapeutic approach. I would also like to thank the participants of the COPE model, who were treated at the Early Psychosis Prevention and Intervention Centre, and the Victorian Health Promotion Foundation, which sponsored the project.

REFERENCES

Barrowclough, C. & Tarrier, N. (1992). *Families of Schizophrenic Patients: Cognitive Behavioural Intervention*. London: Chapman & Hall.

Barrowclough, C. & Tarrier, N. (1994). Interventions with families. In M. Birchwood & N. Tarrier (Eds), *Psychological Management of Schizophrenia* (pp. 53–75). New York: John Wiley & Sons.

Beck, A.T., Rush, A.J., Shaw, B.F. & Emery, G. (1979). *Cognitive Therapy of Depression*. New York: Guilford Press.

Birchwood, M. (1992). Early intervention in schizophrenia: Theoretical background and clinical strategies. *British Journal of Clinical Psychology*, **31**, 257–278.

Birchwood, M. (2000). The critical period for early intervention. In M. Birchwood, D. Fowler & C. Jackson (Eds), *Early Intervention in Psychosis: A Guide to Concepts, Evidence and Interventions* (pp. 28–63). Chichester: John Wiley & Sons.

Birchwood, M. & Macmillan, F. (1993). Early intervention in schizophrenia. *Australian and New Zealand Journal of Psychiatry*, **27**, 374–378.

Birchwood, M., McGorry, P. & Jackson, H. (1997). Early intervention in schizophrenia. *British Journal of Psychiatry*, **170**, 2–5.

Bleuler, M. (1978). *The Schizophrenic Disorders: Long-term Patient and Family Studies* (C. SM, Trans.). New Haven: Yale University Press.

Chadwick, P.J., Birchwood, M. & Trower, P. (1996). *Cognitive Therapy for Delusions, Voices and Paranoia*. Chichester: John Wiley & Sons.

Ciompi, L. (1976). *The Life Course and Aging in Schizophrenia: A Catamnestic Longitudinal Study into Advanced Age*. Berlin: Springer-Verlag.

Coursey, R.D. (1989). Psychotherapy with persons suffering from schizophrenia. *Schizophrenia Bulletin*, **15**, 349–353.

Davidson, L. (1992). Developing an empirical-phenomenological approach to schizophrenia research. *Journal of Phenomenological Psychology*, **23**, 3–15.

Davidson, L. & Strauss, J. (1992). Sense of self in recovery from severe mental illness. *British Journal of Medical Psychology*, **65**, 131–145.

Drury, V. (2000). Cognitive behaviour therapy in early psychosis. In M. Birchwood, D. Fowler & C. Jackson (Eds), *Early Intervention in Psychosis: A Guide to Concepts, Evidence and Interventions*. Chichester: John Wiley & Sons.

Edwards, J. & McGorry, P. (1998). Early intervention in psychotic disorders: A critical step in the prevention of psychological morbidity. In C. Perris & P. McGorry (Eds), *Cognitive Psychotherapy of Psychotic and Personality Disorders: Handbook of Theory and Practice*. Chichester: John Wiley & Sons.

Edwards, J., Cocks, J. & Bott, J. (1999). Preventive case management in first-episode psychosis. In P. McGorry & H. Jackson (Eds), *The Recognition and Management of Early Psychosis: A Preventive Approach*. Cambridge: Cambridge University Press.

Edwards, J., Francey, S., McGorry, P. & Jackson, H. (1994). Early psychosis prevention and intervention: Evolution of a comprehensive community-based specialized service. *Behaviour Change*, **11**, 223–233.

EPPIC (2000). *Trips & Journeys—Personal Accounts of Early Psychosis*. Melbourne: Early Psychosis Prevention and Intervention Centre.

EPPIC (2001). *Case Management in Early Psychosis: A Handbook*. Melbourne: EPPIC.

Erikson, E.H. (1968). *Identity: Youth and Crisis*. New York: W. Norton & Co.

Fowler, D. (2000). Psychological formulation of early episodes of psychosis: A cognitive model. In M. Birchwood, D. Fowler & C. Jackson (Eds), *Early Intervention in Psychosis: A Guide to Concepts, Evidence and Interventions* (pp. 101–127). Chichester: John Wiley & Sons.

Fowler, D., Garety, P. & Kuipers, E. (1995). *Cognitive Behaviour Therapy for Psychosis: Theory and Practice*. Chichester: John Wiley & Sons.

Goldstein, G., Tsuang, M. & Faraone, S. (1989). Gender and schizophrenia: Impressions for understanding the heterogeneity of the illness. *Psychiatry Research*, **28**, 243–253.

Green, M.F. (1993). Cognitive remediation in schizophrenia: Is it time yet? *American Journal of Psychiatry*, **150**, 178–187.

Harding, C., Brooks, G., Ashikaga, T., Strauss, J. & Breier, A. (1987). The Vermont longitudinal study, II: Long-term outcome for DSM-III schizophrenia. *American Journal of Psychiatry*, **144**, 727–735.

Henry, L., Edwards, J., Jackson, H., Hulbert, C. & McGorry, P. (2002). *Cognitively Oriented Psychotherapy for First Episode Psychosis (COPE): A Practitioner's Manual*. Melbourne: EPPIC.

Horowitz, M.J. (1986). Stress–response syndromes: A review of posttraumatic and adjustment disorders. *Hospital and Community Psychiatry*, **37**, 241–249.

Huber, G., Gross, G., Schuttler, R. & Linz, M. (1980). Longitudinal studies of schizophrenic patients. *Schizophrenia Bulletin*, **6**, 592–605.

Jackson, C. & Iqbal, Z. (2000). Psychological adjustment to early psychosis. In M. Birchwood, D. Fowler & C. Jackson (Eds), *Early Intervention in Psychosis: A Guide to Concepts, Evidence and Interventions* (pp. 64–100). Chichester: John Wiley & Sons.

Jackson, H., Hulbert, C. & Henry, L. (2000). The treatment of secondary morbidity in first-episode psychosis. In M. Birchwood, D. Fowler & C. Jackson (Eds), *Early Intervention in Psychosis: A Guide to Concepts, Evidence and Interventions* (pp. 213–235). Chichester: John Wiley & Sons.

Jackson, H., Edwards, J., Hulbert, C. & McGorry, P. (1999). Recovery from psychosis: Psychological interventions. In P. McGorry & H. Jackson (Eds), *The Recognition and Management of Early Psychosis: A Preventive Approach*. UK: Cambridge University Press.

Jackson, H., McGorry, P., Edwards, J. & Hulbert, C. (1996). Cognitively oriented psychotherapy for early psychosis (COPE). In P. Cotton & H. Jackson (Eds), *Early Intervention and Prevention in Mental Health* (pp. 131–154). Melbourne: Australian Psychological Society.

Jackson, H., McGorry, P., Edwards, J., Hulbert, C., Henry, L., Francey, S., Maude, D., Cocks, J., Power, P., Harrigan, S. & Dudgeon, P. (1998). Cognitively-oriented psychotherapy for early psychosis (COPE): Preliminary results. *British Journal of Psychiatry*, **172** (Suppl. 33), 93–100.

Jackson, H., McGorry, P., Henry, L., Edwards, J., Hulbert, C., Harrigan, S., Dudgeon, P., Francey, S., Maude, D., Cocks, J. & Power, P. (2001). Cognitively oriented psychotherapy for early psychosis (COPE): A 1-year follow-up. *British Journal of Clinical Psychology*, **40**, 57–70.

Kessler, R., Foster, C., Saunders, W. & Stang, P. (1995). Social consequences of pscyiatric disorders, I: Educational attainment. *American Journal of Psychiatry*, **152**, 1026–1032.

Kraepelin, E. (1898). *The diagnosis and prognosis of dementia praecox*. Paper presented at the 29th Congress of Southwestern German Psychiatry, Heidelberg.

Kraepelin, E. (1919). *Textbook of Psychiatry*. Edinburgh: Livingstone.

Lewis, S., Tarrier, N., Haddock, G., Bentall, R., Kinderman, P., Kingdon, D., Siddle, R., Drake, R., Everitt, J., Leadley, K., Benn, A., Grazebrook, K., Haley, C., Akhtar, S., Davies, L., Palmer, S., Faragher, B. & Dunn, G. (2002). Randomised controlled trial of cognitive-behavioural therapy in early schizophrenia: Acute-phase outcomes. *British Journal of Psychiatry*, **181** (Suppl. 43), S91–S97.

Markus, H. & Nurius, P. (1986). Possible selves. *American Psychologist*, **41**, 954–969.

McCann, L. & Pearlman, L.A. (1990). *Psychological Trauma and the Adult Survivor, Theory, Therapy, and Transformation*. New York: Brunner/Mazel.

McGorry, P. (1992). The concept of recovery and secondary prevention in psychotic disorders. *Australian and New Zealand Journal of Psychiatry*, **26**, 3–17.

McGorry, P. (1994). The influence of illness duration on syndrome clarity and stability in functional psychosis: Does the diagnosis emerge and stabilise with time? *Australian and New Zealand Journal of Psychiatry*, **28**, 607–619.

McGorry, P. (1995). Psychoeducation in first-episode psychosis: A theoretical process. *Psychiatry*, **58**, 329–344.

McGorry, P., Edwards, J., Mihalopoulos, C., Harrigan, S. & Jackson, H. (1996). EPPIC: An evolving system of early detection and optimal management. *Schizophrenia Bulletin*, **22**, 305–326.

McGorry, P., Henry, L., Maude, D. & Phillips, L. (1998). Preventively-orientated psychological interventions in early psychosis. In C. Perris & P. McGorry (Eds), *Cognitive Psychotherapy of Psychotic and Personality Disorders: Handbook of Theory and Practice* (pp. 213–236). Chichester: John Wiley & Sons.

Ogawa, K., Miya, M., Watarai, A., Nakazawa, M., Yuasa, S. & Utena, H. (1987). A long-term follow-up study of schizophrenia in Japan with special reference to the course of social adjustment. *British Journal of Psychiatry*, **151**, 758–765.

Perris, C. (1989). *Cognitive Therapy with Schizophrenic Patients*. USA: Guilford Press.

Perris, C. (1992). Some aspects of the use of cognitive psychotherapy with patients suffering from a schizophrenic disorder. In A. Werbart & J. Cullberg (Eds), *Psychotherapy of Schizophrenia: Facilitating and Obstructive Factors* (pp. 131–145). Oslo: Scandinavian University Press.

Perris, C. & Skagerlind, L. (1994). Cognitive therapy with schizophrenic patients. *Acta Psychiatrica Scandinavica*, **89** (Suppl. 382), 65–70.

Strauss, J. & Carpenter, W.T. (1981). *Schizophrenia*. New York: Plenum.

Strauss, J., Harding, C., Hafez, H. & Lieberman, P. (1987). The role of the patient in recovery from psychosis. In J. Strauss, W. Boker & H. Brenner (Eds), *Psychosocial Treatment of Schizophrenia* (pp. 160–166). New York: Hans Huber.

Tarrier, N. (1992). Management and modification of residual positive psychotic symptoms. In M. Birchwood & N. Tarrier (Eds), *Innovations in the Psychological Management of Schizophrenia*. Chichester: John Wiley & Sons.

Vallis, T.M. (1998). When the going gets tough: Cognitive therapy for the severely disturbed. In C. Perris & P. McGorry (Eds), *Cognitive Psychotherapy of Psychotic and Personality Disorders: Handbook of Theory and Practice* (pp. 37–62). Chichester: John Wiley & Sons.

Zubin, J. & Spring, B. (1977). Vunerability: A new view of schizophrenia. *Journal of Abnormal Psychology*, **86**, 103–126.

Zubin, J., Magaziner, J. & Steinhauer, S.R. (1983). The metamorphosis of schizophrenia: from chronicity to vulnerability. *Psychological Medicine*, **13**, 551–571.

5 The Dynamics of Acute Psychosis and the Role of Dynamic Psychotherapy

JOHAN CULLBERG
Stockholm Center of Public Health, Sweden

JAN-OLAV JOHANNESSEN
Rogaland Psychiatric Hospital, Stavanger, Norway

Every patient should have the right to tell his/her story

A BRIEF HISTORICAL BACKGROUND

In recent reviews on treatments for psychosis the benefits of psychodynamic therapies are usually negatively valued—even warned against (Lehman et al., 1998; Meuser & Berenbaum, 1990). The reviewers have usually based their conclusions upon psychotherapeutic methods that are today largely abandoned. In addition, the research underlying these firm conclusions has methodological weaknesses. The relative lack of systematic research in modern dynamic methods gives—in contrast to cognitive-behavioural therapy (CBT) methods—the impression of a lack of effects. As this belief is contrary to the clinical experience of many psychiatrists and psychotherapists, including ourselves, we wish to introduce the chapter by giving a historic background of the evolution of dynamic psychotherapy.

The term 'dynamic' underlines the active interaction between the individual and the psychosocial and physical environment. Originating from basic psychoanalytic and anthropological concepts, it is a way of realizing the impact of the psychological development of each individual in modelling his or her coping strategies in combination with the biological prerequisites and the environment. The concept 'psychodynamic' also implies the importance of protective as well as pathogenic psychosocial factors in the individual's reactions to stressful events. Psychodynamic psychotherapy, in addition to increased self-understanding, makes the relationship between the individual and the environment the main focus of the treatment process.

The Heroic Era of Psychoanalytic Cure

These were the long-term psychoanalytically inspired treatments by Sechehaye, Fromm-Reichmann, Searles, Benedetti and others. In intense case studies they depicted journeys into the symbolic world of psychosis with dramatic recoveries, after gaining insight, often

Psychological Interventions in Early Psychosis
Edited by J.F.M. Gleeson and P.D. McGorry. © 2004 John Wiley & Sons, Ltd.

Table 5.1. Systematic studies of psychodynamic treatments of psychosis/schizophrenia

Author(s)	Method	Results	Remarks
May et al. (1968)	Randomized study of four groups of first-episode patients who were given either neuroleptics, psychotherapy, combination of these, or no treatment.	Combination neuroleptics plus psychotherapy was the most effective. Psychotherapy only was no more effective than no treatment.	Low psychotherapeutic competence. Psychotherapeutic methods inadequate according to modern standards. Only inpatient care.
Karon and Van den Bos (1972)	Randomized study of three groups, each consisting of 12 acutely ill schizophrenic patients given either dynamic psychotherapy, psychotherapy plus medication or standardized treatment.	Psychotherapy without medication group significantly better after 2 years.	Unclear diagnostic criteria, small groups, control group not quite comparable.
Sjöström (1985)	14 DSM-III schizophrenic long-term inpatients were given intensive dynamic psychotherapy supervised by an untrained but gifted therapist. Matched comparison group given standard treatment.	Psychotherapy group significantly better results after 6 years—much less neuroleptic medication.	Control group matched but not randomized with experimental group. Treatment conducted or supervised by a formally untrained but gifted therapist.
McGlashan (1984)	163 chronic DSM-III schizophrenic inpatients were given intensive psychoanalytic psychotherapy 4–5 times/week.	14% much better or recovered.	Primarily a chronic group. No systematic social rehabilitation. No efforts to integrate neuroleptic medication.
Gunderson et al. (1984)	95 first-episode DSM-III schizophrenic patients were given either psychoanalytic insight-oriented psychotherapy or supportive dynamic psychotherapy.	Supportive dynamic psychotherapy somewhat better effects. Dynamically best-regarded therapists got better results.	Drop-out over 50%.

Stone (1986)	72 DSM-III schizophrenic patients were given psychoanalytic psychotherapy during a mean of 12 months.	10% recovered, 20% low symptomatic, > 50% residual symptoms, 20% suicided.	Brief treatment periods, unclear treatment policies.
Cullberg (1991)	A case finding study of Swedish DSM-III fully remitted schizophrenic patients treated with long-term dynamic psychotherapy. They were compared with 10 non-recovered patients with the same treatment.	8 cases permanently recovered were found. Some early differences between the groups was the persisting type of auditory hallucinosis in the non-recovered group and the early personality disturbances among the recovered patients.	7 of the 8 recovered patients were treated by therapists, which were supervised by the same therapist as in Sjöström (1985), indicating the importance of selection and technique.
Alanen et al. (1994)	A multi-centre study of 77 first-episode schizophrenia (DSM-III) patients treated with 'need-adapted' psychotherapeutic methods and neuroleptics when needed.	At 5-year follow up 50% did not show any psychotic symptoms and 50% were working. 44% were on neuroleptics. In the 'pure' schizophrenia group full remission in 39% of cases.	Sampling procedures somewhat different between the countries. Results not unfavourable in comparison to other 5-year samples.

through a process of transference interpretation. The popularity of these stories went far beyond psychiatry and may be understood through their telling the old tale of the evil witch-mother being conquered by the wise and enduring therapist. Consequently, a simplified psychoanalytic view on the pathogenic mother was promulgated with a resultant iatrogenic effect upon families of the patients that finally motivated a long-standing backlash against dynamic psychotherapy. The conviction was held that the real treatment for schizophrenia was through psychoanalysis, the main obstacle being the cost for the treatment. However, those cases that were not helped in spite of equally strident efforts were not mentioned.

The mainly negative reports from the May study (May, Tuma & Dixon, 1968) with an experimental design—psychotherapy versus neuroleptics versus milieu therapy versus no treatment—and later the Chestnut Lodge naturalistic study (McGlashan, 1984) contributed to the forceful closure of US psychiatric doors to psychodynamic approaches. Today we know that the psychotherapeutic methods and level of psychotherapeutic skill of therapists participating in these studies were not ideal for long-term schizophrenic patients and that the strict experimental division between psychological and medical treatment may be counter-productive for both approaches.

The influence of the research by Karon and Van den Bos (1972) was, however, important in showing that good results could be achieved, especially during the early phases (see Table 5.1). These reports also incorporated the idealistic assumption that the majority of psychotic patients could recover through adequate psychotherapy, and that there was no clear indication for pharmacological treatments. The deinstitutionalization movement and experiences with group psychiatric treatments catalysed the optimism of the period. It was not until the apparently negative findings of the Chestnut Lodge report (McGlashan, 1984) that the high expectations for psychoanalytic treatments began to fade, even among psychotherapists. However, one should remember that the Chestnut Lodge sample was a negatively selected group of patients—chronic, with long duration of illness, and with multiple admissions to various hospitals. The few, but evident, therapeutic successes must not be forgotten in our efforts to understand why some patients have been helped through such methods.

In 1979 the Finnish psychoanalyst Veikko Tähkä introduced the concept 'psychotherapy as phase-specific treatment' (Tähkä, 1979). He stated that this did not imply a widening of the scope of application of classical technique to the treatment of personality disturbances for which it had not been developed. Instead, he called for the application of analytic *knowledge* to patients who suffer from early and extensive disturbances of personality development. He also stated that very early disturbances in object relations 'may be treatable, but it is very questionable whether they are analysable'. He thus differentiated between *dynamic understanding* and *dynamic treatment* in relation to psychosis.

Others have posited similar arguments from an object-relations perspective. Jackson and Williams (1994), for example, outlined an application of Kleinian concepts to understanding psychotic phenomena in the ordinary clinical setting in their paedagogical text, *Unimaginable Storms*.

The Social Psychiatric Era and the Family Therapy Movement

The advent of sociological and anthropological concepts in psychiatry, in addition to a heightened interest in family dynamics, provided new approaches and new hopes. In Scandinavia (Alanen et al., 1994; Alanen, 1997) large-scale experiments introduced psychodynamic approaches to the treatment of psychosis within the public sector. These were mainly individual treatments during the first years of illness, with a low frequency of sessions. It was hypothesized that early psychotherapeutic intervention would improve the probability of interrupting the progression of the disorder. With the positive and invariably self-confident reports (especially from the Italian family therapy groups), a new direction in dynamic treatment was introduced during the 1970s. Systemic and psychoanalytically informed family approaches were developing internationally. The Turku group showed (Alanen et al., 1985) that the effectiveness was increased when integrating systemic family treatment within the individual treatments. Later, they introduced *need-adapted treatment* (Alanen et al., 1991) that entailed a multifaceted approach with a range of treatment methods for varying situations, across different phases of treatment. Other family treatment teams were more puristic in their approach with—as it seems to us—the inevitable consequence that the therapeutic effect was reduced, or even negative.

Another stage-specific approach was developed during this period by McGlashan and Keats (1989). They outlined a 12-step psychotherapeutic model with a gradual development from relationship-building to using this relationship as both a platform and a focus for the therapy. The empirical studies from this period, which are outlined in chronological order in Table 5.1, seem to give contradictory evidence at first glance. In the light of contemporary research standards these studies suffer from suboptimal definitions and measurement of: (a) diagnosis; (b) length of disorder; (c) therapists' skill; (d) the overall clinical context, and (e) dose of antipsychotic medication. Therefore, even if most of the findings provide support for the beneficial effects of dynamic psychotherapy, we are still lacking integrative experimental studies that could be the basis for unambiguous evidence.

The concept of Expressed Emotion in families (Vaughn & Leff, 1976) and the dramatic lowering of relapse rates with associated psycho-pedagogical approaches (which are not regarded as psychotherapy in its strict sense) produced an increasing interest among psychiatric clinicians in the behavioural methods. This development was paralleled by the, mainly British, application of cognitive-behavioural therapy to psychosis.

The Pragmatic Era of Integrating Different Approaches and Treatment Models

The stress–vulnerability model (Zubin & Spring, 1977), combined with the developments in CBT research, has provided opportunities for amalgamating dynamic and cognitive approaches—one manifestation being Cognitive-Analytic Therapy (Ryle, 1995). Here the psychodynamic concepts of the ego and of self-development, attachment theory, and early development have been integrated with learning theory and cognitive treatment techniques. A low threshold for psychotic breakdown can be conceptualized in *either* biological *or* psychological terms. One important result is that the medical concept of 'the cure' has become less central. Today dynamically trained therapists stress the inherent 'spontaneous' recovery tendencies, building of relationship, supporting the inherent curative forces, working with the post-traumatic stress disorder (PTSD) problems and psychotherapeutically strengthening the personality structures, and attempting to prevent relapses with the goal of diminishing later dysfunction (see Cullberg et al., 2000).

Cognitive models of dysfunctional beliefs or thinking strategies are important new acquisitions for dynamic psychotherapists. Similarly, CBT therapists including Perris, McGorry, Fowler and Birchwood have increasingly incorporated central dynamic constructs such as the search for conceptual meaning, the developmental arrest, mechanisms of defence, and unconscious motivation.

Hogarty has developed a model called 'personal therapy' (Hogarty et al., 1997). It is unclear whether he included his model among the dynamic therapies. However, we find that it satisfies criteria for the dynamic therapies, with an additional emphasis on cognitive techniques. This method is a three-stage, systematic approach in recognition of the sensitivity of many schizophrenic patients. The important, but often neglected fact that it makes no sense to provide advanced psychotherapy for people who have not filled their basic needs for food, housing, a decent economy or meaningful occupation is often poorly reflected in psychotherapy research, along with the need for long-term follow-up. For example, in Hogarty's study positive results of personal therapy were manifested at 3 years follow-up, but not at 2 years.

The demystification of the therapeutic alliance is important for providing a working relationship with a psychotic person. Knowledge about transference/countertransference phenomena is important for understanding its clinical vicissitudes. Symbolization and language formation are important concepts for better understanding some of the phenomena of psychosis. However, the classical, highly regarded psychoanalytic neutrality, the interpretation of symbols, and of unconscious drives are mainly obsolete in modern psychosis treatment. Today's dynamically trained therapists are more active and available as role models. They work on integrating the past and present, sometimes through offering explanations, or interpretations, when the patient is ready. However, the differential diagnosis between unconscious/subconscious conflict states (including early separation traumas or abuse experiences) versus deficiency states [where functional disturbances are regarded either as consequences of early brain disorder or of deficient early care (Killingmo, 1989)] has a value in explaining the type of therapy to which the patient may respond. For example, in cases of chronic psychosis (schizophrenia), a classical working-through of early problems seldom proves constructive or feasible.

Working with the family as important partners is also central in modern dynamic thinking. Family interventions could range from information and support to more explicit psychotherapeutic work with the family system. These approaches, of course, also include an integrative attitude towards the use of medical methods.

In summary, the different types of dynamic therapies have in common the important task of building a relationship between the patient and the therapist in order to help the patient to master his or her life situation.

DYNAMIC UNDERSTANDING OF THE ACUTE PSYCHOSIS

From a dynamic perspective, psychosis is regarded as a breakdown of ego structures (also called psychological coping mechanisms, or psychological defence mechanisms depending on the context used), with a lowering of the capacity to separate between the inner and outer world, thereby creating a chaotic, and extremely anxiety-provoking, subjective disintegration. This process can be understood as a maladaptive crisis reaction to stress that interacts with a specific psychological vulnerability, overwhelming the individual's coping capacity. The dynamic perspective does not constitute a causal model of psychosis but provides an understanding of the dynamic tensions that contribute to the emergence of psychosis (Cullberg 2003).

Continuity between 'normality' and the development of psychotic disorders is assumed, with the transition process commencing in the prodromal phase with subtle disturbances in subjective experience. The prepsychotic person creates private, idiosyncratic explanations to deal with painful confusion that arises from anomalous experiences that are not subjected to the critical testing capacity that normally integrates the inner and outer world. Instead these explanations are products of regressive and 'primitive' thinking that prevails in the acute phases.

For example, a patient's belief that some evil person or organization is controlling his or her thoughts may serve as an explanation of the absurd and frightening confusional state. The anxiety and (secondary) aggressions are projected onto other people, who may be perceived as persecutors. The person may protect himself or herself against the evil gaze of others, by, for example, wearing dark glasses or via alternative avoidant strategies.

When this process accelerates—we do not know how often it is interrupted in the prepsychotic stage by good and supportive occurrences or relations—vocal hallucinations may become prominent, possibly as a sign that the ability to separate thinking and perception is even more disturbed.

This is a common pathway for the first emergence of psychosis. In a smaller percentage we meet a slower progression during months and years, where ego boundaries are maintained, until they collapse abruptly. The pressure of anxiety, together with inability to concentrate and to communicate in a regular fashion, is experienced as a gradual transformation to the self, sometimes into an empty shell or an evil person. Eventually, this becomes impossible to resist and psychotic 'explanations' take over, providing some kind of relief at the cost of losing contact with reality. In our view, this process of becoming ill is typical for the more malignant schizophrenic cases, where an early biological vulnerability may be an important partial explanation. This has much in common with E. Bleuler's (1950) dynamic view on schizophrenia as a personality *trait* that should not be confused with the *state* of being psychotic.

M. Bleuler (1984) advocated a view that deep antagonistic conflicts in the personality between creative abilities (e.g. strong drive impulses during adolescence) and inhibiting external factors (e.g. extreme super-ego pressures) may provoke the latent vulnerability in certain periods of life. In other words, psychological and biological vulnerabilities interact during critical developmental phases to accelerate the onset of psychosis. It is our experience that such psychological contradictions may act as risk factors to later psychotic development.

On the other hand, the dynamic perspective also incorporates the notion of a 'spontaneous' capacity in the ego to 'heal' the psychotic self, provided that the context is supportive. Therefore an imperative in dynamic work is the availability of optimal care during the recovery process, which is taken up below.

CLINICAL ASPECTS

The First Meetings

The immediate task is to create a productive therapeutic meeting, in a *calm setting or milieu* that provides a sense of confidence. It is often preferable to meet the patient in his or her home, with the family, provided the patient has not already arrived at (or been brought to) the clinic. The family is generally highly involved in the process and the sick member often provokes anxiety and sorrow. From a stress–vulnerability perspective, communication styles, the information given by different members, and the supportive and non-supportive elements in the family dynamic are most informative for the therapists.

Offering care to these brittle and anxiety-ridden patients in overcrowded wards that are frequently unstructured, with aggressive and anxiety-provoking atmospheres, must be regarded as counter-therapeutic. This scenario adds additional stress that increases the psychotic withdrawal.

The vignette below provides an example of the difficulties encountered following a lengthy period of untreated psychosis.

Case example: A first home visit

A man called the clinic on recommendation from his GP. His son Stephen, who was 22 years of age, had been increasingly isolating himself in the family's basement during the preceding 6 months, and the father felt highly anxious about him. Stephen had finished job training. Presently he was not working and he rarely left the basement, except for brief meals. He was playing his saxophone loudly during the night and never seemed to sleep. Some years earlier he had been a successful student and a member of a rather good band. When the nurse on call offered a home visit the father became hesitant—he explained he was only seeking advice and he suddenly concluded the call. The next day he called again. Stephen had lit a fire in the garden during the night and kept running in and out of the house. The father again declined the offer of a home visit because he feared his son's reaction, but he wanted to come and talk with the team doctor. Here he was tense and tearful, telling about his son's return from the US after a 1-year stay. The doctor told the father that his reaction was understandable and strongly recommended a home visit, which was now accepted by the father.

At the parents' house the doctor and nurse sat with the father in the drawing room. The mother had placed herself on a chair in the doorway. She indicated that Stephen could be disturbed if they talked too loudly. The doctor asked the father to call on Stephen and to tell him about the visitors. Stephen entered halfway in the basement stairs. The doctor said that they had come because the parents had been worried; they did not know how to help him in the best way.—'I don't need any help.'—'But it must be something that makes your parents uneasy and that prevents you from sleeping enough.'—'I don't need much sleep and I need to practise the saxophone because of a new engagement.'—'Everyone needs sleep and especially if there is an engagement waiting.'—'It is not a problem, just stimulating.'—'Is there anything we could do for you to make it easier for you to have the engagement?'—'No thank-you. Yes, I have backache.'

Commentary: This illustrates rather typical difficulties that are met at a first home visit with a person in pre- or early psychosis. The family is almost paralysed by fear of doing anything wrong. One can also imagine Stephen's apprehension of becoming trapped by psychiatry, and of his own disturbance. Could his disclosure of his backache be an opening for further contact? However, in this case further meetings were resisted, and a few days later the police brought him to the emergency department in an openly psychotic state.

If the family meeting is held in the psychiatric clinic, the room should preferably be rather large, permitting the patient or anyone else to move around. Tea and coffee should be readily available. The meeting time must be flexible. It is also necessary to dose the degree and depth of information provided according to the members' needs and strengths.

In psychodynamic psychotherapy one would also place great emphasis on the *continuity of care*. A trusting and lasting relationship with a consistent contact person is critical for the young psychotic patient, whether the context is individual therapy or the therapeutic milieu. Every new patient requires a primary and a secondary contact person and a responsible psychiatrist whose roles should be fully explained to the family members. In most cases the sick member will be present throughout the family meeting, sometimes he or she may walk in and out.

The meeting usually commences with the staff members (preferably at least two) presenting themselves and their agenda for the meeting. Following the presentation, all family members are encouraged to discuss their problems. Naturally, the family may be focused upon their sick relative, and their various descriptions of the situation may illuminate the family dynamics. The patient may sometimes be aware of being ill and openly discuss it. Mostly, however, the patient ignores his or her problems or they are projected towards other family members. Often the patient can acknowledge problems with poor concentration, tiredness, sleeplessness, etc., which can later provide important motivation for treatment. Delusions or hallucinations should be listened to. Apparent delusional ideas may be questioned in a respectful way but there is no benefit in arguing or refuting the patient's belief. The problem formulations are important to record after the session because the patient often forgets the early formulations.

During the first meetings one should also note stressful preceding events or actual tensions and problems in the family, which may or may not constitute precipitating factors.

Genogram

Generally, components of the family history are revealed during the first meetings. The task of constructing a family genogram may require several sessions. Here the patient's siblings, parents, and grandparents are depicted on a large sheet of paper. All members, dead or alive, will be mentioned, including their special characteristics, mental problems, diseases, etc.

There are several goals in collating this information. Firstly, to *gather information* regarding the family's social, cultural and psychiatric history and *learning to know* the members. Secondly, to establish a *sense of coherence* for the patient and the family concerning the period of illness, and to place it within the history of the family. Often 'skeletons in the closet' may emerge, such as a grandparent's mental disease and the psychological reactions of the parent in question, or a suicide, etc. This information invariably evokes thoughts about what it has been permissible to discuss in the family. Thirdly, the background history provides an opportunity to introduce the concept of 'vulnerability' and to describe the illness as an understandable (even if maladaptive) *psychotic crisis reaction* to the current tensions in the patient. This reduces the dramatic effect of the psychosis and conveys hope, because the concept of crisis to most people implies a self-limiting process. We do not advocate an early interpretation of 'hidden' explanations to the psychosis or the blaming of certain individuals—instead rather obvious connections are made with sources of stress. These, to our experience, are easily recognized in the majority of acute psychoses.

To the inexperienced staff member it may seem surprising to witness how this working with the family genogram often has a positive impact upon the patient's ability to reason coherently, even if the psychotic thinking continues after the meeting.

Planning for the Near Future

A more specific psychosis diagnosis (for example, schizophrenia) is not meaningful during the early period of treatment. Bizarre, confused, or autistic symptoms apparent in the early period of treatment may recede into a more prognostically benign psychosis. Naturally, the clinical status must be evaluated, including possible risks. The affective content, risks for aggressive or antisocial acting out, suicidal proneness, etc. should be continuously evaluated during the early contacts.

A desirable solution is often to let the patient *stay in his or her home*, provided that the family has the capacity to form a holding environment. If the patient is highly anxious, or the mental state is deteriorating, it is preferable to offer an inpatient care situation. Unfortunately, typical psychiatric wards are often anxiety-provoking and loaded with 'high expressed emotion', which is counter-therapeutic and may delay recovery. The commitment often involves rapid and unnecessarily high neuroleptic medication.

This scenario may be avoided if there is access to a so-called *crisis home* with few beds, open doors, and a domestic, non-institutional, low expressed-emotion atmosphere. Here the patient can remain in a relatively private space. This model of care, which is associated with a low risk of serious acting out, is successful in the large majority of first-episode cases (Ciompi et al., 1992; Cullberg et al., 2002). The psychotic anxiety is usually lowered when the patient agrees to stay in the crisis home. In case the patient is very impulsive, or manic, a commitment may be preferable—perhaps with a later transfer to a crisis home.

As 20% or more of acute first-episode psychotic patients recover in a few weeks in a supportive milieu, without specific antipsychotic medication (Cullberg et al., 2002; Lehtinen et al., 2000), we believe it is wise to wait 1 or 2 weeks before prescribing such medication. Benzodiazepines and/or hypnotic medication may be effective during this first period in reducing anxiety and insomnia. When indicated, antipsychotics should be administered in the lowest optimal dose, slowly increasing from 1 to 2 mg-eqs of haloperidol per day, in accordance with the PET-studies of the narrow 'therapeutic window' between antipsychotic response and side-effects (Nyberg et al., 1999).

Repeated family meetings are usually of great value. During the acute psychotic phase individual meetings with the patient should be supportive and reality oriented. Continuous delusions and hallucinations should be met with respectful confrontation regarding their probability and the possibility of a contrary understanding. Often it may be productive to name such experiences as 'psychotic thoughts'. This is especially valuable, when discussing the content of the psychosis and the early signs of relapse during the mainly non-psychotic resolution phase.

Some patients exhibit an obvious need to discuss emotional conflicts in their family situation, and this is often quite feasible even if the psychosis is still present to some degree. The tendency to polarize close relationships can also be addressed in order to promote a more mature capacity for a holding of ambivalent internal representations.

The following case is an example of the need for a combined cognitive and dynamic approach.

Case example: Combined approch

A 30-year-old woman developed an affective psychosis with delusional traits after a period of almost total sleeplessness over several weeks. There was also a brief period with hallucinatory voices. After commitment she was treated with increasing doses of neuroleptics, including depot injections, to no effect. Electroconvulsive therapy was ordered but the patient refused.

After 4 months her case was taken over by a project for first-episode psychotic patients—due to an oversight the patient had not been referred initially. After the first meeting her (apparently ineffective) medication and compulsory status was discontinued, with an agreement that the doctor would see her at regular and frequent intervals. She was greatly relieved not to continue suffering the side-effects of the drugs, which was also helpful in developing the therapeutic alliance. The patient came to the meetings in spite of being very paranoid about the therapist's identity, believing the ward was a disguised police station and that there were hidden microphones, etc.

From the beginning the therapist was working with her anxiety related to her persecutory beliefs. He told her that there were two possibilities as he understood it; the first, that her anxious ideas of being locked up as a victim of unjust prosecution were correct. In that case she urgently needed all protection. The second working hypothesis was that she, in a state of sleeplessness and despair, gradually had started to misinterpret her surroundings. The therapist offered to be her consultant in investigating these hypotheses. He also told her that he realized that she at least had to *pretend* to rely on his honesty in order to cooperate. This intelligent patient, who was a dedicated diary-writer, gradually produced copious material describing her earlier and ongoing experiences in the hospital. These detailed experiences of terror, humiliation and loneliness were also an intricate mixture of her being exposed to stereotypical and incoherent treatment ambitions, and her psychotic interpretations of why this humiliation would continue. Possible alternative interpretations of the events were discussed without the therapist claiming possession of 'the truth'.

Parallel conversations about her marital life continued. She had married her husband at a very young age in an effort to separate from her parental home. There were no children, and there had been no sex life for several years—in fact psychologically the relation had been finished for a long time. Her husband had increasingly behaved in a threatening way during the last year. The patient did not believe that she could manage to live alone after a separation. Six months prior to hospitalization she had met a woman friend who educated her about feminism and about her own separation and new freedom. During this period the patient's nightly quarrels with her husband started and later the sleeplessness—she wanted her husband to 'allow' and support a separation she otherwise did not dare to undertake. This resulted in an increasing feeling of unreality and of being exposed to a gigantic experiment even at her work place. The paranoid ideas, together with her suicidal behaviour, resulted in the compulsory admission to the locked psychiatric ward. The therapy meetings, which started 4 months after admission, continued for a further 4 months until the paranoid system started to loosen and she could accept different joint meetings with her husband, her parents or her work mates where she could discuss their former 'strange' behaviour. The patient did not return home and rented a flat of her own. She gradually regained full insight and psychic strength and returned to her job. She was recommended a private psychotherapist to further explore and work on her low self-esteem.

Commentary: This intelligent but neurotic patient could have been spared a pro-longed and deep suffering if her psychological predicament had been observed from the admission. It was evident that her psychological problems emanated from her inability to solve the conflict between her need to leave her husband and her fear of independence. Her psychosis was triggered by the sleeplessness and enforced by the strange and anxiety-provoking clinical milieu. The psychotherapeutic work was guided by the clinical impression that behind the delusions the patient had a capacity for full recovery. In the first phase the approach was clearly cognitive-behavioural in order to enable a working alliance. When that was achieved her actual dynamic problems could be approached. The deeper neurotic conflicts around sexuality and dependency were largely saved for later working through.

Recovery and Post-Psychotic Depression

When the psychotic thinking is mainly over, a *post-psychotic depressive reaction* may prevail. From a psychodynamic aspect this reaction has several roots. One is the realization that the experiences and behaviour during psychosis were not real, or that the psychical strength has been broken. Acute psychosis is a deep mental trauma to most people and may lower self-esteem and raise hidden thoughts of being 'chronic'. Many patients experience the period around the commitment as humiliating and anxiety-provoking, and they need to talk it over. Also the damage from acting out during the acute phase—be it psychotic telephone calls, disturbed behaviour in the work place, offences towards family members—may later be perceived as irreparable, with feelings of intense shame. Finally, the psychosis-provoking life situation, which may remain unresolved, needs to be tackled. All these experiences may account for the post-psychotic PTSD reaction (McGorry et al., 1991) that can easily be misinterpreted and inappropriately treated as prevailing psychotic reactions. From a dynamic point of view this period may be looked upon as a grief-reaction to the loss of the former self-image. Some patients tend to seal over their experiences, denying that they have been psychotic. These patients have managed to reintegrate their psychological defences but do not have any motivation for exploring the background to their psychosis. Sometimes this also can be a warning sign of continuous schizophrenic thinking under the normalized surface, indicating a need for new treatment efforts, reconsidering both the pharmacological and psychological treatments. These patients are often difficult to motivate in treatment and it is important to attempt to maintain a working relationship so that effective re-engagement in treatment can be established early in the process of a relapse. Hopefully the need to deny the psychotic disorder, and to withstand the narcissistic blow, will be lessened after their next or subsequent episodes of psychosis. Rational discussions can then be held about recognizing early signs and the use of a prophylactic medication.

As ego capacities are improved, the motivation to prevent relapses must be strengthened. This phase is also important with regard to psychotherapy. Of all first-episode patients, 20–40% are motivated for some kind of insight-oriented therapy in this phase. Such therapy may often be a combination of different methods, according to the patient's psychological capacities and the resources of the clinic. In the case of a traumatic upbringing with multiple experiences of early abuse, this may be the first opportunity for the patient to formulate his or her history in depth. Putting words to these early events, which enables the patient to better understand his or her psychological life may, however, require much time. In these cases, so-called brief therapies may be of little help, and long-term treatments, perhaps in an inpatient milieu, may be needed.

On the other hand, the benefit of even brief therapeutic interventions can be repeatedly observed, highlighting an actual separation or developmental crisis, e.g. an unresolved trauma of the early death of a sibling, etc. The suppressed and dissociated memories and emotions act as an unsecured mine, which detonates at a later event, actualizing the original traumatic situation or the specific vulnerability of the patient. Here dynamic psychotherapy may act as an important prophylactic ego-strengthening tool, as shown by the following vignette.

Case example: Eve

Eve, a 35-year-old academic, had strongly opposed becoming pregnant for reasons that were unclear. Finally she had changed her mind because of her husband's deep longing for a child and because she feared that he otherwise might leave her. She had always conducted a well-planned and protected life with an emphasis on aesthetic values. However, the child died just before delivery. A few weeks later she entered a confusional psychosis that was followed by deep depression and a suicidal attempt. She blamed herself for the death of her child because she had not wanted it.

She was referred to a psychotherapist where she reported that her parents, when she was 2 years of age, adopted a 1-year-old boy who developed a severe conduct disorder, that had probably resulted from a brain disorder. The brother concretely demolished her secure world through his aggressive and destructive behaviour and she started to accumulate an intense aggression towards him without being able to show it outwardly. However, Eve became strongly determined not to have a child. After an intensive psychotherapy in combination with antidepressant medication she felt that she had left her early experiences well behind, and she decided to try to become pregnant again. The new child, a girl, has been very satisfactory to her and her husband.

Commentary: Eve's personality traits, with an emphasis on orderliness, control, and aesthetics, probably were defensive reactions to the arrival of the brother. They had been challenged as a reaction to her early experiences and frustration. Her wishes to have a child were conflicting with her early hatred and she carried a deep protest against her pregnancy. Her fantasies about having caused the death of her child could be worked through and she was now able to make a new and free decision.

The most common dynamic therapy is perhaps to identify and to support an ongoing, necessary separation, be it towards a parent or another love–hate object. The acknowledgement of both the positive and negative feelings and the pain in making a choice is an important step towards maturity, and towards higher ego strength. Also, the shame of having been assaulted, which lowers many women's self-esteem, may lessen the ability to accomplish a necessary separation. In such cases, couple therapy, although not always feasible, is often an effective tool.

The actual loss of an important person, sometimes with a deep symbolic significance like a cherished grandparent in an otherwise chaotic childhood, may precipitate a complicated grieving process. Adolescents or young adults may experience a reactive psychosis when they are thwarted in their efforts to work through this complex grieving process. In this context a successful grieving requires a reformulation of the sense of identity and meaning—here, psychotherapy may be concretely life-saving.

SOME PROBLEMS IN THE APPLICATION OF DYNAMIC THINKING

The Therapeutic Attitude

To our experience, modern psychotherapeutic work with psychotic patients is most rationally undertaken with both dynamic and cognitive methods represented in the clinical technique. We would argue that the ability to adapt the treatment to the individual patient's specific needs is a *sine qua non*. To do so, one has to have a clear understanding of the varying phases of a psychotic development, i.e. the prepsychotic phase, the acute psychotic phase, remission, or a chronic phase with more fixed delusional thinking. And, within each subsequent phase, there are subtle periods when the patient will be more oriented to reality, less stressed, providing important therapeutic opportunities.

Depending on personality structure, one patient may be better suited for a predominant emphasis upon CBT, and another for a dynamic approach. We would assert that a 'pure' dynamic or CBT method does not, or should not, exist in psychosis treatment.

If the acute psychotic reaction has mainly subsided, but delusional thinking or verbal hallucinations persist, this indicates a *schizophrenic development* or a long-term paranoid disorder. Sometimes dynamic interpretations may be indicated from a theoretical point of view, but therapists should generally keep such interpretations to themselves until they form the impression that the patient is ready to verbalize these connections, i.e., when the patient expresses some curiosity regarding an actual loss, an ambivalent relationship, or a traumatic experience. A psychotic patient, who has not been working intensely with his or her problematic relations in a secure relationship with an experienced therapist, is even less prepared than a neurotic patient to listen to, and make use of, deep interpretations—irrespective of whether they seem correct from a historic perspective. Long-term psychoanalytic psychotherapies are usually of little benefit to a patient who is suffering from ongoing thought disturbances. In such a case the therapist needs to be a consistent object, or model, for the patient. As mentioned earlier, the psychodynamic techniques for treatment of neurosis, which are taught at psychotherapeutic schools, vary greatly from the approaches required when working with psychotic and other deeply disturbed patients. Sticking rigidly to the therapeutic frame is counter-productive in the work with acutely psychotic persons. The frame must be situated in the therapist's personality, and cannot always be externalized to an inflexible 45-minute session, or to the therapist's office room. Also, the 'neutral' approach must be avoided and replaced by a non-intrusive more personal (which does not mean private!) contact. Even if the therapist's office is the most common environment, you may find your therapeutic work more effective when walking with the patient in the park or when going to a café, or helping to polish the patient's car. The patient may paint or play music at the session. At some point circumstances may permit an interpretation to be made, i.e. to clarify some stressful factor in the patient's past or present.

The 'therapeutic contact' entails non-intrusive warmth, empathic honesty, and—as far as possible—respect for the integrity of the patient in combination with an effort to share an understanding of the patient's problems. It also means a gradual deepening of the knowledge of idiosyncratic risks of destructive actions, which may necessitate time-limited paternalistic interventions.

In this way of working, which mostly is highly rewarding, the personal strains on the therapist may be strong at times. Therefore, it is important that the staff members are provided with formal training in psychotherapy and supervision, as well as a variation of the working situation (changing between in- and outpatient or administrative work). When the psychosis has remitted, in several cases long-term work begins. Tähkä (1979) formulated the specific needs for a psychosis treatment as follows: 'For the psychotic patient we have to become an object, for the borderline patient we have to act as an object and, finally, for the neurotic patient we have to liberate from an object that has become superfluous' (Tähkä, 1979, p. 131). This implies that the psychosis treatment team may need to be continuously accessible, whereas the personality disturbed person must be taught to better relate in his or her own milieu, and the neurotic person helped to liberate from destructive attachments.

Suicidality in Personality Disordered Psychotic Patients

There are some patients who may be diagnosed as schizophrenic and where dynamic psychotherapy may be of specific use in a late phase. These patients are more 'affective' and may make intense emotional contact, which seems adequate even if they seem 'risky' or brittle. The therapeutic problem concerns a coexisting personality disorder of a borderline or possibly a schizotypal character, that easily leads the patients into difficult relations and problematic situations. Because there is a concurrent vulnerability for psychotic reactions in response to stress in these patients, the DSM-IV criteria for schizophrenia may easily be fulfilled. (This is only one example of this diagnosis becoming more and more obsolete.) In these cases, which are not uncommon, the suicidal risk may be strong at periods. Sometimes the therapist may have the feeling that the patient's psychosis is an alternative to suicide. The dynamic psychotherapy is directed towards the personality disturbance as a vulnerability factor. Therefore, it is not very different from working with other deeply disturbed personalities. This may be a painstaking psychotherapeutic experience—both for the therapist and for the patient. The successful cases clearly demonstrate the benefits of undertaking treatments with these patients where otherwise the probability for suicide would be very high (Levander & Cullberg, 1993). Because treatment may take several years, the economic cost may seem high—comparable to the cost of heart transplantation. It must be considered in an assessment of the clinics' total resources, the patient's capacities, and the therapist's professional and emotional maturity (which not always means a formal training!). The need for emotional support for the therapist and for immediate ward admittance in emergency situations must also be recognized.

Antipsychotic Medication

This is a two-edged sword. Its usefulness is not an issue of debate. However, as mentioned earlier, today's PET research on receptor occupancy and antipsychotic effects (Nyberg et al., 1999) clearly show that the patients often have been heavily and sadly overmedicated both in acute and later phase. A lowering of motivation and lessening of the brightness of life becomes as dominant as the antipsychotic effects, when dopamine receptor activities are inhibited in the frontal brain. This reaction is responsible for much of the protest and 'non-compliance' from the patients. Since we simultaneously wish the psychotic period to be brief and the patient to be motivated to work with the recovery process, i.e. not being overly flat or cognitively impaired, low-dose medication principles have proved superior. It is also important to resist the paternalistic temptation, so prevalent in psychiatry, to always be on the safe side regarding relapses, and to prescribe without listening to the patient's often well-founded wishes. When the patient is non-psychotic the medication should be reduced as soon as possible. This policy makes it easier to motivate the patient for a brief increase or new start on medication if needed. On the other hand, an ongoing antipsychotic medication may be a prerequisite for some patients to take part in psychotherapy.

FINAL REMARKS

Working with psychotic patients within a psychodynamic frame of reference means that the patient's clinical care (medical or non-medical) is guided by such an understanding. Many patients may be treated supportively and not insight oriented, according to the needs and resources—the insights mainly being contained within the therapists.

There is today no advantage in distinguishing between a dynamic and a cognitive (or a biologic) approach to working with acute psychoses. The modern dynamic and cognitive theories of human behaviour are widely overlapping—the rest being more complementary than antagonistic, and both sets of therapeutic methods are needed. Controversial elements mainly stem from historical antagonism and irrelevant information that can be reconciled in the clinical setting. People working with psychosis-prone patients should be able to actively change their approach according to the different needs of the patients.

A more complicated matter is the problem of which profession shall have the authority to outline the central therapeutic strategies in the psychosis team. Historically the medical profession has held this privilege. With our developing knowledge of the importance of both psychosocial and biological factors in the development of the brain and in the psychotic individual's functioning, this may be more open to other rational choices.

REFERENCES

Alanen, Y.O. (1997). *Schizophrenia—Its Origins and Need-adapted Treatment*. London: Karnac Books.

Alanen, Y.O., Lehtinen, K., Räkköläinen, V. & Aaltonen, J. (1991). Need-adapted treatment of new schizophrenic patients. Experiences and results from the Turku project. *Acta Psychiatrica Scandinavica*, **83**, 363–372.

Alanen, Y.O., Rakkolainen, V., Rasimus, R., Laakso, J. & Kaljonen, A. (1985). Psychotherapeutically oriented treatment of schizophrenia: Results of 5-year follow-up. *Acta Psychiatrica Scandinavica*, **71** (319), 31–49.

Alanen, Y.O., Ugelstad, E., Armelius, B.Å., Lethinen, K., Rosenbaum, B. & Sjöström, R. (Eds) (1994). *Early Treatment for Schizophrenic Patients*. Oslo: Scandinavian University Press.

Bleuler, E. (1950). *Dementia Praecox or the Group of Schizophrenias* (1st edn, 1911). New York: International University Press.

Bleuler, M. (1984). Das alte und das neue Bild des Schizophrenen. *Schweizer Archiv für Neurologie und Psychiatrie*, **135**, 143–149

Ciompi, L., Dauwalder, H.P., Aebi, E., Truetsch, K., Kupper, Z. & Rutishauser, C. (1992). A new approach of acute schizophrenia. Further results of the pilot project Soteria Bern. In A. Werbart &

J. Cullberg (Eds), *Psychotherapy of Schizophrenia: Facilitating and Obstructive Factors* (pp. 95–109). Oslo: Scandinavian University Press.

Cullberg, J. (1991). Recovered versus non-recovered schizophrenic patients who have had intensive psychotherapy. *Acta Psychiatrica Scandinavica*, **84**, 242–245.

Cullberg, J. (2003). Stressful life events preceding first onset of psychosis. An exploratory study. *Nordic Journal of Psychiatry*, **57**, 209–214.

Cullberg, J., Levander, S., Holmqvist, R., Mattsson, M. & Wieselgren, I.M. (2002). One year outcome in first episode psychosis patients in the Swedish Parachute project. *Acta Psychiatrica Scandinavica*, **106**, 276–285.

Cullberg, J., Thoren, G., Abb, S., Mesterton, A. & Svedberg, B. (2000). Integrating intensive psychosocial and low-dose neuroleptic treatment: A three-year follow-up. In B. Martindale, A. Bateman, M. Crowe & F. Margison (Eds), *Psychosis: Psychological Approaches and their Effectiveness* (pp. 200–209). London: Gaskell.

Gunderson, J.G., Frank, A.F. & Katz, H.M. (1984). Effects of psychotherapy in schizophrenia: II. Comparative outcome of two forms of treatment. *Schizophrenia Bulletin*, **10**, 564–598.

Hogarty, G.E., Kornblith, S.J., Greenwald, D., DiBarry, A.L., Cooley, S., Ulrich, R.F., Carter, M. & Flesher, S. (1997). Three-year trials of personal therapy among patients living with or independent of family, I: Description of study and effects on relapse rates. *American Journal of Psychiatry*, **154**, 1504–1513.

Jackson, M. & Williams, P. (1994). *Unimaginable Storms. A Search for Meaning in Psychosis*. London: Karnac Books.

Karon, B. & Van den Bos, G. (1972). The consequences of psychotherapy for schizophrenic patients. *Psychotherapy: Theory, Research and Practice*, **9**, 11–19.

Killingmo, B. (1989). Conflict and deficit: Implications for technique. *International Journal of Psychoanalysis*, **70**, 65–79.

Lehman, A.F., Steinwachs, D.M., Dixon, L.B., Goldman, H.H., Osher, F., Postrado, L., Scott, J.E., Thompson, J.W., Fahey, M., Fischer, P., Kasper, J.A., Lyles, A., Skinner, E.A., Buchanan, R., Carpenter, W.T. Jr, Levine, J., McGlynn, E.A., Rosenheck, R. & Zito, J. (1998). Translating research into practice: The Schizophrenia Patient Outcomes Research Team (PORT) treatment recommendations. *Schizophrenia Bulletin*, **24**, 1–10.

Lehtinen, V., Aaltonen, J., Koffert, T., Rakkolainen, V. & Syvalahti, E. (2000). Two-year outcome in first-episode psychosis treated according to an integrated model. Is immediate neuroleptisation always needed? *European Psychiatry*, **15**, 312–320.

Levander, S. & Cullberg, J. (1993). Sandra: Successful psychotherapeutic work with a schizophrenic woman. *Psychiatry*, **56**, 284–293.

May, R.A., Tuma, A.H. & Dixon, W.J. (1968). *Treatment of Schizophrenia. A Comparative Study of Five Treatment Methods*. New York: Science House.

McGlashan, T.H. (1984). The Chestnut-Lodge follow-up study: II Long-term outcome of schizophrenia and the addictive disorders. *Archives of General Psychiatry*, **41**, 141–144.

McGlashan, T.H. & Keats, C.J. (1989). *Schizophrenia: Treatment Process and Outcome*. Washington, DC: American Psychiatric Press.

McGorry, P.D., Chanen, A., McCarthy, E., van Riel, R., McKenzie, D. & Singh, B. (1991). Post-traumatic stress disorder following recent-onset psychosis. An unrecognized postpsychotic syndrome. *Journal of Nervous and Mental Disease*, **179**, 253–258.

Mueser, K.T. & Berenbaum, H. (1990). Psychodynamic treatment of schizophrenia: Is there a future? *Psychological Medicine*, **20**, 253–262.

Nyberg, S., Eriksson, B., Oxenstierna, G., Halldin, C. & Farde, L. (1999). Suggested minimal effective dose of risperidone based on PET measured D2 and 5HT2A-receptor occupancy in schizophrenic patients. *American Journal of Psychiatry*, **156**, 869–875.

Ryle, A. (Ed) (1995). *Cognitive Analytic Therapy. Developments in Theory and Practice*. Chichester: John Wiley & Sons.

Sjöström, R. (1985). Effects of psychotherapy in schizophrenia. A retrospective study. *Acta Psychiatrica Scandinavica*, **71**, 513–522.

Stone, M.H. (1986). Explorative psychotherapy in schizophrenia-spectrum patients: A reevaluation in the light of long-term follow up of schizophrenic and borderline patients. *Bulletin of Menninger Clinic*, **50**, 287–306.

Tähkä, V. (1979). Psychotherapy as phase-specific treatment. *Scandinavian Psychoanalytic Review*, **2**, 113–132.

Vaughn, C.E. & Leff, J. (1976). The influence of social factors on the course of psychiatric illness. A comparison of schizophrenic and depressed neurotic patients. *British Journal of Psychiatry*, **129**, 125–137.

Zubin, J. & Spring, B. (1977). Vulnerability—a new view of schizophrenia. *Journal of Abnormal Psychology*, **86**, 103–126.

6 Working with Families in the Early Stages of Psychosis

JEAN ADDINGTON
Department of Psychiatry, University of Toronto, Canada

PETER BURNETT
ORYGEN Youth Health, Melbourne, Australia

INTRODUCTION

The early stages of psychosis are often a frightening and bewildering time for families. Unusual behaviours in a son, daughter or sibling generate emotions such as fear, apprehension, sadness and sometimes guilt and anger. With no previous experience to guide them, families often feel overwhelmed. Yet most young people are still living with their families when the psychosis begins. Families can play a major role in the recovery from psychosis, but without support and understanding from professionals they may find it difficult to see a way through the maze of emotions and problems that inevitably accompany the first psychotic episode. So working constructively with families is an essential component of the management of early psychosis.

The different processes that make schizophrenia a long-term disorder may be most apparent and cause the most damage in the first few years of the illness (McGlashan & Fenton, 1993). Recent research has focused on the deleterious effects of a long duration between the onset of psychotic symptoms and the first effective treatment (Larsen et al., 1996; Loebel et al., 1992) and the potential of a prolonged psychotic state to put individuals at risk. In addition, there are major psychosocial problems that can occur with the onset of psychosis. This collateral psychosocial damage can be extensive and can impose a significant burden of bewilderment, fear and suffering on individuals with the illness and their families. More specifically, these impairments in functioning can disrupt adolescent and young adult development at a particularly important developmental stage. Other disruptive occurrences include the experience of stigma, embarrassment, isolation, loss of mastery and control, decreased self-worth, a disrupted educational and/or professional trajectory, and often a decrease in one's capacity to fully participate in treatment decisions (McGorry, Edwards & Pennell, 1999).

Like any serious illness that can occur during this period of adolescence and young adulthood, one of the implications is that it prolongs the role of the family as caregivers. It has been suggested that as many as 60–70% of individuals presenting with a first episode

Psychological Interventions in Early Psychosis
Edited by J.F.M. Gleeson and P.D. McGorry. © 2004 John Wiley & Sons, Ltd.

of psychosis still live at home with their families (Addington et al., 2001; EPPIC, 1997). Furthermore, as the impact of a psychotic illness continues to affect the psychosocial functioning of the individual, the family is clearly a critical caregiver (Jackson & Edwards, 1992).

It has long been established that families who have a member with schizophrenia undoubtedly experience personal distress, and that burden does exist within such families (Bulger, Wandersman & Goldman, 1993). When family members learn that their relative has developed schizophrenia or another psychotic disorder they experience helplessness, anger, despair and anxiety (Spaniol, Zipple & Lockwood, 1992). They are faced with traumatic role changes that are forced on them without perceived warning. At times they feel that they lack support from and communication with mental health professionals (MacCarthy et al., 1989). Burden is often the result of the addition of the caregiving role to already existing family roles (Schene, 1990). 'Objective burden' involves the disruption to the family/household due to the individual's illness and is usually observable, whereas 'subjective burden' involves the psychological consequences of the individual's illness for the family (Schene, Tessler & Gamache, 1994).

There is a well-established trend for greater burden with greater severity of the individual's symptoms (Birchwood & Cochrane, 1991). In a more recent study it was demonstrated that the more negative items family members endorsed on an experience of caregiving inventory (ECI; Szmukler et al., 1996), the higher the levels of personal and psychological distress among family members (Martens & Addington, 2001). Furthermore, this same study suggested that there was a higher risk of personal distress as opposed to a sense of burden for the family members of those individuals who were experiencing their first onset of schizophrenia. One of the few studies to focus on first-episode patients (Kuipers & Raune, 2000) reported that more than a third of family members demonstrated clear depression and another third demonstrated mild depression. Additionally, social isolation and less constructive coping styles were also evident among family members.

Of course, depression, acute stress and distress in family members are of concern for their own well-being, mental health and quality of life. But as Gleeson et al. (1999) pointed out, it is also a great advantage for the family to remain functional in order to support the individual with psychosis and prevent further deterioration. Here the family can play a very important role in providing a supportive and safe environment to help during the phases of recovery. However, they themselves need to be as healthy as possible in order to manage this caring role despite the tremendous anguish and stress they may be experiencing. Not only is a stressed family unable to provide such a role but they also create a stressful environment which, in turn, runs the risk of symptom exacerbation for the individual with psychosis.

The stressful family environment has been extensively studied using the concept of expressed emotion or EE (Brown, Birley & Wing, 1972; Leff & Vaughn 1985). EE is an empirical construct determined by the presence of a high number of critical comments, hostility or emotional over-involvement elicited from a key relative during a semistructured interview—the Camberwell Family Interview. Numerous studies have shown that high EE is strongly predictive of increased risk of relapse in schizophrenia (see Kavanagh, 1992, for a review). A small number of studies have focused on EE in first-episode patients. Stirling et al. (1991) and Rund et al. (1995) found no correlation between EE and relapse, but the majority of studies (Barrelet et al., 1990; Huguelet et al., 1995; Linszen et al., 1996;

Neuchterlein, Snyder & Mintz, 1992) confirmed a positive association. Further work needs to be carried out in this area to address methodological problems and to assess the impact of potential confounding variables such as duration of untreated psychosis. In our view, all families need psychoeducation and support through the early course of illness, and it would be very useful to be able—easily and reliably—to identify those who would benefit from more intensive therapy. EE offers a potential means of achieving this, although the present measures are too long and detailed for general clinical use. The validity of shorter measures of EE remains equivocal.

FAMILY INTERVENTION

Traditionally, family intervention programmes were specifically designed to address the problems observed in patients with schizophrenia and their families during the post-hospitalization period. These programmes, termed psychoeducational, did not derive from any specific theory of family dynamics or traditional family therapy techniques but from a more empirical perspective. Today the concept of psychoeducational family interventions has achieved worldwide recognition. Although these programmes contain an educational component, they are more sophisticated than education alone.

Various formats have been used successfully, for example, the individual family unit (Falloon et al., 1982; Goldstein et al., 1978; Hogarty et al., 1986; Randolph et al., 1994; Tarrier, Barrowclough & Porceddu, 1988), individual family plus a relatives' group (Leff et al., 1982), relatives only group (Leff et al., 1989), multiple family groups (McFarlane et al., 1995), and parallel patient and relatives' group (Kissling, 1994). These family intervention programmes have been well reviewed elsewhere (e.g. Barbato & D'Avanzo, 2000; Penn & Mueser, 1996).

The published results from these programmes are unequivocal in demonstrating the superiority of family intervention plus medication over medication alone in delaying psychotic relapses. Results from a recent meta-analysis (Pitschel-Walz et al., 2001), examining the impact of family intervention on relapse rates, suggest that the relapse rate can be reduced by 20% if relatives of schizophrenia patients are included in the treatment, with a particularly marked effect if the treatment continued for longer than 3 months. In this analysis the significant effect sizes were low but, considering the questions being asked, they are substantial.

The purpose of this chapter is to focus on interventions for families that (a) have a member who is in the early phases of a psychotic illness or (b) have a member who is experiencing an acute episode of psychosis for the first time. This is an important distinction as these families are different; there is the potential for better outcome by intervening optimally and as early as possible; and ultimately they require a different approach than has traditionally been used for families with a relative who is already experiencing a chronic course of schizophrenia.

FIRST-EPISODE FAMILIES: ARE THEY DIFFERENT?

For those individuals with a more enduring and chronic course of illness, one of the major goals of a family programme is to assist and support relatives in their efforts to manage their family member as helpfully as possible—a reasonable assumption for both chronic and symptomatic clients. Thus the group approach to family interventions is a relatively cost-effective solution. However, for younger clients who do achieve reasonable remissions it may not be appropriate to consider them as 'disabled' and requiring management by others. Instead, one assumption we could work from is that the individual with schizophrenia or other psychotic disorder is capable of taking responsibility for his or her behaviour and can make positive contributions to the improvement of the family climate (Goldstein & Miklowitz, 1995).

The issues facing an individual experiencing a first episode of psychosis are different from those facing a chronically ill patient and his or her relatives (Linzen, 1993). This may be even more apparent for those individuals who are seeking help and are potentially in the very early stages of a psychotic illness. These are individuals who may be in what could be considered the prodromal phase of a psychotic illness or are in an 'at-risk mental' state (Yung et al., 1996).

The impact of these first signs or the first episode is also different for the family since they do not usually have prior experience with psychosis. This can be an extremely strange and bewildering time and there is often diagnostic ambiguity. A diagnosis of schizophrenia or other psychotic disorder cannot be readily given. Indeed, many individuals who present with psychotic symptoms for the first time may not go beyond receiving a DSM-IV diagnosis of schizophreniform disorder or psychotic disorder NOS. Many may develop an affective psychosis. Others may present with psychotic symptoms that are typical of those seen in the prodromal phase of the illness and which may never develop further. Psychoeducation cannot be as specific as with more chronic patients. These unique concerns of first-episode families are being considered in programmes that have a specific focus on working with first-episode patients.

EARLY PSYCHOSIS PROGRAMMES

Early psychosis programmes, as can be seen from many of the chapters in this book, are developing throughout the world. The authors of this chapter work in programmes that are in different countries and hemispheres. These two programmes, one Australian and one Canadian, are very similar philosophically but do have practical differences. Such differences in programmes often reflect the area, the staffing, the population they serve, and the kind of funding they receive.

The Calgary Early Psychosis Program (EPP)

The Early Psychosis Treatment and Prevention Program is a comprehensive programme in Calgary, Canada, serving a population of 930,000 through a publicly funded health care system. The goals of the programme are: early identification of the psychotic illness, reduction in the delays in initial treatment, treatment of the primary symptoms of psychosis, reduction of secondary morbidity, reduction of the frequency and severity of relapse, promotion of normal psychosocial development, and reduction of the burden and stress for families. Referral criteria include experiencing a first episode of non-affective psychosis, and having had no more than 3 months of adequate treatment. Case management, psychiatric management and medication strategies, cognitive-behavioural therapy, group therapy, and family interventions are offered for 3 years, at the end of which patients are referred to other agencies or the care of their family physician. This programme has approximately 180–200 patients at any one time with 75–80% of families being involved in the programme.

In EPP every effort is made to include families as collaborators in the treatment process. All patients have a case manager and a psychiatrist and families are invited to initial assessments and psychiatric clinics. All families are assigned a family worker who works closely with the rest of the team. This close liaison of all staff results in ongoing integration of family interventions, case management and psychiatric management. We have two masters-level clinicians from different disciplines who have special training in family work at the graduate level. These clinicians are dedicated to working specifically with families. This underscores the importance of the family work both within the programme and to the family itself. It also allows for family work to continue should a conflictual situation arise between the patient and the family.

In our family component we are concerned about the impact of psychosis on the family system as well as on subsystems and individual members (EPPIC, 1997; Gleeson et al., 1999). The overall goals are to minimize the disruption to the life of the family and the risk of long-term grief, acute stress and high levels of burden in individual family members and to maximize the adaptive functioning of the family after the acute episode. The specific needs of the family are acknowledged, not only because the family environment may impact the person's experience and recovery but also because the family needs support through a bewildering and distressing period.

The family intervention component of the Calgary programme attempts early engagement in a no-fault atmosphere. We offer families as many sessions as they need—within reason—in the first year in the programme. The result is that, on average, in the first year we have offered families 6–8 sessions on an individual family basis with a focus on education about psychosis, support and learning coping strategies. Several families need many more sessions and these are available; alternatively, several families only want to attend for 2–3 sessions. We try to meet with both the individual with the psychosis and family members together whenever possible. This occurs about 50% of the time. This facilitates an understanding of psychosis and treatment across all family members. We want to help family members to understand the illness, implications of the illness and the potential for recovery. In those individual sessions we offer help with strategies for coping with the disorder. Communication training and problem-solving training are available for those families who have particular difficulties in those areas.

We find that the majority of those first 6–8 sessions occur within the first 6 months of the programme. In the next 6–18 months we offer a short-term family group for those who are interested. This group helps families to meet other families with similar problems and to share solutions to difficulties and gain support. Throughout the next 12–18 months we continue to work with the family to maximize the responsiveness of the family to early warning signs, to facilitate relapse prevention and the preparedness of the family for dealing with crises associated with the psychosis. In the final year of the programme we offer help with discharge planning for families.

The Early Psychosis Prevention and Intervention Centre (EPPIC)

The goals of family work in the EPPIC programme are similar, with a focus on a collaborative approach, emphasizing the important therapeutic role that families can play in a member's recovery from psychosis. However, the model of service delivery is different. The initial responsibility for working with families lies with the case manager who is supported by a psychoeducational programme known as 'Family and Friends Information Sessions'. This is held one night a week for 4 weeks and provides basic information and discussion about psychosis. There are two facilitators who actively encourage the group members to ask questions and discuss their own experiences. The style is very interactive, with a small amount of didactic material. Families are encouraged to attend as soon as possible after their relative enters the programme. Because the individual patients are often very ill at this stage, and also to help families to be open about their own experiences, these sessions are designed for families only. At the same time, case managers and often inpatient staff work at engaging individual families and addressing their specific issues.

The case managers are supported by a family work team which comprises a full-time family worker, and portions of time from a psychiatrist and other staff who have special interest and training in family work. Case-managers refer families for consultation or for more intensive family work when that is indicated—for example, when there is significant distress, family conflict, frequent relapses or slow recovery. Sometimes the family worker works with the case manager and the family, but more often works alone with the family. Another situation in which the family worker plays an important role is when the individual patient is in conflict with the family, or does not want them involved in the treatment, yet is still living with them. Here the case-manager can work with the patient while the family worker works with the family.

The approach to families at this stage is usually a combination of psychoeducation and supportive therapy, recognizing the emotional distress that families understandably experience and encouraging the development of effective and therapeutic coping strategies. However, when patients are slow to recover or suffer frequent relapses, a more structured approach based on cognitive-behavioural principles is used. Again this is available on both an individual family basis and a multi-family group basis. The group in this case is a closed group, which includes patients, and meets fortnightly for 6 months.

THE STAGE MODEL

According to EPPIC (1997; Gleeson et al., 1999) the process of family interaction in early psychosis can be divided theoretically into four main stages that coincide with different stages of the course of the illness. In the first stage, *Before Detection*, during the early prepsychotic phase, families are faced with upheaval and trauma often with little or no real understanding of the changes that are occurring. However, today, with the initiation of both research and intervention in the prodromal or prepsychotic phase, and public education encouraging early help-seeking, we would expect and want to see families at this stage. At this very early stage these families need to access appropriate treatment as soon as possible and need some explanation for the change in behaviour. It is also important at this stage that families receive accurate information about the early warning signs of psychosis and appropriate sources of help, as well as minimizing conflict regarding the young person's behaviour.

In the second stage, *After Detection, Grief and Stress*, families are confronted and may have to deal with the diagnosis and the beginning of treatment. During this stage families need information about the disorder and about their own reactions to stress. This requires practical and emotional support to prevent longer-term problems associated with distress and associated depression. They need to understand what has happened to their relative and what their role will be in his or her treatment and recovery.

In the third stage, *Towards Recovery, Coping, Competence and Adaptive Functioning*, a 'competence paradigm' combined with a stress and coping model offers a way to understand the needs of families. In this paradigm families are seen as competent or potentially competent helpers in the recovery process where the focus will be on family strengths, resources and coping strategies. Although the family may experience competence deficits, these can be strengthened by professional help. Ongoing information regarding treatment during recovery, the appropriate level of care as recovery progresses, and early warning signs of relapse is required.

In the fourth stage, *First Relapse and Prolonged Recovery*, families may need to rethink and even may have to reconstruct their original explanatory model of the psychosis. There will be the need for effective acute phase treatment for relapse and for the family to understand the longer-term prognosis. The family may have to learn how to access other ongoing community supports. Further psychoeducation and communication training might also be required at this stage.

ASSESSING THE FAMILY

The assessment of family needs has to be distinguished from the process of obtaining a collaborative psychosocial history of the patient's presenting problems. This type of assessment can be addressed elsewhere. The focus of the family assessment is immediate concerns in relation to the psychosis (EPPIC, 1997; Gleeson et al., 1999). Furthermore, this assessment should be ongoing throughout the course of the family work.

We want to know the family's current knowledge of psychosis, and their previous experience with the illness. We ask about their understanding of the illness, the treatments and the prognosis, and finally attempt to gain an understanding of their explanatory model of the psychosis. Table 6.1 (adapted from EPPIC, 1997, p. B7) gives examples of questions that could be asked at this point. Secondly, we want to explore the practical impact of the psychosis on the family. This includes the impact on individual family members who may be differentially affected by the psychosis of their relative as well as the impact on regular family routine. Having a family member with psychosis can have practical, cognitive and emotional impacts on the family. Table 6.2 (adapted from EPPIC, 1997, p. B7) gives some examples of questions for exploring the impact of the psychosis on the family.

The third area to be explored is the family's strengths and coping resources. This includes the family's perception of their own strengths and coping resources, their track record of dealing with stress, and their appraisal of resources available to support them. Finally, as we know that patterns of communication in the family can have an impact on the course of psychosis, we therefore want to know how they are relating to and communicating with the ill person. This way we can make sure that they know about: (a) the role of stress in exacerbating symptoms; (b) potentially stressful situations for the ill person; and (c) the difficulty people with psychosis often have when trying to process information.

Table 6.1. Exploratory questions for assessing knowledge about psychosis

---

Previous experience
- Have you had any previous experience with other people with psychosis? If so, how did that compare with the current situation?
- What did you know about psychosis before your relative became unwell?

Previous information provided
- What opportunities have you had to find out about psychosis?
- Have you been given any written information?
- Do you have any questions about any of it?

Symptom/behaviour knowledge
- What do you think are the major symptoms of psychosis that your relative is experiencing?
- Is there anything about your relative's behavior that doesn't make sense?

Explanatory model
- What do each of you think caused the psychosis?
- You've been given the doctor's view; do you have a different idea about where the psychosis came from?

Prognosis
- How does the future for your relative look (over the short term and the long term)?

Treatment
- What medication is your relative taking?
- What have you been told about how these medicines work?
- What do you know about the additional treatments your relative has been receiving?
- Are there any other forms of treatment that you wish your relative was receiving?

Perception of risk
- Do you have any concerns that your relative could be in any danger of self-injury?
- Do you ever worry that your relative could be a threat to anyone?

Other
- Families sometimes have their own opinions even after talking to the doctors.
- Is there anything that you disagree with—for example, the diagnosis or the treatments selected?

Adapted from: Early Psychosis Prevention and Intervention Centre (EPPIC): *Working with Families in Early Psychosis*. No. 2 in a Series of Early Psychosis manuals, Psychiatric Services Branch, Human Services, Victoria, Australia, 1997.

INTERVENTIONS FOR FIRST-EPISODE FAMILIES

Family work should help to empower families to achieve mastery and control over their life circumstances, particularly in relation to the emergence of the psychotic disorder. Generally, interventions are not designed to address dysfunction, but rather to promote coping skills by support and education with the aim of preventing long-term problems. We start by minimizing disruption to the life of the family by making sure that emotional and practical support are available. We need to enhance the adaptive functioning of the family, therefore we offer education about psychosis, skill training in problem-solving, and communication skills. It is important that all members of a family understand psychosis and the available treatment. To minimize the risk of long-term grief, stress, and high levels of burden in individual family members, we offer individual and group-based emotional and practical support and intervention for identified problems. Home-based sessions are not routine but do occur for a minority of the families who find it difficult to attend or are 'harder to reach'.

Interventions focus on psychoeducation, specific strategies, problem-solving and communication training, and group work. These interventions will be described with particular relevance for the different stages.

Table 6.2. Questions for exploring the impact of the psychosis upon the family

---

Practical impact
- What changes to the family routine have occurred?
- Has anyone had to stay home from work recently?
- It is more difficult to do essential daily tasks such as cooking, cleaning?
- Has anyone considered moving out when things have become difficult?
- Has it been difficult to get to sleep because of his or her behaviour?
- When was the last time you had some time to relax and enjoy yourselves?

General health
- Has anyone been getting sick since the psychosis developed?
- Are there any physical health problems in the family?
- Has anyone been tempted to use alcohol or drugs to cope?

Cognitive impact
- Has anyone been preoccupied with particular concerns about the psychosis?
- Are there any bad memories of recent events that stand out?
- Does the future ever look hopeless to anybody because of what is happening?

Emotional impact
- Does anyone have any regrets about anything that has happened?
- Is anyone bothered by feeling scared recently (or edgy, angry, upset, etc.)?
- Does anyone have nightmares because of what has been happening?
- Has anyone been feeling down or depressed after what has happened?
- How much energy does everyone have for doing the everyday things?

Impact on family system
- How do you think the family as a whole is coping?
- What is the family doing to support each other?
- Who would you say is shouldering most of the burden at the moment?
- Who would you say is taking the most responsibility for making decisions?
- Do you have the chance to discuss together the best way to deal with things?
- Does anyone find that it is preferable to stay away from the house these days?

Adapted from: Early Psychosis Prevention and Intervention Centre (EPPIC): *Working with Families in Early Psychosis.* No. 2 in a Series of Early Psychosis manuals, Psychiatric Services Branch, Human Services, Victoria, Australia 1997.

Psychoeducation

In the early phase it is important that families understand the implications of early symptoms for psychosis. Important information includes the risk factors involved with the appearance of prodromal symptoms, attenuated psychotic symptoms or brief intermittent symptoms and the ability to identify either a change or increase in the early symptoms should that happen. Families need to develop an understanding of the explanatory model for these early symptoms because, in this stage, families are so often seeking explanations. Work with the family should focus on helping them to reach a consensus as to the most likely reasons for these early symptoms. Hopefully, this will help to avoid conflict and encourage family members to work together. Families need to learn the treatments that are available and suitable for the young person in this early stage and the treatments that might be available to help to prevent an exacerbation of these early subthreshold symptoms. These would include stress management and treatment for substance use, where this is indicated.

In the second stage, families have usually been confronted with a diagnosis and the start of treatment. Here, they first need information about the disorder. Education for first-episode families includes information about psychosis and its management. Secondly, information should assist families to relate to the young person appropriately, to begin to formulate solutions to practical problems, and to reduce feelings of helplessness. Finally, education offered must be considered in the context of the family's explanatory model. In asking the family to explain their 'theory', beliefs or explanations of the psychotic illness of their relative, the validity of their experience and the importance of their viewpoint are being acknowledged. In addition, the therapist obtains information regarding how the family perceive the psychosis so that the therapist can assess the discrepancy between the family's explanatory model and what he or she, as therapist, might propose. It is essential therefore that the therapist makes these enquiries in a respectful manner and shows a willingness to work with the family's model. This avoids the risk of alienating the family.

Our family education starts with information about the nature of the illness, symptoms and diagnoses. Factors concerning the diagnosis would include symptoms of psychosis, what is illness, and what is not illness-related behaviour. Further information on types of psychosis and diagnostic criteria should be reviewed. Families should understand about the need for a comprehensive assessment, what that entails, and the information that will be forthcoming from that assessment. We need to acknowledge diagnostic uncertainty with this population. Some families may be hearing that a first episode of an unspecified mental illness is emerging which needs treatment to prevent further exacerbation; others may hear that the diagnosis is a first episode of psychosis and the specific diagnosis is as yet unclear; and others may be given a specific DSM-IV diagnosis. As families learn more about the illness and as diagnoses change, families are given information that will help them to understand the nature of the psychotic illness, the prognosis and what these changes might mean.

Once families have a good understanding of symptoms and potential diagnoses, they will find explanations of aetiology and the stress–vulnerability model helpful, particularly if they are presented in a way that makes sense to them. We teach families that this is a brain disorder that is most likely neurodevelopmental. Likening the stress–vulnerability model of psychosis to the stress–vulnerability models of medical illnesses with which families may be familiar can aid understanding. However, there should be a major emphasis on the fact that the psychosis can clearly be made worse or exacerbated by stress and substance use.

For families in the third stage of recovery, coping and adaptive functioning, the relevant psychoeducation will give them a better understanding of some of the illness-related be-haviours they may see and thus lead to better management. Families are educated about the phases of psychosis, issues of secondary morbidity and factors that trigger relapse. A sound knowledge of the early signs of relapse will be helpful. Families are helped to understand the overlap between psychosis-driven behavioural difficulties and typical adolescent mis-behaviours. From routine cognitive assessments, family members can be given information about any obvious impairment so that they may be better able to understand the behaviour of their relative. For example, an explanation to families that their son or daughter may have memory problems helps them to understand better some of the resultant behaviours.

Families need to have a full understanding of the treatments being offered and potential treatments that may be available. This way they will be able to take a more active role in helping the young person manage his or her treatments. In terms of treatment, the importance of continued medication is emphasized as well as the psychosocial treatments such as psychoeducation, individual and group therapy and vocational rehabilitation. Medication must be understood in terms of different types, achieving an optimal dose, possible side-effects and their management, the role of medication in treating positive and negative symptoms, the role of medication in relapse prevention, possible interactions of alcohol and illicit drugs with prescribed medication, the need to monitor medication and, finally, the importance of compliance. Families do need to know that their member is receiving optimal care so that potential conflict around treatment issues is minimized.

The final area of education in this third stage focuses on educating families in ways that they may be able to help manage the illness better. Families are educated in foreseeing and managing crises, defusing situations, setting limits on disturbing behaviour, providing a structured/low-stress environment, responding to psychotic behaviour, knowing when to leave the person alone, and knowing how best to interact with the person. Family education also involves helping families, in particular parents, to change expectations and set more realistic achievable goals with respect to the ill member. Expectations may need to be reviewed and generally 'rescheduled' in order to protect the family and patient from disappointment and disillusionment. To address many of these issues families may need some practical advice, problem-solving training and support in using new skills to help to manage the ill person more successfully.

Families in the fourth stage, i.e. first relapse and prolonged recovery, may need to know more about the longer term prognosis for the individual who continues to have prolonged symptoms. Learning about different medications such as clozapine and its implications is useful here. They may need to know about the availability of other support groups such as self-help and support organizations for families who have a member with schizophrenia, bipolar disorder, and other relevant diagnoses.

Modalities for delivering psychoeducation

There are several options to deliver information to families about psychosis. Multi-family groups are an effective and highly efficient way to impart basic information to families (McFarlane et al., 1995). They also provide opportunities for families to learn from each other's experience and to give support to others. By doing so, they may reduce the sense of isolation and stigma that often accompany psychosis. But it is essential that the group leaders foster an interactive approach rather than a didactic one, so that families learn to be active participants in the process.

Alternatively, education can be offered on an individual basis. For families in the 'first stage before detection', whose family members may be in the prodromal stage of the illness, education should be offered on an individual family basis. Our experience is that it may be difficult for such families to be in a group, particularly with families whose offspring already have a clearly diagnosable psychotic illness (Addington et al., 2001). By offering individual family sessions we can be flexible and adaptable in the presentation of the education.

Interventions: Coping Strategies, Communication Training, and Problem-Solving

Intervention strategies that can be used with families include strategies for coping, communication training and problem-solving training. Families are faced with coping on two fronts: the first is coping with their own personal stress and distress; and the second is coping with the psychosis and subsequent behaviour of their relative. In the second stage, families clearly need practical and emotional support to minimize the impact of the trauma. They need to understand what has happened to their relative. Furthermore, optimal management of psychotic symptoms helps the patient from becoming too dependent on the family. Families need ideas and strategies for coping with a wide range of difficulties. These would include coping with symptoms, understanding medication management, dealing with disturbing behaviours, addressing self-destructive behaviour, and making use of community services. At this stage the therapist must also address caregiver needs. Furthermore, there is the need for identification and treatment of family members who may be at risk of experiencing distress or depression and of more complex family issues.

Communication training is directed at improving communication clarity in general and improving ways of providing positive and negative feedback within the family. Positive, negative and cognitive symptoms can affect communication. Poor or vague communication can have an impact on psychosis. Encouraging open communication and increasing the feedback between family members may decrease the stress within the family. Improved communication can also help to improve communication with other professionals. Through communication training families can learn to better manage interpersonal conflict at home.

It is important to assess problem-solving skills. Many families have good problem-solving skills but need some help with specific problems around psychosis. They may be a family whose normally sound problem-solving skills have been affected by the immediate crises of psychosis, or they may be a family who have poor problem-solving skills regardless of what is happening. Skill training can be used to maximize adaptive functioning of the family. They need to cope with a psychotic illness, deal with stressful life events, manage day-to-day problems and find ways to decrease their stress. Problem-solving training is directed at improving management of day-to-day problems and the management of discrete stressful life events. This is based on the method described in detail by Mueser and Glynn (1999).

Case example: Anna

Anna, a 20-year-old woman suffering from a delusional disorder, believed that her mother was part of the plot against her. Anna's mother felt hurt and frustrated by the repeated accusations and became increasingly angry and then critical with her daughter, resulting in violent confrontations. The family worker focused on psycho-education and communication skills. The psychoeducation helped Anna's mother to accept the accusations as illness-driven rather than a personal attack, and enabled her to frame a more constructive response. Further sessions with Anna's mother alone worked on consolidating the psychoeducation, increasing her own support network and planning 'time out' to reduce the stress that she was experiencing.

Family Groups

In the Calgary programme following the individual family sessions, a multiple family group is available on a weekly basis. This six-session evening group occurs approximately three times per year. The group is available for families after they have been approximately 6 months in the programme and have received education about psychosis. This allows families to be reasonably well informed about psychosis, to be past the initial crises stage, and to be able to benefit from contact with other families.

The purpose of the group is to reduce social isolation, shame and stigma, to provide support, and to reinforce the education already received about psychosis. It can help to increase the knowledge of supports and coping strategies. Such a group offers families the opportunity for open discussion and to exchange information with others, offering increased problem-solving and increased options. At this point in time the group members can be more helpful to one another as they are able to learn from other families who have had similar experiences. The group can be particularly helpful for families who are dealing with a prolonged recovery or for those who have insufficient supports and difficulties coping.

Special Needs

Often families are struggling and present with more difficult or serious problems such as high levels of familial conflict, verbal or physical violence, or extreme levels of tension and distress. There may be multiple family members with psychosis or mental illness, a recent family history of suicide, or severe physical health problems in other members of the family. At times we are presented with families who have recently arrived from non-English-speaking countries.

The above are all examples of family issues not directly caused by the psychosis but which have a major effect on its course and make the process of psychoeducational family work much more difficult. The extent to which they can be addressed within the first-episode service depends upon the training and experience of the family workers. It may require supervision from an experienced family therapist or even referral to another therapist. However, there are advantages in working on all the issues in the one setting, so that fragmentation of therapy and splitting between therapists is avoided. Detailed discussion of the therapeutic strategies employed in these situations is beyond the scope of this chapter, but the following guidelines may be useful (see also Unit E of the EPPIC manual *Working with Families in Early Psychosis*, 1997).

High levels of family conflict

A behavioural approach is most effective. The therapist provides a rationale describing the need to contain conflict so that other aspects of family work (psychoeducation, communication skills training, etc.) can proceed, and asks the family to accept this proposition. When conflict develops, the therapist reminds the family of the agreement to contain the disagreement and focus on the issue at hand; this may need to be repeated several times. If conflict cannot be contained, the therapist may call for time out, either for the whole family or those members who are engaged in the conflict. If conflict still persists, the therapist may use other cognitive techniques, such as asking the whole family to consider the effect of the conflict, how long it has been occurring and whether it leads to any resolution of the problem. Aggression is a particularly difficult expression of conflict. The therapist should state clearly that aggression is not acceptable and explore the experience of family members who have been the victims of aggression, and provide debriefing. Of course, the aggression may be linked to the psychosis, but it may also reflect premorbid behaviour and/or attitudes shared with others in the family. The basis of the aggressive behaviour needs to be discussed, potential triggers identified and problem-solving used to develop new and more constructive ways to express negative feelings or problems.

Language and cultural issues

The most important points here are to be sensitive to and respectful of the family's beliefs and values, and to use professional interpreters. Even if the family appear to have a reasonable command of day-to-day English, the complexity of the subject matter and the emotional nature of issues make accurate communication extremely difficult. It is best not to use family members as interpreters, as this may lead to distortions of the message as well as placing the interpreting family member in a different position from others in the family.

Comorbidity

Comorbid drug and alcohol problems are very common and obviously compound the difficulties associated with the psychosis (Addington & Addington, 2001; Graham et al., 2002). Frequently, they provoke criticism and hostility from other family members, while, for the young person with psychosis, they appear to offer some relief from anxiety and an opportunity to fit in with peers. It is important for the therapist to explore these issues in a non-judgemental way and use strategies such as harm minimization, motivational interviewing and problem-solving to help to develop an approach to the problem that can be accepted by the whole family.

Case example: John

John, a 17-year-old man recovering from his first psychotic episode, continued to smoke cannabis regularly, causing arguments with his parents. The situation was complicated by differences of opinion between his mother and father regarding the best approach to this problem, and his father had tried to prevent John from socializing at all. The family worker met with the family for six sessions. First he heard each member of the family put their views on the issue, and then helped them to see that the current attempts to resolve the conflict were not effective. He allayed some of the parents' fears by stressing the role of the treating team in tackling the cannabis problem, and helped them to negotiate a consistent approach, particularly in regard to limit setting. Both directly and indirectly, he promoted a harm-minimization approach, which helped the parents to see the cannabis use in perspective, and perhaps helped John to see it more clearly in its own right and not through the prism of rebellion against his parents. As a result of this intervention, the level of conflict and criticism was much reduced.

Sexual abuse

Sexual abuse is the most difficult additional problem in working with families of early psychosis patients. Deep feelings of mistrust, anger and identity problems are common, as are distorted relationships and alliances within the family. Often there is denial of the abuse by the perpetrator and sometimes by others in the family. This situation calls for experienced therapists, and if not available within the service, it may be necessary to refer to a specialist service or arrange co-therapy. Mandatory reporting laws may require notification to the appropriate child protection authorities.

When the patient doesn't want the family to be involved

The vast majority of patients are happy for their family to be involved, particularly when this is presented as a routine part of treatment. When patients refuse, the therapist should ascertain if there is a particular reason, and should explain the benefits of family involvement for both the individual and the family. If the patient still refuses, the family should be encouraged to attend group psychoeducation sessions in order to learn general information about the psychosis without breaching the patient's confidentiality. Regional variations in Mental Health legislation may need to be taken into account in such situations. Sometimes the refusal will vanish after the acute phase of illness has been resolved.

Outcome of Family Interventions

Empirical work with first-episode families is clearly limited and there is a need for prospective longitudinal studies. In the Calgary programme, family outcome assessments are conducted initially, at 6 months, at 1 year, at 2 years and at discharge. For the family assessments we use the Psychological General Well-being Scale (Bech, 1993) to determine the level of stress/distress experienced by family members. A high level of distress seems to be a typical result of having a family member with a psychiatric illness, particularly schizophrenia (Barrowclough, Tarrier & Johnston, 1996). The Caregiver Burden Scale (Novak & Guest, 1989) is a self-report inventory that measures the degree of burden family members are experiencing, and the Experience of Caregiving Inventory (ECI; Szmukler et al., 1996) is a self-report measure that consists of ten subscales: eight negative (difficult behaviours; negative symptoms; stigma; problems with services; effects on the family; the need to provide back up; dependency; loss) and two positive (rewarding personal experiences; good aspects of the relationship).

These measures are useful on three levels. First, they provide the therapist with immediate information about the family in terms of their level of distress, current stressors and burden. Secondly, they are often stimulating to the families to enable them to think about what they may be experiencing and help them to put some words to their feeling of distress and conflict. Thirdly, they are useful as outcome measures to assess change over time.

In the Calgary programme, 70% of the first 349 individuals referred to EPP have families involved in the programme. The majority of these families stay involved throughout the course of the programme. When families first came to the programme we found that the most significant predictor of their level of stress and distress was the degree of burden they were experiencing and their experience of caregiving. Families of younger clients tended to be experiencing more distress in the initial few weeks. Increased positive and negative symptoms had a more significant impact on the family's sense of burden and their experience of caregiving than on their actual perceived level of stress (Addington et al., submitted).

Longitudinal outcome data from Calgary suggests that there is a significant improvement in the level of distress and the negative aspects of caregiving at 12 months. Furthermore, continued improvement is observed in the second year after admission to the programme (Addington et al., 2002). Interestingly the family's appraisal of the impact of the illness is a more robust predictor of psychological well-being than symptoms or social functioning (Addington et al., 2002).

Research has clearly emphasized the role of stress as an environmental trigger in schizophrenia. As a result, not only are feelings of distress and burden detrimental to the mental health of the family member but they also may have a negative effect on the well-being of the individual with schizophrenia. We still need to increase our understanding about what impacts the well-being of family members. In terms of further research, two areas are promising. First, there is a need for more qualitative in-depth detail about what is involved in both positive and negative aspects of caregiving and the differences in coping styles between family members. Secondly, the changes families go through over time in response to the impact of having a relative with a psychotic illness need to be addressed. Such a longitudinal study would lead to a more comprehensive understanding of how the coping and response styles of a family change over time from their relative's first onset to periods of recovery and through possible relapses.

CONCLUSION

This chapter has described the family components of two comprehensive services for early psychosis, one in Melbourne, Australia, and one in Calgary, Canada. These two programmes are not philosophically different but do offer a slight variation in their approaches to working with families. We have attempted to describe what we see as necessary components of the work that is needed with these families who have a relative in the very early stages of a psychotic illness or who is presenting with a full-blown psychosis for the first time. By describing both programmes we hope we have offered the reader a wider range of options for use in their own programmes or settings.

REFERENCES

Addington, J. & Addington, D. (2001). Impact of an early psychosis programme on substance use. *The Journal of Psychiatric Rehabilitation*, **25**, 60–67.

Addington, J., Coldham, E., Jones, B., Ko, T. & Addington, D. (2002). Family work in an early psychosis program: A longitudinal study. *Acta Psychiatrica Scandinavica*, **106** (Suppl. 413), 101.

Addington, J., Coldham, E., Jones, B., Ko, T. & Addington, D. (submitted). First episode psychosis: The experience of relatives.

Addington, J., Jones, B., Ko, T. & Addington, D. (2001). Family intervention in early psychosis. *Psychiatric Rehabilitation Skills*, **5**, 272–286.

Barbato, A. & D'Avanzo, B. (2000). Family interventions in schizophrenia and related disorders. A critical review of clinical trials. *Acta Psychiatrica Scandinavica*, **102**, 81–97.

Barrelet, L., Ferrero, F., Szigethy, L., Giddey, C. & Pellizzer, G. (1990). Expressed emotion and first admission schizophrenia: Nine-month follow-up in a French cultural environment. *British Journal of Psychiatry*, **156**, 357–362.

Barrowclough, C., Tarrier, N. & Johnston, M. (1996). Distress, expressed emotion and attributions in relatives of schizophrenia patients. *Schizophrenia Bulletin*, **22**, 691–701.

Bech, P. (1993). *Rating Scales for Psychopathology, Health Status and Quality of Life*. New York: Springer-Verlag.

Birchwood, M. & Cochrane, R. (1991). Families coping with schizophrenia: Coping styles, their origins and correlates. *Psychological Medicine*, **20**, 857–865.

Brown, G.W., Birley, J.L.T. & Wing, J.K. (1972). Influence of family life on the course of schizophrenia: A replication. *British Journal of Psychiatry*, **121**, 241–258.

Bulger, M.W., Wandersman, A. & Goldman, C.R. (1993). Burdens and gratifications of caregiving: Appraisal of parental care of adults with schizophrenia. *American Journal of Orthopsychiatry*, **63**, 255–265.

Early Psychosis Prevention and Intervention Centre (EPPIC). (1997). *Working with families in Early Psychosis*. No. 2 in a Series of Early Psychosis manuals. Victoria, Australia: Psychiatric Services Branch, Human Services.

Falloon, I., Boyd, J.L., McGill, C.W., Razani, J., Moss, H.B. & Gilderman, K.A. (1982). Family management in the prevention of exacerbations of schizophrenia. *New England Journal of Medicine*, **306**, 1437–1444.

Gleeson, J., Jackson, H.J., Stavely, H. & Burnett, P. (1999). Family intervention in early psychosis. In P.D. McGorry & H.J. Jackson (Eds), *The Recognition and Management of Early Psychosis: A Preventive Approach* (pp. 367–406). Cambridge: University Press.

Goldstein, M.J. & Miklowitz, D.J. (1995). The effectiveness of psychoeducational family therapy in the treatment of schizophrenic disorders. *Journal of Marital and Family Therapy*, **2**, 361–376.

Goldstein, M.J., Rodnick, E.H., Evans, J.R., May, P.R. & Steinberg, M.R. (1978). Drug and family therapy in the aftercare of acute schizophrenia. *Archives of General Psychiatry*, **35**, 1169–1177.

Graham, H., Mueser, K., Birchwood, M. & Copello, A. (Eds) (2002). *Substance Misuse in Psychosis: Approaches to Treatment and Service Delivery*. Chichester: John Wiley & Sons.

Hogarty, G., Anderson, C.M., Reiss, D.J., Kornblith, S.J., Greenwald, D. P., Javna, C.D. & Madonia, M.J. (1986). Family psychoeducation, social skills training, and maintenance chemotherapy in the aftercare treatment of schizophrenia. *Archives of General Psychiatry*, **43**, 633–642.

Huguelet, P.H., Favre, S., Binyet, S., Gonzalez, C.H. & Zabala, I. (1995). The use of the Expressed Emotion Index as a predictor of outcome in first admitted schizophrenic patients in a French-speaking area of Switzerland. *Acta Psychiatrica Scandanavica*, **92**, 447–452.

Jackson, H.J. & Edwards, J. (1992). Social networks and social support in schziophrenia: Correlates and assessment. In D.J. Kavanagh (Ed.) *Schizophrenia: An Overview and Practical Handbook* (pp. 275–292). London: Chapman & Hall.

Kavanagh, D.J. (1992). Recent developments in expressed emotion and schizophrenia. *British Journal of Psychiatry*, **160**, 601–620.

Kissling, W. (1994). Compliance, quality assurance and standards for relapse prevention in schizophrenia. *Acta Psychiatrica Scandinavica*, **89** (Suppl. 382), 16–24.

Kuipers, E. & Raune, D. (2000). The early development of expressed emotion and burden in the families of first-onset psychosis. In M. Birchwood, D. Fowler & C. Jackson (Eds), *Early Intervention in Psychosis* (pp. 128–140). Chichester: John Wiley & Sons.

Larsen, T.K., McGlashan, T.H., Johannessen, J.O. & Vibe-Hansen, L. (1996). First-episode schizophrenia: II Premorbid patterns by gender. *Schizophrenia Bulletin*, **22**, 257–269.

Leff, J.P. & Vaughn, C. (1985). *Expressed Emotion in Families*. New York: Guilford Press.

Leff, J., Berkowitz, R., Shavit, N., Strachan, A., Glass, I. & Vaughn, C. (1989). A trial of family therapy versus a relatives' group for schizophrenia. *British Journal of Psychiatry*, **154**, 58–66.

Leff, J.P., Kuipers, L., Berkowitz, R., Eberlein-Fries, R. & Sturgeon, D. (1982). A controlled trial of social intervention in the families of schizophrenic patients. *British Journal of Psychiatry*, **141**, 121–134.

Linzen, D. (1993). *Recent onset schizophrenic disorders: Outcome prognosis and treatment*. Unpublished doctoral dissertation. Netherlands: University of Amsterdam.

Linszen, D., Dingemans, P., Van der Does, J., Nugter, A., Scholte, P., Lenior, R. & Goldstein, M.J. (1996). Treatment, expressed emotion and relapse in recent onset schizophrenic disorders. *Psychological Medicine*, **26**, 333–342.

Loebel, A.D., Lieberman, J.A., Alvir, J.M.J., Mayerhoff, D.I., Geisler, S.H. & Szymanski, S.R. (1992). Duration of psychosis and outcome in first episode schizophrenia. *American Journal of Psychiatry*, **149**, 1183–1188.

MacCarthy, B., Kuipers, L., Hurry, J., Harper, R. & LeSage, A. (1989). Counselling the relatives of the long-term adult mentally ill: I. Evaluation of the impact on relatives and patients. *British Journal of Psychiatry*, **154**, 768–775.

Martens, L. & Addington, J. (2001). Psychological well-being of family members of individuals with schizophrenia. *Social Psychiatry and Psychiatric Epidemiology*, **36**, 128–133.

McGlashan, T.H. & Fenton, W.S. (1993). Subtype progression and pathophysiologic deterioration in early schizophrenia. *Schizophrenia Bulletin*, **19**, 71–84.

McGorry, P.D., Edwards, J. & Pennell, K. (1999). Sharpening the focus: Early intervention in the real world. In P.D. McGorry & H.J. Jackson (Eds), *Recognition and Management of Early Psychosis: A Preventive Approach* (pp. 441–470). Cambridge: Cambridge University Press.

McFarlane, W.R., Lukens, E., Link, B., Dushay, R., Deakins, S.A., Newmark, M., Dunne, E.J., Horen, B. & Toran, J. (1995). Multiple-family groups and psychoeducation in the treatment of schizophrenia. *Archives of General Psychiatry*, **52**, 679–687.

Mueser, K.T. & Glynn, S.M. (Eds) (1999). *Behavioral Family Therapy for Psychiatric Disorders* (2nd Edn). Oakland, CA: New Harbinger Publications, Inc.

Neuchterlein, K.H., Snyder, K.S. & Mintz, J. (1992). Paths to relapse: Possible transactional processes connecting patient illness onset, expressed emotion and psychotic relapse. *British Journal of Psychiatry*, **161** (Suppl. 18), 88–96.

Novak, M. & Guest, C. (1989). Application of a multidimensional caregiver burden inventory. *The Gerontologist*, **29**, 798–903.

Penn, D. & Mueser, K. (1996). Research update on the psychosocial treatment of schizophrenia. *American Journal of Psychiatry*, **153**, 607–617.

Pitschel-Walz, G., Leucht, S., Bauml, J., Kissling, W. & Engel, R.R. (2001). The effect of family interventions on and rehospitalization in schizophenia—A meta-analysis. *Schizophrenia Bulletin*, **27**, 73–92.

Randolph, E.T., Eth, S., Glynn, S.M., Paz, G.G., Leong, G.B., Shaner, A.L., Strachan, A., Van Vort, W., Escobar, J.I. & Liberman, R.P. (1994). Behavioral family management in schizophrenia: Outcome of a clinic based intervention. *British Journal of Psychiatry*, **153**, 532–542.

Rund, B.R., Oie, M., Borchgrevink, T.S. & Fjell, A. (1995) Expressed emotion, communication deviance and schizophrenia. *Psychopathology*, **28**, 220–228.

Schene, A.H. (1990). Objective and subjective dimensions of family burden: Towards an integrative framework for research. *Social Psychiatry and Psychiatric Epidemiology*, **25**, 289–297.

Schene, A.H., Tessler, R.C. & Gamache, G.M. (1994). Instruments measuring family or caregiver burden in severe mental illness. *Social Psychiatry and Psychiatric Epidemiology*, **29**, 228–240.

Spaniol, L., Zipple, A.M. & Lockwood, D. (1992). The role of family in psychiatric rehabilitation. *Schizophrenia Bulletin*, **18**, 341–348.

Stirling, J., Tantam, D., Thomas, P., Newby, D., Montague, L., Ring, N. & Rowe, S. (1991). Expressed emotion and early onset schizophrenia: A one-year follow-up. *Psychological Medicine*, **21**, 675–685.

Szmukler, G.I., Burgess, P., Herrman, H. & Benson, A. (1996). Caring for relatives with serious mental illness: The development of the experience of caregiving inventory. *Social Psychiatry and Psychiatric Epidemiology*, **31**, 137–148.

Tarrier, N., Barrowclough, C. & Porceddu, K. (1988). The community management of schizophrenia: A controlled trial of behavioural intervention with families to reduce relapse. *British Journal of Psychiatry*, **153**, 532–542.

Yung, A.R., McGorry, P.D., McFarlane, C.A., Jackson, H.J., Patton, G.C. & Rakkar, A. (1996). Monitoring and care of young people at incipient risk of psychosis. *Schizophrenia Bulletin*, **22**, 283–303.

7 A Group Psychotherapeutic Intervention during Recovery from First-Episode Psychosis

ASHOK K. MALLA, TERRY S. McLEAN AND ROSS M.G. NORMAN
University of Western Ontario, Canada

INTRODUCTION

Pharmacological intervention is necessary but rarely sufficient for the treatment of psychotic disorders and prevention of their recurrence (Marder & May, 1986; Wyatt 1991). The efficacy of non-pharmacological interventions (psychological and social) in combination with pharmacotherapy has now been well established (Benton & Schroeder, 1990; De Jesus & Steiner, 1994). There has been particularly strong empirical evidence to support the efficacy of family intervention, social skills training, supportive and cognitive psychotherapy and assertive case management. All of these interventions have a positive impact on the course of illness by reducing risk of relapse and rehospitalization, and improving the conditions of patients' lives. There is recent evidence that a stress management programme designed for this patient population and delivered in a group format may provide additional benefits to patients through further reduction in rates of hospitalization even when offered in addition to all of the above interventions (Norman et al., 2002). The efficacy of most of these interventions has been confirmed in effectiveness studies outside the controlled trial environment (Malla et al., 1998). Most national guidelines for treatment of psychotic disorders have now incorporated a variety of psychosocial interventions. Further, their efficacy does not appear to vary as a function of whether the interventions are delivered in an individual or group format or, in the case of family intervention, with the complexity of the content of the intervention (Schooler et al., 1997).

While the results of studies of psychological interventions are extremely encouraging and should vastly improve the lives of the majority of patients with psychotic disorders, a relatively small proportion of patients actually receive these interventions as they have been designed and evaluated (Lehman, Steinwachs et al., 1998; Young et al., 1998). The majority of patients follow the traditionally anticipated poor course and outcome of the illness without the potential benefit of psychosocial interventions. There are likely to be several reasons for this poor implementation of evidence-based psychosocial interventions, despite their low risk of adverse effects. These may include lack of resources for training and dissemination of relevant clinical skills as well as the relatively later stage of treatment at which patients are often offered these interventions. At later stages of the illness patients may be less eager or able to attempt new approaches, families may be more exhausted and/or detached and/or clinicians may have become more resigned to a very limited improvement in the illness. Because a relatively high proportion of patients make only partial recovery after multiple relapses, clinicians may rely on altering medications and not consider the added use of non-pharmacological interventions.

Intervention in the early phases of psychotic disorders provides an opportunity to improve short- and long-term outcome not only by providing treatment early, but also by incorporating psychological interventions in a comprehensive approach to treatment of psychosis after the very first onset (Jackson et al., 1999; Malla et al., 2001). Individuals who have not experienced relapse may be more enthusiastic about psychological interventions and the clinicians may also approach such patients with greater hope. There is, therefore, likely to be considerable interest in psychosocial interventions that may reduce risk of relapse and improve chances of return to a more normal life, thereby protecting the patient from becoming entrenched in the role of a chronic patient in the mental health system. While the evidence for the effectiveness of psychological interventions is generally based on more chronic patients, it would be reasonable to postulate that similar interventions designed to particularly suit the needs of patients in early phases of the illness will be even more beneficial in preventing recurrences of the illness and social decline. Younger patients in early stages of the illness are likely to be more enthusiastic about group interventions in particular because these involve interaction with their peers. In this chapter we will describe the application of group psychotherapy designed to address special needs of patients during the recovery phase of the illness following an initial episode of psychosis.

GROUP THERAPY IN PSYCHOTIC DISORDERS: GENERAL CONSIDERATIONS

Patients with a diagnosis of schizophrenia were provided therapeutic interventions in various group formats long before the introduction of pharmacological treatment (Lazell, 1921). A number of models of group therapy for individuals suffering from psychotic disorders have emerged. These include:

1. Educational approaches, often referred to as 'psychoeducational group therapy', teach patients about the nature of their symptoms and ways of coping with aspects of the illness. They tend to rely on the patient's capacity to acquire knowledge about their illness and the therapist's ability to deliver information that is understandable to the patient. Most of these approaches have used didactic methods to impart information about the illness. While psychoeducational interventions are often provided to the family with good success, very few patients receive such instructions in a manner that takes into account their special needs and possible limitations in processing information in didactic formats. As a result, patients too often learn about their illness from their individual therapist in a rather haphazard fashion without a clear structure and with little consistency between therapists.
2. Psychodynamic approaches emphasize the psychological aspects of the illness, including the impact of intrapsychic conflicts and maladaptive behaviours on their lives. This may include uncovering of presumed unconscious issues and/or interpretations

of transference. In general, psychodynamic group therapy has been provided mostly in long-term inpatient or day hospital settings where the same patients participate for relatively long periods, sometimes extending to years. While such approaches may have their appeal to some patients with long-standing illness, it is generally impractical, uneconomical and not necessarily conducive to achieving the goal of early social integration. Interpersonal approaches tend to address patients' needs to improve their social skills and interpersonal relationships. There is less emphasis on a causative model linking their behaviour and the illness. Improved interpersonal relationships are regarded as the goal, with the implicit understanding that improved relationships will lead to better adjustment to life and coping with the illness.

3. An integrative approach encompasses elements of all of the above models (Kanas, 1999). The objectives are to improve patients' knowledge and ways of coping with the illness, promote their ability to generate discussion about a variety of topics within a supportive environment while recognizing their limitations in tolerating emotionally charged material, and improve their ego functioning as well as social relationships.

The therapeutic approaches used in each of the above models of group therapy are based on the respective theoretical understanding of the nature of psychosis. Evaluations of various models of group therapy in psychotic disorders have generally shown that more interpretive and psychodynamic models have much poorer outcome compared to interpersonal, educative or integrative models and may in fact worsen a patient's condition (Kapur, 1993). The integrative approach has the greatest appeal as it encompasses specific goals of improving patients' coping with symptoms as well as improving interpersonal skills; it provides a more specific framework within which to conduct therapy and is applicable in both in- and outpatient settings. Although there is some evidence that patients respond to the integrative approach with a high degree of group cohesion, subjective satisfaction and reduced anxiety, there have been only a few controlled evaluations of integrative therapy in general, or any evaluations of the impact of group therapy in particular, on short- and long-term outcome in psychotic disorders. It is likely that younger patients may accept and benefit more from group therapy than older patients.

SPECIAL CONSIDERATIONS FOR FIRST-EPISODE PSYCHOSIS (FEP)

Patients being treated for their first episode of psychosis are likely to have very high rates of remission if treated adequately and comprehensively (Loebel et al., 1992; Malla & Norman, 2002). Despite such high rates of recovery, more than 33% of patients are readmitted to hospital within 6 months, 55% within 2 years and 80% within 5 years following treatment of their first episode of psychosis (Geddes et al., 1994; Gitlin et al., 2001; Robinson et al., 1999; Wiersma et al., 1998). It is important to develop ways of intervening during the initial recovery period in order to reduce the risk of relapse. This cannot be achieved without understanding the complex issues associated with increased risk of relapse. These include poor adherence to medication (Fenton, Blyler & Heinssen, 1997; Verdoux et al., 2000), increased substance use (Linszen, Dingemans & Lenior, 1994), impaired insight and understanding of the illness (McGorry & McConville, 1999) and environmental stress (Norman & Malla, 1993).

There are several other considerations that may be of relevance in reducing risk of relapse and improving chances of recovery for young people recovering from their first episode of psychosis. Psychosis will probably interfere with many domains of a young person's developmental trajectory, including academic and vocational achievements, social interactions and peer relations, self-concept and self-esteem, aspects of identity related to psychosexual development, and intimacy and increased independence from parents. In addition, there are likely to be strong concerns about stigmatization by peers, the treatment system, society as a whole and even oneself. Concerns about these issues need to be balanced in trying to prevent a relapse and improve social/occupational functioning and overall quality of life for the individual.

Clear objectives related to the above issues need to be developed for group interventions for persons recovering from a first episode of psychosis. The design of such interventions also need to address the ways in which younger patients with recent onset of illness are likely to differ from the patients for whom psychosocial interventions have been designed in the past. Patients recovering from a first episode are likely to be younger; relatively naïve concerning the mental health care system; have a higher desire to exercise control over their treatment and their future; be more able to articulate their concerns and problems in a group format; have a high potential for substance abuse; and be more impulsive and impatient.

While incorporating the elements we have discussed, it is important that the course of therapy be relatively short in order to retain patients' interest and engagement. The patient's own needs and objectives, which are often different from those of the clinicians, must receive primary attention. Patients' and clinicians' objectives can be paired creatively in order to provide a good shared set of objectives. The mode of delivery also needs to be carefully planned in order to make it acceptable to younger individuals and command their attention. This usually requires flexibility on the part of the therapists, active participation of members, use of multiple media, games, humour, etc. Here we describe an 8-week group therapeutic intervention designed for patients recovering from a first episode of psychosis (FEP).

THE YOUTH EDUCATION AND SUPPORT (YES) GROUP

This group therapy intervention is designed for individuals between the ages of 16 and 25 years but can be modified to suit the needs of even older individuals. Younger patients find the non-stigmatizing title of the group very appealing, particularly when and if they are talking to their peers about their involvement in treatment.

Objectives

The main objective of the group is to assist young patients in the process of recovery through prevention of relapse and resumption of roles relevant to the individual's level of psychosocial development. Specific objectives of the group intervention include:

- reducing the risk of a relapse following complete or partial remission of a FEP;
- improving patients' knowledge about their illness without overwhelming their sense of personal identity;

- assisting patients to develop and/or maintain a sense of identity appropriate to their stage of development;
- improving levels of social and interpersonal skills in order to allow reintegration with peer groups;
- resumption of interpersonal relationships;
- educating patients regarding the effects of use and abuse of alcohol and other substances;
- providing patients with skills to deal with issues of stigma from others and to avoid self-stigmatization;
- improving family relationships and reducing stress and conflict in the family (such as that associated with substance use and medication);
- understanding the nature of prodromal and early warning signs and promoting early detection and intervention of any impending relapse.

Consideration of Issues Related to Group Process

As most patients are relatively naïve to the mental health system and likely to be ambivalent at best about receiving treatment, it is important to inform patients about the group process in general and to describe the specific purpose and content of this intervention. Young people are likely to have acquired their knowledge about 'therapy' from TV or popular 'Hollywood' sources of information and may have developed some misconceptions about the nature and process of therapy. Some may have very negative attitudes about treatment in general, and group therapy in particular, based on old films like *One Flew Over the Cuckoo's Nest* or other peoples' experiences of confrontational and exploratory group therapy. It is also important to the participants to understand the time-limited nature of the intervention, the importance of protection of one's own and others' privacy, the importance of maintaining confidentiality of the material discussed within the group, rules about alcohol and drug use prior to each session and last, but not least, to have objectives of the group intervention clearly explained during the first session.

While the group intervention is structured and delivered according to a written manual, the delivery of material in each session is adapted to the level of intellectual and social functioning of the participating members. For example, within the session on learning about medications, individuals who are functioning at a relatively lower level are asked to learn the class name (i.e. antipsychotic) and dose of their medication, learn to spell it, discuss who to tell and who not to tell and learn relatively concrete reasons for taking the medication. Higher functioning individuals are shown a video regarding neurotransmitter systems and encouraged to learn more details of the mechanism of action for the medications. The intervention is to be delivered in an optimistic and relaxed manner with use of combination of pedagogic techniques; film, games and other media; humour and relaxation exercises. In each session there is a 10-minute refreshment break at the end of the first hour.

The YES group intervention is held weekly for 2 hours over a period of 8 consecutive weeks. It generally involves six to eight members and two therapists. The therapists should have training in individual and group psychotherapy with a good knowledge of psychopathology and the treatment of psychosis. One of the therapists takes primary responsibility for directing the eight sessions. If one therapist is unavailable, the other is able to continue the work with the group. Each group is held in the same location every week. The room must be of adequate size and quiet with comfortable seats arranged in a circle in order to create a milieu conducive to group process. The time at which the group is held is flexible and decided through consensus at the first meeting in order to accommodate the members' other important commitments such as school and work. The total number of sessions can be increased if the members and the therapists believe that otherwise one or more particular themes will not have been adequately addressed. In general, however, it would be unwise to make this intervention longer than 10 to 12 sessions. The themes within each session are paired in order to link the patients' needs and the objectives of the sessions.

Potential group members are patients recovering from a FEP who have achieved sufficient symptomatic stability to tolerate 2 hours of group work. It is important that patients are engaged with a primary therapist who in turn takes a keen interest in facilitating their attendance. The intervention needs to be described to potential members of the group as being related to their lives and not so much to do with psychosis. For most patients this is usually about 3 months after initiating treatment. They are informed about the objectives of the group, importance of the issues to be addressed, the role of psychosocial interventions in the treatment of psychotic disorders and are then asked to make a commitment for 8 weeks. One of the therapists usually meets with prospective members to give information about YES and to help to reduce any anxiety related to participation in the group. Efforts are made to put members at ease and particular attention is given to any member who, in the opinion of the therapists, may need more support. Patients are reassured that personal disclosure is not an expectation in the group, although they may feel comfortable discussing personal concerns in later sessions.

Attendance is encouraged by calling the patients the day before and the same morning, if necessary, to remind them of the session. Rewards such as a coffee pass after each session or a package of lottery tickets after four sessions can be used to increase attendance. Using these techniques in a randomized-controlled trial of a 12-week stress management programme (Norman et al., 2002), we were able to contain the drop-out rates to 6% and 8% for the experimental and control group therapy conditions, respectively.

OUTLINE OF RATIONALE AND CONTENT OF EACH SESSION

Session 1

Introduction to group therapy in general and YES group in particular

It is not necessary for the therapists to have a detailed history but at least one of the therapists should have assessed the patient regarding suitability for the intervention and to get some personal information. While it is preferable that the therapist should not be an individual therapist to any of the members, this is not always possible in smaller programmes and the therapist in that case needs to be particularly cautious about the individual relationship. While members are likely to benefit from a mix of gender, it is unlikely to be achieved given the sex distribution in all first-episode programmes. Having female therapists tends to balance this, for example, by providing opportunities for role-play with male patients.

Procedure
Members are introduced to each other utilizing an 'ice breaker'. The participants are paired up and asked to relate three pieces of information to their partner who will introduce them to

the larger group. The members take various positions in a large room that allows them to talk privately and plan their introductions to the larger group. The therapists participate in this process as needed, often pairing themselves with members who may have more difficulty with the task. After 10 minutes, the group is invited to reassemble and a therapist initiates the task of introducing him/herself to the group, then asks a volunteer from the members to continue by introducing themselves. This is an opportunity for therapists to model social skills by giving positive feedback for the information offered and acknowledging the competence of the member doing the introductions. This segment of the session, in which members are learning about one another, is very important as members are often deciding if they will feel comfortable in the group. For instance, a group with members who had particularly strong educational achievements became very attractive to a highly educated client who had been feeling very stigmatized by the illness and had been reluctant to get involved in a group setting.

The therapists then talk briefly about anxieties associated with joining a group and the benefits of belonging to a group. Some patients may be reassured by comments from the therapists about how members may have attended the first session without being sure why they are there. It is important, therefore, to explore with the members possible reasons for attendance and what they hope to achieve by coming to eight sessions. Articulation of goals can be intimidating for some, therefore, members are provided with a skeleton letter that helps to structure the process of stating their goals. For example, some members write that they want to compare their experiences of the illness to someone else's experiences, they want to learn how to prevent it from recurring, or they want to know more about the medication. The members take about 10 minutes to write themselves a 'Dear Me' letter. The therapists have prepared an envelope with the member's name. Before it is sealed, other members are asked to say something about what they have written. This may be one of the first indications the therapists have about the interests of specific members. With permission from the member, the sealed letters are kept by the therapists and stored for use in Session 8.

Following a 10-minute break for snacks or informal conversation, the second hour of the group begins with the therapists giving an overview of the subsequent seven sessions so that participants will be aware of the subjects to be covered. It is hoped that this discussion will raise the interest of members since the material is designed to be relevant to adolescence and young adulthood as well as providing information about psychosis. For example, group members are made aware that the group will spend 1 hour talking about the use of drugs and alcohol among youth as well as their impact on psychosis. The topic of stigma of medical illnesses is also included, with special attention to mental health and the strategies utilized to cope with it. Our clinical experience, as well as focus group discussions with patients, indicates that these are issues of considerable interest and concern to first-episode patients.

One of the therapists addresses the ground rules for YES. These rules are common to most group work and concern attendance, punctuality, absence, confidentiality, romantic liaisons, use of substances, and expectations for participation at a comfortable level. A list of the rules is distributed. The group is then advised of the concept of a 'check-in' and a 'check-out'. The latter is used at the beginning of the subsequent session and a new check-out will be decided at the end of each session. The check-out in Session 1 is for each member to end the session with one major concern about psychosis that could be explored in this group.

Session 2

Identity/what is psychosis?

Rationale

Poor insight has been associated with poor outcome in schizophrenia and other psychotic disorders (Amador & Kronengold, 1998; McGorry & McConville, 1999). Insight is not a unitary concept and is best understood as being composed of different dimensions that vary between patients and across time for individual patients. The dimensions of insight include ability to recognize the presence of a mental disorder, adhere to treatment and to attribute unusual mental experiences to pathological/abnormal phenomena. While estimations of insight are influenced by assessment methods, a patient's cultural background and other factors, most patients do in fact have some awareness of their illness. Awareness of past aspects of their illness may be greater than that of present illness perhaps as a result of a dispositional shift in the attribution of past experiences (Moore et al., 1979). Whether and how soon this improvement in insight occurs after the first episode has not been directly investigated.

McGorry and McConville (1999) have argued that insight may be better if assessment and intervention were provided during the very early stages of psychosis. The few studies that have examined this issue in first-episode patients suggest that most patients are somewhere between the extremes of identification and denial. It has also been suggested that first-episode patients may be willing to discuss their experiences, but not be willing to accept a label of mental illness in order to avoid internal stigmatization (Moore et al., 1979). Young patients following treatment of a first episode of the illness may fear engulfment, wherein their personal identity is reorganized around the devalued role of the psychotic patient (Lally, 1989). The level of cognitive functioning is also likely to influence acquisition of insight but not necessarily in a linear fashion. Our own experience and reports of our patients support this postulate.

The relationship of impaired insight to poor outcome is likely to be largely mediated through refusal of treatment and/or non-adherence to medication (Marder et al., 1984) and sometimes acting on delusional beliefs. Insight may be an important, but not essential condition for good adherence to treatment (David et al., 1995) especially in younger, recently diagnosed patients. It has been suggested that medication adherence, awareness of illness and attribution of symptoms should be treated as separate constructs in order to avoid a problem of circularity. It is important to pay special attention to the dynamic processes involved in the integration of the psychotic experience by the young person, its effect on his or her self-esteem and the potential trauma occasioned by even one episode. Some degree of denial and rejection of labels of mental illness may be an adaptive mechanism for young people who have experienced their first episode of psychosis (McGorry, 1995).

The second session is, therefore, designed to help patients to recognize and reintegrate their identities apart from the psychosis—which is treated more as a likely traumatic experience. Patients are encouraged to discuss many aspects of their identities (sexual, social, academic, family member, etc.) and the developmental tasks associated with attaining and/or re-establishing them. It is the objective of this session to impart knowledge about psychosis to young patients through discussion of their own experiences while acknowledging their potential need to deny or underestimate the impact of the illness, and explore aspects of their identity not related to their psychosis.

Procedure

Session 2 begins with reintroductions as members may have forgotten the names of co-members. The leader can add information in the form of the person's interests and positive characteristics as each member introduces him/herself. This adds to the establishment of a group process as well as raising self-esteem of individual members. It is essential that leaders be very cognizant of the group process at each session and use information from one session in subsequent meetings. The group therapist also acknowledges the attendance and promptness of the group members and also waits for at least 5 minutes for any late members thus reinforcing the expectation that a participant should call if not able to attend.

As noted before, each session begins with a check-in. The check-in for this session is for each member to identify a character strength that has sustained him or her through the experience of psychosis. Therapists also participate by identifying a character strength that has sustained them through a traumatic event in their own lives. Depending on each participant's comfort and confidence the therapist may ask for some expansion on this character trait. If a member is particularly shy, then it may be too soon to ask for such details. However, if a member is more vocal and confident, this may be a perfect opportunity for him or her to give a detailed example of the strength. This articulation may serve as the first demonstration of self-disclosure for other members.

After this exercise, the therapist will make a few statements about how people go about defining themselves and developing an identity in the adult world. Depending on the membership, the therapist briefly describes adolescent and adult developmental stages or a more generic description of how adolescents and young adults separate from their parents through making independent decisions. There is some discussion of how some of these 'growing up' activities may sometimes be viewed as acting out.

The therapist will then note how a traumatic event like psychosis can interrupt this process and complicate the development of an adult identity. The first example that is often used is that of a young person who develops diabetes. There is discussion of how the disease can place constraints on an individual's behaviour (taking a daily injection, dietary and alcohol restrictions) while maintaining an identity as a peer. The therapist should elicit some of these concerns from group members. An example of a young man at 16 or 17 years of age with psychosis trying to go to school, maintain a peer group, date, etc., is used for discussion of how complicated such milestones can become as a result of the illness.

The therapist emphasizes that whatever the major obstacle, it is very important for the individual to remember who he or she are aside from the illness—son, daughter, basketball player, guitar player, computer nerd, etc., as a means of maintaining a healthy identity. There is also discussion of how people who become enmeshed in illness are more likely to be identified by others as being ill. The therapist will try to stress that psychosis is only one part of who people are and that it must be integrated by individuals as only one aspect of their personality.

As a means of engaging members in the discussion, participants are asked to complete an independent task of describing who they are in a manner that has nothing to do with their illness. A skeleton format is provided to help them to think about this task—full name, ethnic background, role in the family, education/vocation, hobbies, interests, passions, and dislikes. The therapists complete the inventory with the members and then begin the exercise by telling the members 'who am I'. The profiles are shared either by going around the circle or as members volunteer.

If time allows and according to age or level of functioning of the members, a film on self-esteem especially geared to teenagers may be used. Some groups are so talkative that there is neither the time nor a need to change media. In this as in all aspects of the group there is flexibility to tailor content to the levels of functioning, interests, ages, etc., of members. Video films geared to secondary school students are a good resource to explore in this regard.

During the 10-minute break it is likely that some members start to chat with each other, going outside together to smoke or socialize informally. Others prefer to sit with group leaders during the break. It is important that the therapists remain in the group room and socialize as it facilitates group cohesion.

The educational component of the session addresses 'What is Psychosis?' This segment is designed to help members to understand their experience in terms of the vulnerability–stress model. It is important that all members come to understand psychosis as a loss of contact with reality and discuss the major symptoms that indicate this loss. The presentation includes information concerning the stages of psychosis with members identifying the stage they are currently experiencing. Members are also encouraged to list the symptoms of psychosis in terms of changes in ways of thinking, feeling, perceiving, and behaving. There needs to be flexibility in response to clients' needs, the stage and acuity of the initial presentation of their illness, and level of knowledge. For example, some clients may be unfamiliar with different forms of hallucinations, so more time will have to be spent on this topic and several examples offered. Three phases of illness—prodrome, acute psychosis and recovery—are discussed and if any member shows prominent denial of the illness it is important not to push too hard with the idea of illness.

A film can be shown in this segment to enhance the information and make it more meaningful to the members. The possible choices of films or parts of films that can be used for this session to promote discussion include: *First Break*—a national film board of Canada release; and *Reaching Out: the importance of early treatment*— British Columbia (Canada) Schizophrenia Society.

The check-out exercise for this session involves each member describing his or her most significant symptom.

Session 3

Peer pressure and substance use

Rationale

Substance Use Disorder (SUD) is often a comorbid condition in patients with diagnosis of schizophrenia and other serious mental disorders with lifetime prevalence ranging from 48 to 56% (Mueser, Bennett & Kushner, 1995). The prevalence is particularly high for young adult single males (Lehman et al., 1996). Alcohol and cannabis are the most common drugs being used, followed by cocaine. The consequences of substance abuse in patients with psychotic disorders include financial problems, medication non-adherence, high rates of relapse and rehospitalization, violence, legal problems, depression and suicide.

Even moderate use of cannabis, the most commonly abused drug among youth, is widely believed to trigger or increase psychotic symptoms in individuals vulnerable to psychosis (Weil, 1970). In a prospective study of patients with recent onset schizophrenia and related disorders, Linszen, Dingemans and Lenior (1994) reported a strong association between the extent of cannabis abuse and the risk of relapse or increase in psychotic symptoms. These results were independent of the effect of alcohol or other drug use and non-adherence to medication. It is well known that the use of stimulant drugs such as cocaine, amphetamine and its derivatives, LSD and ketamine is strongly related to recurrence of psychotic symptoms in addition to being associated with social decline, violence, suicide and criminal behaviour.

The role of substance abuse in triggering a relapse of psychosis is complex. Most abused drugs, in particular cocaine, amphetamine and its derivatives as well as other stimulants, are likely to directly increase the risk of hallucinations and delusions through their agonistic effect on dopamine in the limbic system. In addition, the relationship between substance use/abuse and relapse of psychosis is likely to be partly mediated through increased social disruption, bringing about stress and non-adherence to medication. Clinicians are invariably convinced about the deleterious effect of cannabis and heavy alcohol use on the course of psychosis in young patients recently diagnosed with psychosis. Our focus groups have confirmed that patients and their families see a strong but complex relationship between substance use (mostly cannabis) and relapse.

The hypothesis that alcohol and drug use by patients with psychotic disorders represent attempts at self-medication to relieve negative symptoms or medication side-effects (Khantzian, 1997) has limited empirical support, particularly in relation to heavy abuse. The reasons given by patients for substance use are similar to those reported by the general population, namely loneliness, boredom, social anxiety and insomnia and, in younger patients, peer pressure. The latter consideration makes any attempt to reduce a young person's substance use particularly problematic as such behaviours are often seen by him or her as being normal for his or her peer group.

Procedure

The check-in exercise involves a sentence completion exercise: 'My friends pressure me most about . . . '. Very often this provides a natural lead-in to the issue of substance use. The therapist initiates discussion about the meaning of using substances in adolescence and young adulthood. Members are then encouraged to talk about the first experience of breaking their parents' rules: smoking (cigarettes or cannabis), lying about whereabouts, breaking curfew, etc. It often evokes memories of the first time members tried alcohol and got drunk or the first time they tried other drugs such as cannabis. In this discussion, as in others, it is important to use terms from the patient's lexicon such as *pot*.

Members are shown a portion of the film *Secret Life of the Brain: Episode 3, The Teenage Brain: A World of Their Own* (PBS Home Video, 2001, Thirteen, WNET New York), followed by discussion of the film using a flip chart to make a list of the effects of marijuana (or other drugs) and stages of intoxication. Besides this list, a list of symptoms of psychosis is written in order to highlight the point that it would be difficult to get rid of psychotic symptoms while taking a substance that triggers them. A discussion evolves around how marijuana is one of the major factors in relapse and how young people often go on to develop chronic mental illness as a result of not being able to stay drug free. It is important that such information be provided in the context of a discussion and not be presented in a way that could be perceived as preaching or imposing therapists' values.

After the break, the educational component for the second part of this session is focused on a jeopardy game, entailing answers to which members provide the questions. For example, to the statement 'Something that may be triggered by stimulants such as pot, bennies, mushrooms, LSD, ecstacy and cocaine' the members would respond by the question 'What is psychosis?' This assesses their level of knowledge regarding drugs and can spark further discussion. Most young people like it because it creates a somewhat competitive atmosphere without being too stressful. In the company of their peers, members often reveal more about their drug use than they may have revealed to their primary clinicians. A survey of personal use of drugs and alcohol is conducted in an informal manner. Members are then asked what they think are safe limits.

If a particular group comprises members who are not drug users, then the emphasis needs to be shifted to alcohol. The use of a film that is informative about the effects of alcohol on the entire body system is advisable. If no members are drug or alcohol users, then a film on smoking or sexually transmitted diseases can be used to provoke some discussion about self-control over harmful behaviour. If all forms of substance use are of relevance to the group members, then this subject may need to be extended to an additional session.

The check-out exercise involves participants identifying one piece of information about drugs and alcohol that they learned during this session.

Session 4

Relationships/medication

Rationale
While the efficacy of antipsychotic drugs in treating psychosis and reducing vulnerability to future relapses is well established, high rates of non-adherence remain a major problem with respect to the effectiveness of antipsychotic medication in the prevention of relapse (Fenton, Blyler & Heinssen, 1997). Following treatment of the first episode of psychosis the risk of relapse over the subsequent 5 years is increased at least five-fold if the patient discontinues antipsychotic medication (Robinson et al., 1999). In a representative sample of first-episode-psychosis patients, Verdoux et al. (2000) found that poor medication adherence ranged from 33 to 44% at each 6-month follow-up assessment over 2 years following treatment of a first episode. They also report that more than half (53%) interrupted their medication against medical advice at least once over the 2-year follow-up.

While non-adherence is sometimes in response to such factors as side-effects, a substantial proportion of patients stop taking medication for more intentional reasons related to lack of insight about the nature of their illness, refusal to acknowledge the possibility of relapse and/or other health-related belief systems. Focus groups conducted with clinical staff, patients and their families suggest the role of additional factors related to non-adherence. These include peer pressure, 'feeling different', misattribution of symptoms to side-effects of medications and cultural attitudes towards medications, particularly among young patients recently diagnosed and recovering from a first episode. Issues related to medication tend to be some of the major foci around which families and patients disagree and tensions often develop around issues of adherence to medication. The two themes of family relationship and medication adherence have, therefore, been combined in the fourth session so that a proper context is created for discussion of medication adherence as well as basic education regarding medication.

Procedure
In the check-in exercise participants are asked to identify a positive or negative change that has occurred in their relationships with parents/spouse since their illness started. This check-in is intended to help the group to focus on issues related to family conflicts. It is common to hear young men relate that it has brought them closer to their fathers. The

therapists can prompt the member for more detail about the conflicts and relationships as is appropriate.

Common issues that emerge during the check-in include rules, curfews, expectations about drug and alcohol use, returning to school, taking treatment, etc. Depending on the age group, a video can be used which highlights young people talking about the difficulty generating or expressing ideas about relationships with parents. If the members are older, then the discussion can be skewed to include the frequency of contact with parents and the type of relationship they are hoping to achieve. One member acts as the recorder while another offers to report to the larger group.

Following the break, the focus is on education about medication. First of all, members' knowledge about their own medication needs to be ascertained in a non-threatening manner. Participants report the name, dose, and time they are to take their medication, and the type of drug they are taking. In addition, enquiries are made to find out if members recognize that the medications are not addictive, know the reason that the medication is prescribed, and appreciate the need for them to be taken consistently. It is also important for participants to explore who they should tell that they take medication, and how to give others information about their medication (physicians/close family members versus acquaintances/work supervisors). Through exploration of their own experience with symptoms and subsequent relief through taking medications members need to be assisted to make the link between medication and hallucinations/delusions/thought disorganization. A discussion of relevant neurotransmitter systems can be very valuable in this respect.

If there are sufficient numbers, the group can be split into two—one to develop a list of physical side-effects while the other develops a list of psychological side-effects of their medication. Members are also encouraged to report any side-effects to their case manager and doctor and be taught specific skills of how to do so assertively. This is especially true of sexual side-effects which patients are generally reluctant to report spontaneously.

A film that gives a good pictorial image of the brain and the affected areas related to the dopamine hypothesis is often presented, depending on time and interest (e.g. *Secret Life of the Brain*, as above). If required, an additional session may be used for this purpose.

The check-out exercise is used to report one positive effect of taking the medication. Responses usually link taking medication with reduction in hallucinations, better organized thinking, etc. Finally, members are given handouts containing information on the respective drugs they are taking.

Session 5

Stigma and strategies

Rationale

It is well recognized that a person with a mental disorder has to deal not only with the direct consequences of the illness in the form of impairment of mental and social functions, but also with the stigma associated with having a mental disorder. There are many contributors to the social stigma of mental illness and its treatment. One of the goals of early intervention in psychosis is to reduce or eliminate stigma by reducing the chronicity of psychotic disorders as well as better education of the public about the nature of psychosis and dispelling misconceptions about its causes and the behaviour of those with psychotic illness.

In addition to dealing with the complexities of social stigmatization, it is important to recognize the implications of self-stigmatization. Diagnosis and treatment of severe mental illnesses are beneficial, but can also carry risks for the individual's self-concept. As alluded to earlier in this chapter, while it is important for individuals recovering from a FEP to be knowledgeable about the nature of their illness, it is equally important to assist them to recognize, protect and integrate the many facets of their identity and not become engulfed by the role of a patient. In this session these issues are further addressed.

Procedure

During check-in members are asked to share their most embarrassing experience that has resulted from psychosis. By this time the group has usually developed some cohesiveness and members are quite interested in each other's experiences (including symptoms).

The therapist begins the discussion by calling upon a member to give a definition of stigma. The therapist may provide some information about the history of the concept of stigma in our society—beginning with the use of branding irons to identify slaves who were seen as property. Then the discussion moves on to medical illnesses where people have experienced stigma, for example, epilepsy (with the image of a sufferer frothing at the mouth and going mad), AIDS, cancer and diabetes (e.g. young people try to keep their peers unaware that they take insulin or need to eat snacks at specified times). Members may be asked to provide a stereotype of an AIDS patient.

The therapist then explains how misunderstanding leads to fear and the development of false beliefs. Participants make a list of how people know that someone in the community is mentally ill. The usual examples of identifying characteristics given by members include ranting and raving on the street, being dirty, unshaven, having uncombed hair, wearing inappropriate clothes, being homeless, etc. The therapist comments that the community bases such stereotypes on their observation of untreated individuals.

Participants are then divided into small groups to discuss the experience of the stigma of mental illness in the home (e.g. parents being too vigilant, family members censoring what they say in case they might upset the person with the illness), at school (e.g. teachers paying particular attention to them, being teased by peers), and work (e.g. being avoided by co-workers, being asked intrusive questions, being left out of social outings).

After the break, video material should be used to focus the discussion. For example, the story of a young man who experiences the results of stigma at university and describes his experience in hospital, symptoms, problems at school, the importance of the support of friends, etc., may be helpful to start the discussion. The latter part of this session is devoted to learning strategies to cope with stigma and to protect oneself from being a victim using role-play.

Examples used are: 'What to say and do if, when filling an official form, you are asked about any illness and medication', or how to respond to insensitive comments like 'I heard you were crazy'.

In the check-out exercise each participant is asked to give a compliment to 'the person next to you' in order that everyone can 'leave the session feeling good about yourself'. The compliment cannot be about choice of clothes; it must concern something more personal.

Session 6

Recovery and social skills

Rationale

The therapeutic benefit of social skills training in the treatment of schizophrenia and related psychotic disorders has been well established (Benton & Schroeder, 1990). While particularly intensive social skills training is required during the chronic phase of the illness, patients in early phases of the illness may have either retained many of their basic social and interpersonal skills, or they may be in a position to regain them with relatively less effort. This is not to deny that there are first-episode patients with major deficits who require intensive skills training over many sessions.

The purpose of Session 6 is to introduce the client to the concept and importance of social skills for maintaining enjoyable and supportive social functioning; and help them to appreciate the importance of developing and practising such skills. The extent to which an individual is capable of meaningful social relationships is related to his or her ability to effectively communicate both verbally and non-verbally.

Procedure

The check-in exercise is for participants to identify the most helpful aspect of treatment for them, other than medication. In response, most members mention the support of other people, such as their parents and/or their case manager.

The therapist comments about the importance of factors in addition to medication in the recovery process. Emphasis is placed on the importance of having the social skills in order to manage the demands of adult life while also managing one's own illness over a long period.

Group members are given a written scenario about a depressed woman who, even after taking antidepressant medication, was left with multiple problems in her home and work life. The members take turns playing the therapist while one of the therapists plays the depressed woman. The experience of this role-play is often very intriguing, particularly as participants become frustrated when the depressed woman does not respond to their suggestions and comments. This frustration provides a natural lead into a discussion regarding the value of more effective communication. One of the therapists then discusses the principles of skill acquisition and verbal and non-verbal communication, initially didactically but later followed by practice.

After the break, the therapists place a pile of index cards in the middle of the table, with each card containing a scenario to role-play. Such scenarios include: refusing to 'light up', ask someone for a date, call someone on the phone and ask them to do something, or make a request to a teacher to hand an assignment in at a later date. Each member of the group is asked to draw a card and role-play the scenario it contains. This session thus promotes an opportunity to role-play around many of the issues discussed in earlier sessions.

In the check-out exercise, each participant is asked to identify one thing that 'you would like to do to improve your communication skills'. It has been our experience that, in response, patients often choose 'being able to make a conversation with someone'.

Session 7

Early warning signs/early intervention

Rationale

Psychotic disorders usually develop gradually over time and are often preceded by non-psychotic 'prodromal' symptoms (Malla & Norman, 1994; Norman & Malla, 1995; Yung & McGorry, 1996). Although these prodromal symptoms are often present before the onset of a first episode of psychosis, their utility is greatest for predicting impending relapse of psychosis. It has been suggested that patients have a distinct and often unique pattern of non-psychotic symptoms and changes in behaviour prior to the first onset that they tend to repeat prior to each relapse (Birchwood, Spencer & McGovern, 2000).

Often patients either do not have a sound knowledge of their unique pattern of warning signs or ignore them and then seek treatment only after a full relapse of psychosis has occurred. Patients following their first episode of psychosis have not as yet had any experience of relapse and are, therefore, unlikely to comprehend the concept of early warning signs prior to a relapse. It is important that they become aware of both the overall concept of warning signs as well as the specific signs that they would have experienced prior to their first episode.

Procedure

The check-in exercise for this session is somewhat amusing and assesses participants' engagement, memory of past conversations, and perception of other group members. Each member is asked to provide the group with three *personal facts*, one of which is untrue, and the next person guesses which one is untrue. The importance of this session is emphasized by reviewing the first session with identified prevention of relapse as a major goal.

The therapist introduces the material with some comments about recovery and the possibility of relapse. Members are reminded that, as there is no real cure, it is important to be able to advocate for oneself in the future. Sheets of paper are distributed and participants are asked to write what they believe to have been the early signs of their illness.

Each group member is then asked to give the story of his or her illness from the very beginning when any change (including even minor changes) in their functioning or feelings was noticed. As the member tells his or her story to the group, the therapist puts the member's name on the flip chart and starts to list the early changes that participants are reporting. Each group member is asked to write his or her symptoms as they evolved. This exercise collectively takes about 1 hour.

After the break, the therapist provides a brief description of the prodromal stage of psychosis using examples from a number of common medical illnesses. The focus is then shifted to psychosis and the list of early symptoms noted from participants' retrospective reports. This list typically includes observations of changes in eating and sleeping, mood changes, growing preoccupations, suspiciousness, paranoia, mild hallucinations, etc. A list of additional warning signs is provided and participants are asked to indicate if any of those are relevant to them. Members are encouraged to add these to their personal list. This list is then typed on an index card, with two copies, one for the patient and the other for his or her case manager. These lists are then used by patients and case managers throughout follow-up in the programme.

In the check-out exercise members are asked to specify the warning signs they would report to their case manager or other clinician/psychiatrist.

Session 8

Review/celebration

Rationale

It is important that participants be given as much opportunity as possible to review and integrate the material covered in earlier sessions. In addition, this session provides a further opportunity to socialize with other members.

Procedure

In the check-in exercise participants are asked to 'Choose a word to describe how you feel about the group coming to an end'.

The therapist then asks all participants to take out their 'Dear Me' letter from Session 1 and add a postscript such as: 'The highlight of the group for me was...' or 'A piece of information I will use from this group is ...'. One of the therapists gives out a review page as an informal assessment about the content of the sessions. Obviously, every effort is made to encourage individual members to see this as an enjoyable exercise and not as a test. The format for this can be flexible. Members may participate individually or as a group.

Finally, all members, including therapists, enjoy a meal together then watch a movie that the group has chosen earlier in the sessions. Members are encouraged to develop friendships with one another beyond the group setting and to utilize what they have learned in the previous 8 weeks in their subsequent individual therapy sessions with their case managers.

EVALUATION

This 8-week group intervention has been evaluated through an open trial comparing group participants with non-participants. Of 131 first-episode psychosis patients who had completed 3 months of treatment in our Prevention and Early Intervention Program for Psychosis (PEPP), 70 participated in the group intervention. The remaining 61 patients did not participate because: (a) the intervention was not available at that point in the development of PEPP; (b) they were not referred by their primary therapist, or (c) they refused to participate. Both groups received novel antipsychotics, intensive case management and family education in the programme. Results show that the two groups did not differ on age, gender, level of education and baseline positive and negative symptoms. Comparative data were available for 68/70 of those who participated, and 59/61 of those not participating. In the participant group, 86% met diagnostic criteria for schizophrenia, schizophreniform or schizoaffective psychosis compared to 53% of the non-participants.

Outcome

Seventy-eight percent of those who received YES group intervention stayed in treatment for a minimum of one year compared to 48% of the non-participant group ($p < 0.001$). At 1-year follow-up, participants in the YES group showed a significantly lower level of negative symptoms (composite total median 11.0 vs 21.5, $p < 0.001$) and a non-significant trend of lower positive symptoms (median 2.0 vs 4.0) and higher rates of remission (74% vs 59%). The results are preliminary and have been summarized for the purpose of this chapter. Details will be provided in a subsequent publication.

CONCLUSION

In this chapter, we have briefly reviewed the role of group therapy in psychotic disorders followed by a detailed description of a group therapy module designed especially for FEP to aid them in their recovery and social reintegration. We have attempted to provide a rationale for each element/session of this intervention followed by some details regarding the process of carrying out the intervention.

REFERENCES

Amador, X.F. & Kronengold, H. (1998). The description and meaning of insight in psychosis. In X.F. Amador & A.S. David (Eds), *Insight and Psychosis* (pp. 15–32). New York: Oxford University Press.

Benton, M.K. & Schroeder, H.E. (1990). Social skills training with schizophrenics: A meta-analytic evaluation. *Journal of Consulting and Clinical Psychology*, **58**, 741–747.

Birchwood, M., Spencer, E. & McGovern, D. (2000). Schizophrenia: Early warning signs. *Advances in Psychiatric Treatment*, **6**, 93–101.

David, A.S., van Os, J., Jones, P., Harvey, I., Foerster, A. & Fahy, T. (1995). Insight and psychotic illness: Cross-sectional and longitudinal associations. *British Journal of Psychiatry*, **167**, 621–628.

De Jesus, M.J. & Steiner, D.L. (1994). An overview of family intervention and relapse on schizophrenia: A meta-analysis of research findings. *Psychological Medicine*, **24**, 565–578.

Fenton, W.S., Blyler, C.R. & Heinssen, R.K. (1997). Determinants of medication compliance in schizophrenia: Empirical and clinical findings. *Schizophrenia Bulletin*, **23**, 637–651.

Geddes, J., Mercer, G., Frith, C.D., Macmillan, F., Owens, D.G.C. & Johnstone, E.C. (1994). Prediction of outcome following a first episode of schizophrenia: A follow-up study of Northwick Park First Episode Study Subjects. *British Journal of Psychiatry*, **165**, 664–668.

Gitlin, M., Nuechterlein, K., Subotnik, K.L., Ventura, J., Mintz, J. Fogelson, D.L., Bartzokis, G. & Aravagiri, M. (2001). Clinical outcome following neuroleptic discontinuation in patients with remitted recent-onset schizophrenia. *American Journal of Psychiatry*, **158**, 1835–1842.

Jackson, H.J., Edwards, J., Hulbert, C. & McGorry, P. (1999). Recovery from psychosis: Psychological interventions. In P.D. McGorry & H.J. Jackson (Eds), *The Recognition and Management of Early Psychosis: A Preventive Approach* (pp. 265–307). Cambridge: Cambridge University Press.

Kanas, N. (1999). Group therapy with schizophrenia and bipolar patients: Integrative approaches. In V.L. Schermer & M. Pines (Eds), *Group Psychotherapy of the Psychoses: Concepts, Interventions and Context* (pp. 129–147). Bristol, PA: Jessica Kingsley Publisher Ltd.

Kapur, R. (1993). Measuring the effects of group interpretations with the severely mentally ill. *Group Analysis*, **26**, 411–432.

Khantzian, E.J. (1997). The self-medication hypothesis of substance use disorders: A reconsideration and recent applications. *Harvard Review of Psychiatry*, **4**, 231–244.

Lally, S.J. (1989). Does being in here mean there is something wrong with me? *Schizophrenia Bulletin*, **15**, 253–265.

Lazell, E.W. (1921). The group treatment of dementia praecox. *Psychoanalytic Review*, **8**, 168–179.

Lehman, A.F., Myers, C.P., Dixon, L.B. & Johnson, J.L. (1996). Detection of substance use disorders among psychiatric inpatients. *Journal of Nervous and Mental Disease*, **184**, 228–233.

Lehman, A.F. Steinwachs, D.M. & the Co-Investigators of the PORT Project (1998). Patterns of usual care for schizophrenia: Initial results from the schizophrenia patient outcomes research team (PORT) client survey. *Schizophrenia Bulletin*, **24**, 11–20.

Linszen, D.H., Dingemans, P.M. & Lenior, M.E. (1994). Cannabis abuse and the course of recent-onset schizophrenic disorders. *Archives of General Psychiatry*, **51**, 273–279.

Loebel, A.D., Lieberman, J.A., Alvir, J.M.J., Mayerhoff, D.L., Geisler, S.H. & Szymanski, S.R. (1992). Duration of untreated psychosis and outcome in first episode schizophrenia. *American Journal of Psychiatry*, **149**, 1183–1188.

Malla, A.K. & Norman, R.M.G. (1994). Prodromal symptoms in schizophrenia: A prospective investigation. *British Journal of Psychiatry*, **164**, 487–493.

Malla, A.K. & Norman, R.M.G. (2002). Early intervention in schizophrenia and related disorders: Advantages and pitfalls. *Current Opinion in Psychiatry*, **15**, 17–23.

Malla, A.K., Norman, R.M., McLean, T.S., Cheng, S., Richwood, A., McIntosh, E., Cortese, L., Diaz, K. & Voruganti, L.P. (1998). An integrated medical and psychosocial treatment program for psychotic patient characteristics and outcome. *Canadian Journal of Psychiatry—Revue Canadienne de Psychiatrie*, **43**, 698–705.

Malla, A.K. Norman, R.M.G., McLean, T.S. & McIntosh, E. (2001). Impact of phase-specific treatment of first episode psychosis on Wisconsin Quality of Life Index (client version). *Acta Psychiatrica Scandinavica*, **103**, 355–361.

Marder, S.R. & May, P.R. (1986). Benefits and limitations of neuroleptics and other forms of treatment in schizophrenia. *American Journal of Psychotherapy*, **40**, 357–369.

Marder, S., Swann, E., Winslade, W.J., Van Putten, T., Chien, C. & Wilkins, J. (1984). A study of medication refusal by involuntary psychiatric patients. *Hospital and Community Psychiatry*, **35**, 724–726.

McGorry, P.D. (1995). Psychoeducation in first episode psychosis: A therapeutic process. *Psychiatry*, **58**, 329–344.

McGorry, P.D. & McConville, S.B. (1999). Insight in psychosis: An elusive target. *Comprehensive Psychiatry*, **40**, 131–142.

Moore, B.S., Sherrod, D.R., Liu, T.J. & Underwood, B. (1979). The dispositional shift in attribution over time. *Journal of Experimental and Social Psychology*, **15**, 553–569.

Mueser, K.T., Bennett, M. & Kushner, M.G. (1995). Epidemiology of substance use disorders among persons with chronic mental illness. In A.F. Lehman & L. Dixon (Eds), *Double Jeopardy: Chronic Mental Illness and Substance Abuse* (pp. 9–25). New York: Harwood Academic Publishers.

Norman, R. & Malla, A. (1993). Stressful life events and schizophrenia II: Conceptual and methodological issues. *British Journal of Psychiatry*, **162**, 166–174.

Norman, R.M.G. & Malla, A.K. (1995). Prodromal symptoms of relapse in schizophrenia: A review. *Schizophrenia Bulletin*, **21**, 527–539.

Norman, R.M.G., Malla, A.K., McLean, T.S., McIntosh, E.M., Cortese, L., Neufeld, R.W.J. & Voruganti, L.P. & Cortese, L. (2002). An evaluation of a stress management program for individuals with schizophrenia. *Schizophrenia Research*, **58** (2–3), 293–303.

Robinson, D.G., Woerner, M.G., Alvir, J., Ma, J., Bilder, R., Goldman, R., Geisler, S., Koreen, A., Sheitman, B., Chakos, M., Mayerhoff, D. & Lieberman, J.A. (1999). Predictors of relapse following response from a first episode of schizophrenia or schizoaffective disorder. *Archives of General Psychiatry*, **56**, 241–247.

Schooler, N.R., Keith, S.J., Severe, J.B., Matthews, S.M., Bellack, A.S., Glick, I.D., Hargreaves, W.A., Kane, J.M., Ninan, P.T., Frances, A., Jacob, M., Lieberman, J.A., Mance, R., Simpson, G.M. & Woerner, M.G. (1997). Relapse and rehospitalization during maintenance treatment of schizophrenia. *Archives of General Psychiatry*, **54**, 453–458.

Verdoux, H., Lengronne, J., Liraud, F., Gonzales, B., Assens, F., Abalan, F. & van Os, J. (2000). Medication adherence in psychosis: Predictors and impact on outcome. A 2-year follow-up of first-admitted subjects. *Acta Psychiatrica Scandinavica*, **102**, 203–210.

Weil, A.T. (1970). Adverse reactions to marijuana, classification and suggested treatment. *The New England Journal of Medicine*, **282**, 997–1000.

Wiersma, D., Nienhuls, F.J., Slooff, C.J. & Giel, R. (1998). Natural course of schizophrenic disorders: A 15-year follow-up of a Dutch incidence cohort. *Schizophrenia Bulletin*, **24**, 75–85.

Wyatt, R.J. (1991). Neuroleptics and the natural course of schizophrenia. *Schizophrenia Bulletin*, **17**, 325–351.

Young, A.S., Sullivan, G., Burnam, M.A. & Brook, R.H. (1998). Measuring the quality of outpatient treatment for schizophrenia. *Archives of General Psychiatry*, **55**, 611–617.

Yung, A.R. & McGorry, P.D. (1996). The prodromal phase of first-episode psychosis: Past and present conceptualizations. *Schizophrenia Bulletin*, **22**, 353–370.

8 Cannabis and Psychosis: A Psychological Intervention

KATHRYN ELKINS

ORYGEN Youth Health and Department of Psychiatry, The University of Melbourne, Australia

MARK HINTON

Camden and Islington Mental Health and Social Care Trust, UK

JANE EDWARDS

ORYGEN Youth Health, Melbourne, Australia

INTRODUCTION

Interest in specific treatment approaches to first-episode psychosis (FEP) has developed in recent years. Substance misuse has emerged as an important target for intervention due to increasing evidence of its detrimental influence on the course of psychosis. In this chapter the prevalence of cannabis use, particularly with regard to first-episode psychosis, is overviewed, and correlates and outcome of substance misuse are outlined. General treatment principles and specific interventions for cannabis use, which are described in the literature, are also outlined. The Cannabis and Psychosis (CAP) intervention developed at the Early Psychosis Prevention and Intervention Centre (EPPIC) is introduced, prefaced by a description of the CAP randomized-controlled trial and the service context. The six phases of CAP are then detailed with emphasis placed on the first two phases, which focus on the engagement of young people in the treatment. Interested readers are referred to a treatment manual and accompanying video for further information.

PREVALENCE AND CORRELATES OF CANNABIS USE

Cannabis use is widespread in Australia (Coffey et al., 2002). Australian rates of lifetime (39%) and current (19% in the past 12 months) cannabis use exceed reports from Canada (28%, 7%), the USA (35%, 9%), Great Britain (25%, 9%) and large-scale surveys from across the European Union (e.g. France (16%, 5%), Denmark (31%, 3%), including the Netherlands with their liberal cannabis laws (18%, 5%). In Australia there is an attitude of tolerance towards cannabis with 25% of the population surveyed reporting regular use of cannabis to be acceptable and 30% supporting its decriminalization; additionally, there has

Psychological Interventions in Early Psychosis
Edited by J.F.M. Gleeson and P.D. McGorry. © 2004 John Wiley & Sons, Ltd.

Table 8.1. Prevalence rates of cannabis misuse in early psychosis available from studies published post-1990

Author (Country)	N	% male	% with cannabis abuse/ dependence	Time under consideration	Setting
Strakowski et al., 1993 (USA)	102	60	7%		First-episode psychosis, inpatient
Linszen et al., 1994 (Netherlands)	93	—	26%	Last year	Recent-onset psychosis, outpatient
King et al., 1994 (UK)	93	—	29% 15% wkly	Lifetime Current	First-episode psychosis, inpatients
Strakowski et al., 1994 (USA)	412	—	4% 8%	Current misuse Lifetime misuse	First-episode psychosis
Hambrecht and Hafner, 1996b (Germany)	232	—	13%	Lifetime	First admission psychosis
Kovasznay et al., 1997 (USA)	98	55	26%[a]	Lifetime	First admission psychosis
Addington and Addington, 1998 (Canada)	113	71	15%	Current	Recent onset psychosis, in- and outpatients
Power et al., 1998 (Australia)	231	72	70%	Lifetime misuse	First-episode psychosis in- and outpatients
Rabinowitz et al., 1998 (USA)	224	65	30%	Lifetime	First admission psychosis
Roder-Wanner and Priebe, 1998 (Germany)	90	33	19%	Lifetime	First admission psychosis
Strakowski et al., 1998 (USA)	77	56	8% 34%	Lifetime abuse Lifetime dependence	First-episode psychosis, inpatients
Cantwell et al., 1999 (UK)	168	60	18%[a]	Current abuse	First-episode psychosis in- and outpatient
Edwards et al., 2002 (Australia)	193	—	30% daily 57%	Current dependence Current abuse	First-episode psychosis in- and outpatient

[a] Authors' calculation from paper.

been a 31% increase in Australian adults reporting recent use of cannabis between 1991 and 1998 (Miller & Draper, 2001).

The prevalence of substance misuse in psychotic populations has been well documented, with rates of substance misuse ranging from 40 to 60% (Cantor-Graae, Nordstrom & McNeil, 2001; Degenhardt & Hall, 2001; Regier et al., 1990), which is 2–5 times that of the general population. Cannabis is undoubtedly the most widely misused illicit substance (Bersani et al., 2002). High rates of use have also been demonstrated in first-episode cohorts, although there is considerable variability in prevalence rates across settings (see Table 8.1). In an Australian FEP group, cannabis was the most widely misused illicit substance

(Edwards et al., 2002) with rates double that of overseas studies, making it the focus of clinical attention.

Cannabis is not benign in its effect on people with psychosis. Accommodation difficulties, financial problems, violence, increased utilization of services, conflict with family and friends, and legal problems are commonly observed in young people who use cannabis (Swofford et al., 2000). Cannabis use in psychotic individuals is associated with higher levels of psychotic and depressive symptomatology, poor treatment compliance, increased suicidality and higher rates of readmission and relapse (Bersani et al., 2002; Drake & Wallach, 1989; Grace, Shenfield & Tennant, 2000; Linszen, Dingemans & Lenior, 1994). Extended and repeated episodes of psychosis are related to increased risk of morbidity and highlight the need for interventions to reduce cannabis misuse (Wiersma et al., 1998).

Cannabis users have been found to have an earlier age of onset of psychosis compared to non-users (Addington & Addington, 1998; Bersani et al., 2002; Cantwell et al., 1999; Hambrecht & Hafner, 1996a, 1996b; Verdoux et al., 1996). The early onset of psychosis may increase the chance of interference in attaining normal adolescent milestones (i.e. completing school, attaining work, developing social networks and establishing independence).

Studies suggest that those individuals experiencing psychosis with a drug misuse disorder have shorter hospitalizations and recover to significantly higher levels of functioning compared to non-drug users (Andreasson, Allebeck & Rydberg, 1989; Arndt et al., 1992; Ries et al., 2000), although these samples did not focus on cannabis misusers alone. Several explanations have been offered for drug-misusers stabilizing more rapidly once in treatment. One favoured explanation is that substance users demonstrate better premorbid functioning, as reflected in their ability to participate in the drug-using subculture (Arndt et al., 1992). An alternative explanation is that drug users experience an acute onset of psychosis (potentially mediated by their drug misuse) and rapid functional decline, coming quickly to clinical attention. The resulting reduction in the duration of untreated psychosis has been associated with a better initial response to treatment (Norman & Malla, 2001). Another hypothesis speculates that drug misuse amplifies symptoms of psychosis and the consequent brief hospitalizations, which curb cannabis use, result in significant symptom benefits (Ries et al., 2000). Considered together, the rapid improvement on abstinence and deleterious effects of continuing substance misuse highlight the need for a reduction in problematic cannabis use in the early phases of psychosis. The first episode is viewed as a critical period for pharmacological and psychological interventions as they are 'likely to have a disproportionate impact relative to interventions later in the course' (Birchwood, Todd & Jackson, 1998, p. 56), and this may be especially true in regard to clients with comorbid cannabis misuse.

REVIEW OF EXISTING TREATMENTS

This section presents a brief review of interventions that have been used in either substance abusing or psychotic populations, and recent trends in modifying substance misuse in psychotic samples.

Interventions for Cannabis Use

The dearth of research on interventions to reduce cannabis misuse may reflect social attitudes to cannabis as 'harmless' and therefore of low priority. Conventional preventative strategies based on education have failed to curb cannabis use in school-age populations (Clayton,

Cattarello & Johnstone, 1996; Dukes, Stein & Ullman, 1997; Ennett et al., 1994; Lynam et al., 1999) and no effective pharmacological agents for cannabis misuse or dependence have been identified (Day, Georgiou & Crome, 2002; Nathan & Gorman, 1998).

Similarly, there are few well-designed studies focused on reducing cannabis misuse in dependent users in the general population. Stephens, Roffman and Curtin (2000) compared 14 sessions of cognitive-behavioural therapy (CBT) as a group intervention and two sessions of individual motivational interviewing (MI), against a delayed treatment control in adults voluntarily seeking treatment for cannabis misuse. All three groups significantly reduced their cannabis use across four follow-up evaluations, over 16 months. Both interventions offered substantial advantages with fewer days of use, number of uses per day, less dependence and fewer related problems than the delayed control condition. However, the representativeness of the sample has been criticized given that, on average, participants had been using cannabis for over 17 years and this was their fifth attempt to cease use.

Copeland et al. (2001) randomized subjects to one of two brief cognitive-behavioural interventions (one session versus six sessions) or a waitlist control. The two treatment conditions promoted abstinence-based goals and included MI plus cognitive-behavioural interventions incorporating goal-setting, behavioural self-monitoring, managing cravings, drug refusal skills, withdrawal management, problem-solving, relaxation training and relapse prevention. Results showed that those in the treatment groups were significantly more likely to be abstinent, reported fewer concerns about control over cannabis and had fewer cannabis-related problems at 24-week follow-up than those in the control group.

Motivational Interviewing in Mental Illness

Over the last decade there has been considerable interest in the use of MI in the treatment of substance misuse (Miller & Rollnick, 1991, 2002). This approach aims to consolidate an individual's commitment to change his or her substance use and was developed initially as a brief intervention for problem drinkers. It has been applied to a wide variety of medical and mental health problems. Among the earliest applications of MI in psychiatric populations was its application to treatment non-adherence. Indeed, compliance therapy (a combination of cognitive therapy and MI to improve medication adherence) was effective in increasing treatment adherence, improving social functioning, attitudes to treatment and levels of insight over a control condition in participants with acute psychosis (Kemp et al., 1998). In another study using MI to improve treatment adherence, Swanson, Pantalon and Cohen (1999) randomized 121 inpatients with psychotic and affective disorders (77% with co-occurring substance use disorders) in an urban psychiatric hospital to either treatment-as-usual (TAU) or TAU with MI (TAU+MI). Significantly more members of TAU+MI kept their initial outpatient appointment following discharge (47% vs 21%) and this result was confirmed when examining results for the dually diagnosed clients alone (42% vs 16%).

Substance Misuse and Psychosis: Recent Trends

Review of recent trends in the treatment literature suggested two promising approaches:

- Cognitive-behavioural therapy (CBT), which has been applied in both groups with psychosis (e.g., Haddock et al., 1998) and those with substance misuse (e.g., Carroll et al., 1994).
- Motivational interviewing (MI) for treating substance misuse (Miller & Rollnick, 1991; Saunders, Wilkinson & Phillips, 1995).

Both treatment approaches assume a non-confrontational, collaborative stance in developing shared treatment goals and emphasize the development of a therapeutic alliance. The studies reported below demonstrate the application of these approaches.

In an important British trial (Barrowclough et al., 2001), individuals with non-affective psychosis and comorbid substance misuse were targeted for treatment. Anticipating that few patients would be motivated to work on issues of substance misuse, the researchers combined MI for substance misuse, CBT for psychosis and a family intervention in a comprehensive 9-month programme to reduce substance misuse. The programme demonstrated benefits over TAU, with less positive psychotic symptoms at initial follow-up, better general functioning and more days abstinent across a 12-month period, although no significant differences in social functioning or total relapse days were found. The multicomponent nature of the intervention limits the attribution of positive benefits to MI, as family intervention and CBT have been shown to be effective in providing similar improvements in outcome (Pilling et al., 2002).

A number of specialist FEP programmes have described 'substance misuse and psychosis' treatments applied within a mental health context (Addington, 2002; Kavanagh et al., 2002). The interventions are brief, highlight engagement initiatives, adopt strategies consistent with MI principles and techniques, have a psychoeducational component focusing on the interaction between substance misuse and psychosis, and incorporate a relapse prevention strategy. Despite the promising findings, these programmes are not specific to cannabis and the evidence does not yet answer the rudimentary question: Can we reduce cannabis misuse with any intervention compared with TAU?

CANNABIS AND PSYCHOSIS (CAP) PROJECT

Overview of a Randomized-Controlled Trial to Reduce Cannabis Use in Early Psychosis

A randomized-controlled trial was conducted which recruited participants within 12 months of referral to EPPIC, who continued to use cannabis after the first 8 weeks of treatment. Cannabis users were randomized to CAP therapy or the control condition, psychoeducation, and were assessed pre- and post-intervention by a rater blind to the treatment condition. All patients continued to receive routine EPPIC case management while engaged in the CAP intervention. The design and early results from the trial are described elsewhere (Edwards et al., 2002).

The CAP Intervention

The Cannabis and Psychosis (CAP) intervention is an individualized, phase-linked intervention aimed at reducing the negative impact of cannabis use on young people with FEP (Edwards et al., 2002). CAP encompasses a harm minimization philosophy which aims to assist clients to understand and minimize the harm associated with ongoing cannabis use. Due to the accumulating evidence that any cannabis use may be 'problematic' for those with a recent-onset psychotic illness (Kavanagh et al., 2002), the target is *any* cannabis use among FEP clients. MI was also considered an essential component of the CAP approach in order to raise motivation and increase commitment to modify cannabis use, because most clients in the early stages of psychosis are precontemplative and highly ambivalent about changing their cannabis use. CAP therapists aim to engage and persuade clients that modification of their cannabis use to 'non-problematic' levels is worthwhile. We have found that assisting clients to develop an understanding of the link between their psychosis and cannabis use provides them with a strong rationale for developing motivation for change. The CAP approach, based on a philosophy of harm minimization, incorporates psychoeducation, MI and CBT techniques and has been detailed in a treatment manual (Hinton et al., 2002) which has an accompanying video.

The Setting: EPPIC, Melbourne, Australia

The EPPIC model aims to reduce the level of both primary and secondary morbidity in clients aged 15–24 inclusive, with early psychosis, by utilizing a dual strategy of early identification and provision of intensive phase-specific treatment for up to 18 months (Edwards, Harris & Herman, 2002). The EPPIC catchment area covers the western metropolitan region of Melbourne, an area served by four geographically based adult mental health services and fewer than 20 private psychiatrists. The region includes a high proportion of people from non-English speaking backgrounds, with low incomes, high unemployment, and low levels of education. The service components of EPPIC include: a mobile youth assessment and treatment team; prevention, promotion and primary care activities; a prodrome clinic; a 16-bed inpatient unit; outpatient case management; family work; a group programme; and a prolonged recovery clinic.

The EPPIC programme has gained research expertise through the development of early intervention CBT programmes for psychosis and complementary prolonged recovery programmes for patients with unrelenting symptoms, namely COPE and STOPP (Herrmann-Doig, Maude & Edwards, 2003; Jackson et al., 2001). Ho and Colleagues (1999) compared four different treatment programmes for dual-diagnosis patients, and found the group with the widest range of treatment components had superior outcomes compared with groups with more limited interventions, which suggests the comprehensive EPPIC service is an ideal environment to pilot innovative interventions.

Considerations of Treatment Group

Young people with early psychosis who are using cannabis present distinct challenges in the development and implementation of a tailored intervention. It is important to:

- take into account the age and developmental stage of the client, including age at illness onset;
- support the attainment of necessary basic skills (e.g. problem-solving), because normal developmental tasks may have been interrupted by the onset of psychotic illness or long-term cannabis use;
- consider the influence of the family and social circle and their attitude to cannabis and other drug use;
- remember that denial is a common characteristic of each disorder and clients may have not initiated help-seeking for psychosis or for cannabis use;
- reassess drug use, readiness to change and mental state frequently, as the clinical picture is often dynamic and complex;
- understand that there can be many losses associated with the onset of illness, and requests to consider changing cannabis use may represent further losses;

- offer adequate support for other comorbidities and social difficulties, using each opportunity to enhance engagement or to make links between cannabis use and current difficulties;
- acknowledge the cognitive difficulties that can arise from heavy cannabis use, illness course, and medication and adapt interventions accordingly;
- capitalize on the window of opportunity afforded in the crisis that brings the client to treatment by assertively offering early treatment before the client 'seals over' by denying the psychosis and refusing to engage in further discussion;
- work to preserve social and family supports, and to re-engage the client in educational/occupational activity to minimize the impact of interruption during recovery.

The Six Phases of CAP

The structure of the CAP intervention follows the six phases described in the transtheoretical model of behaviour change (Prochaska & DiClemente, 1986, 1992), that is, precontemplation (no desire for change), contemplation (ambivalent about change), determination, action (committed to change), maintenance, and relapse. Individuals' motivation to change determines the treatment phase at which they enter the programme (see Table 8.2). Mismatching the phase of treatment with the client's motivation for change compromises rapport and threatens ongoing engagement.

The balance of the chapter will explicate the six phases of CAP. Three techniques, used in the first two phases of CAP, are described in more detail and are illustrated with examples: engagement and assessment, psychoeducation and the decisional balance exercise. The exercises selected serve to illustrate the philosophy and practice of the intervention.

Phase 1: Engagement and assessment

The goal of the first phase of CAP is to engage the client, raise the issue of their cannabis use and elicit a commitment to continue treatment. Engagement is challenging with the FEP group, with a recent trial reporting a 38% drop-out rate after initial treatment (Kavanagh et al., 2002). A thorough assessment is important and can be therapeutic as it may be the first time clients have reviewed their substance use. The assessment should examine current, past and future beliefs about cannabis use, explore individual, family and clinical concerns and clarify the client's motivation for change.

Feedback about the client's cannabis use should be linked with opportunities for education. Responses can include informal discussion about patterns of use and the possible consequences of cannabis use. Feedback can also be formalized, typically in a letter or report reinforcing that the client's individual story has been heard and that each client has been allowed to correct any inaccuracies (Prochaska et al., 1993). Pictorial feedback, for example a simple graph that compares a client's use with the general community, can be helpful. Reflecting data gathered on the practical aspects of cannabis use, such as the cost or the time spent procuring, using and being intoxicated with cannabis, can be a powerful tool.

The language of the assessment must be understandable and acceptable to the young person with psychosis and should communicate confidence and collaboration. All communication used during assessment should be as non-judgemental as possible, avoiding

Table 8.2. Goals and clinical strategies of the six phases of CAP intervention

Phase	Goals	Clinical strategies
1 *Entry*	Engagement Gaining commitment to treatment Raising the issue of *problematic* cannabis use	Case formulation Feedback of findings from assessment Exploring explanatory model of psychosis Exploring views on interaction of cannabis and psychosis Explore readiness to change cannabis use Psychoeducation Explore and problem solve barriers to future attendance
2 *Commitment*	Building commitment to a goal of non-problematic cannabis use	Motivational interviewing Harm reduction Psychoeducation about • Cannabis • Psychosis • Cannabis and psychosis
3 *Goal-setting*	Reinforcing commitment to change Setting a non-problematic cannabis use/non-use goal Development of goal achievement strategies	MI revisited Goal-setting Psychoeducation
4 *Challenges*	Adopting a sound approach to all potential challenges to cannabis-reduction goals	Withdrawal counselling Problem solving Relapse prevention Psychoeducation
5 *Relapse Prevention and Lifestyle*	Examination of factors that are 'threats' to the short-term achievement and long-term maintenance of non-problematic cannabis use Consider positive lifestyle change to support cannabis goals	Relapse prevention Cannabis refusal skills Time management MI revisited Psychoeducation
6 *Maintenance*	Maintenance of motivation to a commitment to non-problematic cannabis use Ongoing consideration of positive lifestyle change to support cannabis goals	Relapse prevention Coping skills Time management Motivational interviewing revisited Reinforcement of psychoeducation
Exit	Termination	Resources

value-ridden labels unless they are terms introduced by the client. For example, the term could be used in a reflection statement 'you said that when you "go overboard" with cannabis, you end up spending a lot of time recovering'.

Case example: Informal feedback

Therapist: Let's recap the information so far. You have used cannabis for many years, mainly with your friends from school and then at your job at the video store. You'd often use it before going to a party or a movie. It was a small part of what you did when you were with those friends, and generally you enjoyed their company as well as the relaxation. Is that correct so far?

Brendan: Yes.

Therapist: Later many of your friends cut down on their use but you started to use more and started to drop out of social activities. Then you quit your job. In the last year you have increased the time you spend smoking dope—and mainly this is something you do on your own in your room at home?

Brendan: Uh-huh.

Therapist: Four months ago you went to see your doctor as you were having trouble sleeping and he said your troubles were "a kind of psychosis". Also, since you stopped work you don't have much money, so sometimes you can't buy things you want like sneakers, or CDs. You're thinking of applying for university, but you're wondering where the money will come from. Also your concentration is poor these days. Since giving up your job you feel bored and sometimes lonely and you want that to change, but it is hard to join in again without having the money to do so. I am interested to hear if I got that all right, and what you make of all of this.

In the above example, the onset of the psychosis has been raised in the feedback, although Brendan did not identify it as related to cannabis use during the assessment. By presenting the two pieces of information together, the young person can make an association.

Formal feedback can be very powerful for clients (Kreuter, Strecher & Glasman, 1999), particularly if the client helps to make the calculations and prepare the feedback report. Reading the summary aloud to the therapist will further emphasize the information and literally place it 'in their voice'. The feedback report can be used in reflective exercises to elicit motivational statements from clients such as: 'This week has been financially tough, and you're upset you can't afford a mother's day present. Sometimes you are shocked at how much money you have spent on cannabis but at the moment you don't want to change that.' An example of a formal feedback sheet used to emphasize monetary costs of using cannabis is shown in Table 8.3.

In this first phase of CAP, the primary goal of the therapist is to move the client towards committing to return for further session(s) even though—at this stage—they may have made no commitment to changing their use. An example follows.

Table 8.3. Example of a Formal Feedback Sheet

How much do you use?

Prepared for Brendan   *29 March 2002*

You have been smoking regularly for the last 6 years.
You reported using cannabis on (30 days) 97% of last month.
You reported you had 15–20 bongs a day, or 510 month, or over 6100 in the last year.
This means you spent $100 per week or $5200 per year using your estimate of average costs.
You consumed 8 cigarettes per day if you used a 50% mix or around 150 packs of cigarettes.
You spent about 3 hours in activities related to smoking cannabis each day, or around 1100 hours
    this year.

Case example: Discussion of commitment to treatment

Client: I'm really not that worried about the money—just having a whinge. I think I can manage it and the psychosis is already getting better.

Clinician: I hear you think it isn't a problem but I want to make sure you have all the information you need to decide about your cannabis use in the future. What you choose to do is up to you, but don't you think it is worth a few more meetings to make sure you know all there is to know about cannabis, especially its relationship to psychosis?

Client: OK—I'm interested to learn what you know, and you might learn a thing or two from me.

Clinician: It will be good to hear about your experience; let's organize to meet the same time for the next two weeks if that suits you.

Phase 2: Building commitment

The objective of the second phase of CAP treatment is to elicit a statement of intent to modify cannabis use to a non-problematic level. Clients need accurate information about both psychosis and cannabis use and their interactive effects to make informed decisions about future cannabis use. Essential areas to be covered are noted in Table 8.4.

Education about both cannabis and psychosis is important as clients with comorbid substance issues are typically poor attendees as outpatients (Swofford et al., 2000) and consequently miss key messages. Psychoeducation provides education, information, and places some responsibility for recovery with the client (McGorry, 1995). Knowledge enables the individual to be an active participant in the management of his or her psychosis and recovery and helps clients to develop an explanatory model of their psychosis and the role of cannabis in their life. The task for the client is to make meaningful links between their cannabis use and the consequences.

Effective education about cannabis and psychosis requires good preparation. Clinicians should develop a collection of relevant and interesting resource materials on the relationship between cannabis and psychosis, including pamphlets, videos and internet sites. It is important to personalize the information, as young people commonly reject what they perceive as 'standard messages'. Material which is relevant to the person's gender, age and educational

Table 8.4. Information about cannabis to be discussed throughout the CAP intervention

1. What is a drug (legal and illegal)?
   - Different types of drugs (depressants, stimulants, hallucinogens)
   - Different types of cannabis
   - How cannabis affects mind and body
   - How changing cannabis use affects mind and body
   - The relationship between cannabis and psychosis
   - Effects of combining illicit drugs with antipsychotic medication

2. Factors affecting substance use:
   - Dependence, tolerance and withdrawal
   - Personal issues
   - Social and cultural issues
   - Family and medical history

3. Harm associated with and reduction strategies when:
   - Obtaining cannabis
   - Using cannabis
   - Intoxicated
   - Withdrawing

4. Treatment:
   - Range of treatments the person will be offered
   - Length of treatment
   - Additional personnel involved in providing treatment (i.e. recruiting help)

level, presented in novel and engaging formats (e.g. good layout, attractive and easy-to-read fonts, appealing graphics with attention-grabbing colour) and offering encouragement to change health behaviour, are better liked and more successful in commanding attention (Bull et al., 2001). Information is more likely to be read, better remembered, viewed as applicable and/or credible, and more persuasive in changing health behaviours when it is tailored to the individual (Skinner et al., 1999). In CAP, documents are constructed and personalized with the client's name. Client relevant examples are added and text boxes or cards are developed with motivational statements tailored to the individual. The impact of both psychosis and cannabis use upon clients' cognitive, motivational and attentional functioning requires that clinicians are highly flexible, and at times creative, in the presentation of information (Carey et al., 2000).

To increase the impact of resource material, it is important to check the client's understanding of the information. Strategies include making summaries, using a question and answer format to check knowledge, and relating the information to the client's experience. Cognitive difficulties and medication effects may mean that information needs to be presented several times and in a number of formats.

Case example: Personalized psychoeducation

Catrina enjoyed word-finding puzzles and had even labelled her information booklet in the manner of a crossword puzzle. However, she was poorly engaged with the service and commented on how boring everything was. In early sessions a word-find puzzle was developed in which she had to locate the answers to questions about cannabis and psychosis from brochures and videos examined together. She found this approach enjoyable and challenging. She later said she was amazed that someone thought that she and the material were important enough to merit this effort.

Table 8.5. Examples of cannabis education resources

Back to Reality: Cannabis and Psychosis—an early psychosis video
Cannabis and Psychosis—an early psychosis treatment manual
Psychosis Fact Sheets—1–4 (can also be downloaded from website)
Cannabis and Psychosis Fact Sheet (can be downloaded from website)
   All available from: Early Psychosis Prevention and Intervention Centre,
   Web: www.eppic.org.au

Cannabis and Psychosis: Information for Health and Welfare Professionals
   Web: www.dhs.vic.gov.au/phd/hdev/cannabis/booklet/contents.htm

What's Your Poison—video (Australian Broadcasting Corporation, 1998)
A Guide to Quitting Marijuana—brochure (Greneyer, Solowij & Peters, 1998)
Mulling it Over—brochure (Bleeker & Malcolm, 1998)
Greening Out: A video on marijuana and its effects—video (Lion Rampant Publishing, 1999)
How Drugs Affect You: Cannabis—brochure (ADF, 2000)
Dealing with Cannabis: A Parent's Guide—brochure (ADF, 1999)
   All available from: Australian Drug Foundation
   Web: www.adf.org.au

Quitting? Cannabis—brochure (Copeland, Swift & Matalon, 2000)
What's the Deal on Grass? Cannabis Facts for Young People—brochure (NDARC)
What's the Deal on Grass? Cannabis Facts for Parents—brochure (NDARC)
What's the Deal on Grass? Talking with a Young Person about Cannabis—brochure (NDARC)
   All available from: National Drug and Alcohol Research Centre
   Web: *www.med.unsw.edu.au/ndarc/*

In the last 3 or 4 years some excellent cannabis resources have been developed which offer accurate and appealing information. Examples of materials are presented in Table 8.5.

Psychoeducation material is explored in a collaborative fashion within a MI framework. Clients typically concur that the information is legitimate and important but may deny its personal relevance, e.g. 'Yeah, I've heard dope is really bad, my cousin is schizophrenic and flipped out using it, but I have never heard voices so it is cool with me.' Regardless of the source of their ideas, always use opportunities to ask for their opinion about the information and to offer more credible material.

Building commitment through motivational interviewing
To achieve behaviour change, a primary component of MI is to focus on the ambivalence associated with decision-making processes in behaviour change. MI draws on models of behaviour change (Prochaska & DiClemente, 1992), theories of self-perception (Bem & McConnell, 1970) and cognitive dissonance (Festinger & Carlsmith, 1959). In brief, the theory of cognitive dissonance proposes that any discrepancy between beliefs and behaviour within an individual leads to tension. If the discrepancy is highlighted, the individual will pursue change to eliminate the tension. Cognitive dissonance is typically resolved by attitudinal change through minimizing, trivializing or dismissing a belief or harvesting new and more consonant beliefs congruent with behaviour. An alternative, but more difficult strategy for most individuals, is to change the dissonant behaviour to make it congruent with the belief. The likelihood of behaviour change is greatest when there is an extreme mismatch between beliefs and behaviour. In CAP, one function of MI is to develop and emphasize inconsistencies between beliefs about cannabis (e.g. cannabis might provoke relapse) and

behaviour (e.g. continuing to smoke cannabis excessively) thus increasing dissonance and promoting motivation for behaviour change, i.e. modifying further cannabis use.

Miller and Rollnick's (2002) four principles of MI were adapted for the CAP programme.

1. *Express empathy*. The clinician seeks and acknowledges, without judgement, the client's perspective on his or her cannabis use, but this does not imply condoning cannabis use. Ambivalence is regarded as a normal part of behavioural change rather than an unreasonable position, or a deficiency of 'will-power'. Particular attention is given to communicating acceptance and understanding, delivering accurate information and dispelling the stigma associated with both disorders.

2. *Develop discrepancy*. The therapist mirrors and amplifies any discrepancy between behaviour and beliefs by exploring the costs of the client's cannabis use and clarifying past, present and future goals in a supportive, therapeutic environment. This creates gaps between the person's self-image, present behaviour and stated goals. A common example is the inconsistency between the client's desire to improve relationships with his or her parents but persistently breaking house rules (e.g. spending all the money on cannabis and failing to pay board).

3. *Roll with resistance*. Individuals are generally more likely to become entrenched in their beliefs than to change them when confronted. Hence, client resistance is a sign that the client views the situation differently and a change of approach is needed. MI discourages therapists from arguing for change, viewing it as counterproductive to the relationship. For example, when an FEP client rejects the label of psychotic illness the therapist does not challenge this view but instead invites exploration of the consequences of cannabis use on areas other than symptoms of psychosis, e.g. impact on finances, social life or study. Techniques such as reflection, reframing and shifting focus are employed to offer new perspectives on the client's situation.

4. *Support self-efficacy*. The onset of psychosis can have a devastating effect on the confidence of a young person. Reflecting on past success in reducing or ceasing cannabis use emphasizes existing skills and achievements and can help to build self-efficacy, reinforcing that change is achievable. Exercises that develop an imagined future sense of self, free from cannabis, can also be used.

Decisional grid exercise

The goal of the decisional exercise is to collaboratively uncover the costs and benefits of using or ceasing cannabis use which have significant *subjective value* to the client. This is achieved by sequentially working through each square of a four-quadrant grid (see example in Figure 8.1). Clinicians use the grid exercise to understand a client's reasons for use but most importantly to prompt the client into arguing for change. Clients need time to generate data on positive and negative aspects and tactful use of examples developed by others, or prompting them with suggestions from earlier sessions can be helpful.

The information generated offers a different perspective, often providing additional information not raised in earlier assessments. Experience with the FEP group suggests that when reviewing the positive effects of using cannabis, clients often focus on short-term benefits of intoxication including a reduction in negative emotional or cognitive states (e.g. anxiety, paranoia or stress) and the augmentation of positive states (e.g. sleep, socializing, confidence, activity or being high). Perceived negative effects of continued cannabis use typically highlight long-term physical problems (e.g. cancer, bronchitis) or biopsychological

	Using cannabis	Cutting down cannabis
Good things	• see friends regularly • not so bored • enjoy the rush • feel less anxious • more relaxed • nothing else I enjoy • sleep better	• More money in hand • Smoke less tobacco • Feel fitter • More clear headed • Less worried about psychosis • Folks/girlfriend stop nagging • Feel less paranoid
Not so good things	• Disapproval from friends and family • Feel bad when my case manager asks me about marijuana • Money problems • Problems with short term memory • Have relapse of psychosis • Might need to return to hospital • Could lose my job • Could run into legal problems	• increased stress and anxiety • feel more depressed • another loss • increased boredom • May lose touch with my mates • No other place to go out

Figure 8.1. Example of decisional balance worksheet

problems (altered pharmacodynamics of medication, craving). Other themes include exacerbation of symptoms, guilt, impact on family, legal and financial consequences, and social isolation (Carey et al., 1999).

Clients typically report that the most concerning negative aspects of abstaining are the short-term difficulties with reducing, rather than abstinence itself. Concerns relating to the discomfort of withdrawal and craving, fears of substance substitution, lost social relationships, boredom and relapse are also reported. Positive aspects of abstaining concern longer-term outcomes such as the alleviation of biophysical problems (more energy, improved efficacy of medication); psychological benefits including reduced symptoms, improved self-esteem, concentration, attention and motivation; and social gains such as better quality relationships, improved financial circumstances, and increased vocational opportunities.

Clients commonly volunteer more negative than positive aspects of cannabis use, even when their level of use is high and they are in the pre-contemplation stage. Clinicians should be cautious when clients rapidly capitulate to view cannabis as detrimental as they have not had sufficient time to process all the information and may merely be attempting to please or placate the therapist.

Once all aspects of use have been explored, a full account of the concerns raised is sought (e.g. 'You think that cannabis might be making your asthma worse, but do you really worry about that often?'). Clients then work to defend the reasons proposed and move towards supporting that position more resoundingly. Interestingly, when completing the grid not all themes are reciprocal, e.g. most see 'high' as a benefit of using but do not report 'missing high' as negative of changing use, making it important to complete all four squares. The examination of both the costs and benefits of cannabis prevents polarizing the client and therapist and helps the clinician to understand the reasons for use, which are often under-explored in standard assessment interviews. Finally, it is important to complete the exercise with the focus on the 'benefits of changing', as the recency effect ensures statements from the last square (i.e. the advantages of modifying cannabis use) will continue to echo in the client's mind.

Clients will often need time to consider the information discussed in the decisional balance grid exercise prior to developing a statement of intent regarding future cannabis use. Once this statement of intent has been established, a collaborative plan can be prepared.

Phase 3: Goal-setting

Once a grid or similar exercise resulting in a statement of intent has been completed, the focus moves to goal-setting. Here the immediate, intermediate and longer-term intention to modify cannabis use may range from achieving abstinence to using identical quantities, but in a less harmful manner. It is important to reassure clients that scepticism and trepidation are common when making changes. Examples of other clients who overcame insecurity and ambivalence about changing cannabis habits can be helpful. Defining the goal (making it measurable and achievable) and establishing a time-line for achievement are key steps. Means of evaluating progress are developed and documentation of the target makes aspirations tangible. Once the goal is selected, threats to goal achievement are identified and the client is motivated to enact the plan, the focus moves to activities to manage challenges.

Phases 4 and 5: Challenges and lifestyle

The focus in latter phases shifts to pre-empting and managing obstacles to goal achievement. The development of a fire drill, similar to the task of developing a relapse prevention plan, is valuable. The drill is a reminder of options for support in difficult times and is presented as a set of straightforward, concrete directions on occasions when a client feels a relapse is imminent, e.g. 'If I feel the need to use cannabis I will distract myself by jogging and remind myself of the reasons I wanted to change.' Psychoeducation is offered regarding withdrawal, managing associated anxiety, and increasing perceived ability to cope. Lifestyle issues which may contribute to relapse (e.g. isolation, boredom, anxiety, anger) are addressed through well-known skills-training interventions such as problem-solving strategies, social-skills instruction, relaxation techniques, sleep hygiene, anger management, drug-refusal skills and activity scheduling.

Identification of supports for monitoring client well-being and reinforcing healthy alternative behaviour is vital. Determining which relationships may pose a threat to achieving cannabis goals and electing to terminate or modify potentially problematic usual social contact may be a formidable task for clients. Generally it is preferable to enlist substance-free family and friends as supports. However, for some clients, the loss of a significant social network, albeit a substance-abusing one, may be more detrimental. In the latter situation assessing the preparedness of social networks to accept a reduction in the client's cannabis use and training the client in refusal skills may be a feasible alternative. A wide spectrum of lifestyle changes, of sufficient magnitude and satisfaction to supplant the previous drug-related activities, needs to be identified and developed.

Phase 6: Relapse prevention

Maintaining any change is a significant challenge. The focus in the final phase of CAP is to reaffirm commitment to maintain gains and momentum towards intermediate and long-term goals. The dynamic nature of the early course of psychosis presents substantial challenges to the initial decision to modify cannabis use, and effort is required to maintain client commitment to cannabis-reduction goals. A booster session is offered after a strategically scheduled break in order to revise psychoeducational messages, rehearse early warning signs, review threats to success, and to update clients' fire drill to reduce the likelihood of relapse.

Relapse of problematic cannabis using patterns post-treatment is the norm. The stage of change model views reversion to cannabis use as a typical but temporary part of the process. The clinical response to relapse is guided by the assessment of the client's readiness for change. For example, if the client re-presents at the action stage, as many often do after brief destructive binges, action strategies are most appropriate. Empathy regarding the difficulty of maintaining change is always offered, and any success achieved in past attempts is stressed to support self-efficacy.

CONCLUSION

> I have a very negative attitude toward marijuana now. Years ago, when I was younger, I loved it. It got me high and I had so much confidence; it made me feel really good. But now when I think back to my symptoms, how bad I was and the problems it caused in my life, I just really think it's not worth it. Ben, 22 (excerpt from *Back to Reality*, Cannabis and Psychosis video)

There are few treatments to assist young people with psychosis to reduce cannabis misuse, however psychological approaches show some promise. The CAP intervention offers a structured treatment approach with a goal of non-problematic cannabis use. Coupling education about links between cannabis and psychosis with techniques for increasing client motivation for change are important aspects of the approach.

ACKNOWLEDGEMENTS

Helpful comments on earlier drafts were provided by Henry Jackson, Simone Pica, Darryl Wade, Leanne Hides, John Gleeson and Peter Eide. The authors gratefully acknowledge the support of The Department of Human Services, Victoria.

REFERENCES

Addington, J. (2002). An integrated treatment approach to substance use in an early psychosis programme. In H. Graham, K.T. Mueser, M. Birchwood & A. Copello (Eds), *Substance Misuse in Psychosis: Approaches to Treatment and Service Delivery*. Chichester, John Wiley & Sons.

Addington, J. & Addington, D. (1998). Effect of substance misuse in early psychosis. *British Journal of Psychiatry*, **172** (Suppl. 33), 134–136.

Andreasson, S., Allebeck, P. & Rydberg, U. (1989). Schizophrenia in users and nonusers of cannabis. A longitudinal study in Stockholm County. *Acta Psychiatrica Scandinavica*, **79**, 505–510.

Arndt, S., Tyrrell, G., Flaum, M. & Andreasen, N.C. (1992). Comorbidity of substance abuse and schizophrenia: The role of pre-morbid adjustment. *Psychological Medicine*, **22**, 379–388.

Barrowclough, C., Haddock, G., Tarrier, N., Lewis, S.W., Moring, J., O'Brien, R., Schofield, N. & McGovern, J. (2001). Randomized controlled trial of motivational interviewing, cognitive behavior therapy, and family intervention for patients with comorbid schizophrenia and substance use disorders. *American Journal of Psychiatry*, **158**, 1706–1713.

Bem, D.J. & McConnell, H.K. (1970). Testing the self-perception explanation of dissonance phenomena: On the salience of premanipulation attitudes. *Journal of Personality and Social Psychology*, **14**, 23–31.

Bersani, G., Orlandi, V., Kotzalidis, G.D. & Pancheri, P. (2002). Cannabis and schizophrenia: impact on onset, course, psychopathology and outcomes. *European Archives of Psychiatry and Clinical Neuroscience*, **252**, 86–92.

Birchwood, M., Todd, P. & Jackson, C. (1998). Early intervention in psychosis. The critical period hypothesis. *British Journal of Psychiatry*, **172** (Suppl. 33), 53–59.

Bull, F.C., Holt, C.L., Kreuter, M.W., Clark, E.M. & Scharff, D.P. (2001). Understanding the effects of printed health education materials: Which features lead to which outcomes? *Journal of Health Communication*, **6**, 265–279.

Cantor-Graae, E., Nordstrom, L.G. & McNeil, T.F. (2001). Substance abuse in schizophrenia: A review of the literature and a study of correlates in Sweden. *Schizophrenia Research*, **48**, 69–82.

Cantwell, R., Brewin, J., Glazebrook, C., Dalkin, T., Fox, R., Medley, I. & Harrison, G. (1999). Prevalence of substance misuse in first-episode psychosis. *British Journal of Psychiatry*, **174**, 150–153.

Carey, K.B., Purnine, D.M., Maisto, S.A., Carey, M.P. & Barnes, K.L. (1999). Decisional balance regarding substance use among persons with schizophrenia. *Community Mental Health Journal*, **35**, 289–299.

Carey, K.B., Purnine, D.M., Maisto, S.A., Carey, M.P. & Simons, J.S. (2000). Treating substance abuse in the context of severe and persistent mental illness: Clinicians' perspectives. *Journal of Substance Abuse Treatment*, **19**, 189–198.

Carroll, K.M., Rounsaville, B.J., Nich, C., Gordon, L.T., Wirtz, P.W. & Gawin, F. (1994). One-year follow-up of psychotherapy and pharmacotherapy for cocaine dependence. Delayed emergence of psychotherapy effects. *Archives of General Psychiatry*, **51**, 989–997.

Clayton, R.R., Cattarello, A.M. & Johnstone, B.M. (1996). The effectiveness of Drug Abuse Resistance Education (project DARE): 5-year follow-up results. *Preventative Medicine*, **25**, 307–318.

Coffey, C., Carlin, J.B., Degenhardt, L., Lynskey, M., Sanci, L. & Patton, G.C. (2002). Cannabis dependence in young adults: An Australian population study. *Addiction*, **97**, 187–194.

Copeland, J., Swift, W., Roffman, R. & Stephens, R. (2001). A randomized controlled trial of brief cognitive-behavioral interventions for cannabis use disorder. *Journal of Substance Abuse Treatment*, **21**, 55–64; discussion 65–56.

Day, E., Georgiou, G. & Crome, I. (2002). Pharmacological management of substance misuse in psychosis. In H. Graham, K.T. Mueser, M. Birchwood & A. Copello (Eds), *Substance Misuse in Psychosis: Approaches to Treatment and Service Delivery* (pp. 259–280). Chichester: John Wiley & Sons.

Degenhardt, L. & Hall, W. (2001). The association between psychosis and problematical drug use among Australian adults: Findings from the National Survey of Mental Health and Well-Being. *Psychological Medicine*, **31**, 659–668.

Drake, R.E. & Wallach, M.A. (1989). Substance abuse among the chronic mentally ill. *Hospital and Community Psychiatry*, **40**, 1041–1046.

Dukes, R.L., Stein, J.A. & Ullman, J.B. (1997). Long-term impact of Drug Abuse Resistance Education (DARE). Results of a 6-year follow-up. *Evaluation Review*, **21**, 483–500.

Edwards, J., Harris, M. & Herman, A. (2002). The Early Psychosis Prevention and Intervention Centre, Melbourne, Australia: An overview. In C. Ogura (Ed.), *Recent Advances in Early Intervention and Prevention in Psychiatric Disorders* (pp. 26–33). Tokyo, Japan: Seiwa Shoten Publishers.

Edwards, J., Hinton, M., Elkins, K. & Anthanasopoulos, O. (2002). Cannabis and first-episode psychosis: The CAP Project. In H. Graham, K.T. Mueser, M. Birchwood & A. Copello (Eds), *Substance Misuse in Psychosis: Approaches to Treatment and Service Delivery*. Chichester: John Wiley & Sons.

Ennett, S.T., Rosenbaum, D.P., Flewelling, R.L., Bieler, G.S., Ringwalt, C.L. & Bailey, S.L. (1994). Long-term evaluation of drug abuse resistance education. *Addictive Behaviours*, **19**, 113–125.

Festinger, L. & Carlsmith, J.M. (1959). Cognitive consequences of forced compliance. *Journal of Abnormal and Social Psychology*, **58**, 203–210.

Grace, R.F., Shenfield, G. & Tennant, C. (2000). Cannabis and psychosis in acute psychiatric admissions. *Drug and Alcohol Review*, **19**, 287–290.

Haddock, G., Morrison, A.P., Hopkins, R., Lewis, S. & Tarrier, N. (1998). Individual cognitive-behavioural interventions in early psychosis. *British Journal of Psychiatry*, **172** (Suppl. 33), 101–106.

Hambrecht, M. & Hafner, H. (1996a). Does substance abuse result in schizophrenia. *Nervenarzt*, **67**, 36–45.

Hambrecht, M. & Hafner, H. (1996b). Substance abuse and the onset of schizophrenia. *Biological Psychiatry*, **40**, 1155–1163.

Herrmann-Doig, T., Maude, D. & Edwards, J. (2003). *Systematic Treatment of Persistent Psychosis (STOPP): A Psychological Approach to Facilitating Early Recovery in Young People with First-Episode Psychosis*. London: Martin-Dunitz, Taylor & Francis Group.

Hinton, M., Elkins, K., Edwards, J. & Donovan, K. (2002). *Cannabis and Psychosis Treatment Manual*. Melbourne: Early Psychosis Prevention and Intervention Centre.

Ho, A. P., Tsuang, J.W., Liberman, R.P., Wang, R., Wilkins, J.N., Eckman, T.A. & Shaner, A.L. (1999). Achieving effective treatment of patients with chronic psychotic illness and comorbid substance dependence. *American Journal of Psychiatry*, **156**, 1765–1770.

Jackson, H., McGorry, P., Henry, L., Edwards, J., Hulbert, C., Harrigan, S., Dudgeon, P., Francey, S., Maude, D., Cocks, J. & Power, P. (2001). Cognitively oriented psychotherapy for early psychosis (COPE): A 1-year follow-up. *British Journal of Clinical Psychology*, **40**, 57–70.

Kavanagh, D., Young, R., White, A., Saunders, J., Shockley, N., Wallis, J. & Clair, A. (2002). Start over and survive: A brief intervention for substance misuse in early psychosis. In A. Copello (Ed.), *Substance Misuse in Psychosis: Approaches to Treatment and Service Delivery*. Chichester: John Wiley & Sons.

Kemp, R., Kirov, G., Everitt, B., Hayward, P. & David, A. (1998). Randomised controlled trial of compliance therapy. 18-month follow-up. *British Journal of Psychiatry*, **172**, 413–419.

King, M., Coker, E., Leavey, G., Hoare, A. & Johnson-Sabine, E. (1994). Incidence of psychotic illness in London: Comparison of ethnic groups. *British Medical Journal*, **309**, 1115–1119.

Kovasznay, B., Fleischer, J., Tanenberg-Karant, M., Jandorf, L., Miller, A.D. & Bromet, E. (1997). Substance use disorder and the early course of illness in schizophrenia and affective psychosis. *Schizophrenia Bulletin*, **23**, 195–201.

Kreuter, M.W., Strecher, V.J. & Glasman, B. (1999). One size does not fit all. *Annals of Behavioral Medicine*, **21**, 276–283.

Linszen, D.H., Dingemans, P.M. & Lenior, M.E. (1994). Cannabis abuse and the course of recent-onset schizophrenic disorders. *Archives of General Psychiatry*, **51**, 273–279.

Lynam, D.R., Milich, R., Zimmerman, R., Novak, S.P., Logan, T.K., Martin, C., Leukefeld, C. & Clayton, R. (1999). Project DARE: No effects at 10-year follow-up. *Journal of Consulting and Clinical Psychology*, **67**, 590–593.

McGorry, P.D. (1995). Psychoeducation in first-episode psychosis: A therapeutic process. *Psychiatry*, **58**, 313–328.

Miller, M. & Draper, G. (2001). *Statistics on Drug Use in Australia 2000* (Drug Statistics Series No. 8 AIHW cat. no. PHE 30). Canberra: AIHW.

Miller, W.M. & Rollnick, S. (1991). *Motivational Interviewing: Preparing People to Change Addictive Behaviour*. New York: Guilford Press.

Miller, W.M. & Rollnick, S. (2002). *Motivational Interviewing: Preparing People to Change Addictive Behaviour* (2nd edn). New York: Guilford Press.

Nathan, P.E. & Gorman, J.M. (1998). *A Guide to Treatments that Work*. New York: Oxford University Press.

Norman, R.M. & Malla, A.K. (2001). Duration of untreated psychosis: A critical examination of the concept and its importance. *Psychological Medicine*, **31**, 381–400.

Pilling, S., Bebbington, P., Kuipers, E., Garety, P., Geddes, J., Orbach, G. & Morgan, C. (2002). Psychological treatments in schizophrenia: I. Meta-analysis of family intervention and cognitive behaviour therapy. *Psychological Medicine*, **32**, 763–782.

Power, P., Elkins, K., Adlard, S., Curry, C., McGorry, P. & Harrigan, S. (1998). Analysis of the initial treatment phase in first-episode psychosis. *British Journal of Psychiatry*, **172** (Suppl. 33), 71–76.

Prochaska, J.O. & DiClemente, C.C. (1986). Towards a comprehensive model of change. In W.R. Miller & N. Heather (Eds), *Addictive Behaviours: Process of Change*. New York: Plenum Press.

Prochaska, J.O. & DiClemente, C.C. (1992). Stages of change in the modification of problem behaviors. In M. Hersen (Ed.), *Progress in Behaviour Modification* (pp. 183–218). New York: Sycamore.

Prochaska, J.O., DiClemente, C.C., Velicer, W.F. & Rossi, J.S. (1993). Standardized, individualized, interactive, and personalized self-help programs for smoking cessation. *Health Psychology*, **12**, 399–405.

Rabinowitz, J., Bromet, E.J., Lavelle, J., Carlson, G., Kovasznay, B. & Schwartz, J.E. (1998). Prevalence and severity of substance use disorders and onset of psychosis in first-admission psychotic patients. *Psychological Medicine*, **28**, 1411–1419.

Regier, D.A., Farmer, M.E., Rae, D.S., Locke, B.Z., Keith, S.J., Judd, L.L. & Goodwin, F.K. (1990). Comorbidity of mental disorders with alcohol and other drug abuse. Results from the Epidemiologic Catchment Area (ECA) Study. *Journal of the American Medical Association*, **264**, 2511–2518.

Ries, R.K., Russo, J., Wingerson, D., Snowden, M., Comtois, K.A., Srebnik, D. & Roy-Byrne, P. (2000). Shorter hospital stays and more rapid improvement among patients with schizophrenia and substance disorders. *Psychiatric Services*, **51**, 210–215.

Roder-Wanner, U.U. & Priebe, S. (1998). Objective and subjective quality of life of first admitted women and men with schizophrenia. *European Archives of Psychiatry and Clinical Neuroscience*, **248**, 250–258.

Saunders, B., Wilkinson, C. & Phillips, M. (1995). The impact of a brief motivational intervention with opiate users attending a methadone programme. *Addiction*, **90**, 415–424.

Skinner, C.S., Campbell, M.K., Rimer, B.K., Curry, S. & Prochaska, J.O. (1999). How effective is tailored print communication? *Annals of Behavioral Medicine*, **21**, 290–298.

Stephens, R.S., Roffman, R.A. & Curtin, L. (2000). Comparison of extended versus brief treatments for marijuana use. *Journal of Consulting and Clinical Psychology*, **68**, 898–908.

Strakowski, S.M., Sax, K.W., McElroy, S.L., Keck, P.E. Jr, Hawkins, J.M. & West, S.A. (1998). Course of psychiatric and substance abuse syndromes co-occurring with bipolar disorder after a first psychiatric hospitalization. *Journal of Clinical Psychiatry*, **59**, 465–471.

Strakowski, S.M., Tohen, M., Flaum, M. & Amador, X. (1994). Substance abuse in psychotic disorders: Associations with affective syndromes. DSM-IV Field Trial Work Group. *Schizophrenia Research*, **14**, 73–81.

Strakowski, S.M., Tohen, M., Stoll, A.L., Faedda, G.L., Mayer, P.V., Kolbrener, M.L. & Goodwin, D.C. (1993). Comorbidity in psychosis at first hospitalization. *American Journal of Psychiatry*, **150**, 752–757.

Swanson, A.J., Pantalon, M.V. & Cohen, K.R. (1999). Motivational interviewing and treatment adherence among psychiatric and dually diagnosed patients. *Journal of Nervous and Mental Disease*, **187**, 630–635.

Swofford, C.D., Scheller-Gilkey, G., Miller, A.H., Woolwine, B. & Mance, R. (2000). Double jeopardy: Schizophrenia and substance use. *American Journal of Drug and Alcohol Abuse*, **26**, 343–353.

Verdoux, H., Mury, M., Besancon, G. & Bourgeois, M. (1996). Comparative study of substance dependence comorbidity in bipolar, schizophrenic and schizoaffective disorders. *Encephale*, **22**, 95–101.

Wiersma, D., Nienhuis, F.J., Slooff, C.J. & Giel, R. (1998). Natural course of schizophrenic disorders: A 15-year follow-up of a Dutch incidence cohort. *Schizophrenia Bulletin*, **24**, 75–85.

9 The First Psychotic Relapse: Understanding the Risks, and the Opportunities for Prevention

JOHN F.M. GLEESON

Department of Psychology, The University of Melbourne, Australia

INTRODUCTION

This chapter integrates the empirical and theoretical literature concerning psychotic relapse with two illustrative first-episode cases. The value of assessing and formulating the individual patient's risks for relapse is demonstrated, with particular reference to the period when the symptoms of the first acute psychotic episode begin to recede. The selection of appropriate psychosocial relapse-prevention interventions is also described.

Case examples: James and David

James is a 20-year-old man, who has been undertaking the third year of his science degree. He lives with his parents and 16-year-old brother. Ten weeks ago he was referred by his family general practitioner to a specialist early psychosis service. For the preceding 3 months he experienced auditory hallucinations and held a belief that he was being followed and kept under surveillance by intelligence service agents who were attempting to implicate him in the spread of AIDS. He was disorganized in his thinking and behaviour, and frightened and perplexed by his experiences. Over the initial weeks of treatment he responded well to careful engagement by a community treatment team who visited him in his home, completed the initial psychosocial assessment, physical investigations and examinations. They confirmed the diagnosis and tailored education for James and his family about the nature of his episode. The team introduced a low-dose atypical neuroleptic, and provided support during the early weeks of his treatment. Soon after the commencement of his treatment James met with his outpatient doctor and case manager, and after 6 weeks of treatment he started to attend a psychoeducation group for young people.

James, his family, and the treating team were at a critical juncture in the course of his psychosis, and in his treatment. On the one hand, James was making very good progress and had a number of very positive indicators for a good long-term outcome—premorbidly he was functioning highly, he had a very supportive family,

Psychological Interventions in Early Psychosis
Edited by J.F.M. Gleeson and P.D. McGorry. © 2004 John Wiley & Sons, Ltd.

and he had a good understanding of the nature of the episode. He was also not using illicit substances. Nonetheless, the treating team was mindful that relapses frequently occur, especially if medication is discontinued following the first episode (Gitlin et al., 2001; Robinson et al., 1999).

David was also 6 weeks into treatment for a first episode of psychosis. In contrast to James, David, an 18-year-old single man, experienced approximately 2 years of active psychotic symptoms before he was referred to a specialist mental health service. His core symptom consisted of a belief that the local Mayor was keeping him under surveillance via a complex system of cameras. In addition, he held erotomanic beliefs involving teachers from his high school. These beliefs were accompanied by a gradual deterioration in his self-care, lowered mood, marked thought disorder, and aggression towards his elderly grandparents, with whom he resided. Over the year preceding the referral to the service, David's consumption of alcohol, cannabis and amphetamines increased markedly, which severely compromised his ability to maintain his place at an inner city school. An assessment of his history of untreated illness highlighted developmental problems consistent with features of schizotypal personality disorder, which were evident from pre-school years. His psychotic illness was preceded by a prolonged prodromal phase beginning with persistent untreated depression at age 15 years. Initially angry with his family for referring him to mental health services, David experienced some relief when the problem was diagnosed, and for a period of several weeks he seemed agreeable to participating in treatment, and, as a consequence, his psychotic symptoms improved significantly.

James and David were at a similar point in their courses of treatment. How should the treating team assess and manage the risk of relapse in the two cases? More generally, what is the likelihood of a psychotic relapse following the first episode? Who is at greatest risk, and when is a relapse most likely to occur? What are the predictors of relapse? Can psychotic relapse be prevented, and if so, what is the most effective approach in the two cases? Finally, if a relapse occurs following the first episode, what is the appropriate response by the treating team?

   The aim of this chapter is to address these questions, by drawing upon research literature and clinical experience within the Early Psychosis Prevention and Intervention Centre (EPPIC)—a specialist early psychosis programme for young people aged 15 to 25 years who are experiencing their first episode of psychosis (Edwards, Harris & Herman, 2002).

RELAPSE RATES AFTER FIRST-EPISODE PSYCHOSIS

Historically, interest in relapse increased significantly in schizophrenia research with the shift towards de-institutionalization in developed countries (Falloon, 1983), although the conceptualization of schizophrenia as an episodic disorder was certainly not altogether new (Meyer, 1922, cited in Falloon, 1983; Ram et al., 1992). Relapse became a focus within first-episode research from the early 1980s onwards (Ram et al., 1992). Twenty-three prospective follow-up studies that have reported relapse rates following a first episode of psychosis were found in the literature using *Medline* and manual journal searches.

Taken together, these investigations, which range in duration from 12 months to 15 years, evinced a high relapse rate over the 10- to 15-year period following onset, with the relapse rate in the range 60–96%. The longest follow-up study, by Wiersma et al. (1998), showed that by 5 years after onset 70% of the patient group had experienced a psychotic relapse and by 9 years the rate was 85%, with no new relapsing patients after this, suggesting that a *safe point* may be reached. The other study with a follow-up longer than 10 years (Eaton et al., 1998) found a relapse rate of 66% for the first relapse and 43% for the second relapse, but this study utilized a more stringent criterion for remission, which may have reduced the overall episode count.

Interestingly, studies which followed-up patients for only 5-year periods found similar relapse rates (range 70–80%), although a range of criteria again were adopted. The highest relapse rate was found in a study by Gitlin et al. (2001), which recorded a 96% relapse rate by 2 years into the study, which followed after an initial 18-month treatment protocol. However, in this study all patients were withdrawn from medication, and a lower threshold for relapse was employed.

The Measurement of Relapse in First-Episode Research and Clinical Practice

The variability in the operationalization of relapse in outcome studies contrasts with recommendations made by Falloon (1983, 1984) for standardized definitions and measurement of relapse. These included the need to: (a) measure qualitative and quantitative aspects of symptom changes; (b) stipulate the duration of symptoms required for a relapse; (c) consider social and treatment variables independently of relapse; and (d) measure symptoms via appropriate objective instruments. However, the lack of consensus criteria across major research centres remains problematic. Relapse has often been confounded with treatment variables, particularly readmission to hospital (Crow et al., 1986; The Scottish Schizophrenia Research Group, 1992; Zhang et al., 1994), and other studies have relied excessively on clinicians' impressions rather than objective rating instruments (Kane et al., 1982).

Duration criteria for psychotic remission have also varied markedly from 8 weeks, 30 days and 3 months respectively (Linszen et al., 1998; Robinson et al., 1999; Wiersma et al., 1998). Other studies (e.g. The Scottish Schizophrenia Research Group, 1992) failed to include any remission duration criteria.

The Department of Psychiatry and Biobehavioural Sciences at UCLA have developed the most widely adopted relapse criteria (Ventura et al., 1989). Precise quantitative and qualitative definitions of remission, relapse, significant psychotic exacerbation following remission and significant psychotic exacerbation following persisting psychotic symptoms were achieved by examining changes in scores on the Brief Psychiatric Rating Scale (BPRS; Overall & Gorham, 1962). These criteria have been adopted in several studies of relapse following first-episode psychosis, including two studies outside of UCLA (Linszen et al., 1994, 1996).

Ten years following Falloon's recommendations, Linszen et al. (1994) argued that objective ratings should be considered in combination with clinical judgement. The authors reported on 69 first-episode patients, diagnosed with DSM-III-R (APA, 1987) schizophrenia or related disorders, aged between 15 and 26 years (see Linszen et al., 1996, for outcome data). The authors applied to the same sample five sets of criteria for defining relapse, as outlined in Table 9.1. The findings indicated that selection of criteria is not a trivial issue, because, while the rates of relapse were similar using different rules, 'disagreement about

Table 9.1. The five criterion sets for relapse utilized by Linszen et al. (1994)

Criterion set 1: UCLA Criteria[a], based on changes on three items of the BPRS: (i) hallucinations, (ii) unusual thought content, (iii) conceptual disorganization.

Criterion set 2: Narrow clinical relapse = (1) hospital readmission due to psychotic symptoms; (2) recurrence or exacerbation of psychotic symptoms; (3) an explicit statement of relapse or exacerbation of psychotic symptoms; and (4) a significant increase of antipsychotic medication. Psychotic symptoms had to be of at least 1 week's duration.

Criterion set 3: Broad clinical definition = as for Criterion set 2, but cases did not need to meet the duration criterion of 1 week.

Criterion set 4: PSE[b] Type I relapse = change of the PSE status on the Index of Definition from non-case (4 or less) to case (5 or above).

Criterion set 5: PSE Type II relapse = increase in caseness from 5 to 7 or from 6 to 8.

---

[a] UCLA criteria sets are described in full in Ventura et al., 1989
[b] PSE = Present State Examination (Wing, Cooper & Sartorius, 1974)

individual cases is considerable' (Linszen et al., 1994, p. 276). They concluded that while objective instruments may provide highly reliable ratings of changes this may not relate directly to clinically salient changes. In other words, perhaps clinicians, for valid clinical reasons, utilize a different set of rules or different thresholds for determining that a relapse has occurred compared with researchers. For example, the clinician may be concerned with small changes in the severity of a specific idiosyncratic symptom for an individual patient, particularly where functioning may be disproportionately compromised. In David's case, for instance, the treating team was very concerned to monitor any re-emergence in his erotomanic beliefs because, in the past, the associated behaviour had caused high levels of distress to his school community, and placed him at added risk of contact with the justice system.

In summary, although specific criteria for the operationalization of relapse have important implications for the categorization of outcome following first-episode psychosis, it has been poorly defined in most follow-up studies. Furthermore, there is a high degree of variability in relapse definitions between the more rigorous studies.

The Construct of Relapse: A Signpost to Chronicity?

The term *relapse*—like *remission*, *recurrence* and *recovery*—denotes a categorical shift in the course of an illness. While the *Australian Oxford Dictionary* defines a relapse as a 'deterioration in a patient's condition after a partial recovery' (Hughes, Michell & Ramson, 1992, p. 963), relapse (and its derivative, *lapse*), have also referred to a worsening or backsliding in behaviour (Bronwell et al., 1986).

Course descriptors, such as relapse, have been acquired by psychiatry from general medicine where the classic use of relapse denoted not only a worsening in symptoms and signs but a reactivation of a dormant pathogen or disease (e.g. secondary tuberculosis). For example, *Butterworths Medical Dictionary* defined a relapse as 'the recurrence of a disease after *seeming* recovery' (MacNalty, 1980, p. 1458). This notion of underlying illness continuity is consistent with the contemporary neurodevelopmental model that assumes a progression (which is not inevitable) in the pathophysiology and neuropathology of early schizophrenia from the neurodevelopmental (premorbid) phase to the deteriorative stage, with a putative critical neuroplastic juncture occurring during the prodromal phase (Lieberman et al., 2001).

Although some investigators have challenged the notion that the 'natural course' of the illness can be observed in contemporary treatment settings (see Shepherd et al., 1989), no challenge to the categorical approach to course of illness has been mounted (see Lader, 1995).

This is surprising because the diagnosis of a *relapse* for some clinicians, consumers, and carers may falsely imply that the progression of *disease* is in fact *inevitable*. Once a relapse is declared, any previous recovery may be retrospectively minimized because the term implies that a disease process has been consistently present, albeit in an inactive state. Likewise, it also implies that any future remission or progress is always precarious— in this sense the diagnosis of a relapse may be an inadvertent signpost to chronicity, and hopelessness, which may reduce the patient's perceived control over the illness, precipitating depression (Birchwood et al., 1993). While, for some, the term may also facilitate awareness of the problem, for other young patients their anxiety may be overly aroused, resulting in a defensive *sealing-over* of curiosity and self-concern and a disengagement from treatment (McGlashan, Levy & Carpenter, 1975).

This is particularly pertinent for first-episode patients who experience a 90% remission rate over the first year of the illness (Lieberman, Jody & Geisler, 1993). If a worsening in symptoms does occur following this initial remission, the use of less categorical terms (e.g. 'setback'), and a more dimensional approach to measurement of change focusing on specific symptoms, may pose less of a threat to the patient's outlook while still facilitating enough self-concern (McGorry & McConville, 1999).

Notwithstanding these caveats regarding the construct of relapse and its measurement, the return of psychotic symptoms to a severe degree after an initial improvement is unequivocally common during the period 2–5 years after the first episode, and almost universal if antipsychotic medication is ceased. The need remains, however, for the treating clinician to balance up the costs and benefits in recommending long-term ongoing prophylaxis for individual first-episode cases.

In assessing and formulating James's and David's individual risk for relapse, the clinical team could have referred to known risk factors, which can be divided into distal and proximal markers. The former aids in discriminating *who* is most at risk of relapse and the latter guides clinical judgements as to *when* relapse is most likely to occur.

RISK FACTORS FOR RELAPSE IN FIRST-EPISODE PSYCHOSIS

Distal Factors

Distal factors are stable enduring factors in the person's history or background. These can be further divided into patient factors (e.g. personality, premorbid adjustment, genetics) and environmental factors (e.g. trauma).

Recently, interest has been revived in the relationship between personality and psychosis, although most of this work has focused upon identifying markers of vulnerability rather than examining the *pathoplastic* or bidirectional relationships between psychosis and personality (see Hulbert, Jackson & McGorry, 1996). Using the framework of the Five Factor Model of personality (McCrae & Costa, 1997), some recent research at EPPIC has suggested that patients with a lower level of agreeableness are more likely to experience a return of positive psychotic symptoms after reaching remission (Gleeson, 2001).

Premorbid adjustment in schizophrenia as a predictor of outcome, including the rate of relapse, has also been studied. A study by Kane et al. (1982) reported significantly worse premorbid adjustment (especially on isolation during pre-adolescence and adolescence) in the subgroup of patients who relapsed compared with those who remained stable over a 1-year follow-up period following the first episode. This was more recently supported in a 5-year follow-up study of first-episode patients (Robinson et al., 1999).

A related paradigm to the premorbid functioning literature is the coping skills literature. Pallanti, Quercioli and Pazzagli (1997), for example, reported data on 41 recent-onset outpatients who met criteria for DSM-III-R (APA, 1987) and RDC schizophrenia (Spitzer, Endicott & Robins, 1978). Importantly, the 39% of patients who relapsed without reporting a severe life event in the previous month scored higher on the Frankfurt scale (Süllwold & Huber, 1986), suggesting that coping resources, including problem-solving skills and social resources, are important protective factors in the pathway to relapse.

In summary, premorbid adjustment has emerged from the literature as a robust predictor of relapse, but further work is required to examine the relationship between relapse and premorbid adjustment which selects from first-episode samples to reduce confounding effects of treatment and to minimize selection bias.

Distal Environmental Factors: Childhood Abuse

The rates of both physical and sexual abuse in childhood in adult psychiatric populations have been found to be approximately twice the estimated rate in the general population (Read, 1997). In a review of 15 studies, Read (1997) reported that childhood abuse has been associated with longer and more frequent hospitalizations, longer periods in seclusion, greater likelihood of suicide attempts and self-harm, and more frequent relapses, in addition to other indicators of more severe psychopathology.

However, it is difficult to conclude from this group of studies that abuse was a complicating factor in the clinical outcome, or if there were instead sampling biases that produced a higher rate of self-reported abuse. To address this limitation, Greenfield et al. (1994) reported on 38 first-episode patients who had a DSM-III-R (APA, 1987) psychotic disorder. Twenty patients reported childhood abuse—a prevalence rate consistent with the group of studies selecting from more chronic patients. Although patients who reported abuse had higher dissociative symptom scores and tended to have longer admissions compared to patients who did not report abuse, there were no differences in recovery rates, and there were no differences on total psychopathology scores. However, the follow-up period was not specified by the authors, and the study was limited by a high drop-out rate and an over-representation of affective psychoses. The authors concluded that the sexual abuse may contribute to an atypical constellation of symptoms, which might not influence the initial recovery process, but may influence longer-term outcome, including relapse. Of course, a history of childhood sexual abuse may also be associated with, and account for, poorer premorbid adjustment and poorer coping skills.

On the basis of known distal factors, David appears to be at heightened risk of relapse. He has a long history of poor premorbid functioning, and has an enduring personality style consistent with low agreeableness. Specifically, he copes with problems by externalizing blame and exploding impulsively when others are unable or unwilling to assist him. Unfortunately this has the effect of evoking criticism from others, particularly his grandparents, which inadvertently increases his anxiety and frustration. He copes with this by isolating himself, drinking alcohol and abusing cannabis. A recurrence of symptoms appears highly likely in the short term.

In reconsidering James' case, he appears, based upon distal factors, to be at relatively low risk of relapse. However, he is part of a population of patients who overall are at high risk of relapse over the longer term (i.e. 3–5 years). The treating team will need to make decisions, within resource limitations, regarding the frequency and duration of follow-up and possible indicators of a pending relapse, even though James' overall risk may be relatively low. The team will also need to carefully consider proximal factors in designing a relapse programme for James and David, also taking into account positive prognostic indicators.

Proximal Factors

Proximal factors assist in estimating the risk of relapse at a particular point in the course of the psychosis. Proximal factors can be divided up into patient behaviours (substance abuse), early warning signs, and environmental factors (life events).

Substance abuse

Despite the common clinical assumption of an association between relapse and cannabis use, there have been surprisingly few empirical studies investigating this issue in first-episode samples. The only exception in the published literature at the time of writing was reported by Linszen, Dingemans and Lenior (1994). The study was conducted during the outpatient phase of treatment that followed a 3-month hospital admission. Cannabis use, measured on self-report, was categorized into mild use (between once per week and once per day) and heavy use (more than one marijuana cigarette per day). Of 93 patients, 26% were cannabis abusers according to DSM-III-R criteria and 54% of these were categorized as heavy users. All but one patient commenced smoking before the onset of psychosis. Of the abusers, 42% experienced a relapse compared to 17% of non-abusers over the 12-month follow-up period of the study. Abusers also had a significantly shorter time to relapse. Furthermore, 61% of heavy users had a relapse compared with 18% of mild users, and there was a greater risk of relapse with longer-term previous use.

More recently consistent use of cannabis over the first 9–12 months of treatment in a first-episode sample at EPPIC ($n = 60$) was associated with a five-fold risk of relapse, which was defined as a return of symptoms to a moderate level or greater. This association remained after controlling for self-reported adherence to medication (Gleeson, 2001).

In James's case, the treating team had no evidence that he was using cannabis or illicit substances. However, the case manager was mindful of the high prevalence of cannabis experimentation in young people in James's age group. For example, a national survey of substance abuse in the Australian general population, which included 14 490 adolescents between the ages of 15–17 years, found that 45% reported using cannabis in the previous 12 months (Reid, Lynskey & Copeland, 2000). Therefore, it was important to include preventive interactive psychoeducation for James, preferably using a variety of sources including the internet video material (EPPIC, 2002), and fact sheets (EPPIC, 1994) to assist him to understand his specific risks in taking up cannabis use in the future, and to prepare him for responding to peer norms and positive cannabis propaganda (Edwards et al., 2002; see Edwards & McGorry, 2002, for a list of psychoeducational resource materials).

In David's case there was an urgent need to address his use of cannabis. Fortunately David was open with his case manager *about* his drug use. There was a need to assess motivation for use and identify any potential dissonance between his behaviour and his goals, and introduce appropriate psychoeducational material as soon as possible (see Elkins, Hinton & Edwards, Chapter 8 this volume).

Life events and interpersonal stress

Stress has been an important factor in studies of schizophrenia, with three main types of studies: (a) comparisons of stress in schizophrenia and other psychiatric conditions; (b) a comparison of stress in schizophrenia and normal controls; and (c) correlational studies examining relationships between antecedent stress and relapse. In schizophrenia research, stress has most often been operationalized as stressful life events, which are commonly measured retrospectively, using weighted checklists of specific events (Brown & Harris, 1978), or in terms of 'Expressed Emotion' (EE) within family environments.

In established schizophrenia the correlational studies have yielded the greatest number of significant findings, usually with elevated stress in the 3 weeks prior to relapse (Norman & Malla, 1993), although some studies have indicated a longer time-frame (e.g. Das, Kulhara & Verma, 1997). The mediating role of behavioural coping patterns have also recently been examined in established schizophrenia. Socially withdrawn patients who were more reluctant to seek help were found in one study to be more likely to experience relapse following stressful events (Hultman, Weiselgren & Ohman, 1997).

A small number of studies have reported life events data in first-episode or recent-onset samples. For example, Ventura et al. (1989) completed a 1-year prospective study of recent-onset outpatients diagnosed with schizophrenia. The authors found a significantly higher number of independent life events in the month prior to relapse when compared with other time periods. A follow-up study demonstrated that the mean number of independent life events prior to relapse was higher in medicated subjects (regimen = 12.5 mg intramuscular fluphenazine decanoate fortnightly) than for medication-withdrawal relapsing patients, which suggested that medication plays an important role in increasing the threshold for relapse (Nuechterlein et al., 1992; Ventura et al., 1992).

The construct of EE is usually divided into three components: expressed hostility, emotional over-involvement, and the number of critical comments directed towards the patient. Relapse rates for patients with schizophrenia over 9-month follow-up periods have been approximately 50% in patients from high EE families compared to 21% from low EE environments (Bebbington & Kuipers, 1994).

The relevance of this finding to the first-episode population is less clear, as a much smaller number of studies have been published with first-episode samples, and findings remain equivocal (see review by Gleeson et al., 1999). More critically, the possibility remains that the emotional response of families at, say, 3 years after onset, may reflect separate family dynamics and processes compared with the initial crisis response to a highly ambiguous behavioural change, often with multiple, unsuccessful attempts to seek help (Lincoln & McGorry, 1995). More widely interpretable elements such as coping, distress, burden and burn-out may be more appropriate constructs to examine. Finally, there is a need for longer-term prospective follow-up studies and premorbid high-risk studies to include families.

Neither David nor James had recently experienced any 'independent' life events. However, the ongoing interpersonal conflict between David and his family posed a significant source of stress. Intervention in the form of emotional support was urgently required for the family to provide them with the opportunity to express anger, anxiety and feelings of shame. In addition psychoeducation was warranted for the family to help them to make sense of his unpredictable behaviour, together with problem-solving sessions with a focus on managing his explosive frustration without inadvertently perpetuating the stress for David or themselves. Assistance for David with his appraisal and response to perceived criticism, and his subsequent problematic use of substances, was also indicated. The treating team decided that the 'vicious' cycle of problems and attempts to cope with them could be diagrammatically mapped out in sessions, and encouragement given to attempt alternative strategies.

FORMULATION OF RELAPSE RISK

A formulation, ideally constructed with the patient, should link his or her lived experience of psychosis with a destigmatizing understanding of the disorder. In this way awareness of psychosis can be developed, distress can be contained but not minimized, and engagement in the therapeutic endeavour can be enhanced through empathy and appropriate optimism. Others have also emphasized the need for overarching models, such as the stress–vulnerability model, to be incorporated into the individual formulation so that the biopsychosocial rationale for treatment can be introduced (Fowler, 2000). Finally, a formulation should promote an informed selection of individualized treatments and preventive interventions.

With these aims in mind, a *relapse prevention model* or *formulation* can be developed with the patient and the patient's carers during the period after remission is reached, which, for the majority of young people, will be in the period 2–6 months after treatment commences (Lieberman et al., 2001). For the subgroup with persistent symptoms, alternative approaches will be required (see Herrmann-Doig, Maude & Edwards, 2003). The relapse formulation should integrate information relating to the risk of relapse after the first episode, including the range of variables outlined in Table 9.2.

In James's case the treating case manager, James and the family agreed that James was making good progress, and that he was in 'early recovery'. His positive premorbid

Table 9.2. Summary of variables incorporated into individual relapse model

Distal variables	• Premorbid adjustment • Duration of untreated illness • Relevant personality issues and coping styles (e.g. comorbid personality disorder)
Proximal	• Assessment of adherence • Substance abuse • Engagement in treatment • Stress • Available resources and supports
Specific individual indicators	• Approximation of early warning signs based on prodromal features

functioning and relatively brief period of untreated psychosis were highlighted as indicators of a low level of relapse risk, together with the supportive and adaptive family environment. In relation to the future, James was eager to return to university and complete his degree, despite significant academic and interpersonal stress in his third year of study. He continued to experience feelings of loss and grief related to a break-up with a girlfriend and he had struggled since early adolescence to assert himself with friends, which was associated with feelings of mild resentment. In the lead-up to his first episode it was noted that the first signs were sleeplessness, generalized worry and tension, followed by vague suspiciousness that consolidated in more definite delusional ideas.

James, the treating team and his parents agreed that achievement at university was important to James, but significant risks to his recovery were posed by returning too soon in the context of residual anxiety. James agreed to work with the case manager over a period of several months to learn more about his individual style of perceiving, and coping with, interpersonal stress and to broaden his repertoire of responses. It was agreed that monitoring for his specific early warning signs would be important as he became more socially active—especially as he faced his fear of explaining his psychosis to his friends and ex-girlfriend. The case manager also agreed to schedule individual sessions with James to discuss at length his ambivalence about remaining on medication for more than 4–6 months.

In David's case the risk of relapse was perceived as very high due to the persistent, long-standing interaction between distal factors (e.g. problems aligning with others) and proximal factors (e.g. cannabis use as a response to interpersonal stress). These factors also posed specific risks to the therapeutic alliance—the treating team anticipated that the 'honeymoon' period of treatment may soon end with David and he may begin to feel resentful and to drop-out of treatment. Given the risk that the relationship would deteriorate in a predictable way, threatening David's well-being, active measures were taken to keep David engaged through practical assistance with housing, and by negotiating control over the process of treatment as much as possible. Themes of 'feeling controlled' were gently broached in discussions about dealing with stressful relationships.

Can Relapse be Prevented?

The successful prevention of relapse is based on the assumptions that (a) it can be accurately predicted, and (b) preventive interventions are available that can be incorporated into service systems.

Recent reviews have highlighted that while there have been very few well-designed studies that have directly addressed the question of whether relapse in schizophrenia can be predicted, the goal of relapse prediction is realistic, especially when the objective measurement of early warning is combined with the judgement of clinicians, carers and patients (Fitzgerald, 2001).

Relapse Prevention Interventions

Interventions for reducing relapse rates have included: (a) monitoring for early prodromal signs in order to facilitate early intervention; (b) compliance therapy to maximize adherence with maintenance medications; (c) family psychoeducation and communication training to reduce interpersonal stress; (d) package approaches which attempt to enhance patient coping skills for potential triggers of relapse; and (e) cognitive interventions.

Early pharmacological intervention

The first group of interventions have typically attempted to intervene with medication at the point when early warning signs of relapse are identified by a clinician, family member, or patient.

In two separate reviews (Birchwood & Spencer, 2001; Herz & Lamberti, 1995) it was concluded that controlled trials of neuroleptic medication, targeted at the point when pro-dromal signs were identified, have shown promise in reducing relapse rates compared with placebo. However, larger reductions in relapse rates (between 12 and 23% over 2 years) have been found in studies that combined maintenance medication (even at low doses) with additional targeted doses in response to putative prodromal signs. However, these studies did not recruit exclusively from first-episode samples, and Birchwood and Spencer (2001) pointed out that it was difficult to clearly establish early warning signs before a relapse had occurred. Moreover, no evidence has been established to indicate that the prodrome prior to the first episode can be used to reliably predict idiosyncratic early warning signs of subsequent relapses.

Compliance interventions

Despite significant reductions in relapse rates associated with neuroleptic medication (Gilbert et al., 1995; Marder, 1999), reviewers have pointed to low compliance rates as a significant obstacle to maximizing their prophylactic potential (Gray, Wykes & Gournay, 2002; Pinikahana et al., 2002). Non-compliance with medication in schizophrenia has been estimated in the range 40–50% (Cramer & Rosenheck, 1998). Estimates in the younger first-episode population have been even higher—approximately 75% non-compliance dur-ing the first 1 to 2 years of treatment (Corrigan, Liberman & Engel, 1990; Gray, Wykes & Gournay, 2002; Kissling, 1992).

Correlates of non-compliance have included longer hospitalizations, more frequent co-ercive treatment, more side-effects (particularly dysphoric reactions), poorer awareness of illness and more negative attitudes towards treatment as predictors of non-compliance (Agarwal et al., 1998; Day & Bentall, 1996). During acute phases, non-compliance has been found to be associated with severity of symptoms and lack of insight, although these factors were less significant in predicting ongoing compliance (McPhillips & Sensky, 1998).

Of particular relevance to the first-episode group, younger age, and shorter duration of illness have also been associated with non-compliance (Agarwal et al., 1998; Day & Bentall, 1996) as well as substance misuse—common in younger male patients (McPhillips & Sensky, 1998). Of course, first-episode patients have less experience of the efficacy of medication and they utilize denial of illness more frequently as a phase-appropriate defence of self-esteem (Kemp et al., 1998).

In order to resolve the cognitive dissonance that is probably aroused by the very first prescription of antipsychotics, the novice consumer, we would assert, requires a destigma-tizing, youth-specific service structure, with therapeutic 'face-validity' extending from the 'shop-front' onwards (Corrigan, Liberman & Engel, 1990; McGorry, 1996).

Specific therapeutic interventions to improve adherence rates have relied upon legal provisions, simplifying medication regimes, depot medications, novel antipsychotics with reduced side-effects, psychoeducation, and behavioural interventions (Healey et al., 1998). Although perhaps necessary in a very small proportion of first-episode patients, the more coercive strategies are a poor substitute for the initial building of trust (Parashos et al.,

2000), and the results from psychoeducational and behavioural strategies have been some-what equivocal (McPhillips & Sensky, 1998). Promise has been shown via the integration of cognitive therapy and motivational interviewing (see Miller & Rollnick, 1991) into a brief intervention, that produced significant differences on measures of insight, attitudes to treatment and observer-rated compliance at 18-month follow-up in the experimental group compared with a group receiving non-specific counselling (Kemp et al., 1998). The sample, drawn from consecutive acute admissions, consisted of 74 subjects with a Diag-nostic and Statistical Manual (DSM-III-R: APA, 1987) diagnosis of a psychotic disorder (predominantly schizophrenia). Importantly, first-admission patients tended to have lower compliance scores than patients with multiple admissions. Clearly this intervention demon-strated promise in preventing relapse. However, it requires further refinement to meet the needs of the first-episode group, perhaps by timing the intervention to the post-acute phase when patients may be confronted for the first time with advice regarding the need for on-going medication for prophylactic reasons, and by involving their family as part of the first-episode 'treatment team' (Gleeson et al., 1999).

In relation to David's case the risk of non-compliance is high, but care should be taken to avoid self-perpetuating coercive solutions that would threaten compliance further over the long term. Early in treatment David was able to associate greater 'clarity of thought' with taking medication. After careful exploration of his perceived problems with medication this advantage was linked by his case manager to his medium-term goals of returning to school, and his desire to feel 'less controlled' by having his own flat.

Family education and communication training

Family-based interventions that have incorporated psychoeducation with communication and problem-solving skills have demonstrated an effect on lowering EE and significantly reducing relapse rates (Mari & Streiner, 1994).

However, only a handful of studies have been published which have incorporated these strategies exclusively with first-episode samples. The results from these studies, in terms of the reduction in relapse rates, have been mixed. One study suggested that attempts to modify family processes of coping during the initial stages of illness led to worse outcomes when the baseline for EE was low (Linszen et al., 1996). More recently, researchers have shown that EE is a dynamic process early in the course of illness, and that the process may be understood as an initially adaptive response to perceived loss and burden (Patterson, Birchwood & Cochrane, 2000).

Other psychosocial 'package' approaches

Complementary psychosocial interventions aimed at preventing relapse in schizophrenia have traditionally commenced at hospitalization with continued therapy following dis-charge, including a focus upon social skills, education about illness and vocational and social activities.

This group of psychosocial interventions have been underpinned by a biopsychosocial model (Glazer, 1993) of relapse that has informed an eclectic package of interventions. Hogarty et al. (1995), for instance, described a personal therapy that aimed to tailor the psychosocial intervention to the specific stressors and resources of patients diagnosed with schizophrenia. Their package of interventions included avoidance, relaxation, social skills training, and criticism management. However, these packages have all been targeted at patients with established schizophrenia, with no specific first-relapse prevention packages described in the literature. A package approach to relapse prevention entitled 'EPISODE II' is commencing at EPPIC, with the active components including individual cognitive therapy, group-based psychoeducation, and family therapy, which will be compared with treatment as usual in patients who have established remission following their first episode of psychosis.

Cognitive interventions

Relapse prevention has also been included as one aim of cognitive-behavioural therapies for positive symptoms of psychosis (Birchwood & Spencer, 2001). Cognitive models, entailing an interaction between enduring self-schema and specific beliefs arising from anomalous prepsychotic experiences, have been developed with the aim of evaluating cognitive interventions targeted at idiosyncratic early warning signs (Gumley & Power, 2000).

Gumley and colleagues recently reported 12-month follow-up data on 144 participants assessed as 'relapse prone' with a diagnosis of schizophrenia or related disorder, who were randomized to treatment as usual or cognitive-behavioural therapy (CBT), which included targeting a phase of therapy to identified early warning signs (Gumley et al., 2003). They described significant advantages for CBT on relapse and readmission rates in addition to overall improvement in positive symptoms, negative symptoms, global psychopathology, and psychosocial functioning.

The authors have argued that the early years of psychosis could be critical in the consolidation of the problematic beliefs that theoretically 'interlock' to produce an iterative interactional process that constitutes a psychological 'engine' of relapse (Gumley, White & Power, 1999).

This paradigm may be particularly useful for understanding the self-perpetuating problems in David's case, by linking his enduring self-schema, and interpersonal schema, regarding 'powerlessness' to his tendency to 'jump to conclusions' of a paranoid nature, especially when reality testing was further compromised through use of cannabis. His self-schema were further confirmed when he elicited criticism and control from others in response to impulsive and desperate attempts to assert himself. However, David's hypervigilance for control remained a significant challenge for the treating team in maintaining a consistent engagement with him.

Over a period of several months James and his case manager were able to build upon their initial formulation of his risk of relapse. Together they identified his propensity to scan his interpersonal world for 'clues to his success or failure in relationships'. James and his case manger explored his tendency to label subtle shifts in relationships as a marker of his 'lack of social skills' which preceded an 'automatic' withdrawal and preoccupation with how others perceived him. This led to a discussion about the limits of measuring his own 'success' in relationships and opened up discussion about paying more attention to his 'satisfaction' with relationships. Behavioural experiments were also designed, involving approaching rather than avoiding others during periods of perceived tension. Low-dose maintenance medication was linked with his perception of increased social ease, although a trial period with no medication was also planned after several further months of stabilization, with the understanding that, in the interim, James should feel free to discuss changes to his perceived cost/benefit balance of maintenance medication.

The treating team remained aware of the possibility of relapse in James's case. Rates of relapse following first-episode psychosis were openly discussed with him, to circumvent 'catastrophization' of relapse and to facilitate 'permission' in the future to disclose changes in mental state. A written plan detailed his possible idiosyncratic early warning signs and likely changes to his treatment in the advent of relapse were also detailed in the plan. This deepened rapport and was associated with a reduced fear of illness and a greater optimism for the future.

SUMMARY AND CONCLUSIONS

In summary, a range of interventions has been found to be significantly effective in reducing the relapse rate in established schizophrenia. However, the number of studies with a focus specifically on prevention of first relapse remains small, although the available findings suggest that first-relapse prevention packages should be age and stage-of-illness appropriate, with a heavy reliance upon education and family-based interventions. In addition, specific attention needs to be given to issues of substance abuse and compliance with medication in the first-episode group, although treatment outcome data on these issues are not yet available. Finally, first-relapse prevention strategies should ideally be nested within a youth-friendly service environment, which stimulates the forging of collaborative relationships between therapists and the young person (McGorry, 1996).

REFERENCES

Agarwal, M.R., Sharma, V.K., Kumar, K. & Lowe, D. (1998). Non-compliance with treatment in patients suffering from schizophrenia: A study to evaluate possible contributing factors. *International Journal of Social Psychiatry*, **44**, 92–106.

APA (1987). *Diagnostic and Statistical Manual of Mental Disorders* (3rd edn, revised). Washington, DC: American Psychiatric Association.

Bebbington, P. & Kuipers, L. (1994). The predictive utility of expressed emotion in schizophrenia: An aggregate analysis. *Psychological Medicine*, **24**, 707–718.

Birchwood, M. & Spencer, E. (2001). Early intervention in psychotic relapse. *Clinical Psychology Review*, **21**, 1211–1226.

Birchwood, M., Mason, R., Macmillan, F. & Healy, J. (1993). Depression, demoralisation, and control over psychotic illness: A comparison of depressed and non-depressed patients with a chronic psychosis. *Psychological Medicine*, **23**, 387–395.

Bronwell, K.D., Marlatt, G.A., Lichtenstein, E. & Wilson, G.T. (1986). Understanding and preventing relapse. *American Psychologist*, **41**, 765–782.

Brown, G.W. & Harris, T. (1978). *Social Origins of Depression: A Study of Psychiatric Disorder in Women*. London: Tavistock.

Corrigan, P.W., Liberman, R.P. & Engel, J.D. (1990). From non-compliance to collaboration in the treatment of schizophrenia. *Hospital and Community Psychiatry*, **41**, 1203–1211.

Cramer, J.A. & Rosenheck, R. (1998). Compliance with medication regimes for mental and physical disorders. *Psychiatric Services*, **49**, 196–201.

Crow, T.J., Macmillan, J.F., Johnstone, A.L. & Johnstone, E.C. (1986). The Northwick Park study of first episodes of schizophrenia, II. A randomized controlled trial of prophylactic neuroleptic treatment. *British Journal of Psychiatry*, **148**, 120–127.

Das, M.K., Kulhara, P.L. & Verma, S.K. (1997). Life events preceding relapse of schizophrenia. *International Journal of Social Psychiatry*, **43**, 56–63.

Day, J.C. & Bentall, R.P. (1996). Neuroleptic medication and the psychosocial treatment of psychotic symptoms: Some neglected issues. In G. Haddock & P.D. Slade (Eds), *Cognitive-Behavioural Interventions with Psychotic Disorders* (pp. 235–264). London: Routledge.

Eaton, W.E., Thara, R., Federman, E. & Tien, A. (1998). Remission and relapse in schizophrenia: The Madras longitudinal study. *Journal of Nervous and Mental Disease*, **186**, 357–363.

Edwards, J. & McGorry, P.D. (2002). *Implementing Early Intervention in Psychosis*. London: Martin Dunitz.

Edwards, J.E., Harris, M. & Herman, A. (2002). The Early Psychosis Prevention and Intervention Centre. In C. Ogura (Ed.), *Recent Advances in Early Intervention and Prevention in Psychiatric Disorders*. Tokyo: Seiwa Shoten Publishers.

Edwards, J.E., Hinton, M., Elkins, K. & Athanasopolous, O. (2002). Cannabis and first-episode psychosis: The CAP Project. In H. Graham, K. Mueser, M. Birchwood & A. Copello (Eds), *Substance Misuse in Psychosis: Approaches to Treatment and Service Delivery* (pp. 283–304). Chichester: John Wiley & Sons.

EPPIC (2002). *Cannabis and Psychosis: An Early Psychosis Treatment Manual and Video*. Melbourne: EPPIC.

EPPIC (Producer) (1994). *A Stitch in Time: Psychosis... Get Help Early—Information Kit* [Video and information kit]. (Available from EPPIC Statewide Services, Locked Bag. Parkville, Vic., Australia 3052).

Falloon, I.R. (1983). Relapse in schizophrenia: A review of the concept and its definitions. *Psychological Medicine*, **13**, 469–477.

Falloon, I.R. (1984). Relapse: A reappraisal of assessment of outcome in schizophrenia. *Schizophrenia Bulletin*, **10**, 293–299.

Fitzgerald, P.B. (2001). The role of early warning symptoms in the detection and prevention of relapse in schizophrenia. *Australian and New Zealand Journal of Psychiatry*, **35**, 758–764.

Fowler, D. (2000). Psychological formulation of early episodes of psychosis: A cognitive approach. In M. Birchwood, D. Fowler & C. Jackson (Eds), *Early Intervention in Psychosis* (pp. 101–127). Chichester: John Wiley & Sons.

Gilbert, P.L., Harris, M.J., McAdams, L. & Jeste, D.V. (1995). Neuroleptic withdrawal in schizophrenic patients: A review of the literature. *Archives of General Psychiatry*, **52**, 173–188.

Gitlin, M., Nuechterlein, K., Subotnik, K.L., Ventura, J., Mintz, J., Fogelson, D.L., Bartzokis, G. & Aravagiri, M. (2001). Clinical outcome following neuroleptic discontinuation in patients with remitted recent-onset schizophrenia. *American Journal of Psychiatry*, **158**, 1835–1842.

Glazer, W.M. (1993). Psychotic relapse: A multisystems perspective. *Journal of Clinical Psychiatry*, **54** (Suppl.), 3–4.

Gleeson, J.F. (2001). *Early signs and risk factors for relapse in early psychosis*. Unpublished PhD thesis, University of Melbourne, Australia.

Gleeson, J.F., Jackson, H.J., Stavely, H. & Burnett, P. (1999). Family intervention in early psychosis. In P.D. McGorry & H.J. Jackson (Eds), *The Recognition and Management of Early Psychosis: A Preventive Approach* (pp. 376–406). Cambridge: Cambridge University Press.

Gray, R., Wykes, T. & Gournay, K. (2002). From compliance to concordance: A review of the literature on interventions to enhance compliance with antipsychotic medication. *Journal of Psychiatric and Mental Health Nursing*, **9**, 277–284.

Greenfield, S.F., Strakowski, S.M., Tohen, M., Batson, S.C. & Kolbrener, M.C. (1994). Childhood abuse in first-episode psychosis. *British Journal of Psychiatry*, **165**, 831–834.

Gumley, A.I. & Power, K.G. (2000). Is targeting cognitive therapy during relapse in psychosis feasible? *Behavioural and Cognitive Psychotherapy*, **28**, 161–174.

Gumley, A., White, C.A. & Power, K. (1999). An interacting cognitive subsystems model of relapse and the course of psychosis. *Clinical Psychology and Psychotherapy*, **6**, 261–278.

Gumley, A., O'Grady, M., McNay, L., Reilly, J., Power, K. & Norrie, J. (2003). Early intervention for relapse in schizophrenia: Results of a 12-month randomized controlled trial of cognitive behavioural therapy. *Psychological Medicine*, **33**, 419–431.

Healey, A., Knapp, M., Astin, J., Beecham, J., Kemp, R., Kirov, G. & David, A. (1998). Cost-effectiveness evaluation of compliance therapy for people with psychosis. *British Journal of Psychiatry*, **172**, 420–424.

Herrmann-Doig, T., Maude, D. & Edwards, J. (2003). *Systematic Treatment of Persistent Psychosis: A Psychological Approach to Facilitating Recovery in Young People with First Episode Psychosis.* London: Martin Dunitz.

Herz, M.I. & Lamberti, J.S. (1995). Prodromal symptoms and relapse in schizophrenia. *Schizophrenia Bulletin*, **21**, 541–551.

Hogarty, G., Kornblith, S., Greenwald, D., DiBarry, A., Cooley, S., Flesher, S., Reiss, D., Carter, M. & Ulrich, R. (1995). Personal therapy: A disorder-relevant psychotherapy for schizophrenia. *Schizophrenia Bulletin*, **21**, 379–393.

Hughes, J.M., Michell, P.A. & Ramson, W.S. (Eds) (1992). *The Australian Concise Oxford Dictionary.* South Melbourne: Oxford University Press.

Hulbert, C.A., Jackson, H.J. & McGorry, P.D. (1996). Relationship between personality and course and outcome in early psychosis: A review of the literature. *Clinical Psychology Review*, **16**, 707–727.

Hultman, C.M., Weiselgren, I. & Ohman, A. (1997). Relationship between social support, social coping and life events in the relapse of schizophrenic patients. *Scandinavian Journal of Psychology*, **38**, 3–13.

Kane, J.M., Rifkin, A., Quitkin, F., Nayak, D. & Ramos-Lorenzi, J. (1982). Fluphenazine versus placebo in patients with remitted, acute first-episode schizophrenia. *Archives of General Psychiatry*, **39**, 70–73.

Kemp, R., Kirov, G., Everitt, B., Hayward, P. & David, A. (1998). Randomised controlled trial of compliance therapy. *British Journal of Psychiatry*, **172**, 413–419.

Kissling, W. (1992). Ideal and reality of neuroleptic relapse prevention. *British Journal of Psychiatry*, **161** (Suppl. 18), 133–139.

Lader, M. (1995). What is relapse in schizophrenia? *International Clinical Psychopharmacology*, **9** (Suppl. 5), 5–9.

Lieberman, J., Jody, D. & Geisler, S. (1993). Time course and biological correlates of treatment response in first-episode schizophrenia. *Journal of Clinical Psychiatry*, **57**, 5–9.

Lieberman, J.A., Perkins, D., Belger, A., Chakos, M., Jarkog, F., Boteva, K. & Gilmore, J. (2001). The early stages of schizophrenia: Speculations on pathogenesis, pathophysiology, and therapeutic approaches. *Biological Psychiatry*, **50**, 884–897.

Lincoln, C.V. & McGorry, P.D. (1995). Who cares? Pathways to psychiatric care for young people experiencing a first episode of psychosis. *Psychiatric Services*, **46**, 1166–1171.

Linszen, D.H., Dingemans, P.M. & Lenior, M.E. (1994). Cannabis abuse and the course of recent onset schizophrenic disorders. *Archives of General Psychiatry*, **51**, 273–279.

Linszen, D.H., Dingemans, P.M., Lenior, M.E., Nugter, M.A., Scholte, W.F. & Van der Does, A. J.W. (1994). Relapse criteria in schizophrenic disorders: Different perspectives. *Psychiatry Research*, **54**, 273–281.

Linszen, D., Dingemans, P., Van der Does, J.W., Nugter, A., Scholte, P., Lenior, R. & Golstein, M.J. (1996). Treatment, expressed emotion and relapse in recent onset schizophrenic disorders. *Psychological Medicine*, **26**, 333–342.

Linszen, D., Lenior, M., de Hann, L., Dingemans, P. & Gersons, B. (1998). Early intervention, untreated psychosis and the course of early schizophrenia. *British Journal of Psychiatry*, **172** (Suppl. 33), 84–89.

MacNalty, A.S. (1980). *Butterworths Medical Dictionary* (2nd edn). London: Butterworth & Co.

McCrae, R.R. & Costa, P.T. (1997). Personality trait structure as a human universal. *American Psychologist*, **52**, 509–516.

Marder, S.R. (1999). Antipsychotic drugs and relapse prevention. *Schizophrenia Research*, **35**, S87–S92.

Mari, J.J. & Streiner, D.L. (1994). An overview of family interventions and relapse on schizophrenia: Meta-analysis of research findings. *Psychological Medicine*, **24**, 565–578.

McGlashan, T.H., Levy, S.T. & Carpenter, W.T. (1975). Integration and sealing over: Clinically distinct recovery styles from schizophrenia. *Archives of General Psychiatry*, **32**, 1269–1272.

McGorry, P.D. (1996). The Centre for Young People's Mental Health: Blending epidemiology and developmental psychiatry. *Australasian Psychiatry*, **4**, 243–247.

McGorry, P.D. & McConville, S.B. (1999). Insight in psychosis: An elusive target. *Comprehensive Psychiatry*, **40**, 131–142.

McPhillips, M. & Sensky, T. (1998). Coercion, adherence or collaboration? Influences on compliance with medication. In T. Wykes, N. Tarrier & S. Lewis (Eds), *Outcome and Innovation in Psychological Treatment of Schizophrenia* (pp. 161–177). Chichester: John Wiley & Sons.

Miller, W.R. & Rollnick, S. (1991). *Motivational Interviewing: Preparing People to Change Addictive Behaviour*. New York: Guilford Press.

Norman, R.M.G. & Malla, A.K. (1993). Stressful life events and schizophrenia, I: A review of the research. *British Journal of Psychiatry*, **162**, 161–166.

Nuechterlein, K.H., Dawson, M.E., Gitlin, M., Ventura, J., Goldstein, M.J., Snyder, K.S., Yee, L.M. & Mintz, J. (1992). Developmental processes in schizophrenic disorders: Longitudinal studies of vulnerability and stress. *Schizophrenia Bulletin*, **18**, 387–424.

Overall, J.E. & Gorham, D.R. (1962). The Brief Psychiatric Rating Scale. *Psychiatric Reports*, **10**, 799–812.

Pallanti, S., Quercioli, L. & Pazzagli, A. (1997). Relapse in young paranoid schizophrenic patients: A prospective study of stressful life events, P300 measures, and coping. *American Journal of Psychiatry*, **154**, 792–798.

Parashos, I.A., Xiromeritis, K., Zoumbou, V., Stamouli, S. & Theodotou, R. (2000). The problem of non-compliance in schizophrenia: Opinions of patients and their relatives. *International Journal of Psychiatry in Clinical Practice*, **4**, 147–150.

Patterson, P., Birchwood, M. & Cochrane, R. (2000). Preventing the entrenchment of high expressed emotion in first episode psychosis: Early developmental attachment pathways. *Australian and New Zealand Journal of Psychiatry*, **34** (Suppl.), S191–S197.

Pinikahana, J., Happell, B., Taylor, M. & Keks, N.A. (2002). Exploring the complexity of compliance in schizophrenia. *Issues in Mental Health Nursing*, **23**, 513–528.

Ram, R., Bromet, E.J, Eaton, W.W., Pato, C. & Schwartz, J.E. (1992). The natural course of schizophrenia: A review of first-admission studies. *Schizophrenia Bulletin*, **18**, 185–207.

Read, J. (1997). Child abuse and psychosis: A literature review and implications for professional practice. *Professsional Psychology: Research and Practice*, **28**, 448–456.

Reid, A., Lynskey, M. & Copeland, J. (2000). Cannabis use among Australian adolescents: Findings of the 1998 National Drug Strategy household survey. *Australian and New Zealand Journal of Public Health*, **24**, 596–602.

Robinson, D., Woerner, M.G., Alvir, J., Bilder, R., Goldman, R., Geisler, S., Koreen, A., Sheitman, B., Chakos, M., Mayerhoff, D. & Lieberman, J.A. (1999). Predictors of relapse following response from a first episode of schizophrenia or schizoaffective disorder. *Archives of General Psychiatry*, **56**, 241–247.

Scottish Schizophrenia Research Group (1992). The Scottish first episode schizophrenia study VIII. Five year follow-up: Clinical and psychosocial findings. *British Journal of Psychiatry*, **161**, 496–500.

Shepherd, M., Watt, D., Falloon, I. & Smeeton, N. (1989). The natural history of schizophrenia: A five year follow up study of outcome and prediction in a representative sample of schizophrenics, *Psychological Medicine Monograph* (15).

Spitzer, R.L., Endicott, J. & Robins, E. (1978). Research diagnostic criteria. *Archives of General Psychiatry*, **35**, 773–782.

Süllwold, L. & Huber, G. (1986). *Schizophrene Basisstörungen*. Berlin: Springer-Verlag.

Ventura, J., Nuechterlein, K.H., Hardesty, J.P. & Gitlin, M. (1992). Life events and schizophrenic relapse after withdrawal of medication. *British Journal of Psychiatry*, **161**, 615–620.

Ventura, J., Nuechterlein, K.H., Lukoff, D. & Hardesty, J. (1989). A prospective study of stressful life events and schizophrenic relapse. *Journal of Abnormal Psychology*, **98**, 407–411.

Wiersma, D., Nienhuis, F.J., Sloof, C.J. & Giel, R. (1998). Natural course of schizophrenic disorders: A 15-year follow-up of a Dutch incidence cohort. *Schizophrenia Bulletin*, **24**, 75–85.

Wing, J.K., Cooper, J.E. & Sartorius, N. (1974). *Measurement and Classification of Psychiatric Symptoms—An Instruction Manual for the PSE and CATEGO Program*. Cambridge: Cambridge University Press.

Zhang, M., Wang, M., Li, J. & Phillips, M.R. (1994). Randomised-control trial of family interventions for 78 first-episode male schizophrenic patients: An 18 month study in Suzhou, Jiamgsu. *British Journal of Psychiatry*, **156** (Suppl. 24), 96–102.

10 Suicide Prevention in Early Psychosis

PADDY POWER
South London and Maudsley NHS Trust, UK

INTRODUCTION

One of the most tragic consequences of psychotic disorders such as schizophrenia is suicide. Ten percent of people with schizophrenia eventually commit suicide (Brown, 1997; Siris, 2001). Indeed, contrary to popular opinion, people with schizophrenia are far more likely to injure or kill themselves than they are to hurt others. The first-episode psychosis population pose a major concern as suicide is much more likely during the early course of schizophrenia (Westermeyer, Harrow & Marengo, 1991), particularly during the first few years after diagnosis (Brown, 1997; Mortensen & Juel, 1993). Furthermore, when schizophrenia develops early in young people, patients are at especially high risk of suicide: in one follow-up study of adolescent onset schizophrenia, 21.5% of males committed suicide (Krausz, Muller-Thomsen & Maasen, 1995).

However, there is encouraging evidence that early intervention can reduce this risk (Power et al., in press; McGorry, Henry & Power, 1998). This chapter will review the literature on suicide and early psychosis and examine interventions that have shown promising results in suicide prevention in psychosis. Some of these interventions have been developed by clinicians at the Early Psychosis Prevention and Intervention Centre (EPPIC) in Melbourne (Power et al., 2003). One particular psychological treatment is called the LifeSPAN Therapy and this has been evaluated in a randomized-controlled trial (Power et al., 2003).

SUICIDE PATTERNS IN FIRST-EPISODE PSYCHOSIS

In clinical practice there are a number of common misconceptions about the relationship between suicide and psychosis. To confirm this, consider the following questions about suicide in psychosis and check your responses with the information described in the remainder of the chapter.

- What percentage of first-episode patients experience suicide ideation, plans, and attempts?
- Are command hallucinations the most common association with suicide attempts?
- Do chronic symptoms heighten the risk of suicide?
- When are first-episode psychosis patients most at risk of suicide?

Psychological Interventions in Early Psychosis
Edited by J.F.M. Gleeson and P.D. McGorry. © 2004 John Wiley & Sons, Ltd.

- Is there any evidence that treatments can reduce the risk of suicide?
- Are people in the prodrome of first-episode psychosis at risk of suicide?

An alarmingly high proportion of first-episode psychosis patients are suicidal by the time they make contact with mental health services (Nordentoft et al., 2002). Studies reveal that at least 50% of first-episode psychosis patients have experienced recent thoughts of suicide and that about 25% have already made a suicide attempt by the time of first contact (Nordentoft et al., 2002). Surprisingly, these features are just as prevalent among patients in the prodromal phase before their first episode of psychosis. In a survey of 25 patients attending a clinic (PACE clinic) for those at ultra-high risk of psychosis, Adlard (1997) found that 20 of the patients (90%) had experienced suicide ideation in the previous 6 months, and 25% had already made an attempt.

Studies suggest that approximately 2% of first-episode psychosis patients will commit suicide within the first year after contact with mental health services (Krausz, Muller-Thomsen & Maasen, 1995). Given that there is such a high prevalence of suicidality among first-episode psychosis patients, what are the features that identify who is most at risk of later suicide? Are psychotic symptoms the predominant factor? Contrary perhaps to conventional expectations, only approximately 10% of suicide attempts in schizophrenia are associated with command hallucinations (Heila et al., 1997). Commenting voices are no doubt associated with suicide thoughts and attempts and the presence of auditory hallucinations does appear to multiply by a factor of 3 the risk of later suicide ideation and suicide attempts. However, strangely, some psychotic features have an opposite effect on suicide risk. For example, the presence of either delusions of reference, somatic delusions, or thought disorder appears to be associated with a relatively reduced risk of suicide (Nordentoft et al., 2002).

Furthermore, the presence of negative symptoms is also associated with a relatively reduced risk of suicide (Fenton & McGlashan, 1991). This may be due to the disorganizing and demotivating effects of negative symptoms on behaviour. Indeed, patients with schizophrenia are not so much at risk of suicide during the acute psychotic phase but during the post-psychotic early recovery phase (Roy, 1982) when positive symptoms have remitted but patients are struggling to recover normal functional ability and reintegrating back into normal life. A range of aggravating and protective factors may interact in a complex and dynamic way during this phase, influencing the fluctuating nature of suicidality during this critical recovery period (Power, 1999).

When are patients with psychosis most at risk of suicide? Is it during the acute psychotic phase of their illness when a person might be expected to be most distressed by his or her psychotic symptoms? There is no doubt that the acute psychotic phase poses a high-risk period but surprisingly, in schizophrenia, the early recovery phase of remission is the time when most suicides actually occur (Roy, 1982), especially for men (Heila et al., 1997). The same pattern is seen in first-episode psychosis (McGorry, Henry & Power, 1998) and possibly even to a greater extent. To summarize, suicide audits (Power et al., 2003) suggest that (a) the risk of suicide is highest around the period of initial contact with services; (b) it dips sharply during the following weeks of acute treatment but rises quickly again during the post-psychotic phase, reaching a second peak about 5 months after first contact then subsiding by month 8; and (c) it rises again to a lesser extent before dropping off by month 18 (see Figure 10.1). It is not clear to what extent suicide occurs before first contact is made

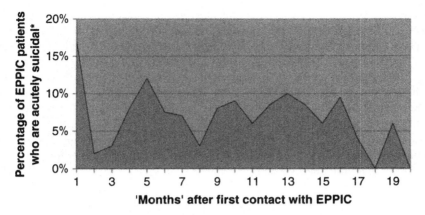

*Ratings: Percentage of EPPIC patients within each monthly period who were rated at the time by
their case managers as being moderately/severely suicidal (score 3–4) within the previous 2 weeks
(using the Suicidality Subscore of the HoNOS scale)

Figure 10.1. Pattern of suicidality during first 20 months of treatment in a first-episode psychosis
population (EPPIC) ($n = 312$)

with services, but undoubtedly a proportion of suicides also occur during this period (given
the high prevalence of suicide attempts before first contact).

Suicide during the acute psychotic phase may result from a wide range of factors, which
are not always directly related to the severity of the psychosis. Patients may kill themselves
by complying with the direct influence of command hallucinations, delusions, or passivity
phenomena (death may not always be intentional, e.g. jumping from a building in the belief
that one can fly). In other patients hallucinations and delusions may cause such severe
distress that death may result from the patient attempting to escape the imagined threats
(again in some cases death may be unintentional, e.g. running out in front of traffic to escape
imagined persecutors). In other acutely psychotic patients, suicide may be a quasi-rational
decision based on a patient's assessment of the situation, e.g. that he or she would be better
off dead than endure a tortured psychotic state any longer. And, finally, in some cases death
may result simply from neglect and dehydration, e.g. Stauder's Lethal Catatonia (Mann
et al., 1986).

Clearly, not all deaths during the acute psychotic phase are true suicides in the strictest
definition of the term. For a legal determination of death by suicide several criteria need to be
fulfilled: the death must be (a) unnatural, (b) self-inflicted and (c) with intent (O'Carroll et al.,
1996). The level of 'intent' is measured by evidence indicating that the person (i) intended to
take the action, (ii) intended to inflict personal harm by that action, (iii) intended to die as a
result of that action, and (iv) at the time of the action, was capable of understanding the likely
consequences of the action. Indeed even in non-psychotic states it may be difficult to be
certain that death was intentional as not infrequently people attempting suicide experience
considerable ambivalence about death and the outcome is heavily dependent on chance and
the lethal nature of the method chosen.

Apart from the acute psychotic phase, why is the early recovery phase so risky? It appears that the high risk of suicide may be more related to the person's individual emotional

and cognitive responses to the psychological and social impact of the illness and relatively unrelated to the acuteness of the primary symptoms of the illness. Suicide ideation and attempts in psychosis are closely associated with the emergence of 'insight' (Amador et al., 1996), 'hopelessness' (Aquilar et al., 1997) and 'depression' (Addington, Addington & Patten, 1998; Power et al., 1998a), features that are particularly evident in the early months after the first episode (Birchwood et al., 2000). Therefore, it is not so surprising that patients become suicidal during this recovery phase, because this is the period when patients emerge from their acute psychosis to face some of the most difficult adjustments to the illness as they struggle to recover normal cognitive and emotional/social functioning. Males appear to take longer than females to regain a premorbid level of functioning after their first episode of psychosis, and little improvement (in negative symptoms) is seen in men within the first year of treatment (Power et al., 1998b). Recovery may be a slow, frustrating and disheartening process for these patients, particularly if they are acutely aware of their own loss in potential.

An additional feature of this recovery phase is, commonly, that acute clinical and social supports are gradually withdrawn in the belief that the high-risk acute phase has abated and the patient might be expected to return to coping with everyday stresses, despite the fragility of his or her functioning and the magnitude of changes to accommodate. It may result in the patient being prematurely returned to the stresses and triggers that precipitated the first episode. The responses of family and social support systems may be crucial during this period. Rejection and alienation may add to a patient's sense of distress, loss, hopelessness and despair.

What is the evidence that psychological and social factors are important determinants of suicide risk during this recovery phase? Higher premorbid IQ, higher socioeconomic background, higher expectations, relatively greater degree of deterioration, loss, stigma, poorer social support and social exclusion/rejection have all been shown to increase the risk of suicide for those with schizophrenia (Siris, 2001).

Which subgroups are at especially high risk of suicide in early psychosis and is it possible to identify the highest risk group from the outset? As with suicide in general it may be the patients who are disadvantaged by multiple comorbid factors who are at greatest risk of suicide.

To give an example from the experience within EPPIC, one of the highest risk subgroups attending the service is the patient with a parent who had committed suicide in the context of a similar illness when the EPPIC patient was approximately 10 years old. Two of the four EPPIC patients (of >1000 cases treated) who committed suicide between 1995 and 1998 had a parent with a history of psychosis and suicide (the two EPPIC patients were unknown to each other). In both cases the parent was of the same gender as the EPPIC patient. Both patients had overwhelming issues to face when becoming aware of their diagnosis. The same pattern has been apparent for other EPPIC patients with similar family histories. Fortunately, their outcome has been less tragic, though not without requiring an intensive level of support and counselling from the service.

SUICIDE PREVENTION IN FIRST-EPISODE PSYCHOSIS

Significant benefits in reducing suicide risk may accrue from better access to more effective treatment of psychosis. In general psychiatric populations, patients who drop out prematurely or who experience an inadequate response to treatment are at greater risk of committing suicide than those who remain engaged in treatment (Dahlsgaard, Beck & Brown, 1998). However, even when treatments are effectively applied, only a few specific pharmacological treatments and cognitive interventions have been shown to reduce the rate of suicide in controlled trials, and their effect appears to be small (Bronisch, 1996; van der Sande et al., 1997a). The same limited effect on suicidality may hold true for pharmacological treatments in schizophrenia (Meltzer, 2002) although a recent large study (InterSePT Study) suggests that clozapine may have a specific effect on reducing suicide ideation (Meltzer, et al., 2003).

There are surprisingly few studies of the effect of psychosocial interventions in suicide prevention (van der Sande et al., 1997a). In their systematic review of randomized-controlled studies ($n = 15$) of psychosocial interventions following suicide attempts, van der Sande et al. (1997a) reported that only two of the studies reported significant reductions in the frequency of subsequent suicide attempts, and this was only with the application of cognitively oriented therapies (Linehan et al., 1991; Salkovkis, Atha & Storer, 1990). The remainder of the studies revealed mixed results (van der Sande et al., 1997a), including their own subsequent study (van der Sande et al., 1997b). None of these studies appears to have involved patients with psychotic disorders despite this group being at particularly high risk of suicide. Also, as yet there are no reports of any of these therapies being adapted for patients with psychotic disorders. Two questions remained unanswered: (a) to what extent do these counselling techniques need to be modified in psychosis, and (b) does this form of counselling reduce the risk of suicide in the subgroup of psychosis patients at particularly high risk?

It is important to note that not all treatments in psychosis may reduce the risk of suicide. Drug treatments carry the potential for side-effects, some of which can induce acutely distressing states of agitation, e.g. akathesia, dysphoria (Meltzer, 2002). Even some standard cognitive interventions for psychosis may aggravate suicidality in suicide prone patients (Power et al., 2003). Enhancing a person's insight into psychosis may carry risks if it is not coupled with enhanced recovery and protection against relapse, hopelessness and depression. Lastly, the effects of dynamics of the service–clinician–patient relationship may be greatly underestimated. Suicides appear to occur frequently around transition phases between services and clinicians. This may be due to a failure to accurately communicate risk between clinicians, but it may also be due to more subtle dynamic factors, e.g. the patient's perception of the service's and clinician's regard for them.

MODELS OF SUICIDE PREVENTION IN FIRST-EPISODE PSYCHOSIS

Given the equivocal and sparse evidence for suicide prevention in psychosis, what should be the elements of a sustainable suicide prevention strategy? Should it be a broad service-wide strategy or should it be a selectively specialized subprogramme targeting those at highest risk? Is it worth the effort and can it be shown to be effective? Is there any point if no suicides have occurred among one's client group? Finally, is there any danger of worsening the problem by some unforeseen and unwanted effect of these strategies?

Unfortunately, there are virtually no service models of suicide prevention in psychosis documented in the literature. The only service model that has been published is the LifeSPAN programme (see description below) at the EPPIC programme in Melbourne, Australia

(Power et al., 2003). The development of this particular service model involved a relatively large investment of staff time and money and was only possible through a research grant. However, a manual (*LifeSPAN Manual*: Power & Bell, in press) has been produced and many of the elements of this model (even the LifeSPAN Therapy) could be introduced into an early intervention service with relatively minimal costs. Alternatively, there are a number of documented suicide risk assessment strategies and protocols that are readily available from a number of early intervention services. These protocols may be seen as relatively simple service-wide suicide prevention strategies. The protocols are generally limited to methods of identifying those at highest risk and to recommendations about closer or more intensive supervision. One of these protocols is available from the Lambeth Early Onset (LEO) service (Edwards & McGorry, 2002) in south London, England, and is called the 'Zoning System' of care (available in both Inpatient and Community-based formats) (Ryrie et al., 1997). Further details are outlined below.

THE LIFESPAN PROGRAM: A SUICIDE PREVENTION PROGRAMME IN EARLY PSYCHOSIS

The LifeSPAN project (Power et al., 2003) was developed by a group of senior clinicians at EPPIC [and the Mental Health Services for Kids and Youth (now ORYGEN Youth Health)] in response to concerns about the suicide rate among the EPPIC population (even though it had already fallen and was relatively low) and the findings of internal suicide audits conducted at EPPIC. The LifeSPAN project group had previously participated in trials of psychological therapies in first-episode psychosis, e.g. COPE therapy (Jackson et al., 1998). The LifeSPAN group recommended the development of a range of suicide prevention strategies at EPPIC that included (a) mechanisms (both clinical and administrative) to enhance the detection and monitoring of these high-suicide-risk patients and (b) a cognitively oriented therapy (LifeSPAN therapy) designed specifically for those at highest risk.

The LifeSPAN group was successful in attracting funding to develop this model of suicide prevention via a 2-year grant (276 000 Australian dollars) for a randomized-controlled trial of the LifeSPAN therapy. It was funded by the Government of Australia as part of the Youth Suicide Prevention Strategy (Power et al., 2003) and operated between 1 January 1997 and 31 March 1999. The programme employed 2.5 effective full-time staff (including two full-time clinical psychologists) at the Mental Health Services for Kids and Youth in Melbourne (now ORYGEN Youth Health). The service provides a catchment-area-based youth mental health service in the Western Region (population 850 000) of Melbourne. The service includes the EPPIC programme: an early psychosis service providing 18-month follow-up for young people (aged 15–25 years) presenting with first-episode psychosis. The LifeSPAN project covered EPPIC as well as the non-EPPIC part of the service (but for the purposes of this chapter only, its involvement in EPPIC is mentioned). EPPIC has an established track record as an optimal model of early intervention in psychosis (McGlashan, 1998). It is a fully integrated service that includes an early detection and crisis assessment team, an acute inpatient unit, an outpatient group programme, assertive follow-up teams and an intensive outreach mobile support team. Its treatments are provided via an individual case management/doctor dyad operating in tandem within an integrated biopsychosocial model and a strong emphasis on low-dose medication, cognitively oriented individual, group and family therapies. Case managers (and many of the doctors) are trained in these therapies and provide them as part of the basic standard clinical care.

Before the introduction of the LifeSPAN project at EPPIC there was neither a standardized protocol of suicide risk assessment nor specific interventions for those identified to be at risk (apart from the norm). However, the standard of clinical training and expertise was high and the level of psychosocial input was also considerably greater than would have been available in generic mental health services. The service had also benefited from recruiting relatively senior clinicians with academic links and from several clinical research projects that often supplemented standard clinical care.

The LifeSPAN project was divided into three phases. The first phase was exploratory and involved an assessment of needs. It included: (a) a suicide audit; (b) surveys of patients' suicidality; (c) surveys of clinicians' routine clinical practice in suicide assessment and risk management; and (d) a re-evaluation of data already available from other studies within EPPIC. The second phase involved the introduction of a routine 'real time' suicide risk-monitoring system into the EPPIC service to identify to clinicians those at highest risk of suicide at any given time. The third phase involved the development, piloting and trial of a suicide prevention therapy (LifeSPAN therapy) for those patients identified to be at highest risk by the risk-monitoring system. This LifeSPAN therapy was evaluated in a randomized-controlled study, with standard clinical care at the service as the comparison condition.

The suicide audit revealed a reduction in the rate of suicide among patients attending the service in comparison to the pre-EPPIC service. Nine (4.25%) first-episode psychosis patients committed suicide (within 2 years of treatment) among the pre-EPPIC cohort of 200 patients in comparison to eight (0.4%) patients in the EPPIC cohort of 1820 patients (Power et al., 2003). A more detailed analysis of the characteristics of the patients who committed suicide before 1998 is reported by McGorry, Henry and Power (1998).

The clinical audit of suicidality involved clinician rating of all patients ($n = 312$) attending the EPPIC service using data from Health of the Nation Outcome Scale (HoNOS) ratings (Wing, 1994) in the study (MHCaSC) at the Centre in 1996 (Buckingham et al., 1998). This data not only provided a more accurate cross-sectional measure of suicidality in those attending the service but identified the phase when EPPIC patients were most at risk. The results revealed an unexpectedly high rate of suicidality with 34% of EPPIC patients being rated as mildly suicidal (score of 1 or 2 on the HoNOS) and 12% moderate/severely suicidal (score of 3 or 4 on HoNOS) within the previous 2 weeks. Significant positive correlations were found between patients' suicidality ratings and their concurrent ratings on HoNOS items of psychosis, depression and substance abuse. The associations were strongest for depression and suicidality scores and weakest for substance use and suicidality (Power et al., 2003). When the duration of contact with EPPIC was analysed, the periods of highest ratings of suicidality were the initial 2 weeks of contact with the service, which peaked again in month 5 afterwards (see Figure 10.1). This confirmed the similar pattern with completed suicides that was seen in the EPPIC suicide audit.

Surveys of EPPIC clinicians' routine clinical practice in suicide assessment and risk management, which included a *concept mapping* exercise (Trochim, 1989), found that EPPIC clinicians perceived that they were able to effectively assess when patients are at risk of suicide, but less able to address the underlying psychological factors. Clinicians rated social support as an important protective factor against suicide; however, they believed that the service did not adequately address this particular need (Power et al., 2003).

Re-evaluation of the effect of existing cognitive-behavioural therapy (CBT) studies at EPPIC suggested that these interventions did not effectively address suicidality in the therapy modules and, indeed, a surprising result from one of the therapy trials even suggested that COPE therapy might be associated with a poorer improvement in suicidality compared to the standard care at the service (Jackson et al., 1998).

The second phase of the LifeSPAN project involved the introduction of a routine suicide risk-monitoring system. After piloting several options, a simple system was introduced that involved an initial suicide risk assessment (using an adapted questionnaire) by clinicians of patients at first contact with the service, followed by subsequent monitoring of patients' suicide risk by routine monthly ratings by case managers using the suicidality item of the Brief Psychiatric Rating Scale (BPRS; Ventura et al., 1993). These ratings were also made at any time if a patient indicated an immediate risk of suicide behaviour. High-risk patients (i.e. with a score of 4 or more on the Expanded Version of the BPRS suicidality subscore) attending the service were identified by this system and were referred and considered for LifeSPAN therapy. However, the shortcoming of this system was that it required continual promotion by the LifeSPAN project staff and the results of the measures only determined whether patients were referred for the LifeSPAN therapy. It did not otherwise influence the service's treatment or patient management protocols. Nor did it provide useful immediate feedback to the multidisciplinary clinical teams regarding patients who were most at risk at any given time. Once the LifeSPAN project finished, the suicide risk identification and monitoring system was discontinued. Essentially it did little to aid clinical practice and was probably perceived as a research tool which did not result in access to extra services for the patient.

The third phase of the LifeSPAN project was the development, piloting, trial and evaluation of the suicide prevention therapy (LifeSPAN therapy). This is described in more detail in the *LifeSPAN Manual* and in an article by Power et al. (2003). LifeSPAN therapy is an individual 10-session cognitive-oriented therapy (LifeSPAN therapy) specifically designed for acutely suicidal young people with psychotic disorders. The therapy drew upon components from other CBT interventions at EPPIC, e.g. Cognitively-Oriented Therapy for Early Psychosis (COPE; Jackson et al., 1998), and suicide prevention manuals such as *Choosing to Live* (Ellis & Newman, 1996) and *Cognitive Therapy of Suicide Behaviour: A Manual for Treatment* (Freeman & Reinecke, 1993). The therapy was provided by one of the project's two clinical psychologists who were independent of the rest of the EPPIC service. There are four phases in the therapy: an initial engagement phase, a suicide risk assessment/formulation phase, a cognitive modules phase, and the final closure/handover phase. The initial two phases aim at a detailed and collaborative risk assessment/formulation of the patient's suicidality, identifying the target foci for the next phase of the therapy. The third phase combines eight modules. The core module further addresses a functional analysis of the patient's suicidality, the rationale for suicide, the quality of hopelessness, and the reasons for living. The additional modules included: problem-solving training, psychoeducation for psychosis, emotional pain tolerance, stress management, self-esteem, help-seeking and social skills training. The selection of a particular combination of the modules is determined by the individual risk assessment/formulation. At the end of the LifeSPAN Therapy the risk formulation and care plan was formally handed over to the case manager in a final joint session with both clinicians and the patient (Power & Bell, in press).

After the initial pilot and development phase of the LifeSPAN therapy, 92 acutely suicidal EPPIC patients were referred to the trial proper of LifeSPAN therapy. Thirty-six of these patients were unwilling (or unable to consent) to participate in the study with the remaining 56 patients agreeing to be randomized (31 into the LifeSPAN therapy group and 25 into the control standard treatment group). Ten of the 31 patients in the LifeSPAN therapy group dropped out before completing the minimum requirement of eight sessions of therapy. This left 21 EPPIC patients who completed the required minimum number of sessions of LifeSPAN therapy.

The LifeSPAN therapists found that engaging the first-episode psychosis group in a verbal dialogue about their suicidality was far more challenging than was the case with a separate non-psychotic group who were recruited from outside EPPIC (in ORYGEN's other programmes). Some of the first-episode psychosis patients lacked the capacity to verbalize or conceptualize their feelings. Others were so withdrawn, guarded, or had residual psychotic features that their concentration or interpretation of the content of sessions was markedly impaired. Perhaps the patients who benefited most were those with clear psychological factors contributing to their post-psychotic depression. These depressive features were not solely a response to the impact of their illness, as one of the striking observations in the LifeSPAN group was the high prevalence of comorbid and premorbid conditions. These comorbid factors posed somewhat independent risk factors for suicide, e.g. histories of social deprivations, poor premorbid functioning, low self-esteem, traumas, sexual abuse, substance use, etc., which contributed partly to the onset of psychosis. Tackling these issues during the fragile recovery phase of psychosis required considerable skill and judgement in balancing the need to acknowledge the issues without overwhelming the person with memories and emotions that could not be tolerated.

Case examples: LifeSPAN

The first case illustrates the complex comorbid factors involved (identifying characteristics have been altered to maintain anonymity).

Peter, who was a 23-year-old man, was referred for LifeSPAN therapy following a suicide attempt approximately 3 months after commencing treatment for paranoid psychosis. He was now acutely depressed and suicidal. He had a history of several other serious suicide attempts several years before his first contact with services. Peter's recent prolonged episode of paranoid psychosis had emerged in the context of heavy marijuana and intermittent alcohol abuse. His drug use had become entrenched early in his teens during a difficult adjustment period after he commenced secondary education and his parents separated. His psychosocial development was equally tragic and he struggled to develop any meaningful relationships beyond one male drug user. This friend subsequently hung himself when the patient was 19 years of age (the patient was the last person to see him hours before his death). By age 20 the patient had been imprisoned briefly for petty criminal activity related to his drug use and had been raped while in jail. When referred to the LifeSPAN therapy after discharge from the EPPIC Inpatient Unit, he had become profoundly depressed, withdrawn, preoccupied, hopeless and suicidal. Antidepressant medication appeared to make little difference. His acute bizarre paranoid psychotic symptoms had remitted with antipsychotic treatment and he had ceased his drug use. However, his cognitive functioning remained impaired and he was experiencing a range of negative-like symptoms. Initially in the LifeSPAN therapy interviews he was a passive participant in sessions. He had great difficulties in articulating his feelings of guilt and worthlessness. In the patient's mind the episode of psychosis confirmed his negative assumptions about himself and his future, reinforcing his determination to end his life. However, it was the long-standing issues that predated the psychosis that proved far more difficult to manage and it was only after several sessions that it was possible to gradually approach the very traumatic nature of the underlying experiences. It was only near the end of the 10 LifeSPAN sessions that it was possible to begin to address these issues at a cognitive level and to help him to visualize a more hopeful future—one in which some of his difficulties might be resolved. At the end of the LifeSPAN sessions his case manager assumed the role of follow-up therapist after attending Peter's final session with the LifeSPAN therapist. He continued to make slow but steady progress over the subsequent months.

The second case example illustrates how even entrenched patterns of cognitions and behaviour can be successfully changed within a relative small number of focused sessions.

John was an 18-year-old unemployed man, living with his parents and two siblings. He was referred to LifeSPAN by his EPPIC case manager because of command auditory hallucinations to kill himself. John had been referred to EPPIC 10 months previously with a history of auditory and visual hallucinations, grossly disorganized behaviour and speech, and social withdrawal. He reported multiple male voices. They sometimes screamed comments such as 'you're a loser', 'freak', 'big fat failure'. Before his referral to LifeSPAN, John had been admitted to the EPPIC Inpatient Unit a total of seven times with suicide ideation associated with these derogatory auditory hallucinations.

John had a long history of 'voices' since age 10 and a more recent history of alcohol dependence. He had started to self-harm in late childhood in the context of social, emotional and physical hardships associated with a physical birth defect. John had several unsuccessful operations to rectify this defect. A month before his referral to EPPIC he had undergone one final operation.

John reported frequent and often violent conflict within the family. He believed that his siblings were unsupportive and despised him because of his physical disability. He said his father had left work to care for him and John felt very dependent on him for any major decisions. John had a long-standing sense of inadequacy. He experienced intense anxiety and loss of control when faced with challenging situations. His subsequent perceived 'failures' and avoidance would result in distressing guilt and self-deprecating ruminations that, in their more intense form, took on the full characteristics of derogatory and command hallucinations. His suicide ideation would arise in this context of overwhelming voices, anger, guilt, despair, self-loathing and hopelessness, often resulting in self-harm. His pattern of suicidal behaviour was further maintained by his difficulty in engaging appropriate help-seeking strategies.

In the LifeSPAN sessions, John engaged well, despite his reported difficulties. He was encouraged by the LifeSPAN therapist to identify and label his feelings and thoughts in distressing situations that led to suicidal thinking and command hallucinations. However, his ambivalence about discussing emotional issues made work slow. Nevertheless, he made good progress in identifying some of these warning signs and developed a collaborative formulation of his suicidality. Previous successful attempts to avoid acting on his suicide ideation were also examined. Elements that had helped him previously were identified and he was encouraged to develop future plans for dealing with these situations. John practised and had some early success with behavioural strategies for managing his suicidality. Other strengths in his coping repertoire were reinforced. John gained confidence in managing otherwise very stressful situations and experiences.

A number of other issues were explored in the LifeSPAN sessions and recommendations were subsequently made to John's treating team. This included his sense of ambivalence and dependence on his father. He was encouraged to consider the benefits of alternative options to diffuse tensions within the family without resorting to hospitalization. Family therapy was recommended by the LifeSPAN therapist to address these issues when the case was handed over to John's treating team. When the LifeSPAN therapist reviewed John's case a year later, John had maintained the gains evident at the end of his LifeSPAN sessions. His suicidality had improved and he had not been rehospitalized.

LifeSPAN Trial Results

The impact of LifeSPAN therapy was evaluated by comparing the outcome of the completers of the therapy group ($n = 21$) versus the control group (standard care) ($n = 21$). Both the therapy and control groups improved progressively over time (initial rating, 10 weeks, and final ratings at 6-month follow-up) on ratings of the Suicide Ideation Questionnaire (SIQ) and the number of suicide attempts (in the 10 weeks prior to each time point) and general ratings of psychopathology (BPRS) (a large number of other ratings were employed but are not reported here). Unfortunately, no significant differences were found between the treatment and control groups in the relative change in these ratings between each time point, although the treatment group did show a trend towards a larger average drop in the SIQ score. The LifeSPAN therapy group (compared to the control group) demonstrated significantly better improvements (using Analysis of Covariance) in scores in the Beck Hopelessness Scale (BHS) at 6 months and at 10 weeks ($p = 0.032$) and at 6 months ($p = 0.014$) and in Quality of Life Scores at 10 weeks ($p = 0.001$) and 6-month follow-up ($p = 0.014$). A positive but moderate (Pearson correlation 0.5–0.7) association was found between the BHS score and the SIQ score at each of the three time points. There was only a weak association between the SIQ score and the number of suicide attempts (in the previous 10 weeks) (Power et al., 2003).

Tragically, two patients in the LifeSPAN study committed suicide. One patient was in the therapy group and the other was in the control group. No other patients committed suicide at EPPIC during the study period (1997–1999). Both patients were outpatients at the time of their suicides. They had been in treatment at EPPIC for between 29 and 35 weeks respectively and committed suicide several weeks before the 6-month LifeSPAN follow-up rating. Both patients had been making reasonably good recoveries but had experienced psychosocial setbacks shortly before their suicides. The two patients had made numerous and serious suicide attempts before their referral to the LifeSPAN study.

The LifeSPAN study was perhaps an overly ambitious project and had many limitations. A number of positive effects of the therapy were observed; and although the analysis was hampered by the relatively small numbers in the trial, it remains an important endeavour, and serves as a useful model on which to develop and evaluate other suicide prevention strategies. A manual has been completed outlining the steps and components of the LifeSPAN therapy and is available from EPPIC.

THE ZONING SYSTEM OF CARE: A PROTOCOL FOR RISK MANAGEMENT

This system (Ryrie et al., 1997) is one of a number of risk management systems available in mental health services but is recommended because of its ease of administration and usefulness in clinical practice. It has been successfully introduced in three teams (acute inpatients, community case management team, and crisis assessment team) within the Lambeth Early Onset (LEO) service in London, England. This is a first-episode psychosis service (Edwards & McGorry, 2002; Garety & Jolley, 2000) based in the Brixton area of south London (population 270 000) and modelled on the EPPIC programme. Since the LEO service began 3 years ago there have been no suicides among its patients.

The zoning system provides 'real time' feedback to all the service's clinicians to alert to which of the patients attending their team are most at risk at any given time. Patients are assessed into three categories of risk (low = green, moderate = amber, high = red) (Ryrie et al., 1997). This assessment is supplemented by a risk assessment questionnaire undertaken when the team makes initial contact with the patient. All new patients to a team are placed in the red zone until the multidisciplinary team decides otherwise at one of its regular clinical review meetings. A highly visible board/chart is kept in each team base with a list of the team's patients in each of the three zones. Any clinician may move a patient up into a higher risk zone at any time if there is concern about the patient, but a patient zone may not be downgraded until the team has made a decision to do so at its clinical review meeting. The zoning system is linked to a patient management protocol that determines the intensity of supervision and contact, e.g. in the community a patient in the red zone may receive daily contact from staff while a patient in the red zone on the inpatient unit must have a nurse to accompany them on leave. The system also determines the frequency of clinical reviews of a patient and means that high-risk-zone patients are frequently evaluated and discussed by the team. It is also a useful audit and management tool for evaluating service demand, incidents, caseloads, and staffing levels. Copies of the protocol are available from the LEO service upon request.[*]

CONCLUSIONS

The prevalence of suicide ideation and behaviours in first-episode psychosis is very high and is usually underestimated by clinicians. Also, clinicians may harbour misconceptions about the factors that place patients at risk and when patients are actually most likely to commit suicide. These biases may lull clinicians into a false sense of security when treating first-episode patients and contribute to a failure to address the issues of suicidality effectively until it is too late.

---

[*] Lambeth Early Onset Service, South London and Maudsley NHS Trust, 108 Landor Road, London SW9 9NT, UK.

Early intervention in itself may reduce the risk of suicide through the indirect effects of improving clinical and functional outcome and preventing worse sequelae emerging. However, early intervention alone is not enough. Introducing suicide risk assessment and audit/management systems into a service may help to identify better the patient group at highest risk. This must, however, be quickly connected to interventions that are likely to minimize the risk once it has been identified. A simple zoning system of risk that determines the intensity of care provision may be one such model. Other interventions such as medication, especially clozapine (Meltzer et al., 2003), cognitive therapies and psychosocial/family interventions may also have important roles. There are some encouraging findings from a small number of recent studies but further evidence is needed to really prove their effectiveness in suicide prevention. The overriding motivation of the LifeSPAN group in developing the LifeSPAN therapy was to offer a therapeutic intervention for the highest risk patients. Even though developing and evaluating the intervention has been a considerable challenge it is the first step and, hopefully, it will encourage others to do likewise.

ACKNOWLEDGEMENTS

The author would like to express his gratitude to Tanya Herrman-Doig for her help with the case examples and also to Richard Bell, Richard Mills, Melanie Davern, Lisa Henry, Hok Pan Yuen, Pat McGorry, and A. Khademy-Deljo, all of whom formed part of the LifeSPAN project. Thanks also to Keith Hawton, Mark G. Williams, Conrad Hauser, Andrew Fuller, Heather Manning, Angela White and Roy Butterham for their advice with the project, and to research, clinical and medical record staff at EPPIC, ORYGEN Youth Health, University of Melbourne for their support. Finally, the author is grateful to the Commonwealth Department of Health and Family Services for their generous funding of the LifeSPAN project.

REFERENCES

Addington, D., Addington, J. & Patten, S. (1998). Depression in people with first-episode schizophrenia. *British Journal of Psychiatry*, **172** (Suppl. 33), 90–92.

Adlard, S. (1997). *An analysis of health damaging behaviours in young people at high risk of psychosis.* FRANZCP dissertation, Melbourne: The Royal College and New Zealand College of Psychiatrists.

Amador, X.F., Freidman, J.H., Kasapis, C., Yale, S.A., Flaum, M. & Gorman, J.M. (1996). Suicidal behavior in schizophrenia and its relationship to awareness of illness. *The American Journal of Psychiatry*, **153**, 1185–1188.

Aquilar, E.J., Haas, G., Manzanera, F.G., Hernandez, J., Gracia, R., Rodado, M.J. & Keshavan, M.S. (1997). Hopelessness and first-episode psychosis: A longitudinal study. *Acta Psychiatrica Scandinavica*, **96**, 25–30.

Birchwood, M., Iqbal, Z., Chadwick, P. & Trower, P. (2000). Cognitive approach to depression and suicidal thinking in psychosis: Ontogeny of post-psychotic depression. *British Journal of Psychiatry*, **177**, 516–521.

Bronisch, T. (1996). The relationship between suicidality and depression. *Archives of Suicide Research*, **2**, 235–254.

Brown, S. (1997). Excess mortality of schizophrenia: A meta-analysis. *British Journal of Psychiatry*, **171**, 502–508.

Buckingham, B., Burgess, P., Solomon, S., Pirkis, J. & Eager, K. (1998). *Developing a Casemix Classification for Mental Health Services: Summary.* Canberra: Commonwealth of Australia, Department of Health and Family Services.

Dahlsgaard, K.K., Beck, A.T. & Brown, G.K. (1998). Inadequate response to therapy as a predictor of suicide. *Suicide and Life-Threatening Behaviour,* **28**, 197–204.

Edwards, E. & McGorry, P. (Eds) (2002). *Implementing Early Intervention in Psychosis: A Guide to Establishing Early Intervention Services.* London: Martin Dunitz.

Ellis, T.E. & Newman, C.F. (1996). *Choosing to Live.* Oakland: New Harbinger Publications.

Fenton, W. & McGlashan, T. (1991). Natural history of schizophrenia subtypes. *Archives of General Psychiatry,* **48**, 969–977.

Freeman, A. & Reinecke, M.A. (1993). *Cognitive Therapy of Suicide Behaviour: A Manual for Treatment.* New York: Springer.

Garety, P. & Jolley, S. (2000). Early intervention in psychosis (Editorial). *Psychiatric Bulletin* **24**, 321–323.

Heila, H., Isometsa, E., Henrisksson, M., Heikkinen, M., Marttunen, M. & Lonnqvist, J. (1997). Suicide and schizophrenia: A nationwide psychological autopsy study on age- and sex-specific clinical characteristics of 92 suicide victims with schizophrenia. *American Journal of Psychiatry,* **154**, 1235–1242.

Jackson, H., McGorry, P., Edwards, J., Hulbert, C., Henry, L., Francey, S., Maude, D., Cocks, J., Power, P., Harrigan, S. & Dudgeon, P. (1998). Cognitively-oriented psychotherapy for early psychosis (COPE): Preliminary results. *British Journal of Psychiatry,* **172** (Suppl. 33), 93–100.

Krausz, M., Muller-Thomsen, T. & Maasen, C. (1995). Suicide among schizophrenic adolescents in the long-term course of illness. *Psychopathology,* **28**, 95–103.

Linehan, M., Armstrong, H., Suarez, A. & Allmon, D. (1991). Cognitive behavioural treatment of chronically parasuicidal borderline patients. *Archives of General Psychiatry,* **48**, 1060–1064.

McGlashan, T. (1998). Early detection and intervention of schizophrenia: Rationale and research. *British Journal of Psychiatry,* **172** (Suppl. 33), 3–6.

McGorry, P.J., Henry, L. & Power, P. (1998). Suicide in early psychosis: Could early intervention work? In R. Kosky & H. Eshkevari (Eds), *Suicide Prevention: The Global Context* (pp. 103–110). New York: Plenum Press.

Mann, S.C., Caroff, S.N., Bleier, H.R., Welz, W.K.R., Kling, M.A. & Hayashida, M. (1986). Lethal catatonia. *American Journal of Psychiatry,* **143**, 1374–1381.

Meltzer, H. (2002). Suicidality in schizophrenia: A review of the evidence for risk factors and treatment options. *Current Science,* **4**, 279–283.

Meltzer, H.Y., Alphs, L., Green, A.I., Altamura, A.C., Anand, R., Bertoldi, A., Bourgeois, M., Chouinard, G., Islam, M.Z., Kane J., Krishnan, R., Lindenmayer, J.P. & Potkin, S. (2003). Clozapine treatment for suicidality in schizophrenia: International Suicide Prevention Trial (InterSePT). *Archives of General Psychiatry,* **60**, 82–91.

Mortensen, P. & Juel, K. (1993). Mortality and causes of death in first admitted schizophrenic patients. *British Journal of Psychiatry,* **163**, 183–189.

Nordentoft, M., Jeppesen, P., Abel, M., Kassow, P., Petersen, L., Thorup, A., Krarup, G., Hemmingsen, R. & Jørgensen, P. (2002). OPUS study: Suicidal behaviour, suicidal ideation and hopelessness among patients with first-episode psychosis. One-year follow-up of a randomised controlled trial. *British Journal of Psychiatry,* **181** (Suppl. 43), S98–S106.

O'Carroll, P.W., Berman, A.L., Maris, R.W., Moscicki, E.K., Tanney, B.L. & Silverman, M.M. (1996). Beyond the Tower of Babel: A nomenclature for suicidology. *Suicide and Life-Threatening Behavior,* **26**, 237–252.

Power, P. (1999) Suicide in early psychosis. In P. McGorry & H. Jackson (Eds), *The Recognition and Management of Early Psychosis: A Preventive Approach* (pp. 338–362). Cambridge: Cambridge University Press.

Power, P. & Bell, R. (Eds) (in press). *LifeSPAN Manual: A Guide to Suicide Prevention in Young People with Mental Illness.* Canberra: Commonwealth Government of Australia.

Power, P., Bell, R., Mills, R., Herrmann-Doig, T., Davern, M., Henry, L., Yuen, H.P., Khademy-Deljo, A. & McGorry, P.D. (2003). Suicide prevention in first episode psychosis: The development of a randomised controlled trial of cognitive therapy for acutely suicidal patients with early psychosis. *Australian and New Zealand Journal of Psychiatry,* **37**, 414–420.

Power, P., Davern, M., Yuen, H.P., Henry, L. & McGorry, P. (1998a). Patterns of suicidality among young people with first episode psychosis. *Second National Conference on Early Psychosis— Realising the Potential.* Hobart.

Power, P., Elkins, E., Adlard, S., Curry, C., McGorry, P. & Harrigan, S. (1998b). An analysis of the initial treatment phase of first episode psychosis. *British Journal of Psychiatry,* **172** (Suppl. 33), 71–77.

Roy, A. (1982). Suicide in chronic schizophrenia. *British Journal of Psychiatry,* **141**, 171–177.

Ryrie, I., Hellard, l., Kearns, C., Robinson, D., Pathmanathan, I. & O'Sullivan, D. (1997). Zoning: A system for managing case work and targeting resources in community mental health teams. *Journal of Mental Health UK,* **6**, 515–523.

Salkovkis, P., Atha, C. & Storer, D. (1990). Cognitive behavioral problem solving in the treatment of patients who repeatedly attempt suicide: A controlled trial. *British Journal of Psychiatry,* **157**, 871–876.

Siris, S. (2001). Suicide and schizophrenia. *Journal of Psychopharmacology,* **15**, 127–135.

Trochim, W.K. (1989). An introduction to concept mapping for planning and evaluation. *Evaluation and Program Planning,* **12**, 1–16.

van der Sande, R., Buskens, E., Allart, E., van der Graaf, Y. & van Engeland, H. (1997a). Psychosocial intervention following suicide attempt: A systematic review of treatment interventions. *Acta Psychiatrica Scandinavica,* **96**, 43–50.

van der Sande, R., van Roojijen, L., Buskens, E., Allart, E., Hawton, K., van der Graaf, Y. & van Engeland, H. (1997b). Intensive in-patient and community intervention versus routine care after attempted suicide. A randomised controlled intervention study. *British Journal of Psychiatry,* **171**, 35–41.

Ventura, J., Lukoff, D., Nuechterlein, K., Liberman, R., Green, M. & Shaner, A. (1993). *Brief Psychiatric Rating Scale (Expanded Version 4.0).* Los Angeles: UCLA Department of Psychiatry and Behavioural Sciences, Clinical Research Center for Schizophrenia and Psychiatric Rehabilitation.

Westermeyer, J., Harrow, M. & Marengo, J. (1991). Risk for suicide in schizophrenia and other psychotic and non-psychotic disorders. *Journal of Nervous and Mental Disease,* **179**, 259–266.

Wing, J.K. (1994). *Health of the Nation Outcome Scale: HoNOS field trials.* London: Royal College of Psychiatrists, Research Unit.

11 Psychological Treatment of Persistent Positive Symptoms in Young People with First-Episode Psychosis

JANE EDWARDS
ORYGEN Youth Health, Melbourne, Australia

DARRYL WADE
ORYGEN Youth Health, Melbourne, Australia

TANYA HERRMANN-DOIG
Chris Mackey & Associates, Clinical Psychology Services, Australia

DONNA GEE
ORYGEN Youth Health, Melbourne, Australia

Effective identification of young people experiencing a prolonged recovery from early psychosis requires a coordinated process in which patients can be consistently monitored, reviewed in a timely fashion and offered intervention from the full spectrum of clinical services. Within this context, cognitive-behavioural therapy provides patients with an opportunity to develop some sense of being able to influence their symptoms and learn strategies to reduce the distress of symptoms. This chapter describes a psychological intervention for individuals experiencing prolonged recovery from first-episode psychosis known as 'STOPP' (Systematic Treatment of Persistent Psychosis) therapy. We outline the rationale for STOPP, provide an overview of key elements of this youth-specific psychotherapy, discuss implementation of STOPP in our clinical service, and conclude with a description of a randomized-controlled trial which is in progress.

PERSISTENT PSYCHOSIS

Persistent psychosis can have profound consequences on a young person, including demoralization, compromised vocational functioning, increased suicide risk and poor illness outcome. An inadequate response to pharmacological interventions can be established relatively early in the course of treatment, signalling the need for more intensive interventions to accelerate recovery. The Early Psychosis Prevention and Intervention Centre (EPPIC),

Psychological Interventions in Early Psychosis
Edited by J.F.M. Gleeson and P.D. McGorry. © 2004 John Wiley & Sons, Ltd.

has sought to establish a treatment practice that detects and targets individuals experiencing prolonged recovery from their first episode of psychosis.

The Clinical Context

EPPIC is a youth-specific clinical service focusing on the early detection and optimal treatment of recent-onset psychosis in people aged 15 to 29 years (Edwards & McGorry, 2002; McGorry et al., 1996). The catchment area for the service is characterized by high unemployment, low incomes, ethnic diversity and a lack of public infrastructure and amenities. EPPIC provides outpatient case management, 24-hour triage, a 16-bed inpatient unit, individual and group-based family work, psychological treatments and an intensive mobile outreach service. Most patients are accepted into EPPIC for a period of 18 months.

Treatment-Resistant Early Assessment Team (TREAT)

The Treatment-Resistant Early Assessment Team (TREAT; Edwards et al., 1998; EPPIC, 2002b) monitors the early recovery of all patients registered at EPPIC. The TREAT coordinator sends queries to case managers and doctors 9 weeks after the acceptance of each patient into EPPIC to determine whether positive or negative symptoms are still present. Patients with continuing psychotic symptoms are reviewed again at 12 weeks and, if the symptoms have not resolved, the case manager and doctor are invited to discuss the patient's treatment and progress at the next weekly TREAT meeting. The TREAT team consists of senior clinicians who consider the case and make treatment recommendations. The team reviews the medication regimen and assesses psychosocial issues such as: the nature of the therapeutic alliance; the young person's response to the illness and coping repertoire; comorbid conditions such as depression and substance misuse; and the effect of the illness on the family, peer network, social and vocational functioning. Of 1072 patients screened by TREAT between 1996 and 2000, 19% continued to experience positive psychotic symptoms at 12 weeks (Edwards et al., 2002).

PSYCHOLOGICAL TREATMENT FOR PERSISTENT PSYCHOSIS

Interest in the use of psychotherapy as an adjunctive treatment for psychosis has been considerable over the past decade. This has been largely due to the application of cognitive-behavioural therapy to the treatment of patients with psychotic illnesses, in particular, the subgroup experiencing persistent positive symptoms. Clinical expertise has been disseminated via the publication of several treatment manuals of cognitive-behavioural therapy for psychosis (e.g. Chadwick, Birchwood & Trower, 1996; Fowler, Garety & Kuipers, 1995; Kingdon & Turkington, 1994). Published research on the efficacy of cognitive-behavioural therapy for individuals with schizophrenia has progressed from single-case studies, case-series reports, and open trials to more sophisticated well-controlled studies. Results have generally been viewed as promising (for recent reviews see Gould et al., 2001; Pilling et al., 2002; Rector & Beck, 2001), although the number of studies and study participants are small (Cormac et al., 2002).

To date, three methodologically sound (i.e. $n > 20$ per group, independent raters, adequate randomization procedures, clear attempts to follow a written treatment manual by well-trained and supervised therapists) randomized-controlled trials evaluating cognitive-behavioural therapy targeting persistent psychotic symptoms in outpatients with chronic disorders have been published (Freeman et al., 1998; Garety et al., 1997; Kuipers et al., 1997, 1998; Sensky et al., 2000; Tarrier et al., 1998, 1999, 2000, 2001) and the results are described below. All three research groups published pilot studies (Garety et al., 1994; Kingdon & Turkington, 1991; Tarrier et al., 1993; Turkington et al., 1996), reflecting substantial experience with this client group. There are two important randomized-controlled trials focusing on accelerating remission during the acute phase of a psychotic illness (Drury et al., 1996a, 1996b; Drury, Birchwood & Cochrane, 2000; Lewis et al., 2002) that are not outlined here, our focus being on positive psychotic symptoms that persist following administration of adequate trials of medication. Readers are also referred to a recent pragmatic randomized trial undertaken by Turkington, Kingdon and Turner (2002), which examines effectiveness of a brief cognitive-behavioural therapy for individuals with schizophrenia, although this study does not specifically target persisting psychotic symptoms.

Three Notable Randomized-Controlled Trials

Kuipers and colleagues (1997) compared cognitive-behavioural therapy plus routine care with routine care alone, and found that the cognitive-behavioural therapy group showed significant reductions on a measure of general psychopathology, and that a higher proportion of patients receiving cognitive-behavioural therapy were considered treatment responders. These improvements were maintained 9 months after the completion of treatment (Kuipers et al., 1998). Rater blindness is a crucial issue, and it should be noted that although the assessments were carried out by independent research workers who were not involved in the therapy, they were not 'totally' blind to the treatment condition.

Tarrier et al.'s (1998) trial, which builds on a study contrasting two cognitive-behavioural approaches (Tarrier et al., 1993), compared three treatment conditions: intensive cognitive-behavioural therapy plus routine care, supportive counselling plus routine care, and routine care alone. The results indicated that the patients receiving cognitive-behavioural therapy showed a greater improvement in positive symptoms than the supportive counselling group and routine care at the 3-month post-baseline assessment (i.e. post treatment). Further, proportionally more cognitive-behavioural therapy patients achieved a clinically significant improvement than the other patients. At 12-month follow-up (Tarrier et al., 1999), the patients who received cognitive-behavioural therapy had less positive symptoms than those who received routine care alone; and there was a trend for those patients who received either cognitive-behavioural therapy or supportive counselling to have less negative symptoms than the patients who received only routine care. In addition, fewer patients who received routine care alone demonstrated clinically significant improvements. At 2-year follow-up (Tarrier et al., 2000), the patients who received routine care alone fared worse on all measures of positive symptoms, negative symptoms, clinically significant change, and number of relapses. There were no differences between the patients who received cognitive-behavioural therapy and supportive therapy on these variables.

Sensky et al. (2000) found no differences between cognitive-behavioural therapy and befriending groups (both in addition to routine care) at the end of 9 months of treatment. However, at assessment 9 months after completion of treatment, the patients who received cognitive-behavioural therapy demonstrated significantly greater improvements on measures of general psychopathology, depression, and negative symptoms. In addition, a higher proportion of these patients achieved clinical improvement.

Overall, the studies suggest that cognitive-behavioural therapy enhances clinical improvement and that the gains are maintained at follow-up. Control treatments are an important consideration, in view of the suggestion that non-specific treatments are associated with improvements, albeit to a lesser extent than cognitive-behavioural therapies. Attention to issues concerning effective treatment components; optimal duration and frequency of cognitive-behavioural therapy; quality of therapeutic input; the impact of treatment on wide symptom domains, social functioning and illness course; and effectiveness and economic evaluations in various 'real world' settings are required. These studies do not consider medication issues beyond dose and/or numbers of patients receiving standard versus atypical antipsychotic medications. The effectiveness (or otherwise) of cognitive-behavioural therapy for persistent psychosis in the face of less than adequate medication is not clinically compelling.

Clozapine

Clozapine is considered superior to typical antipsychotics in terms of effectiveness in reducing overall psychopathology for individuals with treatment-resistant schizophrenia (Chakos et al., 2001; Wahlbeck et al., 1999); it is possible that there is also a role for other atypical antipsychotic medications in individuals with chronic schizophrenia who have a history of suboptimal response to treatment (Tollefson et al., 2001; Volavka et al., 2002). Interestingly, Pinto and colleagues (1999) compared cognitive-behavioural therapy plus social skills training with supportive psychotherapy in patients with treatment refractory schizophrenia who had recently commenced clozapine. The group receiving cognitive-behavioural therapy demonstrated greater improvements in positive symptoms and general psychopathology compared to the supportive therapy group. There were no differences on ratings of negative symptoms. While this suggests that the addition of cognitive-behavioural therapy to clozapine may be useful, the interpretation of results is limited by not having independent raters who were blind to the treatment condition. There is a need for methodologically sound studies of cognitive-behavioural therapy for persistent psychosis that pay serious attention to the adequacy of medication.

FEATURES OF COGNITIVE-BEHAVIOURAL THERAPY FOR PROLONGED RECOVERY IN EARLY PSYCHOSIS

The aims of cognitive-behavioural therapy in prolonged recovery are to:

- reduce the frequency and intensity of psychotic symptoms, if possible;
- reduce the distress associated with psychotic symptoms and minimize their impact on functioning;
- increase capacity to cope with the experiences;
- help patients to develop an understanding of psychosis to reduce potential for relapse and social disability.

Core features of the approach include a collaborative therapeutic alliance between the patient and therapist; use of therapy goals and agendas; linking of thoughts and beliefs to emotion and behaviour; identifying thought biases; and reviewing evidence for beliefs. Coping strategies are introduced to reduce the severity and intrusiveness of hallucinations. Negative self-evaluations are also targeted, since they are often related to the development and/or maintenance of psychotic symptoms (see Bentall et al., 2001; Garety et al., 2001). These tasks are pursued in a non-confrontational 'normalizing' manner.

Psychological Therapy in Early Psychosis

Although many patients with persisting psychotic symptoms would benefit from the addition of psychosocial treatment to medication (Dickerson, 2000), psychological approaches may have greater benefit if used early in the course of the illness (Garety, Fowler & Kuipers, 2000; Jackson et al., 1999). Early intervention offers the opportunity to minimize secondary morbidity which is often associated with long-term illness. A relatively recent onset of psychosis allows comparatively easier access to information about premorbid adjustment and vulnerability factors. Delusional beliefs are also often less rigidly held during this phase of illness.

SYSTEMATIC TREATMENT OF PERSISTENT PSYCHOSIS (STOPP)

STOPP therapy emphasizes an individualized, phase-specific approach to treatment (Herrmann-Doig, Maude & Edwards, 2003). It provides a sequenced yet flexible intervention that targets enduring positive symptoms and distress, while allowing the clinician to 'customize' the treatment to individual patient needs. Cognitively Orientated Therapy for Early Psychosis (COPE) is the basic building block for STOPP therapy; many of the COPE assessment and engagement techniques are relevant to STOPP and will not be covered here. Readers are advised to examine writings on COPE as pre-reading for the sections that follow. Chapter 4 of this volume provides a good starting point, and source materials include other book chapters (Jackson et al., 1996, 1999; Jackson, McGorry & Edwards, 2001), a treatment manual (EPPIC, 2002a), and data papers on a pilot study (Jackson et al., 1998, 2001).

Engagement in Psychological Therapy

Engagement of the young person is central to the therapeutic process. This process requires emotional attunement and empathy from the therapist, which is assisted by understanding young people's specific needs (Jackson et al., 1999, Jackson, McGorry & Edwards, 2001). Young people experiencing prolonged recovery from psychosis often express a sense of hopelessness about their illness, disenchantment with treatment to date, and a desire for a 'quick fix'. In many cases the recent psychotic episode will be their first experience of mental illness and is likely to have led to hospitalization and substantial medical treatment. The common age of onset of psychosis is late adolescence or early adulthood, and it is therefore important to consider developmental issues and identity formation when determining strategies for treatment (Jackson, McGorry & Edwards, 2001).

Individuals experiencing their first episode of psychosis are often confused or suspicious about the reasons for talking about their experiences. They may be reluctant to discuss the possibility of being unwell, and concerned about stigma or receiving judgement from others. Therapists should emphasize the collaborative nature of the treatment, in which the therapist and patient explore the nature and impact of the psychotic experiences and identify ways to improve coping skills.

STOPP therapy consists of four phases:

- Developing a collaborative working relationship
- Exploring and coping with psychosis
- Strengthening the capacity to relate to others
- Finishing and moving on.

Phase 1: Developing a collaborative working relationship

During this phase the therapist and young person work together to establish a consistent and clear therapeutic relationship through:

- evolving a shared formulation of the young person's presenting concerns; and
- creating an agenda for further work.

A thorough assessment provides the opportunity to develop a detailed psychological understanding of the patient's presenting concerns, illness aetiology and response to treatment. A cognitive-behavioural framework is used to assess the specific features of the symptoms and the circumstances in which they occur (Herrmann-Doig, Maude & Edwards, 2003). Patients' explanatory models for their symptoms are elicited. The therapist assesses for trauma which may have resulted either from becoming psychotic or from subsequent treatment (McGorry et al., 1991), and discusses the impact the experience of psychosis may have had on the person.

The individual's personal and family histories are reviewed. This should help the clinician to consider the extent to which premorbid and personality issues might influence engagement and recovery. The clinician learns about the young person's coping resources and style and attempts to understand how the patient's beliefs about self and the world have developed. Issues such as substance misuse, depression, intellectual disability and personality disorders should be covered during the assessment phase as these conditions complicate recovery from psychosis, and accurate identification should facilitate appropriate treatments being offered. Assessment is undertaken by clinical interview and a variety of rating scales can be incorporated (see Box 11.1). Information obtained during assessment is compiled by the therapist and patient into a psychological formulation in an effort to make sense of the individual's persistent psychotic symptoms. An agenda for future sessions is then established through identifying and prioritizing goals for therapy.

In summary, information obtained during assessment, which is then integrated into a shared formulation and treatment agenda, includes:

- the patient's presenting concerns, illness aetiology, and response to treatment;
- the circumstances in which symptoms are experienced;
- the patient's explanatory model for symptoms and the experience of psychosis itself;
- experiences of trauma, stigma or other emotional concerns;
- identity and developmental stage;
- personality and relationship issues;
- beliefs about self and illness;
- comorbid conditions.

Box 11.1. Useful rating scales for STOPP assessment

Brief Psychiatric Rating Scale—Expanded Version (Lukoff, Neuchterlein & Ventura, 1986) is a scale designed to assess the severity of a wide range of psychopathology.

Global Scale of Delusions Severity (John, 2003), a modification of the Maudsley Assessment of Delusions Schedule (Buchanan, et al., 1993), measures degree of conviction, belief maintenance factors, affect related to key belief, amount of action on belief, extent of idiosyncrasy of the key belief, preoccupation with key belief, systematization of key belief, degree of insight, and global severity.

Auditory Hallucination Subscale of the Psychotic Symptom Rating Scales (Haddock et al., 1999) examines the frequency, duration, location, loudness, beliefs about origin, amount of negative content, level and intensity of distress, level of disruption, and degree of perceived control of auditory hallucinations.

Scale for the Assessment of Negative Symptoms (Andreasen, 1984) assesses negative signs and symptoms of psychosis and provides five subscale scores (affective flattening, alogia, anhedonia, and attentional impairment).

Beck Depression Inventory—Short Form (Beck & Beck, 1972) is a self-report inventory designed to assess the severity of depressive symptoms.

Addiction Severity Index (McLellan et al., 1992) is a structured interview designed to assess substance abuse and related treatment problems which allows severity estimates to be made in each of six areas: substance abuse, medical, psychological, legal, family/social, and employment/support.

Case example: Christine

Christine was 22 years old, unemployed and living with her parents in Melbourne. After leaving school she started working in a shop but felt she was unable to continue because she 'couldn't cope' with the demands of the job, especially with the social interactions involved. She was the youngest of three children, her elder brother and sister had both married and left home.

Christine experienced unremitting paranoid delusions that her old friends from school were following her and intending to harm her. She started treatment with an atypical antipsychotic which helped to reduce the distress associated with positive symptoms, but there was no further improvement despite appropriate increases in the dose. After 6 weeks she was switched to another atypical antipsychotic but this was associated with some adverse side-effects. A review by TREAT, 4 months after commencing treatment, recommended treatment with clozapine and referral to STOPP.

Presenting concerns

Christine said she was often uncomfortable around her old friends and felt safe only when at home. These experiences caused her considerable distress, with feelings of anxiety, sadness, loss of pleasure in activities and withdrawal from family.

Christine wanted to return to work or study, but felt hopeless about her ability to achieve this goal as she believed her old friends would interfere with her plans.

Psychological formulation

Christine, as the youngest child, had often been protected within her family and excluded from involvement in family decisions. She had been assessed prior to the onset of her illness as having a low IQ. Christine was shy, had difficulty making friends, and had been socially isolated at school.

Stress associated with leaving school and the transition to work may have exacerbated the development of psychotic symptoms. Christine began to interpret laughter from her school colleagues as being directed at her and was alert to confirmatory evidence such as people looking at her, whispering or laughing. The symptoms were often triggered by social anxiety.

The failure of medication to eliminate her symptoms had increased Christine's doubts about the diagnosis of psychosis and increased her convictions that her beliefs were real.

Hypothesis

Christine's symptoms occurred in the context of a life crisis in which she was unable to cope with increased demands for independence, responsibility and social interaction. Persisting symptoms appeared to protect Christine from confronting difficult and unresolved issues about her development and self-esteem.

Agenda for STOPP intervention

Christine said she was doubtful that anything could change and believed her fears were valid. As a result, the initial agreed goals of therapy focused on practical issues to increase Christine's activity level. She was willing to attend weekly STOPP sessions and to undertake activities at home between sessions.

Phase 2: Exploring and coping with psychosis

This phase allows the therapist and young person to explore the experience of psychosis by:

- discussing the subjective response to psychotic symptoms;
- increasing the patient's knowledge about psychosis;
- considering and using strategies to manage and treat symptoms;
- identifying and learning to tolerate emotional states associated with the discussion and management of the psychotic phenomena.

The therapist can gauge the success of this phase by the extent to which patients can discuss their experience of psychosis with increasing detail and less distress, and effectively implement strategies to deal with the phenomena.

Psychoeducational resources, including videos and pamphlets (for source details see Appendix 1 of Edwards & McGorry, 2002), can be used to provide information about the causes and treatment of psychosis, and to reassure patients that their experience is understandable. The variable rate of recovery is emphasized, peer experiences of psychosis are shared, and comorbid conditions are discussed. Education about medication (benefits, types, doses and side-effects) is provided.

During this phase, further information is obtained from the patient about the range and type of coping strategies that are currently used or have been used in the past, and the circumstances in which they have been used. Patients are encouraged to keep a log-book to record the time, place and circumstances in which symptoms were experienced. This may help to identify patterns of symptoms, make sense of the phenomena and trial coping strategies. If young people have trouble undertaking this outside sessions then the patient and therapist can make retrospective diary entries together in the session.

Additional coping strategies are introduced where possible to help the young person to expand and improve upon his or her repertoire of techniques for dealing with symptoms. These include methods to reduce tension, distraction, and focusing on the nature of symptoms. The reader is referred to a number of excellent texts for details of relevant psychological techniques (Chadwick, Birchwood & Trower, 1996; Fowler, Garety & Kuipers, 1995; Haddock & Slade, 1996; Kingdon & Turkington, 1994, 2002).

Socratic dialogue and reality testing (Box 11.2) are used to question the evidence for assumptions on which delusional beliefs are based. Questionnaires to elicit, and determine the extent of, positive psychotic symptoms can provide ideas about how these questions may be phrased. 'Cue cards' are also used to help the patient to challenge some of these assumptions between sessions.

Box 11.2. Examples of Socratic questions

1. What do you think is the likelihood that this explanation could be true?

2. You said . . . , but I'm a bit confused about how that could be. Could you explain what makes you think . . . ?

3. Have you asked anyone else what they think about . . . ?

4. What would need to happen for you to doubt that this is true?

5. Have there been times where you thought . . . would occur and it didn't? How do you explain it?

In this phase the patient is encouraged to persist with life goals and tasks and foster a sense of hope for the future, despite experiencing symptoms. Problem-solving and cognitive strategies can assist this process.

In summary, during phase 2 the therapist assists the young person to explore and cope with psychosis by:

- providing knowledge about the causes of psychosis and medication;
- exploring coping strategies used now and in the past;
- introducing alternative coping strategies such as tension reduction, distraction and focusing;
- using Socratic dialogue and reality testing;
- encouraging persistence with life goals;
- addressing anxiety-provoking situations.

Case example: Christine (continued)

Christine acknowledged that her worries were interfering with her quality of life but she was convinced that her concerns were valid. However, she also accepted that she may have psychosis, although she was unsure what the term 'psychosis' actually meant. Providing Christine with factual information about psychosis was a priority.

Because Christine had impaired memory and concentration due to her illness, psychoeducation was provided in a variety of forms to ensure that she understood and remembered the messages. A 'normalizing' model of psychoeducation was provided, making use of diagrams and a number of videos and personal stories of others, so that she knew she was not the only person to experience the illness. This allowed her the opportunity to reconsider the validity of her beliefs.

Interventions to cope with Christine's 'worries' initially focused on anxiety-reduction techniques, including relaxation and breathing strategies.

Gentle reality testing was started, concentrating first on less strongly-held beliefs—for instance, that the neighbours were spying on her or that there were cameras in her walls. She was asked to consider alternative explanations and review the evidence for her beliefs.

Graded behavioural experiments were also used to challenge her beliefs. For example, she would go for a short walk with her father who would help her to check if neighbours were watching. A further step was to go shopping and check whether she really would see her troublesome former friends. When this didn't occur, she was able to think about going out more.

Christine was encouraged to explore her life goals. Combined with cognitive strategies to address negative beliefs about herself, this gradually increased her self-confidence and she began to attend a cooking group with other patients recovering from first-episode psychosis.

Phase 3: Strengthening the capacity to relate to others

This phase aims to increase the patient's sense of integration by:

- exploring and reaffirming different aspects of self;
- attending to psychotic beliefs about others;
- providing opportunities for self-reflection.

Success is demonstrated by:

- an increase in the capacity to identify and challenge erroneous beliefs;
- an ability to explain why psychosis developed and possible reasons for symptoms occurring;
- an awareness of personal strengths;
- a willingness to tackle new challenges.

In this phase the therapist returns to a focus on the developmental history of the patient, with particular emphasis on self-evaluation and evaluation of significant others. An exploration of previous and current relationships, as well as interests and opinions, provides an opportunity to identify unhelpful assumptions and how they may have developed. The patient and therapist are then able to consider how the young person may come to view himself or herself and his or her world in more constructive ways.

Where it is clear the patient has minimal opportunity for self-development, as a consequence of either psychosis or premorbid social limitations, the therapist and patient work together to enhance social skills.

The process aims to link symptomatology and personal difficulties—for example, by drawing connections between emotional responses to situations and the exacerbation of psychotic symptoms.

In summary, Phase 3 explores the patient's capacity to relate to others through:

- discussion of self-evaluation and evaluation of others;
- identification of unhelpful beliefs about self and others;
- linking symptomatology with personal difficulties.

Case example: Christine (continued)

Identity
Christine aimed to increase her self-confidence and independence. Her coping response to persisting symptoms had been to isolate herself and reduce the likelihood of paranoid experiences. She was encouraged to be more independent through graded exposure and gentle challenging techniques.

Christine had initially attended appointments and group programmes with her father, but she finally agreed to try EPPIC's patient transport system and travel a little more independently. However, she developed paranoid ideas that the transport company would tell her former friends. The therapist explored the evidence for her concerns and discussed confidentiality. At first she agreed to meet the transport service at a point away from her house, and finally agreed to be collected from home.

Exploring core beliefs
Christine saw herself as a dependent person who needed to rely on her parents to make life choices, and recognized that this limited her capacity to pursue her interests. She was encouraged to set personal goals, particularly in the areas of vocation and health. She began to attend a gym and used an employment service to help her to find a job.

Although Christine and her therapist had agreed that it was important to increase her social supports, she continued to have difficulty trusting others. Social skills training and discussing her interpretation of conversations helped her to engage better in social situations. She was able to identify links between her increased anxiety in social situations and her tendency to misinterpret benign interactions as threatening.

Phase 4: Finishing and moving on

This final phase facilitates a positive closure of the therapeutic relationship and maximizes the likelihood of continued progress. Three areas are addressed:

- Dealing with issues of loss and disappointment
- Planning for the future
- Handing over to other team members.

Successful completion of this phase will include discussion of the patient's experience of the therapy sessions, collaborative identification of areas for further personal development, clarification of goals for the future, and identification of resources for ongoing support.

Sessions should include discussion and reflection on previous experiences of leaving relationships, as well as the current experience of saying goodbye. This is conducted in a supportive way, to encourage open and honest reflection on both the positive and difficult aspects of therapy and what the young person has gained from the sessions. A problem-solving approach is used to encourage the patient to consider how to tackle future goals or manage early signs of illness relapse. Where necessary, the therapist challenges the young person's self-defeating beliefs about his or her capacity to manage future situations. A handover session is conducted with the treatment team to facilitate a smooth transition to continuing care.

Case example: Christine (continued)

Christine continued to hold many of her delusional beliefs at the conclusion of the STOPP sessions, but they were less dominant and did not interfere as much with her quality of life. She was able to go out more often with friends and attend a recovery group programme, and she felt more comfortable and safe in her own home. Christine also reported improvement in her mood and self-esteem. Her progress and future goals were reviewed.

Christine felt quite anxious about her future and was reluctant to finish sessions. These fears were addressed directly with Christine and the case worker who would be her main point of contact in the future.

Finally, Christine and her therapist reviewed the progress they had made, identifying many improvements in her function and her quality of life.

IMPLEMENTING STOPP AT EPPIC

Most therapists undertaking STOPP at EPPIC are clinical psychologists who are also involved in other aspects of the clinical programme. STOPP therapists are required to have training in cognitive-behavioural therapy, experience in working with young people with early psychosis, and a willingness to participate in supervision. It is feasible that clinicians from other disciplines join the STOPP team; however, it is often challenging for other clinicians to access training in cognitive-behavioural therapy, in contrast to the situation in the UK (Kingdon & Pelton, 2002). Interestingly, a psychiatrist and senior registrar who had received training in cognitive therapy overseas participated as STOPP therapists while working at EPPIC for 12 months.

Therapists are guided by an orientation pack that includes the STOPP manual (Herrmann-Doig, Maude & Edwards, 2003), academic papers, and assessment and rating scales. A senior clinical psychologist, who is a member of TREAT, facilitates supervision meetings and coordinates the allocation of new referrals to STOPP therapists.

When possible, STOPP patients are seen at least weekly for up to 24 sessions. Farhall and Cotton (2002) evaluated the implementation of a psychological treatment for symptoms of psychosis in a routine mental health service, and noted the modal number of sessions to be 18, similar to the reports of Sensky et al. (2000) and Kuipers et al. (1997). A benefit of placing some restriction on the number of sessions is that it encourages 'throughput'— maximizing the number of patients who have the opportunity to access an individual therapist, and allowing therapists to gain experience with a diverse range of presenting problems.

Therapist Supervision

Weekly peer supervision meetings are conducted for administrative, educational and supervision requirements. This is a key component in professional development and the maintenance of high-quality clinical practice (Spence et al., 2001). Supervision acknowledges that patients with a serious mental illness and persistent psychotic symptoms usually have a range of difficult and complex problems that may challenge any individual therapist. It also enables training for psychologists whose specialist skills are often under-used in case management models of care. Case presentations allow therapists to readily obtain assistance with assessment, case formulation and implementation of therapeutic strategies and techniques.

Discussion With Other Team Members

It is important for the STOPP therapist to communicate with other clinicians involved in the patient's treatment, not only to obtain assessment information and to discuss progress, but also to engage them as potential allies in treatment. This will require some elaboration of the treatment approach. Lectures and/or workshops can be offered within the treatment facility, in addition to dissemination of relevant review and research papers. For busy mental health clinicians, brief handouts may also be helpful, such as 'Dealing with Voices' in Box 11.3 accompanied by further discussion.

Box 11.3. A handout for health clinicians

DEALING WITH VOICES

It can be useful to approach 'Dealing with voices' on a number of levels, including increasing skills in coping with them when they occur, increasing the curiosity about and psychological understanding of the voices, trying to make some connections in terms of both their occurrence and content with the person's life story and internal world, and increasing the person's understanding of self as separate from illness and symptoms.

1. Coping strategies

Most people spontaneously try some form of distraction. It can be useful to focus on a limited number of strategies they are already using and help them to employ those strategies systematically. The literature suggests that the most successful distraction techniques are those that involve meaningful information and cognitive processing, and also that use vibration of the vocal cords. The use of distraction techniques alone

---

does not seem to increase confidence about dealing with voices and may contribute to maintaining anxiety about them, so it is advised to try some focusing strategies that also tend to function as a form of exposure. Depending on the frequency and duration of the voices, some techniques are more useful than others.

(a) *Distraction techniques*
• Using headphones, paying active attention to music/sounds selected
• Naming things in field of vision as quickly as one can
• Counting backwards, and other versions of arithmetic
• Reading out loud
• Psychoeducation about psychosis and symptoms
• Humming, singing.

(b) *Focusing techniques*
It can be helpful to set this up in a graded fashion in conjunction with learning how to remain calm while experiencing the voices. The idea would be to get the person to report particular dimensions of the voice *as they occur*, e.g. loudness, location, gender, age, tone, and content, with the aim being to be able to do this without a change in arousal level. There have been some reports that getting the person to repeat the content in the wording of their own thoughts—e.g. convert 'you are an idiot' to 'I am an idiot'—is effective, though this would seem to be a very confrontational method for some patients.

2. Identifying triggers and patterns

A thorough and basic cognitive-behavioural analysis of the phenomena will strengthen the use and rationale for the coping strategies and offer other avenues for intervention, i.e. dealing with the precipitant situations, arousal, cognitions at the onset of the voices. It is also useful from the point of view of increasing the person's curiosity about the phenomena and introducing the idea that there may be psychological connections that have some personal meaning.

3. Exploring the meaning of the voices

• Psychoeducation about psychosis and symptoms
• Identifying a range of possible alternative explanations for the experiences (where 'auditory hallucinations' is only one possible explanation)
• Constructing tests related to beliefs and evidence for beliefs about origin, cause, meaning, etc.
• Making gentle connections between content of voice and disowned thoughts about themselves
• Exploring possible psychological functions the voices may have.

4. Strengthening sense of self and separating self from illness

Asking patients to spend some time looking at the impact of being unwell on how they think about themselves, and the impact of still not being completely well; their views about mental illness and recovery; what has changed or remained the same since being unwell; what type of people are they; what are their hopes and fears; what are the gaps in their knowledge about themselves; and other relevant information.

CONCLUSION

TREAT currently oversees a randomized-controlled trial (the Recovery Plus Study) which attempts to establish the relative and combined effectiveness of the early introduction of STOPP and clozapine. Consecutive first-episode patients not achieving a predefined level of remission after the initial 12 weeks of treatment are randomized into one of four groups for a further 12-week period of: clozapine; clozapine plus STOPP; standard antipsychotic therapy; or standard antipsychotic therapy plus STOPP. All groups receive case management services. Fortnightly assessments are undertaken, with 3-month and 18-month follow-ups. The recruitment phase of the study ceased in 2002 and results are expected to be available by 2004.

Author Notes

Writing of this chapter was assisted by a Research Program and Project Grant from the Victorian Health Promotion Foundation (1999–2001). Dana Maude drafted the 'Dealing with Voices' handout. Tony James assisted with editing and Sue Leitinger with references.

REFERENCES

Andreasen, N.C. (1984). *The Scale for the Assessment of Negative Symptoms (SANS)*. Iowa City: University of Iowa.

Beck, A.T. & Beck, R.W. (1972). Screening for depressed patients in family practice, A rapid technique. *Postgraduate Medicine*, **52**, 81–85.

Bentall, R.P., Corcoran, R., Howard, R., Blackwood, N. & Kinderman, P. (2001). Persecutory delusions, a review and theoretical integration. *Clinical Psychology Review*, **21**, 1143–1192.

Buchanan, A., Reed, A., Wessley, S., Garety, P., Taylor, P., Grubin, D. & Dunn, G. (1993). Acting on delusions (2): The phenomenological correlates of acting on delusions. *British Journal of Psychiatry*, **163**, 77–81.

Chadwick, P., Birchwood, M. & Trower, P. (1996). *Cognitive Therapy for Delusions, Voices and Paranoia*. Chichester: John Wiley & Sons.

Chakos, M., Lieberman, J., Hoffman, E., Bradford, D. & Sheitman, B. (2001). Effectiveness of second-generation antipsychotics in patients with treatment-resistant schizophrenia. A review and meta-analysis of randomized trials. *American Journal of Psychiatry*, **158**, 518–526.

Cormac I., Jones, C., Campbell, C. & Silveira da Mato Neto, J. (2002). Cognitive behaviour therapy for schizophrenia (Cochrane Review). In *The Cochrane Library* (Issue 4). Oxford: Update Software.

Dickerson, F.B. (2000). Cognitive behavioral psychotherapy for schizophrenia, a review of recent empirical studies. *Schizophrenic Research*, **43**, 71–90.

Drury, V., Birchwood. M. & Cochrane, R. (2000). Cognitive therapy and recovery from acute psychosis, a controlled trial, III: Five-year follow-up. *British Journal of Psychiatry*, **177**, 8–14.

Drury, V., Birchwood, M., Cochrane, R. & Macmillan, F. (1996a). Cognitive therapy and recovery from acute psychosis, a controlled trial, I: Impact on psychotic symptoms. *British Journal of Psychiatry*, **169**, 593–601.

Drury, V., Birchwood, M., Cochrane, R. & Macmillan, F. (1996b). Cognitive therapy and recovery from acute psychosis, a controlled trial, II: Impact on recovery time. *British Journal of Psychiatry*, **169**, 602–607.

Edwards, J. & McGorry, P.D. (2002). *Implementing Early Intervention in Psychosis. A Guide to Establishing Early Psychosis Services*. London: Dunitz.

Edwards, J., Maude, D., Herrmann-Doig, T., Wong, L., Cocks, J., Burnett, P., Bennett, C., Wade, D. & McGorry, P.D (2002). A service response to prolonged recovery in early psychosis. *Psychiatric Services*, **53**, 1067–1069.

Edwards, J., Maude, D., McGorry, P.D., Harrigan, S. & Cocks, J.T. (1998). Prolonged recovery in first-episode psychosis. *British Journal of Psychiatry*, **172** (Suppl. 33), 107–116.

EPPIC (2002a). *Cognitively-Oriented Psychotherapy for Early Psychosis*. No. 4 in a series of early psychosis manuals. Melbourne: Early Psychosis Prevention and Intervention Centre.

EPPIC (2002b). *Prolonged Recovery in Early Psychosis. A Treatment Manual and Video*. Melbourne: Early Psychosis Prevention and Intervention Centre.

Farhall, J. & Cotton, S. (2002). Implementing psychological treatment for symptoms of psychosis in an area mental health service, the response of patients, therapists and managers. *Journal of Mental Health*, **11**, 511–523.

Fowler, D., Garety, P. & Kuipers, E. (1995). *Cognitive Behaviour Therapy for Psychosis: Theory and Practice*. Chichester: John Wiley & Sons.

Freeman, D., Garety, P., Fowler, D., Kuipers, E., Dunn, G., Bebbington, P. & Hadley, C. (1998). London–East Anglia randomized controlled trial of cognitive-behavioural therapy for psychosis, IV: Self-esteem and persecutory delusions. *British Journal of Clinical Psychology*, **37**, 415–430.

Garety, P., Fowler, D. & Kuipers, E. (2000). Cognitive-behavioral therapy for medication-resistant symptoms. *Schizophrenia Bulletin*, **26**, 73–86.

Garety, P., Fowler, D., Kuipers, E., Freeman, D., Bebbington, P., Hadley, C. & Jones, S (1997). London–East Anglia randomized controlled trial of cognitive-behavioural therapy for psychosis, III: Predictors of outcome. *British Journal of Psychiatry*, **171**, 420–426.

Garety, P., Kuipers, E., Fowler, D., Chamberlain, F. & Dunn, G. (1994). Cognitive behavioural therapy for drug-resistant psychosis. *British Journal of Medical Psychology*, **67**, 259–271.

Garety, P.A., Kuipers, E., Fowler, D., Freeman, D. & Bebbington, P.E. (2001). A cognitive model of the positive symptoms of psychosis. *Psychological Medicine*, **31**, 189–195.

Gould, R.A., Mueser, K.T., Bolton, E., Mays, V. & Goff, D. (2001). Cognitive therapy for psychosis in schizophrenia, an effect size analysis. *Schizophrenia Research*, **24**, 335–342.

Haddock, G. & Slade, P. (Eds) (1996). *Cognitive Behavioural Interventions with Psychotic Disorders*. London: Routledge.

Haddock, G., McCarron, J., Tarrier, N. & Faragher, E.B. (1999). Scales to measure dimensions of hallucinations and delusions, the psychotic symptom rating scales (PSYRATS). *Psychological Medicine*, **29**, 879–889.

Herrmann-Doig, T., Maude, D. & Edwards, J. (2003). *Systematic Treatment of Persisting Psychosis. A Guide for Facilitating Recovery from First-Episode Psychosis*. London: Dunitz.

Jackson, H., McGorry, P.D. & Edwards, J. (2001). Cognitively oriented psychotherapy for early psychosis (COPE). Theory, praxis, outcome and challenges. In P. Corrigan & D. Penn (Eds), *Social Cognition and Schizophrenia* (pp. 249–284). Washington, DC: APA Press.

Jackson, H.J., Edwards, J., Hulbert, C. & McGorry, P.D. (1999). Recovery from psychosis, psychological interventions. In P.D. McGorry & H.J. Jackson (Eds), *Recognition and Management of Early Psychosis: A Preventive Approach* (pp. 265–307). Cambridge: Cambridge University Press.

Jackson, H.J., McGorry, P.D., Edwards, J. & Hulbert, C. (1996). Cognitively-oriented psychotherapy for early psychosis (COPE). In P. Cotton & J. Jackson (Eds), *Early Intervention and Preventative Application of Clinical Psychology* (pp. 131–154). Melbourne: Australian Psychological Society.

Jackson, H.J., McGorry, P.D., Edwards, J., Hulbert, C., Henry, L., Francey, S., Cocks, J., Power, P., Harrigan, S. & Dudgeon, P. (1998). Cognitively orientated psychotherapy for early psychosis (COPE). Preliminary results. *British Journal of Psychiatry*, **172** (Suppl. 33), 93–100.

Jackson, H.J., McGorry, P.D., Henry, L., Edwards, J., Hulbert, C., Harrigan, S., Dudgeon, P., Francey, S., Maude, D., Cocks, J. & Power, P. (2001). Cognitively oriented psychotherapy for early psychosis (COPE). A 1-year follow-up. *British Journal of Clinical Psychology*, **40**, 57–70.

John, C.H. (2003). *The Global Scale of Delusional Severity (GSDS). A 17-item measure of the severity of delusional symptoms*. Manuscript in preparation.

Kingdon, D. & Pelton, J. (2002). Training in CBT for psychosis. In D. Kingdon & D. Turkington (Eds), *The Case Study Guide to Cognitive Behaviour Therapy of Psychosis* (pp. 183–190). Chichester: John Wiley & Sons.

Kingdon, D. & Turkington, D. (1991). The use of cognitive-behavioural therapy with a normalizing rationale in schizophrenia. Preliminary report. *Journal of Nervous and Mental Disorder*, **179**, 207–211.

Kingdon, D. & Turkington, D. (Eds) (1994). *Cognitive-Behavioural Therapy of Schizophrenia*. New York: Guilford Press.

Kingdon, D. & Turkington, D. (Eds) (2002). *The Case Study Guide to Cognitive Behaviour Therapy of Psychosis*. Chichester: John Wiley & Sons.

Kuipers, E., Fowler, D., Garety, P., Chisholm, D., Freeman, D., Dunn, G., Bebbington, P. & Hadley, C. (1998). London–East Anglia randomized controlled trial of cognitive-behavioural therapy for psychosis, III: Follow-up and economic evaluation at 18 months. *British Journal of Psychiatry*, **173**, 61–68.

Kuipers, E., Garety, P., Fowler, D., Dunn, G., Bebbington, P., Freeman, D. & Hadley, C. (1997). London–East Anglia randomised controlled trial of cognitive-behavioural therapy for psychosis, I: Effects of the treatment phase. *British Journal of Psychiatry*, **171**, 319–327.

Lewis, S.W., Tarrier, N., Haddock, G., Bentall, R., Kinderman, P., Kingdon, D., Siddle, R., Drake, R., Everitt, J., Leadley, K., Benn, A., Grazebrook, K., Haley, C., Akhtar, S., Davies, L., Palmer, S., Faragher, B. & Dunn G. (2002). Randomised controlled trial of cognitive-behavioural therapy in early schizophrenia: Acute-phase outcomes. *British Journal of Psychiatry*, **181** (Suppl. 43), 91–97.

Lukoff, D., Neuchterlein, K.H. & Ventura, J. (1986). Manual for the Expanded Brief Psychiatric Rating Scale. *Psychiatric Bulletin*, **12**, 594–602.

McGorry, P.D., Chanen. A., McCarthy, E., Van Riel, R., McKenzie, D. & Singh, B.S. (1991). Post-traumatic stress disorder following recent-onset psychosis: An unrecognized postpsychotic syndrome. *Journal of Nervous and Mental Disease*, **179**, 253–258.

McGorry, P.D., Edwards, J., Mihalopoulos, C., Harrigan, S.M. & Jackson, H.J. (1996). EPPIC: An evolving system of early detection and optimal management. *Schizophrenia Bulletin*, **22**, 305–326.

McLellan, A.T., Kushner, H., Metzger, D., Peters, R., Grisson, G., Pettinati, H. & Argeriou, M. (1992). The fifth edition of the Addiction Severity Index. *Journal of Substance Abuse Treatment*, **9**, 199–213.

Pilling, S., Bebbington, P., Kuipers, E., Garety, P., Geddes, J., Orbach, G. & Morgan, C. (2002). Psychological treatments in schizophrenia, I. Meta-analysis of family intervention and cognitive behaviour therapy. *Psychological Medicine*, **32**, 763–782.

Pinto, A., La Pia, S., Mennella, R., Giorgio, D. & DeSimone, L. (1999). Cognitive-behavioural therapy and clozapine for clients with treatment-refractory schizophrenia. *Psychiatric Services*, **50**, 901–904.

Rector, N.A. & Beck, A.T. (2001). Cognitive behavioral therapy for schizophrenia: An empirical review. *Journal of Nervous and Mental Disease*, **189**, 278–287.

Sensky, T., Turkington, D., Kingdon, D., Scott, J.L., Scott, J., Siddle, R., O'Carroll, M. & Barnes, T.R. (2000). A randomised-controlled trial of cognitive-behavioural therapy for persistent symptoms in schizophrenia resistant to medication. *Archives of General Psychiatry*, **57**, 165–172.

Spence, S.H., Wilson, J., Kavanagh, D., Strong, J. & Worrall, L. (2001). Clinical supervision in four mental health professions, a review of the evidence. *Behaviour Change*, **18**, 135–155.

Tarrier, N., Beckett, R., Harwood, S., Baker, A., Yusupoff, L. & Ugarteburu, I (1993). A trial of two cognitive-behavioural methods of treating drug-resistant residual psychotic symptoms in schizophrenia patients, I. Outcome. *British Journal of Psychiatry*, **162**, 524–532.

Tarrier, N., Kinney, C., McCarthy, E., Humpreys, L., Wittkowski, A., Yusupoff, L., Gledhill, A., Morris, J. & Humpreys, L. (2000). Two-year follow-up of cognitive-behavioral therapy and supportive counseling in the treatment of persistent symptoms in chronic schizophrenia. *Journal of Consulting and Clinical Psychology*, **68**, 917–922.

Tarrier, N., Kinney, C., McCarthy, E., Humpreys, L., Wittkowski, A., Yusupoff, L., Gledhill, A., Morris, J. & Humpreys, L. (2001). Are some types of psychotic symptoms more responsive to cognitive-behaviour therapy? *Behavioural and Cognitive Psychotherapy*, **29**, 45–55.

Tarrier, N., Wittkowski, A., Kinney, C., McCarthy, E., Morris, J. & Humphreys, L. (1999). Durability of the effects of cognitive-behavioral therapy in the treatment of chronic schizophrenia: 12-month follow-up. *British Journal of Psychiatry*, **174**, 500–504.

Tarrier, N., Yusupoff, L., Kinney, C., McCarthy, E., Gledhill, A., Haddock, G. & Morris, J. (1998). Randomised controlled trial of intensive cognitive behaviour therapy for patients with chronic schizophrenia. *British Medical Journal*, **317**, 303–307.

Tollefson, D.G., Birkett, M.A., Kiesler, G.M. & Wood, A.J. (2001). Double-blind comparison of olanzapine versus clozapine in schizophrenic patients clinically eligible for treatment with clozapine. *Biological Psychiatry*, **49**, 52–63.

Turkington, D., Kingdon, D. & Turner, T. (2002). Effectiveness of a brief cognitive-behavioural therapy intervention in the treatment of schizophrenia. *British Journal of Psychiatry*, **180**, 523–527.

Turkington, D., John, C.H., Siddle, R., Ward, D. & Birmingham, L. (1996). Cognitive therapy in the treatment of drug-resistant delusional disorder. *Clinical Psychology and Psychotherapy*, **3**, 118–128.

Volavka, J., Czobor, P., Sheitman, B., Lindenmayer, J.-P., Citrome, L., McEvoy, J.P., Cooper, T.B., Chakos, M. & Lieberman, J.A. (2002). Clozapine, olanzapine, risperidone, and haloperidol in the treatment of patients with chronic schizophrenia and schizoaffective disorder. *American Journal of Psychiatry*, **159**, 255–262.

Wahlbeck, K., Cheine, M., Essali, A. & Adams, C. (1999). Evidence of clozapine's effectiveness in schizophrenia: A systematic review and meta-analysis of randomized trials. *American Journal of Psychiatry*, **156**, 990–999.

12 Cognitive Therapy and Emotional Dysfunction in Early Psychosis

MAX BIRCHWOOD

Early Intervention Service, Birmingham, UK

ZAFFER IQBAL

Leeds Mental Health Teaching NHS Trust, UK

CHRIS JACKSON

Early Intervention Service, Birmingham, UK

KATE HARDY

South West Yorkshire Mental Health NHS Trust, UK

Cognitive therapy for psychosis has developed rapidly throughout the 1990s and into the new millennium, ignited by the systematic, pioneering work of Chadwick and Lowe (1990). This study, using multiple baseline single case methodology, showed that it was possible to engage people with psychosis in a collaborative fashion and to systematically explore the logical and empirical bases for their delusions. This process of 'collaborative empiricism' was found to weaken strongly held delusional beliefs. This breakthrough work has led to a proliferation of randomized-controlled trials and an assured place for cognitive-behavioural therapy (CBT) in the therapeutic armamentarium. Curiously, a secure theoretical framework has not informed CBT for psychosis; if anything, only now is the basis for its effectiveness beginning to be understood (Garety et al., 2001). The primary outcomes for the trials of CBT have been the positive symptoms of psychosis, assessed using the same scales widely used in trials of neuroleptic medication, predominantly the Brief Psychiatric Rating Scale (BPRS) (Overall & Gorham, 1962) and the Positive and Negative Syndrome Scale (PANSS) (Kay, Fiszbein & Opler, 1987). This is reflected in meta-analyses (Cormac, Jones & Campbell, 2002) where the Cochrane plots parallel those for studies of neuroleptics; indeed the CBT trials reports are almost identical to pharmacological studies. CBT, in other words, is widely regarded and evaluated as a 'quasi-neuroleptic'. This has not unexpectedly led to resistance and, at times, hostility, as professional territory is challenged (McKenna, 2003). The results of the randomized-controlled trials (RCTs) have demonstrated efficacy in symptom reduction and led to the therapy being taken seriously by the mental health community and by research funders. We will argue, however, that CBT is, in both theory and practice, a therapy to reduce emotional dysfunction and distress and that its application with delusional beliefs is something of an anomaly. We will argue that CBT should define a clear niche in

Psychological Interventions in Early Psychosis
Edited by J.F.M. Gleeson and P.D. McGorry. © 2004 John Wiley & Sons, Ltd.

resolving distress, life disruption and the emotional dysfunction that arises from psychosis, and that the resolution of positive symptoms should become a secondary outcome. We will first develop this argument by reference to the nature of CBT, then review the efficacy of the RCTs in resolving emotional dysfunction, including the first-episode trials. We review the evidence for the presence and prevalence of emotional dysfunction in first-episode psychosis and the different processes governing the development and maintenance of these 'comorbidities'. We will argue that CBT in early psychosis will fail to resolve distress and emotional dysfunction unless it moves away from the positive symptoms *per se* and focuses on the different psychological pathways to emotional dysfunction.

EMOTIONAL DISTRESS AND PSYCHOTIC SYMPTOMS

There can be little doubt that the experience of voices and delusions is often immensely distressing. Freeman, Garety and Kuipers (2001) document the level of depression among a group of people with persecutory delusions and report that over 80% were at least moderately depressed on the Beck Depression Inventory (BDI) with a mean score of 23. Furthermore, 75% of the same sample were anxious and the mean delusional distress score was 8 (out of 10). Birchwood and Chadwick (1997) and Birchwood et al. (2000b) similarly find that 7 out of 10 voice hearers were depressed (BDI > 15) and over 80% found their voices 'very distressing'. This is in line with the general assumption that depression 'follows the same course' as psychotic symptoms (Birchwood et al., 2000a). However, data from community samples shows that distress is not an inevitable consequence of psychotic experience (van Os et al., 1999) and in young children who hear voices, distress/depression and can develop over time, linked to the appraisal of the voices as powerful and malevolent (Escher et al., 2002).

WHAT IS CBT FOR PSYCHOSIS?

CBT draws its strength from the traditions of Beck and Ellis and is quintessentially a therapy for emotional dysfunction: depression, anxiety, trauma, anger, etc. In these applications of CBT, there are clearly articulated models of the relationship between cognition and dysfunctional affect. These cognitions then become the focus for therapy. In psychosis a consensus is beginning to emerge about a cognitive model of the formation and maintenance of positive symptoms (Garety et al., 2001). This revolves around the appraisal of anomalous experience and the operation of perceptual and reasoning biases involved in the processing of social information. It also proposes that affective disturbance can independently influence this process and 'contribute to the maintenance of the psychotic appraisal' (p. 192). It is arguable that dysfunctional schema arising from anomalies of development contribute to treatment resistance and relapse proneness. Garety's cognitive model brings emotion into the discourse on schizophrenia and to the development of positive symptoms in particular. The cognitions addressed in psychosis are either the delusions themselves ('I have been put under surveillance by MI6') or beliefs linked to low self-esteem ('I deserve to be punished'), which are believed to lock the individual into a deluded view of the world (Bentall & Kinderman, 1998). The assumption is that delusions and hallucinations *per se*

Table 12.1. Cognitive therapy in psychosis: 10 common elements

Engagement strategies appropriate for psychosis
Assessment and individual formulation
Coping strategy enhancement
Psychoeducation: normalizing rationale
'Verbal challenge': resolving inconsistencies in beliefs
Challenging the evidence for beliefs: Reaction to hypothetical contradiction (RCTH)
Challenging power and omnipotence of persecutor(s), including voices
Empirical testing of beliefs
Viewing content of delusions/voices in life context (e.g. trauma, neglect)
Improving self-concept and self-worth

generate their own dysfunctional affect (e.g. fear) and that reducing the frequency of voices or the strength of delusional conviction will reduce distress and behavioural disruption.

CBT for psychosis has been developed in the UK in four centres: London (Fowler, Kuipers & Garety, 1995), Newcastle (Kingdon & Turkington, 1994), Manchester (Tarrier et al., 1999) and Birmingham (Chadwick, Birchwood & Trower, 1996). They each have a distinctive characteristic and theoretical emphasis, but have much in common, which we distil into 10 core elements (see Table 12.1).

The therapeutic stance requires taking the client's perspective seriously and retains the classic Beckian approach of 'collaborative empiricism'. Working with delusional beliefs consumes the majority of time, usually organized around a shared formulation, which attempts to understand the meaning of psychosis and the content of symptoms in the individual's life context. Some elements, for example relapse prevention, are emphasized in some approaches (Fowler, Kuipers & Garety, 1995) but not others (Chadwick, Birchwood & Trower, 1996). In all versions of CBT, the targeting of particular beliefs is democratically agreed with the client.

RANDOMIZED-CONTROLLED TRIALS: IMPACT ON DEPRESSION AND DISTRESS

Table 12.2 lists all the RCTs of CBT for psychosis, noting whether each measured depression or distress linked to delusions. The trials included are all those in the Pilling et al. (2002) review, plus four reported since 2002. The COPE trial of Jackson et al. (2001) is included as it incorporates many of the elements listed in Table 12.2 and includes an explicit focus on 'comorbidity'. These trials have shown a decisive impact on psychotic symptoms (Pilling et al., 2002) with an effect size of 0.6 rising to 0.93 at follow-up (Gould et al., 2001). Twelve trials are included, nine of which measured depression as a secondary outcome. Four measured distress—either using the Psychotic Symptom Rating Scales (PSYRATS: Haddock, McCarron & Tarrier, 1999), which includes distress subscales, or the Personal Questionnaire Rating Scale Technique (PQRST: Brett-Jones, Garety & Hemsley, 1987). In no study was distress separately analysed (*N.B.* PSYRATS uses the distress scale to compile total scores for hallucinations or delusions).

Overall, three of the nine studies measuring depression reported an improvement in depression score attributed to CBT (Drury et al., 1996b; Garety et al., 1994; Sensky et al., 2000; Turkington, Kingdon & Turner, 2002). All of these were secondary measures taken

Table 12.2. Randomized-controlled trials of CBT in psychosis and their impact on depression and distress

Study	Inclusion criteria	CBT procedure	Control procedure	Follow-up	Results	Measure of depression used	Does therapy alleviate depression better than control? CBT end	Follow-up	Effect size	Distress from symptoms targeted and measured?
Rector et al. (2003)	DSM-IV diagnosis of schizophrenia or schizoaffective disorder, persistent +ve and −ve symptoms for 6 months assessed. Non-organic or concurrent substance abuse. No past treatment with behavioural or CBT.	(n = 24) 6 months: engagement and assessment, education of cognitive model, coping skills, psychoeducation with normalization, relapse prevention. Targets +ve and −ve symptoms; guided discovery, behavioural self-monitoring and cognitive strategies.	(n = 18) Enriched treatment as usual (ETAU).	Post-treatment and 6 months.	Significant clinical effects seen for +ve, −ve and overall symptoms for CBT group but no difference between groups at post-treatment. CBT showed significant reduction in −ve symptoms at follow-up.	BDI	No	No	n/a	No
Durham et al. (2003)	ICD-10 and DSM-IV diagnosis of psychosis, schizophrenia, schizoaffective or delusional disorder. 16–65 years of age, known to psychiatric services, suffering from positive symptoms and stabilized on antipsychotics for 6 months.	(n = 22) 9-month treatment phase over 20 sessions: engagement, education, therapeutic alliance, formulation, problem list, normalization, coping strategies, relaxation training and problem solving.	1. Supportive psychotherapy (SPT) (n = 23). 2. TAU (n = 21).	Baseline, 3 months.	Modest treatment effects reported at follow up. CBT led to greater improvement in overall symptom severity. No treatment effects found for auditory hallucinations.	n/a	n/a	n/a	n/a	PSYRATS; no treatment effect for hallucinations, but reduction in severity of delusions from CBT and SPT combined.

Study	Population	Intervention (n)	Assessment	Results	Depression measure			Effect size	Comments
McGorry et al. (2002)[a]	First prodromal episode ultra-high-risk group, 14–30 years, highly symptomatic and moderately disabled by symptoms.	(n = 31) Specific preventive intervention (SPI): low dose risperidone for 6 months and modified CBT (targets: stress management, depression, −ve and +ve symptoms, comorbidities). (n = 28) Needs based intervention (NBI).	Baseline, 6 months and 12 months.	No significant difference between SPI and NBI. Progression to acute psychosis at 6 month follow-up. NNT = 4:1	Hamilton Rating Scale for Depression	No	No	n/a	No
Lewis et al. (2002)[a]	Early psychosis, non-organic or primary substance misuse; DSM-IV schizophrenia or related disorder.	(n = 101) CBT for 5 weeks: engagement, education, problem list generation, intervention, monitoring. 1. (n = 106) Supportive counselling. 2. (n = 102) Routine care alone.	Baseline, 2, 3, 4, 5 and 6 weeks.	Trend for CBT group to improve fastest up to Week 5 but difference is not maintained.	n/a	n/a	n/a	n/a	PSYRATS; no difference seen in rate of change between treated and routine care groups on delusions and hallucinations scales.
Turkington et al. (2002)	ICD-10 diagnosis of schizophrenia, 18–65 years, non-organic or primary substance misuse.	(n = 257) CBT: assessment, engagement, case formulations, symptom management, adherence, working with core beliefs and relapse prevention – 6 sessions. (n = 165). Treatment as usual.	Assessed 9 months after therapy ended.	CBT superior in lowering symptoms and promoting insight. Higher attrition in treatment as usual group.	Montgomery–Asberg Depression Rating Scale	Yes	n/a	0.29	No
Jackson et al. (2001)[a]	FEP, 16–30 years. Non-organic or primary substance misuse; DSM-III-R schizophrenia or related disorder.	(n = 44) Cognitively oriented psycho-therapy: engagement, assessment, adaptation and comorbidity targeted. 21 sessions (mean). 1. (n = 21) Refused CBT and treatment as usual in FEP service. 2. (n = 15) No CBT or FEP service.	Baseline, treatment end, 12 months.	All end-of-treatment differences were sustained over 12 months on the BPRS, SANS, QoL and I/SO.	BDI	No	No	n/a	No

(cont.)

Table 12.2. (*cont.*)

Study	Inclusion criteria	CBT procedure	Control procedure	Follow-up	Results	Measure of depression used	Does therapy alleviate depression better than control? CBT end	Follow-up	Effect size	Distress from symptoms targeted and measured?
Tarrier et al. (2001)	DSM-III-R diagnosis of schizophrenia and related disorder, 18–65 years, non-organic or primary substance misuse.	(n = 24) CBT: coping strategy enhancements, problem-solving, cognitive-behavioural relapse prevention—20 sessions.	1. (n = 21) Supportive counselling and routine care. 2. (n = 27) Routine care.	Assessed at baseline and 3 month follow-up.	Hallucination and delusions showed improvement with CBT. No effect on affective symptoms.	BDI	No	n/a	n/a	No
Sensky et al. (2000)	DSM-IV and ICD-10 diagnosis of schizophrenia, 16–60 years, not primary substance misuse.	(n = 46) CBT: normalizing, collaborative critical analysis of beliefs, reattribution, coping strategies, guided discovery—9 months.	(n = 44) Befriending.	Assessed at baseline, 9 months and 9 month follow-up.	Both interventions resulted in significant reductions in symptoms. CBT continued to improve at 9 months.	Montgomery–Asberg Depression Rating Scale.	Yes	Yes	0.21	CBT aimed to reduce distress and disability but no measurement of distress employed.
Bradshaw (2000)	DSM-IV criteria for schizophrenia, 18–60 years, non-organic or primary substance abuse	(n = 8) Day treatment programme and CBT weekly over 3 years: engagement and education, behavioural treatment and cognitive treatment.	(n = 7) Day treatment programme.	Assessed at end of 3-year treatment.	Both groups showed improvement in psychosocial functioning but effect greater in the CBT group.	n/a	n/a	n/a	n/a	No

Study	Inclusion criteria	Intervention	Control	Assessment	Outcome	Measure			Effect size	Notes
Kuipers et al. (1997) Garety et al. (1997) Kuipers et al. (1998)	Schizophrenia or related disorder. Non-organic or primary substance misuse.	(n = 28) CBT for 9 months, improving, coping strategies, developing a shared model, modifying beliefs and dysfunctional schema, management of social disability and relapse.	(n = 32) Routine care.	Assessed at baseline, 3, 6, 9 and 18 months.	Only BPRS showed significant improvement for CBT group. Cognitive flexibility regarding delusions predicted good outcome. Improvement maintained at 9 months after therapy.	BDI	No	No	n/a	Personal questionnaires: measured conviction, preoccupation and distress with delusions and hallucinations. No change seen in scores post CBT but significant improvement reported at 18-month follow-up for delusions.
Drury et al. (1996a, 1996b, 2000)	DSM-IV criteria for schizophrenia and related disorder. Non-organic or primary substance abuse.	(n = 20) Cognitive therapy: individual CT, group CT, family engagement, structured activity programme from ward—max of 6 months.	(n = 20) Recreation and support group.	Follow-up at 9 months and 5 years.	CT group showed a faster rate in decline of +ve symptoms over 12 weeks. No difference in relapse at 5 years. CT group report less entrapment due to illness.	Psychiatric Assessment Scale (PAS)	Yes	Yes	0.34	Personal questionnaire: Conviction and preoccupation reported as decreasing but no report of distress at end of CBT or follow-up.
Tarrier et al. (1993)	DSM-III-R criteria for schizophrenia, 16–65 years, non-organic.	1. (n = 15) Coping strategy enhancement (CSE) 2. (n = 12) Problem-solving (PS) treatment lasted 5 weeks	(n = 14) Waiting period.	Assessed at baseline, 6 weeks and followed up at 6 months	CBT showed improvement on symptom related assessments CSE more effective than PS.	Psychiatric Assessment Scale (PAS).	No	No	n/a	No

[a] First-episode or prodromal (high-risk) patients.

at the end of treatment, suggesting that the impact of the CBT upon psychotic symptoms is also responsible for a decrease in the depressed affect associated with them. Two studies described a longer-term improvement in depression at the 9-month follow-up (Drury et al., 1996b; Sensky et al., 2000). In the Drury et al. (1996b) study, this may have reflected the attempt to challenge secondary appraisals of psychosis (e.g. loss, shame) that informed their CBT programme. Additionally, Tarrier et al. (2001) reported an improvement in mood following the alleviation of positive symptoms at the end of treatment. In summary, three out of the nine trials measuring depression reported that a reduction in the targeted psychotic symptoms was associated with a reduction in depression (and in one case mood improvement: Tarrier et al., 2001) at the end of therapy. The mean effect size of those studies reporting a significant effect was 0.28 compared to the effect size of 0.65 (all studies) for psychotic symptoms, with more gains with time (EF = 0.93) (Gould et al., 2001). Of the four studies measuring delusional distress, one (Durham et al., 2003) reported a reduction in the severity of delusions on the PSYRATS (distress scale aggregated in the delusions scale score) and another (Kuipers et al., 1998) reported an improvement in delusional distress (on PQRST) only at follow-up. Considering the high level of depression and distress associated with positive symptoms, and the scale of the impact of CBT on the positive symptoms, it is surprising that the impact of CBT on depression occurred only in a minority of studies and with low effect size. These results call into question the assumption that easing distress and depression in psychosis will follow from the treatment of positive symptoms alone.

In the next section, therefore, we examine the assumption that emotional disturbance in psychosis will be relieved by a reduction in psychotic symptoms alone.

PATHWAYS TO EMOTIONAL DYSFUNCTION IN FIRST-EPISODE PSYCHOSIS

Emotional dysfunction and schizophrenia have long been uncomfortable bedfellows. It was Bleuler who first argued that problems of affect lie at the heart of schizophrenia and that the symptoms on which we all focus—the hallucinations and delusions—are merely 'accessory' and common to many forms of disorder. This view gave way to the now familiar distinction between affective and non-affective psychosis and to Jaspers' hierarchical approach to diagnosis, wherein affective symptoms are 'trumped' by the presence of schizophrenia in terms of diagnosis and treatment. Yet emotional dysfunction is pervasive in non-affective psychosis. Sometimes (and perhaps unhelpfully) referred to as 'comorbidity', these include: depression, usually accompanied by hopelessness and suicidal thinking; social anxiety, usually accompanied by social avoidance and problems with forming relationships; and traumatic [post-traumatic stress disorder (PTSD)] symptoms. It is now widely acknowledged that the prodromal and early stages of psychosis 'set the scene' for the development of the long-term illness trajectories, social disabilities and psychological comorbidities embodied in the concept of schizophrenia (Birchwood, Todd & Jackson, 1998; Harrison et al., 2001; Jones et al., 1993, Wiersma et al., 1998). Emotional dysfunction, in common with the core symptoms and disabilities, develops rapidly and aggressively during the prodrome and early phase (Harrison et al., 2001). These comorbidities are considerable and include depression and suicidal thinking, an impaired capacity to form and maintain interpersonal relationships, drug misuse, social anxiety and social avoidance, post-traumatic symptoms, and disturbed relationships within the family. Though assumed to be linked to psychosis, little research has been done to determine how these co-occurring emotional disorders develop. However, they are substantial at the first episode: over 50% report post-psychotic depression (PPD: Addington, Addington & Patten, 1998; Birchwood et al., 2000a) and the early phase is a high-risk period for suicide (Mortensen & Juel, 1993; Verdoux, 2001; Westermeyer, Harrow & Marengo, 1991); while over one-third report traumatic reactions sufficient to qualify for PTSD, in particular, unwanted intrusions of images surrounding the first episode and its treatment (McGorry et al., 1991). A marked and persistent fear of social interaction (e.g. social anxiety disorder) has been observed in 50% of people with schizophrenia (Cossof & Hafner, 1998). To complicate matters further, these comorbidities are also comorbid with one another; for example, the overlap between PTSD and depression (Bleich et al., 1997; Strakowski et al., 1995) and between drug misuse and suicidality (Verdoux et al., 1999).

It is tempting to characterize these emotional problems as integral to psychosis and the accompanying loss of functioning and it is perhaps for this reason that the pathogenesis of these emotional comorbidities is not understood and few effective treatments are available (Jackson & Iqbal, 2000; Lewis et al., 2002). This is particularly important because the presence of comorbidities increases the probability of early relapse, for example misuse of cannabis (Linszen, Dingemans & Lenior, 1994), and their presence during the prodrome may act as risk factors for transition to psychosis (Strakowski et al., 1995). In order to improve our understanding and to develop new treatments we need to make a clear distinction between three core, but not mutually exclusive, pathways: emotional disorder that is *intrinsic* to the psychosis diathesis; a *psychological reaction* to it; and the product of *disturbed developmental pathways* resulting from developmental trauma.

Emotional Disorder as Intrinsic to Psychosis

The clearest example of the first relationship is depression and psychosis. The second generation of factor analytic studies of psychotic symptoms yielded additional dimensions of depressive symptoms (McGorry et al., 1998; van Os et al., 1999). When orthogonality is not imposed on these factors, the dimensions co-vary in patient (Peralta & Cuesta, 1999) and community samples (Stefanis et al., 2002). Depression is nearly always part of the first-episode prodrome (Jackson, McGorry & McKenzie, 1994), which recedes with the positive symptoms (Birchwood et al., 2000a). In a similar vein, the problems of social anxiety and social avoidance in the context of active psychotic symptoms may be traced directly to the symptoms themselves. Patients with persecutory delusions often deal with the perceived threat to their well-being through avoidance of high-risk social encounters; in cognitive therapy this is one of a class of 'safety behaviours' which function to reduce threat (Freeman, Garety & Kuipers, 2001). Social disengagement can also be traced to the content of command hallucinations that can directly undermine trust in others (Beck-Sander, Birchwood & Chadwick, 1997). Many studies also report correlations between negative symptoms, particularly alogia and affective flattening, and social disengagement (Chapman et al., 1998).

The therapeutic implications of this pathway to emotional disorder lie in the treatment of core psychotic symptoms and, in relation to first-episode psychosis, the reduction in duration of untreated psychosis.

Emotional Disorder as a Psychological Reaction to Psychosis

Here the emphasis is on the pathway from psychosis as a challenging or traumatic life event to the adaptation by individuals and their families. Post-psychotic depression (PPD) is known to occur some months after recovery (Addington, Addington & Patten, 1998) and has been shown to be predicted by how patients appraise the personal threat of this shattering life event: where the individual appraises psychosis as leading to *loss* of social goals, roles and status—as a source of *shame* from which escape is thwarted, i.e. *entrapment* by a supposed malignant disorder—this predicts the later emergence of PPD with hopelessness (Iqbal et al., 2000). In this study, first-episode patients had a higher rate of PPD (over 50%) linked to heightened awareness of the diagnosis and its implications. There is also evidence that relatives' and patients' appraisals of psychosis are linked as they jointly attempt to adapt to this major life event (Patterson, Birchwood & Cochrane, 2000). Where symptoms persist, depression has been attributed to the perceived power of voices and not voice frequency or volume (Birchwood et al., 2000b), or persecutory delusions (Freeman, Garety & Kuipers, 2001), and to the *subjective* experience of negative symptoms (Liddle et al., 1993). In general, the distress occasioned by persisting symptoms has been shown to operate through a 'psychological filter'; in other words, the experience of psychotic phenomena *per se* does not generate distress, it is how it is perceived and coped with.

With regard to traumatic reactions, these do not appear to be linked to 'objective' trauma of psychosis, e.g. compulsory admission, as would be required for a DSM-IV diagnosis (McGorry et al., 1991; Priebe, Broker & Gunkel, 1998). In non-psychotic PTSD, attention now focuses on the *perceived* threat of traumatic events and how people cope (Ehlers & Clark, 2000). In psychosis, patients may perceive themselves at risk of injury or death from supposed persecutors (Freeman, Garety & Kuipers, 2001), voices (Birchwood et al., 2000b) or from others in a disturbed psychiatric ward, but its impact on trauma is as yet unknown. With regard to social anxiety, it is known that patients perceive themselves to be shamed and socially subordinated by others because of their psychosis and patient status (Gilbert et al., 2001; Haghighat, 2001). In non-psychotic social anxiety, patients fear criticism and humiliation in social encounters which drives social avoidance (Clark, 2001). It has been argued that social anxiety and avoidance in psychosis may be underpinned by a similar process, namely social shame and fear of discovery (Jackson & Iqbal, 2000).

The therapeutic emphasis in this pathway focuses on patients' appraisals (beliefs) of the threat posed by the diagnosis, by voices and by perceived social shame. We believe that therapy aimed at promoting adaptation to psychosis must focus exclusively on the resolution of appraisal of shame and entrapment by psychosis, in a coherent and theoretically driven way. 'Scattershot' approaches involving many components—for example, psychoeducation, supportive psychotherapy, relapse prevention etc.—do, we believe, risk losing the focus on these core appraisals and confusing the client.

Emotional Disorder Arising from Developmental Anomaly and Trauma

Birth cohort (e.g. Isohanni et al., 1998) and retrospective studies (Jones et al., 1993) reveal that first-episode psychosis is often preceded by social difficulty and emotional disorder as well as by low-level 'psychotic' experience stretching back into early adolescence (Poulton et al., 2000). These childhood antecedents of a developing psychosis will unfold in a social environment and there is now considerable evidence that social factors influence morbidity and outcome, for example urban living, particularly deprivation (van Os et al., 2003; Pederson & Mortensen, 2001), membership of marginalized social groups (Bhugra et al., 1997), the impact of migration (Bhugra, 2000) and the (favourable) correlates of 'developing nation' status (Harrison et al., 2001). The unfolding antecedents of psychosis will also affect 'normal' social and psychological development leading, perhaps, to low self-esteem,

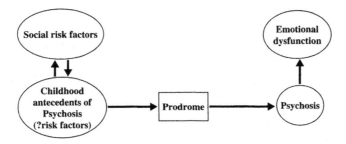

(A) The classical model of emotional dysfunction

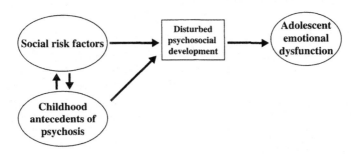

(B) The developmental model of emotional dysfunction

Figure 12.1. Psychosis (A) and developmental (B) pathways to emotional dysfunction

difficulty in establishing relationships, and susceptibility to stress. The science of developmental psychopathology (Rutter, 2000) shows that continuity exists between adolescent and adult characteristics, including depression and risk of suicide (Fombonne et al., 2001), which occurs in a dimensional, and not a categorical way, influenced by the social and familial context (Rutter, 2000). There is also considerable *dis*-continuity between adolescent and adult emotional functioning; for example, Andrews and Brown (1995) showed that positive life events in late adolescence can serve to restore a disturbed developmental trajectory to within normal limits. The domains of emotional functioning also interact; for example, social anxiety increases the developmental risk of adolescent depression (Stein et al., 2001). A strong case can be made that the variance in comorbid emotional disorder in first-episode psychosis is a product in part of these unfolding, disturbed, developmental pathways triggered by the psychosis diathesis (see Figure 12.1).

Childhood trauma and problems of parental attachment can predispose individuals to adult depression (Brown et al., 1990). There is evidence of a high rate of traumatic histories in people with psychosis, including sexual abuse (Greenfield et al., 1994), unwanted pregnancy (Myhrman et al., 1996) and dysfunctional parental attachment (Parker, Johnston & Hayward, 1988; Tienari, 1994). Such traumatic histories may also render patients prone to PPD and other emotional disorders. In PTSD, traumatic responses to violent crime have been shown to be more likely in those who have a history of childhood trauma who appraise the event as more personally threatening (Andrews et al., 2000). These histories and developmental anomalies have been hypothesized to influence cognitive schema that govern the processing of self and social information (Birchwood et al., 2000b; Garety et al., 2001). Such schema have been observed to be active in the emotional response to psychosis in the way in which the voice hearer appraises the interpersonal significance of the voice (i.e. of power and omnipotence: Birchwood et al., 2000b) and also in the distress and persistence of voices in young adolescents (Escher et al., 2002).

This pathway to comorbid emotional disorder in first-episode psychosis may therefore arise due to developmental disturbance leading to (a) dysfunctional cognitive schema that affect adaptation to psychosis and its symptoms, and (b) adolescent emotional disorder that shows continuity into adulthood.

The therapeutic implications of this pathway lie in the focus on disturbances in 'normal' developmental processes in adolescence and their continuity with emerging psychopathology with a particular therapeutic focus on dysfunctional schema of self and others.

Implications for CBT

We have proposed that distress arising from psychotic symptoms and the emotional dysfunctions will arise from pathways that are not necessarily driven by positive symptoms or primary psychotic experience alone. 'Standard CBT', which focuses on delusional beliefs (including beliefs about voices) and self-evaluative beliefs will not address all of these pathways and may fail, therefore, to fully treat emotional dysfunction and the psychological factors influencing the perception of threat and distress from supposed persecutors (Birchwood, 2003). Moreover, we would argue that it may be possible to reduce distress and behaviour arising from psychosis, without changing the core psychotic experience itself. For example, in our recent work with command hallucinations (Byrne et al., 2003), we demonstrated that by focusing on the voice hearer's appraisal of the power and omnipotence of voices, this itself reduced depression and despair, and compliance with voices' commands, but it did not lead to a decrease in the frequency of hallucinations *per se*. Returning to the opening theme of this chapter, we believe the time has come to shift attention from CBT as a quasi-neuroleptic, to CBT as a therapy to relieve distress associated with psychotic experience and the 'comorbid' emotional dysfunctions. This broader focus for therapy has been advocated by Jackson, McGorry and colleagues (2001) for some time and is particularly apposite in early psychosis where these disorders develop at, or before, the first episode. CBT has, we believe, a *distinctive* role to play in relieving distress, which is more in keeping with its natural roots in emotional dysfunction. However, there is not yet an understanding of the pathways to the emotional dysfunctions and validated cognitive models to inform CBT in psychosis; but, we do have some well-developed models in non-psychotic disorders that can serve as an excellent platform for research (Birchwood, 2003).

Finally, to illustrate these points, we outline two cases where the origin of emotional dysfunction lies (1) with the psychotic symptoms themselves and (2) through the pathways described above.

Case example: 1. Phil—psychotic symptoms without distress

Phil is a 25-year-old factory worker who lived at home with his mum and girlfriend. He was initially referred to psychiatric services by his GP after complaining about hearing voices and having difficulties concentrating at work.

During his initial assessment with the psychiatrist, Phil admitted to a number of psychotic symptoms including second- and third-person auditory hallucinations, visual hallucinations and hearing his own thoughts spoken aloud in his head. He described his brain as being 'overactive' and his sleep was disturbed. He was quickly referred to his local community mental health team where he was assessed by a psychiatrist and diagnosed with early psychosis. Consequently, he was prescribed olanzapine and referred for cognitive-behavioural therapy.

Prior to the commencement of CBT a baseline assessment on the PANSS (Kay, Fiszbein & Opler, 1987) confirmed that Phil was experiencing a relatively high level of psychotic symptomatology. Despite this, further standardized assessment indicated that Phil was not particularly distressed by these symptoms, as indicated by his low scores on the Calgary Depression Scale (CDS: Addington, Addington & Maticka-Tyndale, 1993) and high self-ratings on the Robson Self-Esteem Questionnaire (Robson, 1989):

PANSS (Kay, Fiszbein & Opler, 1987)
    Positive   18
    Negative   12
    General   29
    Total   59
Calgary Depression Scale   2 (no significant depression)
Robson Self-Esteem   163 (1 s.d. above mean for non-psychiatric controls)

However, Phil did admit that his four voices were distracting and an irritant and he would have preferred that they did not exist. Phil also stated that he would often become 'fed up' on some days. This was often short lived, however (lasting 1 or 2 days at a time), and appeared to be more related to a failure to live up to his high perfectionist standards (e.g. 'I must be 100% successful at all jobs I am given at work') and problems identifying what he wanted to do with his life (i.e. his valued goals) rather than as the result of negative appraisals of his psychotic symptoms *per se*. For instance, there was no evidence that he felt either humiliated or entrapped by his psychosis in that he saw it as reason for not fulfilling his life goals and achieving the social and psychological status he sought (Rooke & Birchwood, 1998). He did, however, report a long history of chronic back pain, which had resulted in Phil having long periods of time off work.

Upon the commencement of CBT, Phil identified his main problem as his perfectionist thinking and his inability to identify and execute valued life goals (i.e. find the right job) rather than his voices or other psychotic symptoms. Since the onset of his psychosis 18 months previously Phil had learnt to cope with his voices by using a number of distraction techniques, including listening to music through a personal stereo and conversing with his work colleagues.

In view of the fact that the psychotic symptoms were not identified by Phil as being a primary source of distress, this ceased to become the primary focus of the CBT. Instead, therapy evolved around a formulation that took into account the other sources of entrapment in Phil's life, including his inflexible perfectionistic standards, low frustration tolerance and chronic back pain.

Case example: 2. Andy—distress without psychotic symptoms

Andrew is a 22-year-old man of Greek-Cypriot descent who, approximately a year ago, was admitted to an inner city psychiatric unit after experiencing a first episode of psychosis. Since being discharged from the unit he has lived at home with his mother and younger brother after a short period of time staying with his grandmother in a different part of the city.

Andrew recalled first hearing a voice approximately 3 months prior to his admission, which followed a period of long-term cannabis use and a growing interest in Islam, much to the consternation of his Catholic family. At the time he believed that this was the result of one of his neighbours living in the house opposite attempting to communicate with him telepathically.

He started to have delusions that he was a prophet and that his family were devil worshippers who were plotting against him in an attempt to deliberately try to drive him mad. He felt very threatened and anxious and avoided going out. After a while he soon believed that his voices were coming from Cyprus where his father lived. At this point he decided to go back to Cyprus to visit his father, bought an airplane ticket and made his way to the airport. However, his family alerted the police and he was detained at the airport under the UK Mental Health Act and taken to a psychiatric unit.

During his admission he was treated with antipsychotic medication and his psychotic symptoms quickly remitted. Upon discharge from hospital he went to live with his grandmother in another part of the city because his mother was concerned that he would come under the negative influence of some of his old friends who took drugs and were involved in petty crime.

Five months later, after a period of outpatient appointments with his psychiatrist, Andrew was referred for CBT. At baseline, PANSS scores revealed no significant psychotic symptomatology apart from some fleeting ideas of reference. However, baseline assessments of other comorbid problems revealed elevated scores on depression and hopelessness:

PANSS
    Positive   11
    Negative   12
    General   29
    Total   52
CDS   6 ('moderate depression')

Upon compilation of a problem list at the beginning of therapy, Andrew identified his main difficulty as a 'lack of confidence in social situations' or, more specifically, a fear of being negatively evaluated by his peer group (i.e. social anxiety). Andrew described a pattern of overt and covert avoidance (i.e. safety behaviours), which had led to increased isolation and distressing symptoms of anxiety triggered by either interpersonal situations or the anticipation of interpersonal situations. Upon further investigation it transpired that the onset of Andy's social anxiety had most likely occurred *after* his first episode of psychosis. Premorbidly he described himself as 'socially confident and relaxed in the company of his friends'.

A formulation of Andrew's social anxiety, based on the original model of Clark and Wells (1995), placed emphasis on Andrew's processing of self as a social object (i.e., how he thought others perceived him). It also drew attention to Andrew's dysfunctional beliefs and rules about how he thought he *should* behave when he was with other people. Andrew believed that he needed to be quiet and uncontroversial in social situations so that people would like him and not reject him ('I must not upset people or else they will reject me'). Safety behaviours linked to these beliefs included keeping quiet, not offering any controversial opinions and sticking to safe topics such as the weather. Unsurprisingly he came across as uninteresting and uninterested, which appeared to produce genuine negative reactions and rejection from some of the people on the periphery of his social network. He gradually began to avoid more and more social situations and became increasingly socially isolated from his social network. As a result, he felt a sense of failure and became moderately depressed.

After sharing this formulation with Andrew, CBT focused upon breaking this cycle of avoidance and safety behaviours as well as addressing and challenging the underlying beliefs that were helping to maintain Andrew's social anxiety. Behavioural experiments tested his belief that he would be rejected if he said anything that people were not in full agreement with. Video work and role-play also provided Andrew with direct feedback of his social presentation when trying to be non-controversial as opposed to 'his normal self'.

Andrew found this approach useful and soon became less anxious and avoidant of social situations. His confidence slowly returned and he enrolled in a college course at his local university.

CONCLUSION

CBT for psychosis has come through a major period of growth with notable improvements in the specification of the therapy and sophistication of the research trials. CBT has shown reliable and worthwhile benefits in reducing psychosis symptoms approaching that of the neuroleptics, but its impact on depression and distress pales by comparison. We believe this paradox arises from a simplistic model of distress in psychosis, which subordinates emotional dysfunction to the (positive) psychosis symptoms. There is good evidence that emotional dysfunction arises from pathways untouched by CBT for psychosis as currently practised. In our view, if CBT is to advance and fulfil its potential, it must stop trying to emulate the neuroleptics and return to its theoretical and applied home in the emotional dysfunctions.

REFERENCES

Addington, D., Addington, J. & Maticka-Tyndale, E. (1993). Assessing depression in schizophrenia: The Calgary Depression Scale. *British Journal of Psychiatry*, **163** (Suppl. 22), 39–44.

Addington, D., Addington, J. & Patten, S. (1998). Depression in people with first-episode schizophrenia. *British Journal of Psychiatry*, **172** (Suppl. 33), 90–92.

Andrews, B. & Brown, G.W. (1995). Stability and change in low self-esteem: The role of psychosocial factors. *Psychological Medicine*, **25**, 23–31.

Andrews, B., Brewin, C.R., Rose, S. & Kirk, M. (2000). Predicting PTSD symptoms in victims of violent crime: The role of shame, anger, and childhood abuse. *Journal of Abnormal Psychology*, **109**, 69–73.

Beck-Sander, A., Birchwood, M. & Chadwick, P.D. (1997). Acting on command hallucinations: A cognitive approach. *British Journal of Clinical Psychology*, **36**, 139–148.

Bentall, R.P. & Kinderman, P. (1998). Psychological processes and delusional beliefs: Implications for the treatment of paranoid states. In T. Wykes, N. Tarrier & S. Lewis (Eds), *Outcome and Innovation in Psychological Treatment of Schizophrenia* (pp. 119–144). Chichester: John Wiley & Sons.

Birchwood, M. (2003). Pathways to emotional dysfunction in first episode psychosis. Editorial: *British Journal of Psychiatry*, **182**, 373–375.

Birchwood, M. & Chadwick P.D. (1997). The omnipotence of voices, III: Testing the validity of the cognitive model. *Psychological Medicine*, **27**, 1345–1353.

Birchwood, R. & Spencer, E. (2003). Psychotherapies for schizophrenia. *WPA Series in Evidence and Experience in Psychiatry* (Eds. Mario Maj & Norman Sartorius). Chichester: John Wiley & Sons.

Birchwood, M., Todd, P. & Jackson, C. (1998). Early intervention in psychosis. The critical period hypothesis. *British Journal of Psychiatry*, **172** (Suppl. 33), 53–59.

Birchwood, M., Iqbal, Z., Chadwick, P. & Trower, P. (2000a). Cognitive approach to depression and suicidal thinking in psychosis, I. Ontogeny of post-psychotic depression. *British Journal of Psychiatry*, **177**, 516–521.

Birchwood, M., Meaden, A., Trower, P., Gilbert, P. & Plaistow, J. (2000b). The power and omnipotence of voices: Subordination and entrapment by voices and significant others. *Psychological Medicine*, **30**, 337–344.

Brett-Jones, J., Garety, P. & Hemsley, D.R. (1987). Measuring delusional experiences: A method and its application. *British Journal of Clinical Psychology*, **26**, 257–265.

Bhugra, D. (2000). Migration and schizophrenia. *Acta Psychiatrica Scandanavica*, **102** (Suppl. 407), 68–73.

Bhugra, D., Leff, J., Mallett, R., Der, G., Corridan, B. & Rudge, S. (1997). Incidence and outcome of schizophrenia in whites, African-Caribbeans and Asians in London. *Psychological Medicine*, **27**, 791–798.

Bleich, A., Koslowsky, M. & Dolev, A. (1997). Post-traumatic stress disorder and depression: An analysis of comorbidity. *British Journal of Psychiatry*, **170**, 479–482.

Bradshaw, W. (2000). Integrating cognitive-behavioural psychotherapy for persons with schizophrenia into a psychiatric rehabilitation program: Results of a three year trial. *Community Mental Health Journal*, **36**, 491–500.

Brett-Jones, J., Garety, P. & Hemsley, D. (1987). Measuring delusional experiences: A method and its application. *British Journal of Clinical Psychology*, **26**, 257–265.

Brown, G.W., Andrews, B., Bifulco, A. & Veiel, H. (1990). Self-esteem and depression, I: Measurement issues and prediction of onset. *Social Psychiatry and Psychiatric Epidemiology*, **25**, 200–209.

Byrne, S., Trower, P., Birchwood, M., Meaden, A. & Nelson, A. (2003). Command hallucinations: Cognitive theory, therapy and research. *Journal of Cognitive Psychotherapy*, **17**, 67–84.

Chadwick, P.D.J. & Lowe, C.F. (1990). Measurement and modification of delusional beliefs. *Journal of Consulting and Clinical Psychology*, **58**, 225–232.

Chadwick, P.D., Birchwood, M. & Trower, P. (1996). *Cognitive Therapy for Delusions, Voices and Paranoia*. Chichester: John Wiley & Sons.

Chapman, M., Hutton, S. & Duncan, L.J. (1998). Core negative symptoms and social functioning: West London first-episode schizophrenia study. *Schizophrenia Research*, **29**, 1.

Clark, D.M. (2001). A cognitive perspective on social phobia. In R. Crozier & L.E. Alden (Eds), *Handbook of Social Anxiety: Concepts Relating to the Self and Shyness* (pp. 224–276). Chichester: John Wiley & Sons.

Clark, D.M. & Wells, A. (1995). A cognitive model of social phobia. In R. Heimberg, M. Liebowitz, D.A. Hope & F. Schneier (Eds), *Social Phobia: Diagnosis, Assessment and Treatment* (pp. 187–209). New York: Guilford Press.

Cormac, I., Jones, C. & Campbell, C. (2002). Cognitive behaviour therapy for schizophrenia. *Cochrane Library*, Issue 3. Oxford: Update Software.

Cosoff, S.J. & Hafner, R.J. (1998). The prevalence of comorbid anxiety in schizophrenia, schizoaffective disorder and bipolar disorder. *Australia and New Zealand Journal of Psychiatry*, **32**, 67–72.

Drury, V., Birchwood, M. & Cochrane, R. (2000). Cognitive therapy and recovery from acute psychosis: a controlled trial—III: Five-year follow-up. *British Journal of Psychiatry*, **177**, 8–14.

Drury, V., Birchwood, M., Cochrane, R. & Macmillan, F. (1996a). Cognitive therapy and recovery from acute psychosis: A controlled trial—I: Impact on psychotic symptoms. *British Journal of Psychiatry*, **169**, 593–601.

Drury, V., Birchwood, M., Cochrane, R. & Macmillan, F. (1996b). Cognitive therapy and recovery from acute psychosis: A controlled trial—II: Impact on recovery. *British Journal of Psychiatry*, **169**, 602–607.

Durham, R.C., Guthrie, M., Morton, R.V., Reid, D.A., Treliving, L.R., Fowler, D. & Macdonald, R.R. (2003). Tayside–Fife clinical trial of cognitive behavioural therapy for medication-resistant psychotic symptoms. Results to 3-month follow-up. *British Journal of Psychiatry*, **182**, 303–311.

Ehlers, A. & Clark, D.M. (2000). A cognitive model of posttraumatic stress disorder. *Behaviour Research and Therapy*, **38**, 319–345.

Escher, S., Romme, M., Buiks, A., Delespaul, P. & Van Os, J. (2002). Independent course of childhood auditory hallucinations: A sequential 3-year follow-up study. *British Journal of Psychiatry*, **181** (Suppl. 43), S10–S18.

Fombonne, E., Wostear, G., Cooper, V., Harrington, R. & Rutter, M. (2001). The Maudsley long-term follow-up of child and adolescent depression. 1. Psychiatric outcomes in adulthood. *British Journal of Psychiatry*, **179**, 210–217.

Fowler, D., Kuipers, L. & Garety, P. (1995). *Cognitive Behaviour Therapy for Psychosis: Theory and Practice*. Chichester: John Wiley & Sons.

Freeman, D., Garety, P.A. & Kuipers, E. (2001). Persecutory delusions: Developing the understanding of belief maintenance and emotional distress. *Psychological Medicine*, **31**, 1293–1306.

Garety, P.A., Fowler, D., Kuipers, E., Freeman, D., Dunn, G., Bebbington, P., Hadley, C. & Jones, S. (1997). London–East Anglia randomised controlled trial of cognitive behavioural therapy for psychosis, II: Predictors of outcome. *British Journal of Psychiatry*, **171**, 420–426.

Garety, P.A., Kuipers, E., Fowler, D., Chamberlain, F. & Dunn, G. (1994). Cognitive behavioural therapy for drug resistant psychosis. *British Journal of Medical Psychology*, **67**, 259–271.

Garety, P.A., Kuipers, E., Fowler, D., Freeman, D. & Bebbington, P.E. (2001). A cognitive model of the positive symptoms of psychosis. *Psychological Medicine*, **31**, 189–195.

Gilbert, P., Birchwood, M., Gilbert, J., Trower, P., Hay, J., Murray, B., Meaden, A., Olsen, K. & Miles, J.N. (2001). An exploration of evolved mental mechanisms for dominant and subordinate behaviour in relation to auditory hallucinations in schizophrenia and critical thoughts in depression. *Psychological Medicine*, **31**, 1117–1127.

Gould, R.A., Mueser, K.T., Bolton, E., Mays, V. & Goff, D. (2001). Cognitive therapy for psychosis in schizophrenia, an effect size analysis. *Schizophrenia Research*, **24**, 335–342.

Greenfield, S.F., Strakowski, S.M., Tohen, M., Batson, S.C. & Kolbrenar, M.L. (1994). Childhood abuse in first-episode psychosis. *British Journal of Psychiatry*, **164**, 831–834.

Haddock, G., McCarron, J. & Tarrier, N. (1999). Scales to measure dimensions of hallucinations and delusions: The psychotic symptom rating scales (PSYRATS). *Psychological Medicine*, **39**, 879–889.

Haghighat, R. (2001). A unitary theory of stigmatisation: Pursuit of self-interest and routes to destigmatisation. *British Journal of Psychiatry*, **178**, 207–215.

Harrison, G., Hopper, K., Craig, T., Laska, E., Siegel, C., Wanderling, J., Dunn, K.C., Ganev, K., Giel, R., an der Heiden, W., Homberg, S.K., Janca, A., Lee, P.W., Leon, C.A., Malhotra, S., Marsella, A.J., Nakane, Y., Sartorius, N., She Skoda, C., Thara, R., Tsirkin, S.J., Varma, V.K., Walsh, D. &

Wiersma, D. (2001). Recovery from psychotic illness: A 15- and 25-year international follow-up study. *British Journal of Psychiatry*, **178**, 506–517.

Iqbal, Z., Birchwood, M., Chadwick, P. & Trower, P. (2000). Cognitive approach to depression and suicidal thinking in psychosis, 2: Testing the validity of a social ranking model. *British Journal of Psychiatry*, **177**, 522–528.

Isohanni, I., Jarvelin, M.R., Nieminen, P., Jones, P., Rantakillio, P., Jokelainen, J. & Isohanni, M. (1998). School performance as a predictor of psychiatric hospitalization in adult life. A 28-year follow-up in the Northern Finland 1966 Birth Cohort. *Psychological Medicine*, **28**, 967–974.

Jackson, C. & Iqbal, Z. (2000). Psychological adjustment to early psychosis. In M. Birchwood, D. Fowler & C. Jackson (Eds), *Early Intervention in Psychosis* (pp. 74–102). Chichester: John Wiley & Sons.

Jackson, H.J., McGorry, P. & McKenzie, D. (1994). The reliability of DSM-III prodomal symptoms in first episode psychotic patients. *Acta Psychiatrica Scandinavica*, **90**, 375–378.

Jackson, H., McGorry, P., Henry, L., Edwards, J., Hulbert, C., Harrigan, S., Dudgeon, P., Francey, S., Maude, D., Cocks, J. & Power, P. (2001). Cognitively orientated psychotherapy for early psychosis (COPE): A 1 year follow-up. *British Journal of Clinical Psychology*, **40**, 57–70.

Jones, P.B., Bebbington, P.E., Foerster, A., Lewis, S.W., Murray, R.M., Russell Sham, P.C., Toone, B.K. & Wilkins, S. (1993). Premorbid social underachievement in schizophrenia: Results from the Camberwell collaborative psychosis study. *British Journal of Psychiatry*, **162**, 65–71.

Kay, S.R., Fiszbein, A. & Opler, L.A. (1987). The positive and negative syndrome scale (PANSS). for schizophrenia. *Schizophrenia Bulletin*, **13**, 261–276.

Kingdon, D. & Turkington, D. (1994). *Cognitive-Behavioural Therapy of Schizophrenia*. London: Guilford Press.

Kuipers, E., Fowler, D., Garety, P., Chisholm, D., Freeman, D., Dunn, G., Bebbington, P. & Hadley, C. (1998). London–East Anglia randomised controlled trial of cognitively behavioural therapy for psychosis, III: Follow-up and economic evaluation at 18 months. *British Journal of Psychiatry*, **173**, 61–68.

Kuipers, E., Garety, P., Fowler, D., Dunn, G., Bebbington, P., Freeman, D. & Hadley, C. (1997). London–East Anglia randomised controlled trial of cognitively behavioural therapy for psychosis, I: Effects of the treatment phase. *British Journal of Psychiatry*, **171**, 319–327.

Leff, J. (1990). Depressive symptoms in the course of schizophrenia. In L.E. DeLisi (Ed.), *Depression in Schizophrenia* (pp. 3–23). Washington, DC: American Psychiatric Press.

Lewis, S., Tarrier, N., Haddock, G., Bentall, R., Kinderman, P., Kingdon, D., Siddle, R., Drake, R., Everitt, J. & Leadley, J. (2002). Randomised controlled trial of cognitive-behavioural therapy in early schizophrenia: Acute-phase outcomes. *British Journal of Psychiatry*, **181** (Suppl. 43), S91–S97.

Liddle, P.F., Barnes, T.R.E., Curson, D.A. & Patel, M. (1993). Depression and the experience of psychological deficits in schizophrenia. *Acta Psychiatrica Scandinavica*, **88**, 243–247.

Linszen, D.H., Dingemans, P.M. & Lenior, M.E. (1994). Cannabis abuse and the course of recent-onset schizophrenic disorders. *Archives of General Psychiatry*, **51**, 273–279.

McGorry, P.D., Bell, R.C., Dudgeon, P.L. & Jackson, H.J. (1998). The dimensional structure of first episode psychosis: An exploratory factor analysis. *Psychological Medicine*, **28**, 935–947.

McGorry, P., Chanen, A., McCarthy, E., Van Reil, R., McKenzie, D. & Singh, B.S. (1991). Post-traumatic stress disorder following recent-onset psychosis: An unrecognized postpsychotic syndrome. *Journal of Nervous and Mental Disease*, **179**, 253–258.

McGorry, P.D., Yung, A.R., Phillips, L.J., Yuen, H.P., Francey, S., Cosgrave, E., Germano, D., Bravin, J., McDonald, T., Blair, A., Adlard, S. & Jackson, H. (2002). Randomised controlled trial of interventions designed to reduce the risk of progression to first episode psychosis in a clinical sample with subthreshold symptoms. *Archives of General Psychiatry*, **59**, 921–928.

McKenna, P. (2003). Is cognitive-behavioural therapy a worthwhile treatment for psychosis? *British Journal of Psychiatry*, **182**, 477–479.

Mortensen, P.B. & Juel, K. (1993). Mortality and causes of death in first admitted schizophrenic patients. *British Journal of Psychiatry*, **163**, 183–189.

Myhrman, A., Rantakallio, P., Isohanni, M., Jones, P. & Partanen, J. (1996). Unwantedness of a pregnancy and schizophrenia in the child. *British Journal of Psychiatry*, **169**, 637–640.

Overall, J.E. & Gorham, D.R. (1962). The Brief Psychiatric Rating Scale. *Psychological Reports*, **10**, 799–812.

Parker, G., Johnston, P. & Hayward, L. (1988). Prediction of schizophrenic relapse using the parental bonding instrument. *Australian and New Zealand Journal of Psychiatry*, **22**, 283–292.

Patterson, P., Birchwood, M. & Cochrane, R. (2000). Preventing the entrenchment of high expressed emotion in first episode psychosis: Early developmental attachment pathways. *Australian and New Zealand Journal of Psychiatry*, **34**, S191–S197.

Pedersen, C.B. & Mortensen, P.B. (2001). Evidence of a dose–response relationship between urbanicity during upbringing and schizophrenia risk. *Archives of General Psychiatry*, **58**, 1039–1046.

Peralta, V. & Cuesta, M.J. (1999). Dimensional structure of psychotic symptoms: An item-level analysis of SAPS and SANS symptoms in psychotic disorders. *Schizophrenia Research*, **38**, 13–26.

Pilling, S., Bebbington, P., Kuipers, E., Garety, P., Geddes, J., Orbach, G. & Morgan, C. (2002a). Psychological treatments in schizophrenia: I. Meta-analysis of family intervention and cognitive behaviour therapy. *Psychological Medicine*, **32**, 763–782.

Poulton, R., Caspi, A., Moffitt, T.E., Cannon, M., Murray, R. & Harrington, H. (2000). Children's self-reported psychotic symptoms and adult schizophreniform disorder. A 15-year longitudinal study. *Archives of General Psychiatry*, **57**, 1053–1058.

Priebe, S., Broker, M. & Gunkel, S. (1998). Involuntary admission and posttraumatic stress disorder symptoms in schizophrenia patients. *Comprehensive Psychiatry*, **39**, 220–224.

Rector, N.A., Seeman, M.V. & Segal, Z.V. (2003). Cognitive therapy for schizophrenia: A preliminary randomised controlled trial. *Schizophrenia Research*, **63**, 1–11.

Robson, P. (1989). Development of a new self-report questionnaire to measure self-esteem. *Psychological Medicine*, **19**, 513–518.

Rooke, O. & Birchwood, M. (1998). Loss, humiliation and entrapment as appraisals of schizophrenic illness: A prospective study of depressed and non-depressed patients. *British Journal of Clinical Psychology*, **37**, 259–268.

Rutter, M. (2000). Risks and outcomes in developmental psychopathology. *British Journal of Psychiatry*, **177**, 569.

Sensky, T., Turkington, D., Kingdon, D., Scott, J.L., Scott, J., Siddle, R., O'Carroll, M. & Barnes, T.R. (2000). A randomised controlled trial of cognitive-behavioural therapy for persistent symptoms in schizophrenia resistant to medication. *Archives of General Psychiatry*, **57**, 165–172.

Stefanis, N.C., Hanssen, M., Smirnis, N.K., Avramopoulos, D.A., Evdokimidis, I.K., Stefanis, C.N., Verdoux, H. & Van Os, J. (2002). Evidence that three dimensions of psychosis have a distribution in the general population. *Psychological Medicine*, **32**, 347–358.

Stein, M.B., Fuetsch, M., Muller, N., Hofler, M., Lieb, R. & Wittchen, H.U. (2001). Social anxiety disorder and the risk of depression: A prospective community study of adolescents and young adults. *Archives of General Psychiatry*, **58**, 251–256.

Strakowski, S.M., Keck, P.E. Jr, McElroy, S.L., Lonczak, H.S. & West, S.A. (1995). Chronology of comorbid and principal syndromes in first-episode psychosis. *Comprehensive Psychiatry*, **36**, 106–112.

Tarrier, N., Beckett, R., Harwood, S. & Baker, A. (1993). A trial of two cognitive-behavioural methods of treating drug-resistant residual psychotic symptoms in schizophrenic patients, I: Outcome. *British Journal of Psychiatry*, **162**, 524–532.

Tarrier, N., Kinney, C., McCarthy, E. & Wittkowski, A. (2001). Are some types of psychotic symptoms more responsive to cognitive behaviour therapy? *Behavioural and Cognitive Psychotherapy*, **29**, 45–55.

Tarrier, N., Yusupoff, L., Kinney, C., McCarthy, E., Gledhill, A., Haddock, G. & Morris, J. (1999). Randomised controlled trial of intensive cognitive behavioural therapy for patients with chronic schizophrenia. *British Medical Journal*, **317**, 303–307.

Tienari, P. (1994). Interaction between genetic vulnerability and family environment: The Finnish adoptive family study of schizophrenia. *Acta Psychiatrica Scandinavica*, **84**, 460–465.

Turkington, D., Kingdon, D. & Turner, T. (2002). Effectiveness of a brief cognitive-behavioural therapy intervention in the treatment of schizophrenia. *British Journal of Psychiatry*, **180**, 523–527.

van Os, J., Gilvarry, C., Bale, R., van Horn, E., Tattan, T., White, I. & Murray, R. (1999). A comparison of the utility of dimensional and categorical representations of psychosis. *Psychological Medicine*, **29**, 595–606.

van Os, J., Hanssen, M. & Bijl, R.V. (2000). Strauss (1969). revisited: A psychosis continuum in the general population? *Schizophrenia Research*, **45**, 11–20.

van Os, J., Hanssen, M., Bak, M., Bijl, I. & Vollebergh, W. (2003). Do urbanicity and familial liability coparticipate in causing psychosis? *American Journal of Psychiatry*, **160**, 477–482.

Verdoux, H. (2001). Predictors and outcome characteristics associated with suicidal behaviour in early psychosis: A two-year follow-up of first-admitted subjects. *Acta Psychiatrica Scandinavica*, **103**, 347–354.

Verdoux, H., Liraud, F., Gonzales, B., Assens, F., Abalan, F. & van Os, J. (1999). Suicidality and substance misuse in first-admitted subjects with psychotic disorders. *Acta Psychiatrica Scandinavica*, **100**, 389–395.

Westermeyer, J.F., Harrow, M. & Marengo, J.T. (1991). Risk for suicide in schizophrenia and other psychotic and nonpsychotic disorders. *Journal of Nervous and Mental Disease*, **179**, 259–266.

Wiersma, D., Nienhuis, F.J., Slooff, C.J. & Giel, R. (1998). Natural course of schizophrenia disorders: A 15-year followup of a Dutch incidence cohort. *Schizophrenia Bulletin*, **24**, 75–85.

13 Principles and Strategies for Developing Psychosocial Treatments for Negative Symptoms in Early Course Psychosis

PAUL R. FALZER, DAVID A. STAYNER AND LARRY DAVIDSON
Yale University School of Medicine, USA

INTRODUCTION

Since the early 1970s, when Strauss and Carpenter introduced the concept of negative symptoms into schizophrenia research (see Strauss, Carpenter & Bartko, 1974), studies of negative symptoms focused principally on their evolution and their role in influencing the disorder's long-term course and outcome (Davidson & McGlashan, 1997). In the intervening years, most investigations were predicated on the assumption that dramatic positive symptoms such as delusions and hallucinations preceded the onset of negative symptoms. Notwithstanding some notable exceptions, including Carpenter's notion of a 'deficit syndrome' that comprises a primary disease process (Carpenter, Heinrichs & Wagman, 1988), negative symptoms were viewed generally as secondary effects of positive symptoms. The following description, from Andreasen's influential book *The Broken Brain* (1984), captures the commonly held view that negative symptoms are the residue of the positive symptoms that were believed to have preceded them:

> Delusions, hallucinations, and disorganized speech tend to occur early in the illness. As it progresses, these symptoms sometimes 'burn out'. The patient is then left only with prominent negative or defect symptoms. Looking at things superficially, one might think that a person is better off no longer hearing voices or feeling persecuted. Indeed, one might think the patient is better off once he has lost his capacity to feel intensely. But the 'burned-out' schizophrenic is an empty shell—he cannot think, feel, or act. The schizophrenic who hears voices can hope that medication will drive away the voices and that he can return to a relatively normal life. The schizophrenic with defect symptoms has lost the capacity both to suffer and to hope—and at present, medicine has no good remedy to offer for this loss. (pp. 62–63)

In addition to the notion that negative symptoms are derivative and difficult to treat, negative symptoms also were construed as difficult if not impossible to assess reliably, owing their purported similarity to other conditions such as affective, personality, and substance-related disorders. Given these beliefs, it is not surprising that comparatively little effort has been focused to date on developing or testing treatments that are specifically targeted to reducing negative symptoms. The idea of assessing and treating negative symptoms early

Psychological Interventions in Early Psychosis
Edited by J.F.M. Gleeson and P.D. McGorry. © 2004 John Wiley & Sons, Ltd.

in the course of psychosis, when their continuity with either depressive or normal affective states may be most prominent, has not attracted much attention.

Recent studies of early course psychosis (Addington & Addington, 1993), including important studies of the prodromal period prior to onset of frank psychosis (Häfner et al., 1999; Hambrecht, Häfner & Loeffler, 1994), present a different picture of negative symptoms. These studies suggest that negative symptoms may actually precede the onset of positive symptoms, and this finding supports the notion that a deficit syndrome may lie at the core of the disease process. In addition to their calling for a reassessment of the importance of negative symptoms in early course psychosis, such studies imply that we would do well to develop interventions that target this dimension of the disorder.

In this chapter, we first review current knowledge concerning the nature and course of negative symptoms before exploring these possibilities in greater detail. We address the questions: Do negative symptoms in fact constitute an important dimension in early course psychosis? If so, are negative symptoms responsive to intervention? Given the increasing prominence of negative symptoms and associated cognitive deficits early in the course of psychosis, we expect that research on intervention strategies will emerge in the near future as the object of considerable attention. With this chapter, we hope to suggest a few principles and strategies for conducting forays into this relatively unexplored terrain.

NEGATIVE SYMPTOMS: A BRIEF HISTORY

Though the distinction between positive and negative symptoms of disorder was first proposed in mid-nineteenth-century medicine (Berrios, 1985), it was not applied to psychiatry until the early 1970s. Nonetheless, similar delineations appear in the earliest investigations of schizophrenia. For instance, consider Kraepelin's distinction between the pervasive and structural aspects of what, at the time, was called 'dementia præcox':

> On the one hand we observe a *weakening of those emotional activities which permanently form the mainsprings of volition*. In connection with this, mental activity and instinct for occupation become mute. The result of this part of the morbid process is emotional dullness, failure of mental activities, loss of mastery over volition, of endeavor, and of ability for independent action ... The second group of disorders ... consists in the *loss of the inner unity* of the activities of intellect, emotion, and volition in themselves and among one another ... This annihilation presents itself to us in the disorders of association ... in incoherence of the train of thought, in the sharp change of moods as well as in desultoriness and derailments in practical work. (Kraepelin, 1919, pp. 74–75)

With characteristic care and elegance, Kraepelin depicts a deficit state—the absence of an ability essential to normal human functioning, and an emptiness manifested by dullness, failure, and loss. The notion that schizophrenia is a deficit condition is prominent also in Minkowski's writings, as he writes:

> Schizophrenia, after a more or less lengthy period of time, is likely to progress and to form a lasting and characteristic deficiency. It also seems progressively to destroy something essential in the human personality. (Minkowski, 1970, p. 72)

The deficit that is characteristic of schizophrenia has been studied extensively, with most efforts aimed at a question that was posed by Kraepelin a century ago: What is the pathogenesis of schizophrenia and how many morbid processes are at work? Though the question has yet to be answered, schizophrenia is currently conceived as a heterogeneous condition, a mixture of persistent signs and symptoms—positive, negative, and disorganized—that have no singular defining characteristic (see Carpenter et al., 1993). This heterogeneous conception predicates the current diagnostic nomenclature, which does not theorize or speculate about aetiology, but instead divides the disorder into symptom-based subtypes (American Psychiatric Association, 1994). Two of these subtypes, the *paranoid* and *disorganized*, comprise primarily of positive symptoms, whereas a third, the *catatonic*, comprises mainly of negative symptoms.

The idea of delineating by subtypes can be traced to Bleuler's early clinical investigations (Bleuler, 1950), and has been supported by recent factor analytic studies (see Andreasen & Olsen, 1982; Arndt, Alliger & Andreasen, 1990). Bleuler's clinical investigations, along with Kraepelin's, comprise much of the current lore about schizophrenia. But perhaps Bleuler's most significant contribution to modern psychiatry is his effort to identify a set of symptoms that are fundamental and *pathognomonic*—that is, symptoms that appear in every case of this disorder and in no other. Bleuler conceived of schizophrenia as principally a disorder of cognition or thought process, in other words, a thought disorder. Foremost among his fundamental symptoms was a *loosening of associations* (now called 'positive thought disorder') (1950, p. 13). The attempt to identify pathognomonic symptoms occupied much of psychiatry's empirical research in the 1960s and 1970s. The most popular theory of the time was articulated by Schneider (1959), whose clinical investigations suggested that certain *positive* symptoms are 'first rank', or what Bleuler would have called fundamental (see Crichton, 1996; Crowhurst & Coles, 1989; Peralta & Cuesta, 1999).

For over a decade, research in descriptive psychiatry was predicated on the hope that a pathognomonic symptom would be discovered, and that this discovery would expedite the effort to discern the cause of schizophrenia. Considerable evidence supports the hypothesis that there are fundamental symptoms, and a host of studies have discerned a relationship among positive symptoms, thought disorder, and language. For instance, auditory hallucinations are related to a disturbance in semantic content and in the neural processes that affect verbal memory (Hoffman et al., 1994; Hoffman & Rapaport, 1994). Memory disturbance is also implicated in the production of loosely associated and clanging expressions (Kerns et al., 1999), and in the production of ambiguous linguistic references (Docherty et al., 1996). Hoffman's studies on 'discourse planning' indicate that persons with schizophrenia are deficient in constructing meaningful discourse (Hoffman, Stopek & Andreasen, 1986), and recent work suggests that a deficiency in discourse planning is related to the presence of positive symptoms (Meyer & Pratarelli, 1997).

However significant, these studies fail to support Schneider's hypothesis about first-rank symptoms. Large-scale investigations conducted in the late 1960s found that first-rank symptoms frequently appear in other disorders (Carpenter & Strauss, 1973; Strauss, Carpenter & Bartko, 1974). Florid thought disorder occurs frequently and dissipates rather quickly, but even the most florid examples of 'word salad' and 'neologism' are found in bipolar disorder as well (Andreasen, 1979a). A link between symptoms and aetiology should be evident in comparing the course of schizophrenia in persons who present fundamental symptoms to those without first-rank symptoms. But course cannot be predicted from first-rank symptoms alone (Carpenter, Strauss & Muleh, 1973; Harding, Zubin & Strauss, 1987). Clearly, the link between positive symptoms and aetiology is more complex than Bleuler and Schneider envisioned, and a lack of contiguity between symptoms and course further complicates the search for aetiology.

Table 13.1. The dimensions of schizophrenia

Symptom	Representative items	Dimension
Anhedonia	Diminished recreational interest and activity; diminished sexual interest and activity; diminished ability to feel intimacy or closeness	Negative
Affective flattening	Unchanging facial expression; decreased spontaneous movement; lacking expressive gestures; poor eye contact; affective nonresponsivity; lack of vocal inflections	Negative
Avolition	Poor grooming and hygiene; impersistence at goal-directed activities; lack of physical energy	Negative
Alogia	Poverty of speech[a]; poverty of content of speech[b]; blocking[b]; increased latency of response[a]; perseveration[b]	Negative/ disorganized
Attentional impairment	Social inattentiveness[a]; inattentiveness during mental testing[b]	Negative/ disorganized
Hallucinations	Voices commenting, voices conversing; somatic, tactile; olfactory, or visual hallucinations	Psychotic
Delusions	Persecutory, grandiose, religious, somatic delusions; delusions of reference, of being controlled, of mind reading; thought broadcasting, thought insertion, thought withdrawal	Psychotic
Bizarre behaviour	Bizarre clothing and appearance, bizarre social and sexual behaviour; aggressive and agitated behaviour; repetitive or stereotyped behaviour	Disorganized
Formal thought disorder	Derailment; tangentiality; incoherence; illogicality; circumstantiality; pressure of speech; distractible speech; clanging	Disorganized

[a] Loads highest on the negative dimension.
[b] Loads highest on the disorganized dimension.
Adapted from Andreasen et al. (1995).

It was fortuitous that during a trans-Atlantic airplane flight in the early 1970s, Strauss discussed his findings about the lack of contiguity between positive symptoms and course with J.K. Wing, and Wing was inspired to explain these findings by invoking J. Hughlings Jackson's distinction between positive and negative symptoms (see Berrios, 1991; Jackson, 1931; Landis, 1945). This conversation led Strauss to query his longitudinal data about the relationship between course and negative symptoms (Strauss & Carpenter, 1977). His finding of a significant association led another investigator, T.J. Crow, to suggest that positive and negative symptoms may comprise distinct syndromes. Crow's concept of a 'positive versus negative' schizophrenia was quickly appropriated by other researchers, who posited that Bleuler's putatively fundamental concepts of loose association and thought disorder have distinct negative and positive aspects (Andreasen, 1979a, 1979b; Andreasen & Grove, 1986). Subsequent factor analytic studies led to the formulation of the 'dimensional' view of schizophrenia as a complex syndrome with positive, negative, and mixed subtypes. The dimensions and related symptoms are identified in Table 13.1.

The dimensional view has now disabused us of the idea that schizophrenia is a homogeneous condition with pathognomonic symptoms; moreover, it rectifies the belief that the path to the aetiology of schizophrenia passes inevitably through positive symptoms. The dimensional view has invigorated research into the function, measurement, and possible treatment of negative symptoms. As a result, we know that a schizophrenic disorder with a high concentration of negative symptoms is associated with an earlier and more insidious onset, poor premorbid functioning, poorer long-term functioning, cognitive deficits, and fewer instances of remission (Davidson & McGlashan, 1997; Fenton & McGlashan, 1991). Negative symptoms also are predictors of poor treatment outcome and progressive deteriorating course (Bailer, Braeuer & Rey, 1996; Fenton, 2000; Hwu et al., 1995). Finally, and in contrast to the long-standing view that negative symptoms are derivative of positive symptoms and have later onset, recent studies suggest that negative symptoms are more likely than positive symptoms to be precursors of a schizophrenic disorder (Häfner et al., 1993).

After two decades of concentrated research into the putative dimensions of schizophrenia, questions about pathogenesis, course, and treatment response remain unanswered (see Carpenter et al., 1993). Table 13.1 indicates that the syndrome consists of at least three dimensions—two comprised principally of positive symptoms and one of negative symptoms (see Brekke, DeBonis & Graham, 1994). Evidence about the course of symptoms over time suggests that all three dimensions tend to change in union, but independently of one another (Arndt et al., 1995). What makes this finding particularly important is that most people with schizophrenia have a mix of positive and negative symptoms (Marneros, Rohde & Deister, 1995). There is considerable variation in course and duration, even among persons with predominantly negative symptoms (Fenton & McGlashan, 1991; Mojtabai, 1999).

For some clinicians and researchers, descriptive psychiatry's focus on negative symptoms was indicative of a 'Kraepelinian revolution' (Compton & Guze, 1995). The dimensional view, however, tends to abridge the concept of *deficit* that is central to Kraepelin's conception of dementia præcox (McGlashan, 1998). For this reason among others, researchers became less sanguine about the prospect of explicating the dimensions of the syndrome and began to take a different, almost diametrical, tack of isolating a homogeneous substrate. These efforts produced refinements such as 'type I and type II schizophrenia' (Crow, 1985) and the 'deficit syndrome' (Carpenter, Heinrichs & Wagman, 1988). For both approaches, negative symptoms and cognitive deficits dominate the clinical picture (see Buchanan et al., 1990; Penades et al., 2001). For persons with type II schizophrenia or the deficit syndrome, negative symptoms persist over time (Amador et al., 1999; Penades et al., 2001). These symptoms diminish the ability to initiate or sustain goal-directed activity and lead to a curtailing of interests in ideas and events of the world (see Kirkpatrick et al., 1989; Mueser et al., 1991). In addition, they adversely affect social adjustment and lead to a poor treatment outcome (Mueser et al., 1991; Tek, Kirkpatrick & Buchanan, 2001).

Notably, the principal attributes of the deficit syndrome are *primary* negative symptoms and a diminished quality of life (Kirkpatrick & Buchanan, 1990). A 'primary' symptom of schizophrenia is a product of the disorder itself. By contrast, a 'secondary' symptom is a product of a different disorder, such as depression or substance abuse, a result of treatment such as a medication side-effect, or an effect of the primary disorder such as apathy that results from repetitive experiences of rejection.

In previous work, we depicted the severest instances of the deficit syndrome, in which people are observed to be 'sitting dormant for long periods, uninterested in social participation, offering little or no eye contact, and exhibiting little verbal or nonverbal evidence of any mental or emotional activity' (Davidson, Stayner & Haglund, 1998, p. 99). However, social awkwardness, impoverishment, alienation, and interpersonal dysfunction are evident even in less severe cases (Davidson, Stayner & Haglund, 1998, pp. 100–101). As McGlashan (1998) noted, the loss that accompanies a deficit process tends to be progressive; in some cases it is irreversible. For persons with the deficit syndrome, schizophrenia is more than a debilitating mental disorder, it becomes a way of life. By insidious means, schizophrenia takes a person over and becomes inextricably connected to what that person is and may become. It transforms one's sense of self as experienced inwardly and alters one's identity in the world of others (Estroff, 1993).

The ontological alteration that we have depicted here contributes to the difficulty acknowledged in the diagnostic nomenclature of distinguishing negative symptoms from ordinary behavior (American Psychiatric Association, 1994, p. 189). Making this distinction is problematic for several reasons. First, the clinical picture is typically incomplete, obscured by positive symptoms and their treatment, and contaminated by the need to intervene quickly. Rarely do trained clinicians have the luxury of observing negative symptoms manifest over time. Second, even when the opportunity for sustained observation presents itself, a complex of factors can affect the clinical presentation. For example, positive symptoms can mask negative symptoms, the treatment of positive symptoms can produce secondary negative symptoms, and symptoms of other conditions such as affective disorder and substance abuse can emerge as positive symptoms diminish. Finally, as suggested by Strauss and colleagues (1989), negative symptoms may reflect a variety of psychological and social processes and compensatory mechanisms, some of which are actually adaptive.

One example of the potentially adaptive nature of what might appear to an objective observer to be a negative symptom is provided in the ethnographic and qualitative research of Corin and Lauzon (also see Corin, 1998; Corin & Lauzon, 1992). An important study conducted by these investigators suggested that young males with schizophrenia in Montreal were able to be more successful in living independently by maintaining themselves on the social periphery. Participants with lower rates of rehospitalization were found to have minimized contacts with family members and circumscribed their social interactions. The investigators depicted this behaviour as *positive withdrawal*—a way of protecting oneself against the demands of social and familial relationships. Though such a posture may appear to others as merely symptomatic of social and emotional withdrawal, the authors concluded that it *also* has an intentional and productive character. They depict positive withdrawal 'as enabling the person to find inner peace, to settle things with oneself; in solitude, one is left with oneself, one is able to move at one's own rhythm, one takes the time to master things, to advance slowly, to think' (Corin & Lauzon, 1992, p. 274). Here is a case of (secondary) negative symptoms accommodating (primary) negative symptoms: behaviours that evidence and sustain the deficit are the very behaviours that compensate for its existence.

A complex clinical picture is complicated further by the transactional nature of the social environment. Consider, for instance, the compounding effect of burden and stigma on symptoms and course. Because the burden that is felt by families and other caretakers increases with greater symptom severity and longer duration (Perlick et al., 1992), persistent negative symptoms can prove more burdensome than positive symptoms (Fadden, Bebbington & Kuipers, 1987). Burden leads to isolation, partly because the stigma of schizophrenia extends to caretakers (see Goffman, 1963). In turn, burden and isolation lead some caretakers to overlook the subtle, almost imperceptible, distinction between symptoms and ordinary behaviour (see Bland, 1989; Brewin et al., 1991). Attributing inaccurately some elements of a person's behaviour to a psychiatric disorder may result from stigma and concomitantly perpetuate it (Davidson, Stayner & Haglund, 1998). However, mistakenly attributing symptomatic behaviour to the person contributes to relapse (that is, decompensation and rehospitalization), which eventually amplifies the burden (Barrowclough, Johnston & Tarrier, 1994; Rund et al., 1995).

TREATMENT OF NEGATIVE SYMPTOMS

The brief history in the previous section suggests that we are only beginning to develop the kind of in-depth understanding of negative symptoms that is requisite to formulating new, effective, interventions. As we noted above, negative symptoms tend not to be responsive to medication. Though studies show that atypical antipsychotics may have beneficial effects (see Hamilton et al., 1998; Llorca et al., 2000; Meltzer et al., 1989; Wahlbeck et al., 1999), pharmacologic treatment has only marginal value when negative symptoms predominate (Breier et al., 1994; Buchanan et al., 1998; Chakos et al., 2001). Assertive case management, the other standard treatment of choice for schizophrenia, has been shown to reduce rehospitalization rates (Dixon, 2000; Ziguras & Stuart, 2000) but it has not consistently demonstrated the ability to reduce symptoms, positive or negative, or to enhance quality of life (Mueser et al., 1998). Cognitive-behavioural therapy for persistent symptoms in schizophrenia has produced, in one randomized-controlled trial, a sustained reduction in negative symptoms over a 9-month follow-up period, which was compared with befriending which was associated with only a transient reduction in negative symptoms (Sensky et al., 2000). Cognitive therapy shows promise in treating negative symptoms, particularly as an adjunctive therapy, but evidence to date is not sufficient to warrant its general use in treating prodromal symptoms or first-episode schizophrenia (Turkington, Kingdon, & Chadwick, 2003).

Novel strategies must be developed that are capable of diminishing the deleterious effects of negative symptoms, particularly the burden and disruption that occurs in the early course of psychosis. The remainder of this chapter is devoted to articulating four principles that may be useful in developing such interventions. These principles are based on several years of research (Davidson et al., 1997, 2001; Falzer, 2002). The first is a general principle about working with persons who present negative symptoms. The other three are specific to early course interventions and include strategies for working with persons in group or individual contexts.

Principle #1: Use negative symptoms as a point of reference and target what these symptoms disrupt and prevent

Positive and negative symptoms play distinct roles in formulating medical and psychosocial interventions. Positive symptoms in themselves are legitimate targets of intervention. For instance, reducing the frequency and intensity of auditory hallucinations is a viable treatment goal, as is increasing the number of activities that require sequential tasks. By contrast, treatment goals that directly target negative symptoms appear forced or inconsequential. For instance, two features of *alogia* are slowed speech rate and impoverished content. How would we phrase a treatment goal that calls for the person, in effect, to speak faster and more meaningfully? More important than targeting a reduction in negative symptoms *per se* is identifying what these symptoms *disrupt* and *prevent*. Once the practical consequences of negative symptoms are known, we can formulate interventions that are designed to minimize the disruption and promote activities of everyday life that have become remote, infrequent, or inaccessible.

Since quality of life and social functioning diminish even prior to the first episode of psychosis (Browne et al., 2000; Häfner et al., 1995), it is important to target any disruption precipitated by negative symptoms as quickly as possible. Symptoms provide a point of reference; they assist providers in identifying early signs of deterioration (Birchwood et al., 1989; King & Shepherd, 1994), and aid in correctly identifying the sources of disruption. For instance, social and emotional withdrawals are negative symptoms of schizophrenia, but they also are related to major affective disorders, substance abuse, and sundry personality disorders. A sound diagnostic formulation clarifies the clinical picture and promotes effective treatment planning. Equally, formulating viable treatment goals requires that we understand what these symptoms are disrupting.

Principle #2: Preserve and re-establish social, familial, and educational ties

Once they are severed, a person's ties to others and to normative educational, vocational, social, and recreational activities are harder to restore. A substantial proportion of the effort that is involved in rehabilitating people later in the course of illness focuses on restoring social relationships and encouraging participation in meaningful educational, vocational, social, and recreational activities. Much of this work would not be needed if persons were able to maintain the involvements that were lost during the early stages of the disorder. From the outset, efforts can be directed at enhancing, preserving, or renewing the person's investments in these important areas of function, so that crucial ties are not be broken.

Strategies for preserving ties and involvement in meaningful activities include:

- Education of family, friends, and other members of the person's natural support system (such as teachers, employers, and landlords), in order to destigmatize psychosis and engender continued acceptance despite the illness. Such programmes that are undertaken during the early stages of psychosis improve clinical outcome, even for persons with poor premorbid functioning (Rund et al., 1994).
- Establishment of *in vivo* supports that enable a person to remain in mainstream educational and vocational settings. Most people learn skills for independent living, educational and vocational success, and social and recreational gratification within a social context comprising their peers. People early in the course of a psychotic disorder are at risk of losing their previous peer group or of not being able to keep pace with this group as they continue to grow through late adolescence into early adulthood. No individual, particularly an individual at the early stages of psychosis, should be expected or encouraged to undergo the journey of recovery alone.
- Framing of medications and other treatments as a means of remaining on or resuming on a normal developmental trajectory (for instance, staying in school, focusing attention on creative activities such as music or art). The preponderance of empirical evidence supports the claim that early intervention leads to a better symptomatic and functional outcome, a greater likelihood of remission, less overall disability, fewer severe negative symptoms, and less cognitive impairment (Loebel et al., 1992; McGorry et al., 1996; Scully et al., 1997).

Principle #3: Affirm the capacity of individuals to be responsible for their own recovery

No one can do the work of recovery for someone other than the person him- or herself; the best we can offer are opportunities, encouragements, and support for persons to take the steps that can achieve their goals. One of the more frustrating aspects of psychosocial interventions for psychosis is that no one can do the work of rehabilitation *for* the person. Yet, the notion persists that treatment ought to 'make people better'. Even the language of traditional medical and psychosocial practice implies that the person whose recovery is at issue should maintain a passive role: she ought to be *patient*; he is *receiving treatment*. Some mental health providers complain bitterly about the lack of motivation of people they are working with. It is easy to misconstrue the apathy, withdrawal, and lack of energy characteristic of negative symptoms for moral or personal failings. But rather than blame either the person or the disorder, we can appeal to the person to catalyse and consolidate the energies that remain. Engaging persons as active agents who are primarily responsible for their recovery may be the most difficult task of all. Yet, once the task is accomplished, dividends begin to accrue.

Strategies for offering appealing opportunities, encouragement, and support include:

- Begin by reviewing the person's major areas of need, interest, and aspiration (e.g. graduating from high school, having a girlfriend, learning how to drive). People are more likely to try things they either enjoyed previously or think they will enjoy, perhaps having wanted to try before.
- Build on existing strengths and remaining areas of confidence, so that these may be extended to other parts of the person's life (e.g. a person who is good at math might be a good cashier).
- Focus on activities that the person might enjoy, appreciating that enjoyable and pleasurable experiences provide a counterbalance to negative symptoms, and enticing the person to increase his or her participation in relationships and activities.
- Persist in viewing the person (as opposed to the provider of treatment) as the agent of change. Provide opportunities for the person to contribute something of value rather than simply being a recipient of the others' beneficence.
- Recognize that interests, talents, aspirations, and gifts are idiosyncratic; thus, interventions that work for one person may not work for others. The importance of individualizing and specifying treatment interventions, a premise of individualized treatment planning, should not be minimized as the interventions are formulated and implemented.

Principle #4: Do not attempt to eliminate fear and anxiety from daily living

In the course of their recovery, persons must learn to monitor and adjust their expectations and environmental demands in order to match their level of comfort. As with normal development, anxiety can be a healthy means of spurring progress. Efforts to encourage persons to maintain ties to others and continue their involvement in activities should be made with consideration to the painful and frightening aspects of psychosis. Intense feelings of social loss, alienation, anger, and rejection can manifest even in the midst of a celebration. Acknowledging the profoundly negative feelings that accompany celebratory moments is a way of reflecting an ambivalence that at times can become overwhelming. Similarly, people may need to share experiences of isolation and loss, of feeling misunderstood, having family members being fearful and rejecting. These experiences may also include a desire to withdraw in the face of overwhelming symptoms and being unable to control them, or upon recalling actions that have harmed others or led to legal problems. Sharing such experiences can serve to temper a person's growing sense of being alone, unique, or isolated.

Strategies for enabling the person to tolerate a healthy amount of anxiety include:

- Encouraging people to recognize and share their problems, the limitations they face, and the changes that occur because of their illness. In order to avoid their being overwhelmed or paralyzed by feelings of demoralization, powerlessness, and fatalism, persons can learn, with the assistance of service providers, that some problems may be insurmountable at present, but resolvable over time.
- Assisting persons in distinguishing an acknowledgement of psychiatric symptoms from acquiescence to the illness. The former facilitates effective treatment and problem-solving, whereas the latter leads persons to identify themselves with a diagnostic label and become absorbed in the role of 'patient'.
- Combating the person's loss of control by using opportunities that arise to identify specific ways in which the person's decisions and actions impact on his or her life and on the lives of others.
- Taking advantage of opportunities to identify and recall positive changes and improvements in the person's life. Remembering these changes can awaken hope in the possibility of further improvement and recovery. For instance, some people have described how their experiences of symptoms have changed as a result of medications, the gradual lifting of a debilitating depressive episode, or the fading of auditory hallucinations.
- Finally, it is important to realize that positive changes and events also can be sources of stress, so that people can be prepared for the increased demands that often come with gains in functioning.

CONCLUSION

Little is currently known, and there is much to learn, about the prevalence and nature of negative symptoms early in the course of psychosis. However, recent studies suggest that negative symptoms play an increasingly important role in shaping the long-term course and outcome of the disorder, and early intervention may represent the best hope for attenuating the course of schizophrenia and minimizing its disruption. Owing principally to research on negative symptoms, we recognize schizophrenia as a heterogeneous syndrome. Recent studies of schizophrenia's long-term course have debunked the myth of a singular, progressive, course. They provide ample support for the claim that eventual recovery from psychosis is not only possible, but likely (see Harding et al., 1987; Harding & Zahniser, 1990). Owing to these studies and to the considerable progress that has been made since the 1970s, when research on negative symptoms began in earnest, our sights are set higher: we are no longer asking whether recovery from schizophrenia is possible, but how to reduce the time for recovery and how to minimize the disruption that the disorder inflicts on individuals, their families and communities.

Exploring the nature of negative symptoms in greater depth and detail can assist us in overcoming the obstacles that are preventing these goals from being achieved. The most urgent task is to develop innovative psychosocial interventions that are capable of addressing these symptoms early in the course of illness. As noted above, it is easier to preserve a person's ties to others and the world at large than to restore these ties once they are severed. We have yet to implement consistently the kinds of early interventions that effectively assist persons in maintaining their involvements in meaningful relationships and activities. Clearly, adopting a 'wait-and-see' approach only leads to persons falling behind their developmental trajectories and ensuring their ultimate disability. Perhaps the ideas in this chapter articulate some elements of what may eventually comprise an alternative.

REFERENCES

Addington, J. & Addington, D. (1993). Premorbid functioning, cognitive functioning, symptoms and outcome in schizophrenia. *Journal of Psychiatry and Neuroscience*, **18**, 18–23.

Amador, X.F., Kirkpatrick, B., Buchanan, R.W., Carpenter, W.T. Jr, Marcinko, L. & Yale, S.A. (1999). Stability of the diagnosis of deficit syndrome in schizophrenia. *American Journal of Psychiatry*, **156**, 637–639.

American Psychiatric Association (1994). *Diagnostic and Statistical Manual of Mental Disorders* (4th edn). Washington, DC: American Psychiatric Association.

Andreasen, N.C. (1979a). Thought, language, and communication disorders, II: Diagnostic significance. *Archives of General Psychiatry*, **36**, 1325–1330.

Andreasen, N.C. (1979b). Thought, language, and communication disorders, I: Clinical assessment, definition of terms, and evaluation of their reliability. *Archives of General Psychiatry*, **36**, 1315–1321.

Andreasen, N.C. (1984). *The Broken Brain: The Biological Revolution in Psychiatry*. New York: Harper & Row.

Andreasen, N.C. & Grove, W.M. (1986). Thought, language, and communication in schizophrenia: Diagnosis and prognosis. *Schizophrenia Bulletin*, **12**, 348–359.

Andreasen, N.C. & Olsen, S.A. (1982). Negative v. positive schizophrenia: Definition and validation. *Archives of General Psychiatry*, **39**, 789–794.

Andreasen, N.C., Arndt, S., Alliger, R., Miller, D. & Flaum, M. (1995). Symptoms of schizophrenia: Methods, meanings, and mechanisms. *Archives of General Psychiatry*, **52**, 341–351.

Arndt, S., Alliger, R.J. & Andreasen, N.C. (1990). The distinction of positive and negative symptoms: The failure of a two-dimensional model. *British Journal of Psychiatry*, **158**, 317–322.

Arndt, S., Andreasen, N.C., Flaum, M., Miller, D. & Nopoulos, P. (1995). A longitudinal study of symptom dimensions in schizophrenia. *Archives of General Psychiatry*, **52**, 352–360.

Bailer, J., Braeuer, W. & Rey, E.R. (1996). Premorbid adjustment as predictor of outcome in schizophrenia: Results of a prospective study. *Acta Psychiatrica Scandinavica*, **93**, 368–377.

Barrowclough, C., Johnston, M. & Tarrier, N. (1994). Attributions, expressed emotion, and patient relapse: An attributional model of relatives' response to schizophrenic illness. *Behavior Therapy*, **25**, 67–88.

Berrios, G.E. (1985). Positive and negative symptoms and Jackson: A conceptual history. *Archives of General Psychiatry*, **42**, 95–97.

Berrios, G.E. (1991). Positive and negative signals: A conceptual history. In A. Marneros & N.C. Andreasen (Eds), *Negative versus Positive Schizophrenia* (pp. 8–27). New York: Springer-Verlag.

Birchwood, M., Smith, J., Macmillan, F., Hogg, B., Prasad, R., Harvey, C. & Bering, S. (1989). Predicting relapse in schizophrenia: The development and implementation of an early signs monitoring system using patients and families as observers: A preliminary investigation. *Psychological Medicine*, **19**, 649–656.

Bland, R. (1989). Understanding family variables in outcome research in schizophrenia. *Australian and New Zealand Journal of Psychiatry*, **23**, 396–402.

Bleuler, E. (1950). *Dementia Praecox and the Group of Schizophrenias* (Zinkin, J., Trans.). New York: International Universities Press.

Breier, A., Buchanan, R.W., Kirkpatrick, B. Davis, O.R., Irish, D., Summerfelt, A. & Carpenter, W.T. (1994). Effects of clozapine on positive and negative symptoms in outpatients with schizophrenia. *American Journal of Psychiatry*, **151**, 20–26.

Brekke, J.S., DeBonis, J.A. & Graham, J.W. (1994). A latent structure analysis of the positive and negative symptoms in schizophrenia. *Comprehensive Psychiatry*, **35**, 252–259.

Brewin, C.R., MacCarthy, B., Duda, K. & Vaughn, E. (1991). Attribution and expressed emotion in the relatives of patients with schizophrenia. *Journal of Abnormal Psychology*, **100**, 546–554.

Browne, S., Clarke, M., Gervin, M., Waddington, J.L., Larkin, C. & O'Callaghan, E. (2000). Determinants of quality of life at first presentation with schizophrenia. *British Journal of Psychiatry*, **176**, 173–176.

Buchanan, R.W., Brief, A., Kirkpatrick, B., Ball, P. & Carpenter, W.T., Jr (1998). Positive and negative symptom response to clozapine in schizophrenic patients with and without the deficit syndrome. *American Journal of Psychiatry*, **155**, 751–760.

Buchanan, R.W., Kirkpatrick, B., Heinrichs, D.W. & Carpenter, W.T. (1990). Clinical correlates of the deficit syndrome in schizophrenia. *American Journal of Psychiatry*, **147**, 290–294.

Carpenter, W.T. Jr & Strauss, J.S. (1973). Cross-cultural evaluation of Schneider's First-Rank Symptoms of schizophrenia: A report from the international pilot study of schizophrenia. *American Journal of Psychiatry*, **131**, 682–687.

Carpenter, W.T. Jr, Heinrichs, D.W. & Wagman, A.M.I. (1988). Deficit and nondeficit forms of schizophrenia: The concept. *American Journal of Psychiatry*, **145**, 578–583.

Carpenter, W.T. Jr, Strauss, J.S. & Muleh, S. (1973). Are there pathognomonic symptoms in schizophrenia? An empiric investigation of Schneider's First-rank symptoms. *Archives of General Psychiatry*, **28**, 847–850.

Carpenter, W.T. Jr, Buchanan, R.W., Kirkpatrick, B., Tamminga, C. & Wood, F. (1993). Strong inference, theory testing, and the neuroanatomy of schizophrenia. *Archives of General Psychiatry*, **50**, 825–831.

Chakos, M., Lieberman, J., Hoffman, E., Bradford, D. & Sheitman, B. (2001). Effectiveness of second-generation antipsychotics in patients with treatment-resistant schizophrenia: A review and meta-analysis of randomized trials. *American Journal of Psychiatry*, **158**, 518–526.

Compton, W.M. & Guze, S.B. (1995). The neo-Kraepelinian revolution in psychiatric diagnosis. *European Archives of Psychiatry and Clinical Neuroscience*, **245**, 196–201.

Corin, E. (1998). The thickness of being: Intentional worlds strategies of identity, and experience among schizophrenics. *Psychiatry*, **61**, 133–146.

Corin, E. & Lauzon, G. (1992). Positive withdrawal and the quest for meaning: The reconstruction of experience among schizophrenics. *Psychiatry*, **55**, 266–281.

Crichton, P. (1996). First-rank symptoms or rank-and-file symptoms? [Editorial]. *British Journal of Psychiatry*, **169**, 537–540.

Crow, T.J. (1985). The two-syndrome concept: Origins and current status. *Schizophrenia Bulletin*, **11**, 471–486.

Crowhurst, B. & Coles, E.M. (1989). Kurt Schneider's concepts of psychopathy and schizophrenia: A review of the English literature. *Canadian Journal of Psychiatry*, **34**, 238–243.

Davidson, L. & McGlashan, T.H. (1997). The varied outcomes of schizophrenia. *Canadian Journal of Psychiatry*, **42**, 34–43.

Davidson, L., Stayner, D. & Haglund, K.E. (1998). Phenomenological perspectives on the social functioning of people with schizophrenia. In K.T. Mueser & N. Tarrier (Eds), *Handbook of Social Functioning in Schizophrenia* (pp. 97–120). Boston, MA: Allyn & Bacon.

Davidson, L., Stayner, D.A., Lambert, S., Smith, P. & Sledge, W.H. (1997). Phenomenological and participatory research on schizophrenia: Recovering the person in theory and practice. *Journal of Social Issues*, **53**, 767–784.

Davidson, L., Stayner, D.A., Lambert, S., Smith, P. & Sledge, W.H. (2001). Phenomenological and participatory research on schizophrenia: Recovering the person in theory and practice. In D.L. Tolman & M. Brydon-Miller (Eds), *From Subjects to Subjectivities: A Handbook of Interpretive and Participatory Methods. Qualitative Studies in Psychology* (pp. 163–169). New York: New York University Press.

Dixon, L. (2000). Assertive community treatment: Twenty-five years of gold. *Psychiatric Services*, **51**, 759–765.

Docherty, N.M., Hawkins, K.A., Hoffman, R.E., Quinlan, D.M., Rakfeldt, J. & Sledge, W.H. (1996). Working memory, attention, and communication disturbances in schizophrenia. *Journal of Abnormal Psychology*, **105**, 212–219.

Estroff, S.E. (1993). Identity, disability, and schizophrenia. In S. Lindenbaum & M. Lock (Eds), *Knowledge, Power, and Practice* (pp. 247–286). Berkeley CA: University of California Press.

Fadden, G., Bebbington, P. & Kuipers, L. (1987). The burden of care: The impact of functional psychiatric illness on the patient's family. *British Journal of Psychiatry*, **150**, 285–292.

Falzer, P.R. (2002). *Social capital, rhetorical practice, and negative symptoms of schizophrenia.* Paper presented at the First International Congress of Psychiatric Trainees on Science, Ethics and Philosophy, Turku, Finland.

Fenton, W.S. (2000). Heterogeneity, subtypes, and longitudinal course in schizophrenia. *Psychiatric Annals*, **30**, 638–644.

Fenton, W.S. & McGlashan, T.H. (1991). Natural history of schizophrenia subtypes. II. Positive and negative symptoms and long-term course. *Archives of General Psychiatry*, **48**, 978–986.

Goffman, E. (1963). *Stigma: Notes on the Management of Spoiled Identity.* Englewood Cliffs NJ: Prentice-Hall.

Häfner, J., Loeffler, W., Maurer, K., Hambrecht, M. & an der Heiden, W. (1999). Depression, negative symptoms, social stagnation and social decline in the early course of schizophrenia. *Acta Psychiatrica Scandinavica*, **100**, 105–118.

Häfner, H., Maurer, K., Loeffler, W. & Riecher-Roessler, A. (1993). The influence of age and sex on the onset and early course of schizophrenia. *British Journal of Psychiatry*, **162**, 80–86.

Häfner, H., Nowotny, B., Loeffler, W., an der Heiden, W. & Maurer, K. (1995). When and how does schizophrenia produce social deficits? *European Archives of Psychiatry and Clinical Neuroscience*, **246**, 17–28.

Hambrecht, M., Häfner, H. & Loeffler, W. (1994). Beginning schizophrenia observed by significant others. *Social Psychiatry and Psychiatric Epidemiology*, **29** (2), 53–60.

Hamilton, S.H., Revicki, D.A., Genduso, L.A. & Beasley, C.M. Jr (1998). Olanzapine versus placebo and haloperidol: Quality of life and efficacy results of the North American double-blind trial. *Neuropsychopharmacology*, **18**, 41–49.

Harding, C.M. & Zahniser, J.H. (1990). Empirical correction of seven myths about schizophrenia with implications for treatment. *Acta Psychiatrica Scandinavica*, **90** (Suppl. 384), 140–146.

Harding, C.M., Zubin, J. & Strauss, J.S. (1987). Chronicity in schizophrenia: Fact, partial fact, or artifact? *Hospital and Community Psychiatry*, **38**, 477–486.

Harding, C.M., Brooks, G.W., Ashikaga, T., Strauss, J.S. & Breier, A. (1987). The Vermont longitudinal study of persons with severe mental illness: I. Methodology, study sample, and overall status 32 years later. *American Journal of Psychiatry*, **144**, 718–726.

Hoffman, R.E. & Rapaport, J. (1994). Preliminary findings. In A.S. David (Ed.), *The Neuropsychology of Schizophrenia* (pp. 255–267). Hove, UK: Lawrence Erlbaum.

Hoffman, R.E., Stopek, S. & Andreasen, N.C. (1986). A comparative study of manic vs schizophrenic speech disorganization. *Archives of General Psychiatry*, **43**, 831–838.

Hoffman, R.E., Oates, E., Hafner, R.J., Hustig, H.H. & McGlashan, T.H. (1994). Semantic organization of hallucinated 'voices' in schizophrenia. *American Journal of Psychiatry*, **151**, 1229–1230.

Hwu, H.G., Tan, H., Chen, C.C. & Yeh, L.L. (1995). Negative symptoms at discharge and outcome in schizophrenia. *British Journal of Psychiatry*, **166**, 61–67.

Jackson, J.H. (1931). *Selected Writings*. London: Hodder & Stoughton.

Kerns, J.G., Berenbaum, H., Barch, D.M., Banich, M.T. & Stolar, N. (1999). Word production in schizophrenia and its relationship to positive symptoms. *Psychiatry Research*, **87**, 29–37.

King, C. & Shepherd, G. (1994). Early signs monitoring through a period of relapse in a highly symptomatic chronic schizophrenia patient. *Behavioural and Cognitive Psychotherapy*, **22**, 147–152.

Kirkpatrick, B. & Buchanan, R.W. (1990). Anhedonia and the deficit syndrome of schizophrenia. *Psychiatry Research*, **31**, 25–30.

Kirkpatrick, B., Buchanan, R.W., McKenney, P.D. & Carpenter, W.T.J. (1989). The Schedule for the Deficit Syndrome: An instrument for research in schizophrenia. *Psychiatry Research*, **30**, 119–123.

Kraepelin, E. (1919). *Dementia Praecox and Paraphrenia* (R.M. Barclay, Trans.). Edinburgh, UK: E. & S. Livingstone.

Landis, C. (1945). Intellectual deterioration and disorganization. *Institute of Living*, **13**, 218–221.

Llorca, P.M., Lancon, C., Farisse, J. & Scotto, J.C. (2000). Clozapine and negative symptoms: An open study. *Progress in Neuro Psychopharmacology and Biological Psychiatry*, **24**, 373–384.

Loebel, A.D., Lieberman, J.A., Alvir, J.M., Mayerhoff, D.I., Geisler, S.H. & Szymanski, S.R. (1992). Duration of psychosis and outcome in first-episode schizophrenia. *American Journal of Psychiatry*, **149**, 1183–1188.

Marneros, A., Rohde, A. & Deister, A. (1995). Validity of the negative/positive dichotomy of schizophrenic disorders under long-term conditions. *Psychopathology*, **28**, 32–37.

McGlashan, T.H. (1998). The profiles of clinical deterioration in schizophrenia. *Journal of Psychiatric Research*, **32**, 133–141.

McGorry, P.D., Edwards, J., Mihalopoulos, C., Harrigan, S.M. & Jackson, H.J. (1996). EPPIC: An evolving system of early detection and optimal management. *Schizophrenia Bulletin*, **22**, 305–326.

Meltzer, H.Y., Bastani, B., Kwon, K.Y., Ramirez, L.F., Burnett, S. & Sharpe, J. (1989). A prospective study of clozapine in treatment-resistant schizophrenic patients: I. Preliminary report. *Psychopharmacology*, **99** (Suppl.), 68–72.

Meyer, S.L. & Pratarelli, M.E. (1997). Language planning processing in schizophrenia using the active or passive voice. *Journal of Nervous and Mental Disease*, **185**, 53–55.

Minkowski, E. (1970). *Lived Time: Phenomenological and Psychopathological Studies* (N. Metzel, Trans.). Evanston, IL: Northwestern University Press.

Mojtabai, R. (1999). Duration of illness and structure of symptoms in schizophrenia. *Psychological Medicine*, **29**, 915–924.

Mueser, K.T., Bond, G.R., Drake, R.E. & Resnick, S.G. (1998). Models of community care for severe mental illness: A review of research on case management. *Schizophrenia Bulletin*, **24**, 37–74.

Mueser, K.T., Douglas, M.S., Bellack, A.S. & Morrison, R.L. (1991). Assessment of enduring deficit and negative symptom subtypes in schizophrenia. *Schizophrenia Bulletin*, **17**, 565–582.

Penades, R., Gasto, C., Boget, T., Catalan, R. & Salamero, M. (2001). Deficit in schizophrenia: The relationship between negative symptoms and neurocognition. *Comprehensive Psychiatry*, **42**, 64–69.

Peralta, V. & Cuesta, M.J. (1999). Diagnostic significance of Schneider's First-Rank Symptoms in schizophrenia: Comparative study between schizophrenic and non-schizophrenic psychotic disorders. *British Journal of Psychiatry*, **174**, 243–248.

Perlick, D., Stastny, P., Mattis, S. & Teresi, J. (1992). Contribution of family, cognitive and clinical dimensions to long-term outcome in schizophrenia. *Schizophrenia Research*, **6**, 257–265.

Rund, B.R., Moe, L., Sollien, T., Fjell, A., Borchgrevink, T., Hallert, M. & Naess, P.O. (1994). The psychosis project: Outcome and cost-effectiveness of a psychoeducational treatment program for schizophrenic adolescents. *Acta Psychiatrica Scandinavica*, **89**, 211–218.

Rund, B.R., Oie, M., Borchgrevink, T.S. & Fjell, A. (1995). Expressed emotion, communication deviance and schizophrenia. *Psychopathology*, **28**, 220–228.

Schneider, K. (1959). *Clinical Psychopathology* (M.W. Hamilton, Trans.). New York: Grune & Stratton.

Scully, P.J., Coakley, G., Kinsella, A. & Waddington, J.L. (1997). Psychopathology, executive (frontal) and general cognitive impairment in relation to duration of initially untreated versus subsequently treated psychosis in chronic schizophrenia. *Psychological Medicine*, **27**, 1303–1310.

Sensky, T., Turkington, D., Kingdon, D., Scott, J., Siddle. R., O'Carroll, M., Scott, J.L. & Barnes, T.R.E. (2000). A randomised controlled trial of cognitive-behavioural therapy for persistent symptoms in schizophrenia resistant to medication. *Archives of General Psychiatry*, **57**, 165–172.

Strauss, J.S. & Carpenter, W.T. Jr (1977). Prediction of outcome in schizophrenia: III. Five-year outcome and its predictors. *Archives of General Psychiatry*, **34**, 159–163.

Strauss, J. S., Carpenter, W.T. Jr & Bartko, J. (1974). The diagnosis and understanding of schizophrenia: Part III. Speculation on the processes that underlie schizophrenic symptoms and signs. *Schizophrenia Bulletin*, **1** (11), 61–69.

Strauss, J.S., Rakfeldt, J., Harding, C.M. & Lieberman, P. (1989). Psychological and social aspects of negative symptoms. *British Journal of Psychiatry*, **155** (Suppl. 7), 128–132.

Tek, C., Kirkpatrick, B. & Buchanan, R.W. (2001). A five-year followup study of deficit and nondeficit schizophrenia. *Schizophrenia Research*, **49**, 253–260.

Turkington, D., Kingdon, D. & Chadwick, P. (2003). Cognitive-behavioural therapy for schizophrenia: Filling the therapeutic vacuum. *British Journal of Psychiatry*, **183**, 98–99.

Wahlbeck, K., Cheine, M., Essali, A. & Adams, C. (1999). Evidence of clozapine's effectiveness in schizophrenia: A systematic review and meta-analysis of randomized trials. *American Journal of Psychiatry*, **156**, 990–999.

Ziguras, S.J. & Stuart, G.W. (2000). A meta-analysis of the effectiveness of mental health case management over 20 years. *Psychiatric Services*, **51**, 1410–1421.

14 Making Sense of Psychotic Experience and Working Towards Recovery

RUFUS MAY

Centre for Citizenship and Community Mental Health, Bradford University, UK

This chapter will describe the process of making sense of psychotic experiences and promoting recovery in Early Psychosis Services. It will focus on some of the concepts, therapeutic strategies and actions that are likely to aid the recovery process. I am a clinical psychologist who has spent the last 7 years working psychosocially with people whose problems have been diagnosed as psychotic. I have also had the experience as an 18 year old of receiving psychiatric treatment for psychosis and being diagnosed with schizophrenia. I will consider some of the basic principles we can learn from the growing recovery literature in order to better promote self-help and recovery for the person who has psychotic experiences. I will imagine the different ways that we, as professionals and patients, might understand psychotic experiences as meaningful events in the context of people's social lives. I will argue that rather than attempting to reduce psychotic experience, the focus of our work should be on reducing the debilitating nature of the experience so that people can freely get on with their lives. I aim in this chapter to reflect on practical considerations for working with psychosis that derive from both subjective wisdoms as well as the usual professional sources.

MY EXPERIENCE OF PSYCHOSIS

From September 1986 to November 1987, I was treated for psychosis. This included several involuntary hospital admissions. Initially, I had experienced sleep deprivation and was very confused, holding some grandiose and paranoid beliefs involving espionage and science fiction theories. I perceived the television and radio as having interactive messages for me. I also entertained spiritual beliefs focusing on battles between good and evil and having special powers of communication. My concentration was extremely poor. I was in a high state of vigilance, fear and tension, leading to chest pains. Perhaps due to having a family history of problems diagnosed as schizophrenia, clinicians quickly made a diagnosis of schizophrenia. My parents were informed and told that I would need to take medication for the rest of my life. However, 14 months after my initial psychiatric admission I stopped taking my depot injection of medication and disengaged with psychiatric services. I have not since received or used psychiatric services.

As a patient, I did not receive any specialist psychological interventions. The main interventions I received were pharmacological, ideological ('you must accept you have a serious mental illness') and eventually occupational therapy. I believe that I came very close to developing a long-term sick role as a 'schizophrenic' because the expectation all around me was that I would not be able to rebuild my life. Rather, I was encouraged to passively adjust to a serious 'mental illness' with a maintenance-style medication regime. The belief held by hospital staff was that I would be powerless to influence the return of psychotic symptoms that could at any moment strike again. For me to escape this prophecy, it felt like wading through miles and miles of swamp. This was an incredibly lonely journey. I had no guides, no specialist support, and no stories of success. With hindsight, my own understanding of my initial psychotic reaction is that my drift into a psychotic world was the result of dissociative psychological strategies that allowed me to withdraw from a social reality from which I felt alienated. Motivated by the poor care I received and witnessed, I decided to train as a psychologist so that I might influence change in therapeutic approaches in the mental health system.

I now work in Bradford mental health services in England as a Clinical Psychologist. My aim in this chapter is to reflect on how recovery from psychotic experience can be best promoted, given the evidence from personal accounts and clinical research. In another publication I have reflected on what was and what was not helpful to my recovery process (May, 2000). In retracing my route to recovery I highlighted enabling personal narratives (stories of success and possibility), meaningful activities, and social inclusion opportunities (housing, work and educational opportunities) as being important turning points. I would like here to reflect on four areas that are important for practitioners to address if they are to be helpful in enabling people's recoveries. These areas are clinical language, the recovery process, medication and a whole-person approach.

CLINICAL LANGUAGE

Being given a diagnosis of schizophrenia was not helpful for me. It created a learned hopelessness in me and my family, who resigned themselves to the established belief I would always be ill, unable to work and always need antipsychotic medication. There is a deeply held assumption that schizophrenia is a disease-like degenerative process. Thus the category of schizophrenia is associated with a failure to recover and a gradual deterioration in social functioning (Blackman, 2001; McGorry, 1991; White, 1987). It is more helpful to see each individual's mental health as a unique and evolving story, which is importantly influenced by social and relational experiences.

Compared with traditional diagnostic categories, a focus on individual experiences provides a better framework for understanding psychosis on both empirical and practical grounds (Bentall, 1990). The British Psychological Society report, *Recent Advances in Understanding Mental Illness and Psychotic Experiences*, suggested that individual formulations may be more useful than diagnostic categories (BPS, 2000). Moreover, there is generally a practical benefit to moving away from clinical language and the concept of mental illness to a more holistic flexible language about 'mad' experience. Traditionally clinical language has risked colonizing people's experiences and beliefs (Dillon & May, 2002). The danger of clinical language is that it objectifies the individual concerned, presenting that person as a passive victim of an active pathology. Therefore, the use of traditional clinical language risks compounding the sense of anxiety and powerlessness that the patient will experience. Consequently, there are strong arguments for an increased emphasis on valuing the subjective experience of psychosis and the meanings people attach to their experiences. I find it helpful to use terms such as *voices* and *disturbing or alternative beliefs*, rather than the terms hallucinations and delusions. This more inclusive language helps to increase an understanding of clients' perspectives of their experiences and ways they might best enhance their coping abilities. This *demedicalizing* of the experience also highlights the fact that it is not the voices or unusual beliefs that are the problem, rather the person's relationship with these experiences will determine how distressing they are (Morrison, 1998; Romme & Escher, 2000).

RECOVERY PROCESSES

The concept of schizophrenia was unhelpful to me. A more helpful concept would have been recovery, but unfortunately this was never discussed. In discussing recovery I am not implying the medical concept of 'cure'. Rather I am using the definition made by Anthony (1993) who suggests that recovery from serious mental health problems is a multidimensional concept: social and psychological recovery processes are seen as being as important as clinical recovery (Coleman, 1999). Clinical recovery is defined by a reduction in 'symptoms' (e.g. voices and unusual beliefs). Social recovery describes the development of meaningful social relationships and roles, vocational activities and access to decent housing. Psychological recovery describes the process of developing ways to understand and manage psychotic experiences and regain some sense of structure in one's life. These distinctions are important as, currently, services and research focus too heavily on clinical recovery. However, if someone can recover socially and psychologically, clinical recovery may be irrelevant to the quality of that person's life. For example, there are many people who live successful lives who hear voices. They have ways of managing their voices so that their experiences do not hold them back from getting on with their lives. Anthony's (1993) definition of recovery includes dimensions of self-esteem, adjustment to disability, empowerment and self-determination.

The recovery concept being discussed was originally used by the physical disability movement in America. It has since then been used by mental health service users internationally. A recovery vision looks at the whole person from his or her own point of view. It focuses on people's strengths, hopes, wishes and achievements, as well as on ways to manage difficulties.

'For some of us Recovery means learning to cope with our difficulties, gaining control over our lives, achieving our goals, developing our skills and fulfilling our dreams' (Ron Coleman, 1999, p. 103). The following eight principles have been adapted from Anthony (1993), who described them as important in understanding a recovery-based approach to serious mental health problems:

- Each person's recovery is different.
- Recovery requires other people to believe in and stand by the person. Other people/opportunities play an important part in enabling the person to make this recovery journey.
- Recovery does not mean cure. It does not mean the complete disappearance of difficulties.
- Recovery can occur without professional help. Service users hold the key to recovery.

- Recovery is an ongoing process. During the recovery journey there will be growth and setbacks, times of change and times where little changes.
- Recovery from the consequences of mental distress (stigma, unemployment, poor housing, loss of rights, etc.) can sometimes be more difficult than recovery from the distress and confusion itself.
- People who have or are recovering from confusion and distress have valuable knowledge about recovery and can help others who are recovering.
- A recovery vision does not require a particular view of mental health problems.

Recovering Social Identity

Initially when a person realizes that he or she has been identified as psychotic and is therefore different to others, a sense of loss of one's normality often follows. This can feel very threatening. Cast as psychotic one has entered a taboo identity in Western society, with connotations of being socially, morally and genetically inferior. A real sense of social failure and despair can set in. In addition one may feel disabled by the psychotic experiences themselves. At the time of hospitalization I found it useful to see myself as 'burnt out', that I needed rest but that I could make a full recovery. However, I knew that I could not go back and undo the fact that I had 'gone loopy'. It took me some time to come to terms with this. Consequently, there may be a period of time when one has to mourn the loss of a former identity and reassess one's expectations and values (Ridgway, 2001). Many young people will value the information in the normalizing literature (Kingdon & Turkington, 1994). It is often useful to challenge traditional prejudices about psychotic experiences—for example, many people find it useful to see their experiences not as pathology but rather as a meaningful and adaptive response to adversity (Read & Harre, 2001), and others will benefit from reading accounts by people who value or have found meaning in their psychotic experiences (e.g. Barker, Campbell & Davidson, 1999; Read, 2001; Romme & Escher, 1993).

Recovery and Narratives of Possibility

My recovery was about gaining other people's confidence in my abilities and potential. Behind that there was the physical recovery, which required rest, therapeutic activities and good food. However, the toughest part was changing other people's expectations of what I could achieve. It involved seeking out contexts where my contribution was welcomed and valued. To approach new settings with confidence it was important for me to resist adopting an identity dominated by an illness model (see Deegan, 1993; Thornhill, Clare & May, in press, for other accounts). In another paper I have focused on how combating a 'mental-illness-saturated' view of myself required access to some alternative positive stories about my identity (May, 2000). For example in planning my recovery, I found it helpful to remember a teacher from my childhood who had said about me: 'This boy will do well.' The literature on narrative approaches illustrates the benefits of creating spaces where people who have had psychotic experiences can explore enabling narratives about themselves and their lives (e.g. White, 1987, 1996; White & Epston, 1990).

Recovery Themes

From the studies that have looked at personal recovery accounts I will describe some recurrent themes (see Davidson & Strauss, 1992; Ridgway, 2001; Young & Ensing, 1999):

The importance of supportive others

A consistent theme in accounts of recovery is that there is always at least one person who has stood by that person, and treated him or her with dignity and value. Having people around you who give you space but who also believe in your abilities and potentials is a huge asset. We may be able to learn from stories of recovery in the disability movement where the importance of support networks or 'circles of friends' is described (e.g. Pearpoint/Snow, 1998). These structures both reduce the likelihood of burden on any one person and give the individual a range of relationships within which one can enhance and rebuild one's confidence and social skills.

Hope

Hope is a key ingredient in successful recoveries, but, traditionally, this has been lacking in mental health services. Therefore stories of success are important ingredients in both information given to service users and training for mental health workers. From my own experience, positive stories written by people who have made good recoveries would have given hope and been inspirational. Therefore, every early psychosis services should have a 'recovery library', containing positive media and personal accounts of experiencing psychosis and getting on with one's life. Involving mental health workers who have experienced psychosis in early intervention programmes is another excellent way to promote positive expectations of people's outcomes.

A coherent account of experience

Ridgway's (2001) review of recovery accounts concluded that while denial may be an important initial coping strategy (Deegan, 1994), finding a way of understanding one's difficulties is an important aspect of recovery. However Ridgway (2001) observed that adopting an illness model is not necessary for recovery. Recovery does not require a singular view of psychosis. This fact challenges traditional approaches that assume that there is a correct and insightful way to understand psychotic experience. Organized understandings of unusual experiences and mind states may be developed in a diverse set of frameworks (Romme & Escher, 2000). For example, as alternatives or complements to medical or psychological frameworks many people find spiritual, paranormal and sociopolitical frameworks useful to make sense of their experiences. A coherent account may not see psychotic experiences as wholly negative; many people who function well socially find their voice hearing or alternative beliefs informative and metaphorically meaningful.

Spiritual beliefs

Spiritual beliefs and activities are reported widely to be helpful in people's recovery stories (Young & Ensing, 1999). Mrs M.L. is a Rastafarian living in England who described the importance of faith in her recovery:

> My problem was that I could not be myself living in a country that does not accept black people. But through the voices I found myself—my identity, which has everything to do with my racial history and my own past.... How have I come through my particular fire? Because I trusted completely in JAHOVIAH! All my thoughts are inside my head now. (Romme & Escher, 1993, p. 124)

Acknowledging the importance and validity of spiritual belief systems and activities allows people to maintain authorship of their lives in the way that works most fruitfully for them. There is scope for good partnership work with local religious organizations, which have a different yet often valuable wisdom about healing and recovery processes.

Building a positive personal and social identity

This is about gaining access to conversations and activities that enable one to feel good about oneself. However, this is not about promoting a relentless self-awareness. It includes having opportunities to carry out valued activities that contribute to and introduce one to the world of others so that one is less preoccupied with one's own inner world (Harrop & Trower, 2001). For example, doing voluntary work and later paid work with adults with learning disabilities was significant in my own development of a more positive sense of identity. This was an activity that enabled me to be less preoccupied with my own deficiencies and inadequacies and instead focus on connecting to and assisting in the lives of others. Harrop and Trower (2001) also observed the dangers of psychological preoccupation with deficits of thought and behaviour. Thus services are likely to be more motivating and appealing if they have a solution focus, rather than a deficit focus: i.e. focusing on strengths, competencies, achievements and abilities (O'Hanlon & Rowan, 1998). Such psychological assets do not exist in a social vacuum. For many people progressing in their social recovery may be about searching for contexts where their abilities and attitudes are noticed and appreciated. Voluntary and community-based projects are often of value here, with less of a clinical focus than health-based services. Therefore, early psychosis services that are not based in the voluntary sector would do well to make strong links with more community based organizations (e.g. colleges, community centres, voluntary organizations, employers, etc.). 'Recovery groups' where members are encouraged to share stories, learn skills together (e.g. personal development, social awareness, etc.) and exchange self-help strategies are effective at building morale and competency for many. A key principle that I make explicit with members of recovery groups is that everyone in the group has wisdom and expertise about his or her own life (see Dillon & May, 2002). How successfully services promote recovery for individuals will be determined by their ability to truly collaborate with this wisdom and expertise. Young people are more likely to engage in such recovery groups if they are positive, lively events that are relevant to their interests. I would suggest that the young people involved are invited from the start in the planning of the aims, the content and the ground rules of such groups.

Becoming active; the individual moving to a position of taking responsibility for, and active involvement in his/her recovery

Traditionally, mental health services have to some extent encouraged passive adjustment to an assumed 'illness'. The recovery literature suggests that this is only likely to foster dependence and passivity. Rather, the challenge is to create environments that recruit the person as an active agent in his or her recovery. This is likely to evoke a more functional sense of self (Davidson & Strauss, 1992). Thus a recovery-oriented service needs to offer accessible information and choices to the people with whom they are working; share decision-making; negotiate care; encourage the use of advance directives; and support people to take informed risks. Ron Coleman, ex-psychiatric patient and mental health consultant, described how recovery requires one to invest in personal agency:

We must become confident in our own abilities to change our lives; we must give up being reliant on others doing everything for us. We need to start doing these things for ourselves. We must have the confidence to give up being ill so that we can start being recovered. (Coleman, 1999, p. 16)

Respectfully challenging a person who is showing signs of passivity to take greater responsibility is a very important skill in working with some young people with psychotic presentations. It is important to build strong rapport. Furthermore, this will require the workers to be very open about who they are, what their feelings are and what their roles are, if they are to challenge the person they are working with. Challenging someone has to be done in a non-aggressive way, emphasizing the long-term benefits of becoming more active and responsible as well as creating space to acknowledge difficult feelings involved in interpersonal interaction.

There are many reasons why a person will show signs of passivity. Sedative effects of medication can encourage a lazy approach to life. Inner thoughts or internal dialogue may also be very seductive, avoiding the need for outside interaction. An outward appearance of disengagement with the world will act protectively against the possibility of social rejection and loneliness. Subjectively the person may feel some sense of power and security in being socially silent.

People who exhibit passivity (often clinically described as negative symptoms) will benefit particularly from an approach that is assertive, creative and persistent. I recommend the use of a range of mediums to engage with the person and, if possible, to engage with family members and or friends in this process. These can include: reading poetry, discussing topical ideas, story-telling, discussing and listening to music, going on countryside walks, outdoor activities and sport. One young man with whom I worked was willing to engage with me once I had asked him if he felt more powerful since he talked less. He nodded that this was the case. Our recovery work together then consisted of thinking about how he could interact more with the world without losing that sense of power and control he obtained from his socially withdrawn state. As I have indicated, a range of physical and creative activities may help to facilitate the person to recover a more active role in his or her life, but, as ever, these always need to be carefully negotiated with the individual. Retrospectively, one man has described to me how he understood his passive state as a state of shock about traumatic life events. Interestingly he described how he was always listening to what was being said to him, despite his comatosed presentation. Traditionally many clients who present in such withdrawn states have been over-medicated, and this may often exacerbate the problem of relating to the world.

Emotional Recovery

Traditionally, professionals' approach to psychosis has prioritized thought disorder over the emotional content of psychotic experiences. While it has been assumed that some empathic work takes place, this has not been emphasized sufficiently. I would like to suggest that emotional work is a crucial consideration in addressing psychotic problems. Firstly, for many it is about emotionally validating clients' experiences. This is equally important in relation to psychotic experiences themselves, the experiences of receiving mental health services, and the social consequences of these experiences. For example, giving clients space to express their angry feelings about prejudices they have experienced has, in my experience, often been a valuable part of building a good relationship with them.

Evidence suggests that persecutory delusions act in an emotion manner to protect a low self-esteem (Bentall & Kaney 1994; Lyon, Kaney & Bentall, 1994). In my experience, if you can help clients to build up their sense of personal resilience and social value, the influence of persecutory ideas can be greatly reduced. A persecutory idea, though distressing, will also make one feel important and responses help to structure one's daily routine. In other words, these beliefs provide one with a sense of meaning and purpose. If, as therapists, we want people to give up such ideas they will need to be replaced by beliefs that provide people with increased meaning and purpose.

Cognitive belief modification techniques for paranoid beliefs—those that teach people to think more rationally using guided discovery techniques—are in danger of being overvalued in psychological approaches. Cognitive work that endeavours to shift persecutory beliefs risks undermining the emotionally protective function provided by the persecutory belief. Such interventions are in danger of, firstly, alienating the client from the therapist and, secondly, increasing the client's vulnerability to a depressive state. The solution is to give people the choice about the best way to proceed. For example, whether they should explore the reality of their beliefs or pursue ways to live with the paranoid ideas. In my experience clients are very able, given informed choices, to make good decisions about the course of their recovery work.

Drayton, Birchwood and Trower (1998) carried out a study that looked at the relationship between comorbid depression and recovery-coping styles for people with psychosis. Depression was found to be related to more frequent psychotic relapses and poorer social functioning. This was also related to perceptions of poorer parenting in childhood. It is therefore of key importance to address these emotional aspects of the lives of people with psychotic experiences. This can include self-esteem work for some. Others will benefit from counselling that addresses significant past emotional experiences. For example, one client with whom I worked was preoccupied with disturbing ideas about being related to a mass murderer. After engaging in a course of supportive counselling relating to the loss of a child who had been taken from her by social services, she became far less preoccupied with, or bothered by, her disturbing ideas. The traditional emphasis in clinical work on prioritizing thought disorder for intervention needs to be replaced by a paradigm that acknowledges the emotional and psychological functions of psychotic experience.

Psychosis as a Post-Traumatic Reaction

Romme and Escher (2000) described how, for voice hearers, the emotional processes recognized as important to recovery from trauma are extremely relevant. Romme and Escher's work suggested that many psychotic experiences are linked to earlier experiences of trauma. Many studies have found a high correlation between psychotic experience and past experiences of adversity and trauma (e.g. Greenfield et al., 1994; Mueser et al., 1998; Ross, Anderson & Clark, 1994). Many personal recovery accounts report finding emotional explanations useful in making sense of their experiences. Jasna Russo (2001) describes her journey into madness as one of protest against her past experiences of oppression and abuse:

> I was meant to be a manufactory of pleasure—you touch me and I enjoy .... I was meant to belong to one man and feel secure with him, because he was my father. ... Madness was about all the suppressed feelings and fears and disgust coming out at the same time. ... Being crazy was also about wanting everything at the same time and having to have it immediately. I can't say I miss that intensity, but it gave me the feeling that change is possible. I discovered how much I wanted

to want and that my life could change into something I wanted. . . . I'm glad I didn't remain the one who was able to stand it all, the one behind the walls of an impermeable world all on my own, all unhappy. (Russo, 2001, pp. 38–39)

An advantage of the post-traumatic explanation of psychosis is that it gives the psychotic process a functional role. Rather than being just an affliction, such psychological processes as splitting off from experience and dissociation can be seen as adaptive strategies that have enabled the person to survive adversity (Warner, 2000). For many this is a more coherent and enabling story than the bio-medical narrative about psychosis. Therefore it is worth reflecting on the circumstances which aid recovery from trauma. Herman's (1992) work, focusing on recovery by traumatized war veterans and sexual abuse survivors, described the value of the following four stages in healing processes:

- A healing relationship
- Safety
- Remembrance and mourning
- Reconnection.

It is important to note that many people may not be prepared to explore past distressing events. Making sense of past emotional experiences is therefore only relevant for some. For others, psychological or group work might be about focusing on resources, coping strategies and meaningful activities. My work with people suggests that clients have a wisdom and expertise about the line of inquiry that might be most helpful to them, and when; therefore, the important principle is to offer people choices about directions of therapy and recovery work. In my experience, once clients feel safe and trust the therapist or group they are attending, they are able to make good decisions about the course of their recovery work.

Living and Coping with Alternative Beliefs

Kaffman (1981) in a study of 34 families where there was a 'paranoid patient' found, firstly, that there was always an element of truth and reality underlying persecutory belief systems and, secondly, that past and present relationships played an important role in generating and activating the beliefs. Exploring the meaningfulness of people's persecutory beliefs and their relevance to their social lives and past experiences is often an extremely helpful and validating process. Persecutory beliefs that appear delusional to professionals often have significant metaphorical and affective value for some patients. Thus they may represent real experiences of persecution and powerlessness. As an alternative to the conventional view of paranoid belief systems as pathological cognitive states, in applying a developmental perspective, persecutory ideas can be seen as understandable responses to past threatening experiences. Persecutory frameworks can be adaptive in eliciting safety behaviours in times of emotional adversity.

Rather than challenging the rationality of their alternative beliefs, many people find it useful in their recovery work to accept the possibility that their unusual beliefs are correct and develop appropriate coping strategies that enable them to improve their social functioning and sense of well-being. An example from my own work is Ben who, in a recovery group, brought the problem that he was being persecuted by the local bus drivers shouting abuse at him as they drove past his home. Some group members felt that he might be paranoid, while others looked at how he was coping with the experience. It was suggested to Ben that: 'It seems there are two ways forward with this problem, you can check out the reality of the experience to see if you are correct or not, or you can accept from your point of view the reality of the experience and focus on ways to not let these experiences stop you from getting on with your life in the way you want to.' Ben chose the latter solution; he was much keener to build up his self-esteem and coping abilities than focus on whether or not he was making perceptual errors.

A psychologist, Tamasin Knight (2002) described the personal benefits of working within the reality of unusual belief systems:

> At 16 years old, I became convinced that many things, including food packaging and my hands, were infected with a fatal disease. A couple of years later I became convinced that the water supply had been contaminated so was refusing to drink. Resulting from the first of these experiences I was referred to clinical psychology . . . my beliefs were very strong so cognitive approaches were unable to shift them. On both the above occasions hospital admission was seriously considered and perhaps it was the fear of this that motivated me to try and find effective ways of helping myself. By this method I accepted my beliefs, and eventually found ways of overcoming or getting round them—by saying to myself statements such as 'yes, my hands are infected with disease so I must find ways of eating without touching the food with my hands, if the food packaging is contaminated, can I find ways of decontaminating the packaging?' and 'OK, the water supply is contaminated so I'll only drink imported water'. (Knight, 2002, p. 4)

Knight's own success using such techniques allowed her to avoid psychiatric admission and go on to higher education. At the time of writing, Knight is in the process of carrying out a piece of national research, looking at service-users' coping strategies within alternative belief systems. The literature on coping strategy enhancement is also relevant to this approach (Yusupoff & Tarrier, 1996).

Therefore, it should not be automatically assumed that persecutory beliefs themselves are the primary problem, as they might be part of the solution. Rather it is the person's relationship with the persecutory idea that should be focused on. If individuals can find ways to cope within belief systems, this may be part of an important way to take back more control over their lives and decrease their sense of powerlessness. The following questions may be useful to consider:

- How can we as helpers support individuals to decrease the disempowering nature of disturbing ideas in a way that is most helpful to them?
- How can the individuals relate to such ideas in a way where they are able to feel safer and negotiate wider social realities?

While rationalizing techniques may help some people I suggest that it is important to present a range of options in how best they can psychologically manage their relationship with alternative belief systems and ideas. What is clear is that people require safe places to make sense of socially taboo experiences and ideas, in the context of their wider social experiences.

MEDICATION

The psychological effects of neuroleptic drugs are important to consider in any psychological approach with people being treated for early psychosis. Though these drugs are often described as antipsychotic, neuroleptic (meaning 'nerve seizing') may be a more accurate description of their action. How can we explain the experience of taking neuroleptic drugs? David Healy (1997) in his book *Psychiatric Drugs Explained* described how, in the 1950s, the original understanding of how neuroleptics worked concluded that they produced a feeling of detachment—of not being bothered by what had previously been bothering. This description very much fits with my own experience of neuroleptics. Unfortunately, this 'feeling of detachment' not only applied to my disturbing ideas but also to recovery processes such as creative thinking, problem-solving and motivation to pursue purposeful activities. There is a danger that if antipsychotic medication is used in a long-term fashion, its dissociative effects may suspend individuals' abilities to recover complex psychosocial abilities.

It was very difficult for me as an 18-year-old man on medium doses of neuroleptics to do all the learning one needs to do about social skills, about emotions, about career skills and about one's sense of identity and drive. Six months after my third psychiatric admission I was at Art College trying to not let hand tremors affect my painting, and always feeling half a second out of time with the other students. When I came off medication, people observed how much more in touch with myself I seemed, both emotionally and intellectually. I was suddenly able to express more complex thought processes again. My decision to cease taking medication received no support from the psychiatrists. My actions were seen as non-compliance and no supportive services were offered to me. I was left to cope with the withdrawal effects alone. This was risky—the first two attempts to withdraw resulted in readmissions, which were at least partly contributed to by mania-like withdrawal effects. Withdrawal syndromes often produce psychotic experiences and are often mistakenly assumed to be the 'illness' returning (Thomas, 1997; Warner, 1994). This misattribution can increase helplessness in the person concerned.

If people choose to move beyond maintenance medication as part of their recovery from psychosis, it is important to provide them with specialist support. For example, this could include:

- How best to gradually reduce doses. Research suggests that gradually titrated withdrawal produces the most successful outcomes (Breggin & Cohen, 1999).
- Education about the withdrawal effects to look for.
- Education about how these effects are caused.
- Strategies to deal with withdrawal states (e.g. temporarily increasing the reduced dose, temporary doses of benzodiazepines or other short-term medication, relaxation techniques, alternative therapies).

At present this type of support rarely occurs, making successful withdrawal less likely and recurrences more traumatic. While the current trend in treatment approaches is towards the use of low-dose 'atypical' antipsychotics, these drugs are not without their problems. They can lead to significant weight gain, which can undermine morale and reduce confidence levels, as body-image is an important source of self-esteem for most people. Emotional and generalized cognitive blunting, increased sleep and lethargy are common. The widespread long-term 'maintenance' approach to the use of these drugs is concerning. The risks of disability caused by medication need to be considered and compared to the risk of increased level of psychotic experiences. Each person will have to make informed decisions about what is most suitable in the management of recovery. For example, in my own case, I may experience more unusual ideas than if I were taking neuroleptic medication, but I have learned ways to incorporate them into my life so that they are life enhancing. If I took a maintenance dose of medication my overall level of motivation and cognitive abilities would be reduced so much that I would be unable to function socially and professionally at my current level.

It is important to shift the ideology of services so that psychopharmacology is seen as just one of the tools people can use to recover from early psychosis. In Finland, psychosis services operate according to psychotherapeutic principles. Alanen (1997) described the 'needs-adapted treatment' approach where medication is seen as an adjunct. Medication treatment strategies are seen as time limited and are constantly reviewed as part of a broader approach to recovery. People in early psychosis programmes can make very good long-term recoveries from early psychosis with no or minimal neuroleptic treatment (Martensson, 1998; Mosher & Burti, 1994; Warner, 1994). The therapeutic superiority of drug-based treatment regimens has been questioned when compared with the successful long-term outcomes from drug-free therapeutic programmes. Examples of the latter include The Soteria project in San Francisco and the Sater project in Sweden, both of which demonstrated superior long-term outcomes compared to control groups given standard treatment (Martensson, 1998; Mosher & Burti, 1994). In the first 2–3 years the drug-free patients required more care and services but after this time period they showed significantly better outcomes on both clinical and social measures of performance. Warner (1994) presented a detailed review of drug-free approaches and suggested that adults with well-developed social networks prior to psychotic episodes fare better without any neuroleptic treatment whatsoever. Despite the evidence, Western state-funded services rarely offer drug-free therapeutic services. Unfortunately, drug companies sponsor many psychosis training events and appear to have a vested interest in promoting a biomedical understanding of psychosis and maintenance-style medication regimens. Hopefully in the future we will move to a more collaborative approach to drug management, which uses antipsychotic medication in a less pervasive, more flexible style.

An important part of the engagement process should be in involving the client in a 'partnership manner' in making informed decisions about prescribing strategies. Healy (1997) produced a study showing that people with psychosis could be trained to 'cleverly self-prescribe' their medication, which included stopping it completely and using increases according to stress levels. The people who were self-managing their medication achieved more socially without clinical deterioration in comparison to their controls, who were on maintenance drug regimens. Clearly the way forward is a collaborative approach to prescribing, where one can make informed decisions about how best to use medication or not, and to get on with life.

WORKING WITH THE WHOLE PERSON

Valuing the Person's Subjective Perspective and Wisdom

A recovery-oriented approach suggests a move away from observing the person's behaviour and trying to interpret it in terms of clinical models to an approach that starts from valuing and respectfully understanding the person's experiences from his or her perspective. This is about a whole-person approach, working on the problems that the client presents in the way he or she wants to work with them.

Adopting a whole-person approach means that a consideration of the person's present difficulties with psychotic experiences needs to be balanced with an appreciation of important non-clinical aspects of personhood. These include a consideration of the person's developmental life experiences, achievements, abilities and potentials. Social references of personhood also need consideration. For example, the gender, family, peer, aesthetic and cultural contexts within which people define themselves.

Culture and a Whole-Person Approach

It is important to consider the impact of different cultural expectations on how clients might want to respond to their difficulties. For example, as a young Western man it was very important for me to demonstrate autonomy and preserve my newly acquired physical attributes. It meant that I experienced the psychiatric treatment I received as emasculating as it made me physically weaker, sexually impotent and encouraged a dependent relationship with psychiatry.

Veronica Dewan described how a cultural understanding demystified what had been seen as a problem only medicine would solve:

> During my first admission to a psychiatric ward in 1990, I resisted all three White English male psychiatrists who told me that drugs were the only treatment that would help me. The fourth psychiatrist had an Indian partner and children of dual heritage. Within minutes of meeting me she asked if I had ever been offered psychotherapy . . . I now have a psychotherapist who is a black woman of African Caribbean and English heritage. She works in a way that takes account of the whole of me. She understands the damage caused by racism, and how the process of assimilation has profoundly and painfully distorted my identity and truth. She gives me hope that my identity can have its own meaning. My psychotherapist is now the only mental health professional involved in my care. (Dewan, 2001, p. 46)

Thus to relate to the person we really need to be creative in how we move beyond the illusory focus of the 'clinical gaze'.

CONCLUSION

Psychosis is not just an individual problem. My own 'madness' was about disconnecting from a world with which I struggled to identify. Therefore in my work with people I am keen to consider how we can make the world around them one that is worth connecting to and negotiating with.

Traditionally the problem with being seen to be psychotic is that one is isolated with this experience, and is set aside as fundamentally different and inferior. The way to combat this isolation is to create safe spaces where unusual experiences can be shared and made sense of. As soon as we start to share commonalities, the power of the isolation of the experience is broken down. Meaningful accounts of psychosis that allow us to connect with others and make choices about our lives are essential to any recovery process. In sharing unusual experiences and different ways of making sense of them we are no longer mad. The experience that is identified as psychotic can be incorporated into social identity, using a range of explanatory frameworks, including emotional, spiritual and psychosocial paradigms. Therefore, being prepared to think flexibly about our approach to people with psychotic experiences on an ongoing basis is an important part of developing recovery-oriented services. Services for psychosis have traditionally employed overly medicalized and didactic treatment approaches. Creating a more enabling approach involves recruiting the expertise of personal experience into therapeutic services. Recovery stories are an important source of hope and motivation for people with psychotic experiences. Recovery accounts demonstrate that people benefit from being able to make sense of their psychotic experience in the context of their past and present social experiences, in the way that feels most comfortable to them. Making sense of psychosis and engaging in meaningful activities also requires reliable and enabling community networks. Truly helpful services enable people to take an active role in their recovery. Such services are likely to be those that avoid imposing clinical labels and definitions, stress the possibilities for recovery, adopt a collaborative approach to decisions about therapies, and relate to the person rather than the 'symptoms'.

ACKNOWLEDGEMENT

Thanks to Anne Cooke for advice and support in the initial preparation of this chapter.

REFERENCES

Alanen, Y. (1997). *Schizophrenia: Its Origins and Needs-Adapted Treatment*. London: Karnac Books.

Anthony, W.A. (1993). Recovery from mental illness: The guiding vision of the mental health service system in the 1990's. *Psychosocial Rehabilitation Journal*, **16** (4), 11–23.

Barker, P., Campbell, P. & Davidson, B. (Eds) (1999). *From the Ashes of Experience: Reflections on Madness, Survival and Grow*. London: Whurr Publications.

Bentall, R.P. (Ed.) (1990). *Reconstructing Schizophrenia*. London: Methune.

Bentall, R.P. & Kaney, S. (1994). Abnormalities of self-representation and persecutory delusions: A test of a cognitive model of paranoia. *Psychological Medicine*, **26**, 1231–1237.

Blackman, L. (2001). *Hearing Voices, Embodiment and Experience*. London: Free Association Books.

Breggin, P. & Cohen, D. (1999). *Your Drug May be Your Problem: How and Why to Stop Taking Psychiatric Medications*. Cambridge, MA: Perseus Publishing.

The British Psychological Society Report (2000). *Recent Advances in Understanding Mental Illness and Psychotic Experience*. Leicester: The British Psychological Society.

Coleman, R. (1999). *Recovery: An Alien Concept*. Gloucester: Handsell Press.

Davidson, L. & Strauss, J. (1992). Sense of self in recovery from severe mental illness. *British Journal of Medical Psychology*, **65**, 131–145.

Deegan, P. (1993). Recovering our sense of value after being labelled. *Journal of Psychosocial Nursing*, **31**, 7–11.

Deegan, P. (1994). Recovery: The lived experience of rehabilitation. In W.A. Anthony & L. Spaniol (Eds), *Readings in Psychiatric Rehabilitation* (pp. 149–162). Boston: Boston University Center for Psychiatric Rehabilitation.

Dewan, V. (2001). Life Support. In J. Read (Ed.), *Something Inside So Strong: Strategies for Surviving Mental Distress* (pp. 44–49). London: Mental Health Foundation.

Dillon, J. & May, R. (2002). Reclaiming experience. *Clinical Psychology*, **17**, 25–77.

Drayton, M., Birchwood, M. & Trower, P. (1998). Early attachment experience and recovery from psychosis. *British Journal of Clinical Psychology*, **37**, 269–284.

Greenfield, S.F., Strakowski, S.TM., Tohen, M., Batsom, S.C. & Kolbrener, M.L. (1994). Childhood abuse in first-episode of psychosis. *British Journal of Psychiatry*, **164**, 831–834.

Harrop, C. & Trower, P. (2001). Why does schizophrenia develop at late adolescence? *Clinical Psychology Review*, **21**, 241–266.

Healy, D. (1997). *Psychiatric Drugs Explained.* London: Mosby.

Herman, J.L. (1992). *Trauma and Recovery.* New York: Basic Books.

Kaffman, M. (1981). Paranoid disorders: The core of truth behind the delusional system. *International Journal of Family Therapy*, **3**, 29–41.

Kingdon, D.G. & Turkington, D. (1994). *Cognitive-Behavioural Therapy of Schizophrenia.* New York: Guilford Publications.

Knight, T. (2002). Alternatives to sectioning in correspondence. *Clinical Psychology*, **12**, 4.

Lyon, H.M., Kaney, S. & Bentall, R.P. (1994). The defensive function of persecutory delusions: Evidence from attribution tasks. *British Journal of Psychiatry*, **164**, 637–646.

Martensson, L. (1998). *The Case Against Neuroleptic Drugs.* Switzerland: The Voiceless Movement (Mouvement Les Sans Voix).

May, R. (2000). Routes to recovery from psychosis: The roots of a clinical psychologist. *Clinical Psychology Forum*, **146**, 6–10.

McGorry, P.D. (1991). The schizophrenia concept in first episode psychosis: Does it fit and is it harmful? *Dulwich Centre Newsletter*, No. **4**, 40–44.

Morrison, A.P. (1998). Cognitive behaviour therapy for psychotic symptoms in schizophrenia. In N. Tarrier & A. Wells (Eds), *Treating Complex Cases: The Cognitive Behavioural Therapy Approach* (pp. 195–216). New York: John Wiley & Sons.

Mosher, L.R. & Burti, L (1994). *Community Mental Health. A Practical Guide.* New York: W.W. Norton & Company.

Mueser, K.T., Trumbetta, S.L., Rosenberg, S.D., Vidaver, R., Goodman, L.B., Osher, F.C., Auciello, P. & Foy, D.W. (1998). Trauma and posttraumatic stress disorder in severe mental illness. *Journal of Consulting and Clinical Psychology*, **66**, 493–499.

O'Hanlon, B. & Rowan, T. (1998). *Solution Oriented Therapy for Severe Mental Illness.* New York: John Wiley & Sons.

Pearpoint, J. (1998). *From Behind the Piano* and (Joint Publication) Snow, J.A. (1998) *What's really Worth Doing and How To Do It.* Toronto: Inclusion Press.

Read, J. (2001). *Something Inside So Strong: Strategies for Surviving Mental Distress.* London: Mental Health Foundation.

Read, J. & Harre, N. (2001). The role of biological and genetic causal beliefs in the stigmatisation of 'mental patients'. *Journal of Mental Health (UK)*, **10**, 223–235.

Ridgway, P. (2001). Restorying psychiatric disability: Learning from first person narratives. *Psychiatric Rehabilitation Journal*, **24**, 335–343.

Romme, M. & Escher, S. (1993). *Accepting Voices.* London: Mind Publications.

Romme, M. & Escher, S. (2000). *Making Sense of Voices: A Guide For Mental Health Professionals Working With Voice-Hearers.* London: Mind Publications.

Ross, A. Anderson, G. & Clark, R. (1994). Childhood abuse and the positive symptoms of schizophrenia. *Hospital and Community Psychiatry*, **45**, 489–491.

Russo, J. (2001). Reclaiming Madness. In J. Read (Ed.), *Something Inside So Strong: Strategies for Surviving Mental Distress* (pp. 36–39). London: Mental Health Foundation.

Thomas, P. (1997). *The Dialectics of Schizophrenia.* London: Free Association Books.

Thornhill, H., Clare, L. & May, R. (in press). Escape, enlightenment and endurance: Narratives of recovery from psychosis. Special issue of *Anthropology and Medicine*.

Warner, R. (1994). *Recovery from Schizophrenia: Psychiatry and Political Economy.* London and New York: Routledge.

Warner, S. (2000). *Understanding Child Sexual Abuse. Making the Tactics Visible.* Gloucester: Handsell Publishing.

White, M. (1987). Family therapy and schizophrenia: Addressing the 'in the corner' lifestyle. *Dulwich Newsletter*, Spring edition.

White, M. (1996). Power to our journeys. *American Family Therapy Academy Newsletter*. Summer edition, 11–16.

White, M. & Epston, D. (1990). *Narrative Means to Therapeutic Ends*. London: W.W. Norton & Co.

Young, S.L. & Ensing, D.S. (1999). Exploring recovery from the perspective of people with psychiatric disabilites. *Psychiatric Rehabiliation Journal*, **22**, 219–231.

Yusupoff, L. & Tarrier, N. (1996). Coping strategy enhancement. In G. Haddock & P. Slade (Eds), *Cognitive Behavioural Interventions with Psychotic Disorders*. London and New York: Routledge.

15 Psychological Therapies: Implementation in Early Intervention Services

GRÁINNE FADDEN, MAX BIRCHWOOD, CHRIS JACKSON AND KAREN BARTON

Early Intervention Service, Birmingham, UK

INTRODUCTION

In order to deliver high-quality early intervention services, clinicians need to incorporate into their therapeutic repertoire interventions with demonstrated efficacy. One task, as already discussed in this book, will be to establish a reliable body of evidence-based psychological interventions for early psychosis. However, there is also the challenge of how to disseminate established research findings so that they are employed in routine practice. This is an area that is unfortunately under-researched and the final stage of any research study—the dissemination of results—is often the one that is neglected and under-funded (Palmer & Fenner, 1999). Frequently, there is a reliance on publications and presentations at conferences as a means of getting results disseminated. However, there is a substantial amount of evidence that these methods are ineffective (Freemantle et al., 1995; Grol, 1992; Lomas, 1991), and that publishing material without an accompanying implementation strategy is unlikely to produce a change in practice.

A good example of the gap between research evidence and the adoption of evidence-based psychosocial approaches into practice is that of psychoeducational family interventions. There is a large and consistent body of evidence, which is almost unprecedented in the area of mental health, that demonstrates the effectiveness of these approaches. This is well documented in numerous reviews (Dixon & Lehman, 1995; Fadden, 1998; Goldstein & Miklowitz, 1995; Mari, Adams & Streiner, 1996; Penn & Mueser, 1996; Pilling et al., 2002). However, these family approaches have not been implemented in practice, and evidence suggests that they are not available routinely in mental health services in the United States (Dixon et al., 1999; Johnson, 1994; Lehman, Steinwachs et al., 1998), the United Kingdom (Department of Health, 1995), or in other European countries (Magliano et al., 1998), almost two decades after the earlier studies were published (Falloon et al., 1982; Leff et al., 1982).

In this chapter, we will describe a strategic approach to the implementation of evidence-based approaches to care that is currently being employed in the West Midlands of England. There are two strands to the strategy: an in-service cascade training model, and a University training programme. Both methods incorporate involvement with the broad mental health

Psychological Interventions in Early Psychosis
Edited by J.F.M. Gleeson and P.D. McGorry. © 2004 John Wiley & Sons, Ltd.

service system, and involve a range of strategic interventions with service managers and planners. While both of the programmes are concerned with training the mental health workforce to work across a range of services, we will refer throughout the chapter to specific issues relating to the implementation of psychological therapies in early intervention services.

Blocks to Implementation

In order to develop an effective implementation strategy, it is important to understand the complexity of barriers to the adoption of particular interventions into routine care. It is clear that there is greater difficulty implementing psychosocial interventions than biological innovations into routine practice (Department of Health, 1995; Lehman, Steinwachs et al., 1998). Previous surveys have demonstrated that model-training packages *per se* do not result in changes in clinical practice. Kavanagh et al. (1993) and Fadden (1997) demonstrated that, following the receipt of training in family work, the majority of therapists were unable to put their training into practice because of obstacles in the systems in which they were employed. There were also issues relating to staff skills, attitudes and experience. While some studies have demonstrated success in training small numbers of staff (Bailey, Burbach & Lea, 2003), the task of training large numbers of staff with varying degrees of skill and motivation is much more complex.

Prior to the inception of the two West Midlands training programmes, an understanding of the barriers to implementation was derived from experience of previous attempts at training staff in this area, and from an audit of the staff and services in the West Midlands Region. Some core issues in the implementation of psychosocial interventions were identified.

Planning, development and delivery of early intervention services

In the development of any new service, there is frequently a focus among planners and those charged with commissioning and developing services to focus on structures and capacity rather than on activities. Thus there is discussion around the number of teams, staff mix on teams, and where they will be based. There is much less frequently a discussion around which therapies or interventions the staff will be expected to deliver, or an examination of what training is required to ensure that this happens. Equally, the philosophy and values of the new service are often not made explicit. In the absence of attention to these issues, it is much more likely that staff bring with them the values and practices that prevailed in the setting in which they were previously employed. This scenario is more likely in situations where there are tight deadlines or targets around the establishment of services. Newstead and Kelly (2003), for example, highlight the risk of authorities rushing the development of services in order to meet current government targets in the UK relating to the development of early intervention services by 2004.

New services require new ways of working. Many individual and family psychological interventions require out-of-hours work, and many traditional services operate Monday to Friday, 9 am to 5 pm working patterns. Many staff have chosen community (rather than inpatient) posts for this reason. They perceive that there are no rewards and no incentives for out-of-hours working. Other service factors, such as short-term thinking on the part of management, responding to crises, having busy caseloads, multiple priorities, and clashes of training initiatives, all impede the capacity to provide psychosocial interventions.

The perception of psychosis as a biological disorder

In the majority of mental health services, at least in the UK, biological models and their associated treatments are seen as the most important, with psychological approaches being seen as secondary, optional or adjuncts even when there is strong evidence to support them (Fadden & Birchwood, 2002). Staff frequently comment that if individual and/or family psychological interventions are not offered, there are no adverse consequences for them. An audit in the West Midlands area (Fadden & Birchwood, 2002) revealed a lack of confidence among professionals in asserting the importance of psychosocial approaches in general, and this was identified as linked to the prevailing and powerful biological reductionist culture. Along with this goes a focus on care of the individual rather than of a social system. This is a specific barrier to the delivery of interventions that address the needs of family and friends as well as those of the individual. Issues of diagnostic and prognostic uncertainty for those adhering strongly to biological models are inevitable when dealing with early psychosis. This often leads to staff avoiding questions from individuals and family members because they are worried about questions to which the answers are unclear.

Training of staff in psychosocial interventions

An audit of clinical skills of mental health professionals in the West Midlands (Fadden & Birchwood, 2002) revealed a poor base level of skill in psychosocial interventions, and low numbers of individuals trained specifically to implement them. While training courses in psychosocial interventions have been widely available in the UK, their uptake has been low in comparison with the overall level of need, and has tended to depend on individual motivation and opportunity. Where staff had received training, they tended to be isolated and usually unidisciplinary professionals operating in community teams where the team culture did not support psychosocial interventions. There was also a lack of availability of skilled supervision on an ongoing basis in the area.

The majority of mental health staff receive very little training in how to work psychologically with young people with psychosis and their families in their professional training, and it is not routine on training curricula. For instance, in the in-service family training programme, 72% of staff across the different disciplines reported that they had never received any training in family work prior to joining the programme. They lack confidence therefore in even the basics of talking with families and coping with their distress and anger. This lack of confidence is often projected onto the family, who are described as 'not the right kind of family', or as being 'unsuitable'. Similarly, in individual psychological work with those experiencing their first episode of psychosis, an individual's tendency to deny what is happening, or to express anger to services, can be viewed as a characteristic of an individual or illness, rather than a phase of adjustment.

Staff opting to work in new early psychosis services are often drawn from community teams and other established mental health settings. This gives rise to a host of experience and confidence issues specific to working with young people in an early phase of psychosis and their families. Those coming from adult mental health services often lack confidence in dealing with children and adolescents, while those drawn from child services frequently perceive that their knowledge of psychotic disorders is scanty. Many lack recent prolonged exposure to acute psychosis, and find the 'rawness' and intensity of emotion to which they are exposed difficult to cope with. Those whose primary experience is in working with individuals find it difficult to cope with issues of confidentiality, and find it challenging to

Table 15.1. Threats to engagement

Threat	Example
Failure in empathy	Phenomena outside of therapist's experience, e.g. hallucination, bizarre beliefs
Therapist beliefs	Psychosis is beyond the scope of cognitive therapy and symptoms will not change
Client's beliefs	The therapist will view his or her experience in the context of 'madness' and only wants to increase medication or 'test' the client
The therapeutic relationship	The client has a bad experience of relationships and perceives them as threatening
Reframing of delusions	Client does not feel that he or she is believed because the therapist wants to class a delusion as a belief (B), not a fact (A)
Rationale for questioning delusions	The therapist moves too soon into identifying the delusion as the problem, before the client is ready

Source: From P. Chadwick, M. Birchwood & P. Trower (1996). *Cognitive Therapy for Hallucinations, Delusions and Paranoia.* © John Wiley & Sons, Ltd. Reproduced with permission.

have to take the views of all family members into account. They get caught up in dilemmas derived from their individualistic ways of working in relation to whether they are an ally for the young person or the family.

Some identify with the families and think that they could be in a similar situation with their own children in the future. On the whole, most of these workers have little experience in helping people to cope with issues related to grief, loss, and adjustment to changed expectations and dreams which are so common in early psychosis, and feel out of their depth in addressing these in therapy. They frequently describe worries about opening a 'can of worms' that they will not be able to control or manage. A final issue relates to their lack of experience of the complex range of service systems such as education, probation, and voluntary services which work with young people involves.

Barriers to engagement

At an individual and family level, implementation of psychosocial interventions is dependent upon clients and relatives engaging in a therapeutic process. In relation to family work, therapists identify engagement as the most difficult stage of therapy (Fadden & Birchwood, 2002). Chadwick, Birchwood and Trower (1996) identified what they considered to be the principal problems when engaging clients with psychosis in cognitive therapy (see Table 15.1). It is very probable that these also apply to other psychosocial interventions.

Each threat can be seen as an obstacle to be negotiated if the therapist is previously aware that there might be a problem. Chadwick and colleagues concluded that clients should be eased gently into the therapeutic alliance to minimize the risk of arousing anxiety, thereby making them more likely to disengage. Although important with all client groups, this message is especially so with young psychosis sufferers. The therapist may become part of the delusional belief—for example, an agent of the Government who has been sent to spy on them. Even in milder forms, clients who have had a bad experience of mental health services may see the therapist as a doctor who will increase medication or send them back to hospital if they say the 'wrong' thing.

In this environment it is very difficult to establish a trusting relationship and this requires persistence, reassurance and patience. Even clients who appear eager to talk may have the wrong impression of therapy because of their disordered thought processes. For example, someone with grandiose delusions may feel special because he or she has been singled out for therapy and could be let down when the truth is discussed. With first-episode clients, the skills of the therapist should include use of non-threatening body language, introductory subjects (e.g. the client's other pastimes, football, etc.), and everyday language.

There is still very little research into why it is difficult to engage some clients in psychological therapies. In one of the few studies that explored this issue, Tarrier and colleagues found that the three main reasons clients gave for dropping out of cognitive therapy for psychosis were (1) they did not feel that therapy was useful for their problem, (2) they feared it would aggravate their symptoms, and (3) their previous experiences of help-seeking had not been fruitful (Tarrier et al., 1998). Fifty-six percent of clients also stated that their symptoms had already disappeared by the time they received cognitive therapy and that they were no longer bothered by them.

Denial of the disorder as a way of coping with its negative consequences, especially stigma, and the need for medication, has been described as a 'sealing over' strategy (McGlashan, Levy & Carpenter, 1975). This is manifest clinically in more problematic engagement. Conversely, the 'integrating' client is more curious about his or her problems, is more willing to discuss them and is open to help. Such 'integrative' coping styles, although associated with better engagement, are independent of insight (Drayton, Birchwood & Trower, 1998; Tait, Birchwood & Trower, 2003), suggesting that motivational therapies may be of more use during the 'sealing' phase because they do not modify insight but instead intervene at the 'level of the individual's psychological defences to treatment...' (Tait, Birchwood & Trower, 2003, p. 127).

Coping style is a psychological response to the experience of psychosis which reflects the client's underlying readiness for psychological help. In other words, if the person is denying the existence of the disorder, he or she may not be ready for the pressures and challenges of therapy. However, much can still be done in terms of establishing a positive relationship, and starting the process of engagement.

Obviously, it is easier to engage clients when they are in the integration phase. Initially the integration style of recovery was seen as more positive because clients would be active in monitoring their own mental health and taking steps to prevent relapse. One aim of psychological therapy is to help clients to move from the sealing-over phase to the integration phase (Jackson et al., 1998). However, the integration phase may itself bring new challenges because clients who have accepted their problems and their consequences in terms of long-term prognosis are more likely to be at risk of depression, hopelessness and even suicide (Jackson & Iqbal, 2000). The therapist needs to be aware of these risks and address them. Recovery style appears to be a state characteristic, dependent on adjustment to illness, and not entirely a trait characteristic as formerly proposed (McGlashan, Levy & Carpenter, 1975; Tait, Birchwood & Trower, 2003; Thompson, McGorry & Harrigan, 2003). In the initial phase of recovery from acute psychotic illness, clients tend to adopt an integrative style but this shifts towards a sealing-over approach as recovery begins, perhaps because the implications of illness become clearer, and clients believe they can 'put it all behind them and move on' (Tait, Birchwood & Trower, 2003).

It is however, very tempting for the clinician to focus on the integrating client. Given less than optimal resources within a service, it appears to make more sense to concentrate efforts on clients who appear to want help. But this may mean that clients who are severely ill may 'slip through the net' of psychosocial intervention. Staff may feel less than confident delivering psychological interventions to those who at first seem reluctant to engage in a therapeutic relationship. A recent study of the role of a shared case formulation in cognitive-behavioural therapy (CBT) for psychosis (Chadwick, Williams & Mackenzie, 2003) showed that its benefit was more for the therapist than the client in cementing an optimistic, energetic collaborative relationship. This may need to be addressed in further staff training. Implementing CBT and family interventions in practice requires more careful appreciation of the barriers to engagement in both client *and* therapist.

THE WEST MIDLANDS REGION, UK

The West Midlands Region was the traditional industrial and manufacturing centre of England. The region covers a population of 5 million people, and in 1997 when both programmes were developed, it was divided into 17 different health service geographical areas known as 'Trusts'. Following a number of mergers, there are currently 13 different areas. The Trusts vary in size, ranging from a population of 250 000 in the smallest, to 1.2 million in the largest, which covers the city of Birmingham. There are other smaller cities in the Region, as well as large rural areas. All of the Trusts are part of the National Health Service, and there are very few private services available. Some parts of the Region are among those with the highest levels of social deprivation in England. It is an area that is rich in cultural diversity, with many different ethnic groups living in Birmingham and some of the nearby districts.

PSYCHOSOCIAL TRAINING PROGRAMMES IN THE WEST MIDLANDS

Both the in-service training programme in family work ('Meriden'), developed and led by Dr Gráinne Fadden, and the University-based programme in Community Mental Health ('RECOVER'), were initiated in 1997, with the ambitious aim of training all mental health staff in the Region in psychosocial interventions. The cascade-training programme was aimed at rapidly training large numbers of staff in family interventions. In the context of the powerful culture of evidence-based practice in health services in the UK, and the Government's endorsement of psychosocial interventions in its Mental Health Strategy (Department of Health, 1998), it was felt that a strategic approach to training and implementation of these interventions throughout the West Midlands should be undertaken. Both programmes received explicit backing from the Regional National Health Executive—a fact that gave them a clear status as being valued, important, and having the support of the Department of Health. The aims of the programmes continue to be supported by further recent Department of Health policies (Department of Health, 2002a, 2002b).

The programmes have some common features: both were financed through top-sliced Regional funds, by which 'free' training is available to staff within the 17 Trusts. An independent evaluation of each was commissioned. One of the aims of both programmes was to develop a supervisory infrastructure within mental health services throughout the West Midlands, and to create an alliance with services at the highest level to facilitate and encourage the implementation of psychosocial interventions in routine practice. However, both programmes use quite different methods to ensure that these aims are achieved.

Neither programme focuses specifically on staff who work in early intervention services, rather these staff are trained alongside those who work in a range of mental health services.

MERIDEN, THE FAMILY INTERVENTIONS CASCADE TRAINING PROGRAMME

In addition to those outlined above, the specific aims of this programme were as follows:

- To raise the profile of families and other supportive persons in the lives of service users in the mental health system.
- To encourage the development of family sensitive services.
- To ensure that evidence-based family work is available to those living in the Region who would benefit from it.
- To train 1000 therapists initially in the skills needed to offer therapeutic interventions to people with serious mental health problems and their families.

Because of the scale of the task, a cascade model of training was adopted as the only one that would be likely to be successful in training a large number of staff in a short space of time. This involved the training of staff in each Trust to become trainers and supervisors. These therapists drawn from all professions could then offer training courses within their own services.

We were aware that the barriers to implementation were mainly related to staff skills and issues in service systems. A two-tier approach was adopted which incorporated staff training and interventions in the systems in which therapists worked. In order for the project to be successful, it was seen as crucial to enlist the support of management at all levels in the 17 Trusts across the Region before any training was offered.

Step 1: Contact with Senior Management

The Chief Executives in all 17 Trusts that were in place at the start of the programme were contacted, and the programme and its aims were explained to them. If they were interested in being involved, they were offered an introductory half-day workshop in their Trust to explain the project to their staff, and to outline the commitment that participation in the project would require. A link person was identified in each Trust to coordinate a venue for the workshop, and to invite relevant personnel.

Step 2: Introductory Workshops

The 17 Trusts in the Region agreed to host an introductory workshop, which was presented by the Director of the Programme and a Regional Consultant in Public Health. The coordinators were asked to ensure that all relevant senior managers from health, social services and the purchasing authorities attended the workshop, that was also open to senior clinicians.

The workshop provided background information on the programme, and outlined the evidence supporting the effectiveness of family interventions. Participants were informed that training, supervision and materials would be funded centrally, and that the commitment from Trusts was in terms of staff time, management support, and the provision of venues for in-service training courses. Local barriers and potential solutions were identified. It should be noted that many of the issues that impacted on the implementation of family work, such as caseload size, were not identified by staff at this early stage. Trusts were then asked to decide if they wished to take part in the project.

Step 3: Selection of Trainers for the Programme

The 17 Trusts in the Region made a commitment to take part in the project, though one postponed joining at this early stage because of pre-existing commitments to other training. Each of the participating Trusts was asked to select members of staff with the necessary skills to train as therapists to work with families in the first instance, and later as trainers. Between two and five members of staff were selected per Trust depending on the size and geography of the area covered. In all, 43 mental health professionals from different disciplines—nursing, psychology, psychiatry, social work and occupational therapy—entered this first training phase of the programme to train as therapists and trainers.

Step 4: Family Therapy Skills: Training and Supervision

In April 1998, the 43 professionals who had been selected attended a training course in psychoeducational family interventions. In the 6-month period between April and October 1998, they put their skills into practice, offering therapy to families in the areas in which they worked. Their skills were evaluated, and they were required to produce case reports and audiotapes of therapy sessions in addition to an academic essay. The 16 Trusts were divided into four supervision groups, each consisting of staff from four neighbouring Trusts. Therapists continued to receive ongoing supervision and training one day per month, and attendance was high, as staff could attend supervision in another Trust if unable to attend their own. The venue for supervision rotated among the Trusts, with each Trust hosting a training day once every 4 months. This helped to maintain the profile of the programme in the various Trusts. Issues affecting the implementation of the interventions in practice which arose during this period continued to be addressed at senior management level, and solutions were sought to resolve them.

Step 5: Training the Trainers

Thirty-five staff representing the 16 Trusts attended a course in October 1998 to train as trainers and supervisors in psychoeducational family interventions. Once again their competence in the necessary skills was evaluated and monitored. They then held a series of training courses within their own Trusts for multidisciplinary groups of staff—a process that is still continuing. Over the course of the programme, four further courses have been held in order to increase the numbers of trainers and supervisors, as the numbers of trained therapists increased.

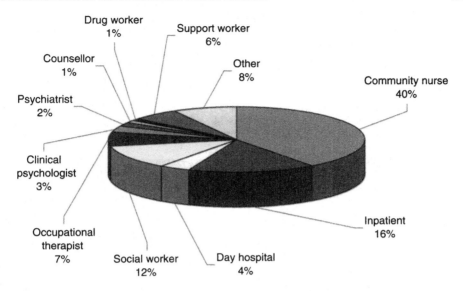

Figure 15.1. The Meriden programme: professional breakdown of therapists ($n = 1272$)

CURRENT SITUATION

Since the first therapists were trained in April 1998, 1272 therapists from different disciplines have been trained within the cascade training programme, and a total of 143 training courses have been held across the various Trusts. All the initial training courses were monitored by an external evaluator to check the consistency of the content, and to ensure that the quality of the presentations is maintained. All new trainers are evaluated on two occasions to monitor their presentation and group facilitation skills. While the earlier courses trained a greater proportion of staff who worked in community settings, later courses involved inpatient staff, and people from voluntary agencies have also been trained. A welcome recent development is the training of family members and service users as therapists. The breakdown of those trained by profession is given in Figure 15.1.

In the University programme, described later, over 150 therapists have been trained over four intakes including over 30 in early intervention programmes. Over a period of 5 years, therefore, 1272 therapists have been trained in family work in the region and 117 in CBT. There are now 100 trainers/supervisors in family work spread throughout the Region. These represent the various disciplines working in mental health services, and one carer has been trained as a trainer. This is an area that, hopefully, will develop as the programme progresses.

The therapists' fidelity to the family intervention model is measured through the provision of therapy tapes at five different stages of the therapy process. These are evaluated by an independent researcher using the Hahlweg Rating Scale (Durr & Hahlweg, 1996), which was designed specifically for rating psychoeducational family work. The initial cohort of trainers demonstrated high ratings at all points of the therapy process, and this has been sustained in subsequent cohorts, as shown in Table 15.2. Therapists are rated as maintaining fidelity to the approach, with mean scores of 22.3 for engagement, 25.4 for assessment, 27.4 for information giving, 29.8 for communication skills training, and 28.1 for problem-solving.

Table 15.2. Fidelity to the family therapy model: Hahlweg Rating Scale

Taped session	Range of possible scores	Mean	S.D.	n
Engagement	0–29	22.3	4.84	48
Assessment	0–29	25.4	2.88	31
Education	0–34	27.4	4.92	20
Communication skills	0–34	29.8	4.00	17
Problem-solving	0–34	28.1	3.79	14

Table 15.3. Mean number of families seen—cohorts 1–6 at 3 years

Cohort	Mean no. of families	Cohort	Mean no. of families
1	4.6 ($n = 16$)	4	2.3 ($n = 22$)
2	2.5 ($n = 35$)	5	1.2 ($n = 15$)
3	2.8 ($n = 13$)	6	1.9 ($n = 10$)

According to Durr and Hahlweg (1996), scores above 20 indicate more than adequate fidelity to the model.

Implementation

One of the key factors of concern when setting up this programme was that therapists would be able to implement what they had learned in practice. The first cohort of trained therapists continues to see an increasing number of families as time goes on. The mean number of families seen by them was 2.7 at 6 months, 3.2 at 1 year, 3.8 at 2 years, and 4.6 at 3 years. Later cohorts appear to have increasing difficulty in implementing their training in practice, as is shown in Table 15.3. They encounter a range of difficulties related to their heavy workload, difficulties integrating this work into their clinical practice, and concerns about their own level of skill. Poor data returns from some of the trained personnel has introduced a further difficulty.

A recent survey of therapists who received the cascade training programme was conducted in order to establish some of the problems encountered when trying to implement family work in clinical practice. As can be seen in the list in Box 15.1, difficulties tended to be related to service issues, skill/experience in family work, and some issues to do with attitude and conflicts with demands in therapists' personal lives. It is interesting to note that, over the period of the programme, there is little change in the issues reported by staff as causing problems, indicating how difficult it is to bring about changes in attitudes and working practices that have become entrenched over time. Anyone setting up early intervention services needs to be aware of this, and to address training and attitudinal issues from the outset.

In addition to the generic training, specific modules around early psychosis are provided. These cover topics such as dealing with diagnostic uncertainty, loss, the needs of siblings, dealing with therapists' own emotional reactions, and negotiating among different members. In addition, joint training has been held with staff from adult mental health services and child and adolescent services in order to enhance communication and understanding among the two groups. A special project has been conducted through the Meriden Programme to

---

Box 15.1. Top ten implementation difficulties encountered by therapists

---

Difficulties encountered at 6 months

- Integration with my caseload demands responsibilities at work
- Allowance of time from the service to do the intervention
- Availability of appropriate clients
- Engagement of clients or families
- Integration of family work with my outside interests or responsibilities
- Availability of time in lieu or overtime for appointments
- Keeping family discussions on track
- Knowledge and skills in behavioural techniques
- Work with families using other models
- Clash of family sessions and other clinical needs of the clients and/or families

Difficulties encountered at 36 months

- Integration with my caseload demands responsibilities at work
- Allowance of time from the service to do the intervention
- Work with families using other models
- Availability of appropriate clients
- Integration of family work with my outside interests or responsibilities
- Engagement of clients and their families
- Availability of time in lieu or overtime for appointments
- Clash of family sessions and other clinical needs of the clients and/or families
- Keeping family discussions on track
- Clashes of family sessions with crises with other clients

---

identify issues and produce recommendations for these two groups to work together more effectively (Gillam et al., 2003).

Strategies that Have Proved to be Helpful

At a managerial level a number of strategies have been implemented to try to overcome some of the resistance to change. Management links have been identified in each Trust, and a process of ongoing audit, feedback and problem-solving of difficulties is continuous throughout the programme. Developing implementation policies, amending job descriptions to include specific reference to psychosocial approaches, setting targets for managers relating to the implementation of family work and other psychological therapies have all proved to be useful. Recently, there has been a focus on the training of managers via workshops to help them with the difficulties they face in encouraging an attitude change in their staff. The key role played by management in the successful implementation of new approaches has also been identified in other studies (Smith & Velleman, 2002).

'Ringfencing' time and money to allow for the implementation and supervision of psychosocial interventions is sometimes useful. It is particularly helpful for therapists who are learning new skills to have some protected time immediately following training courses. Addressing the issue of working unsociable hours, by assessing how individual therapists can be helped to achieve a satisfactory balance between their personal and working lives, is also an effective strategy. We have also found it useful within our early intervention service to nominate 'product champions' who can promote and oversee the implementation of interventions such as relapse prevention or family work by other team members. This strategy has also been employed in other services (Smith & Velleman, 2002). We have also found it useful to set realistic and achievable targets for the implementation of psychosocial interventions, which can be reviewed weekly through team meetings and monitored through clinical governance structures and individual supervision. This will allow the team to monitor (e.g. via a database) 'who needs what and whether they got it'.

On an individual level, good supervision and support in implementing psychosocial interventions should not be treated as a luxury but should be 'built-in' to clinical work from the start. Continued professional development and training should, ideally, be encouraged at a managerial level and a programme of in-house 'top-up' training organized by those responsible for the implementation of that particular psychosocial intervention. Clinicians' time will always be precious. How it is prioritized remains key to the implementation of psychosocial interventions.

In terms of family interventions, it is anticipated that a further 3 years of work within the Trusts will be required to ensure that family work is fully embedded in the 'core' business of services. The cost of the programme to date is £550 000 which, considering the scale of the programme, is very cost-effective.

'RECOVER': THE COMMUNITY MENTAL HEALTH PROGRAMME

The second programme was conceived by Professor Birchwood, in conjunction with Professor Sheehan (Mental Health lead in the government agency responsible for the delivery of healthcare within the West Midlands Region) as a partnership between the local mental health services and the University.

The mental health services in the West Midlands are responsible for nominating and releasing staff to engage with the programme, and this is facilitated through the close collaboration achieved between the Regional Executive and the Chief Executives of each of the Mental Health Trusts. Each Mental Health Trust is promised, in return, a supply of fully trained staff, plus support to enable the staff to be appropriately supervised (see below). The University of Birmingham is responsible for the provision of the taught respects of the programme itself and in developing the supervision structure. Thus, the programme is unique in the UK and perhaps elsewhere, in the strategic approach taken to training. It is underpinned by the highest level of collaboration between key agencies necessary to make a dramatic impact on the skill-base of mental health workers routinely engaged in clinical practice with the severely mentally ill, including those working with early psychosis.

THE UNIVERSITY PROGRAMME: AIMS

It was felt that, in order to train all front-line staff in psychosocial intervention (PSI) skills, their training had to be broader than PSI and should embrace a thorough and deep understanding both of traditional psychiatry and of the structure, funding and organizational aspects of mental health service delivery. We aimed, in other words, to develop a group of practitioners, not only skilled in PSI, but confident in their role as service innovators.

The programme explicitly adopted a value-base focused around the express needs of service users and their carers. Critical to the success of the programme, however, was the creation of an infrastructure within the mental health services in the West Midlands to support the trainees from the programme. The experience of the implementation of PSI elsewhere has emphasized the risk of drift in the 'fidelity' of therapists to the core principles of the interventions.

Multidisciplinary Nature of the Programme

The programme is organized by the University of Birmingham and operates as a multidisciplinary partnership between university departments, including Psychology, Psychiatry, Social Work, Nursing and Primary Care. The programme is open to a multidisciplinary audience and also to non-professionals. The course is structured as a modular programme, but at the present time it remains linear in nature. There are three levels: Certificate, Diploma and Masters. Each level requires the successful completion of the previous level, and trainees can exit at any of these levels. This usually occurs according to the aptitude of the student and also the needs of the local service.

CONTENT OF THE COURSE

1. Certificate Level

Foundation course

The skill base and background of the workforce was found to be extremely varied. The foundation course is intended to bring the group to a similar level and to develop confidence for those who have been away from formal study for some time. The foundation provides a conceptual basis for cognitive-behavioural therapy and family intervention, and includes user-focused practice, current legislative and policy issues, and emphasizes reflection on the values of clinical practice and mental health services in general.

Phenomenology and drug treatment

This module enables students to sharpen their understanding and assessment of psychotic symptoms. Training in a range of instruments to assess symptoms is provided, including the SCAN (WHO, 1992) and the PANSS (Kay, Fiszbein, & Opler, 1987). The limitations and side-effects of neuroleptic medication are covered and currency is given to low-dose strategies, particularly in first-episode psychosis, using typical and atypical preparations.

Consumer participation

This module takes a consumer perspective, including specific ways in which consumers can be brought into the design and implementation of services in order to promote a consumer-led ethos in clinical practice. Service consumers contribute to the teaching of this module, and a service consumer has been appointed as a lecturer in the programme.

Cognitive-behavioural therapy

This module provides the main clinical focus in conjunction with problem-based assessment strategies and provides discrete areas of skill-based interventions, including: early signs methodology for relapse prevention; individual and group psychoeducation for individuals and families; 'compliance therapy' for medication adherence; and group approaches to working with those who hear voices. The module emphasizes the acquisition and implementation of CBT skills. However, in recognition of the diverse professional and skill backgrounds of students, it does not aim to train 'cognitive therapists', but therapists who are able to implement the CBT skills developed for psychosis.

Working in community teams

This module presents and evaluates service protocols for assertive outreach teams, home treatment teams and early intervention teams. It includes considerable emphasis on the interagency collaboration and on promoting truly multidisciplinary, consumer-focused approaches.

2. Diploma Level

The Diploma is taught during the second year and requires successful completion of the Certificate to a criterion level. The Diploma concentrates on a range of PSI skills, building upon those developed in the first year. These include:

- *Family intervention:* This is organized in conjunction with the in-service cascade training programme described above.
- *Cognitive therapy:* This level of CBT focuses exclusively on the cognitive approaches to delusional thinking developed in the UK (Chadwick, Birchwood & Trower, 1996; Fowler, Garety & Kuipers, 1995), and includes the process of engagement, disputing delusional beliefs, and reality testing. It includes both beliefs about voices and also other delusional ideas, and is taught within the very practical framework described by Nelson (1997).
- *Early intervention:* In the UK there has been some considerable development in the conceptual basis and implementation of early intervention in psychosis (Birchwood, Fowler & Jackson, 2000), with the requirement that, by the year 2004, specialized early intervention programmes will be available to support all young people with their first episode of psychosis (Department of Health, 2000). This module has two related aims: firstly, to encourage students to examine their service's ability to engage and to sustain intervention during the early 'critical period' of psychosis to prevent traumatic reactions and suicidal thinking; secondly, it includes CBT to promote individual adaptation to a psychosis to prevent traumatic reactions and suicidal thinking, and further teaching around the specialized task of promoting families' early adjustment to the experience and diagnosis of psychosis.
- *Complex critical assessments:* The problems of 'comorbid' substance misuse and risk issues are addressed in this module. These 'complex' assessments are supported by CBT interventions to reduce the use and impact of substance misuse within a 'harm-reduction' framework.

- *Ethical and legal aspects:* This covers the ethical and medico-legal issues in mental health care. Key national legislation and policy documents as they relate to the mentally ill are presented and analysed in detail.
- *Interagency collaboration:* This module requires advanced understanding of the relationship between healthcare agencies, primary care, social care agencies and the voluntary sector. Trainees are taught the skill of network mapping and how this relates to the coordination of care in the individual case.

3. Masters Level

The Masters level takes place in the third year and aims to teach research skills, including service evaluation skills. This is achieved through tuition in experimental methodology and statistics, with considerable emphasis on critical appraisal of scientific literature. Students are required to undertake a research project using either conventional hypothesis-driven research, or consumer-oriented qualitative recording of service audit/evaluation.

ASSESSMENT

The programme assesses each module through structured assignments which are exclusively of a practical and applicable nature. For example, the CBT modules require a forward assessment of the implementation of CBT techniques; the early intervention includes completion of a mini-audit of care for first-episode psychosis; and in the consumer participation module, trainees are asked to develop a strategy to promote consumer involvement in the delivery of mental health care, and to begin its implementation. The assignments are intended to provide an assessment of competence and to be of practical value to the mental health services and their consumers. The assignments also include reference to relevant academic literature of which the trainee is expected to demonstrate mastery.

SUPPORT AND SUPERVISION

Students are recommended to the programme in groups of four, and are expected to operate as a team within each mental health service. This provides mutual support. In addition, they are expected to continue as a team, forging links with other graduates of the programme to create the 'critical mass' of trained therapists, and the infrastructure to support PSI. These teams are multidisciplinary. Each mental health service also nominates a senior member of their service whose job it is to meet regularly with the trainees, to support them with any difficulties or barriers to implementation, and, where appropriate, to provide supervision in relation to their areas of expertise.

A network of CBT and family intervention tutors/supervisors has now been established throughout the Midlands. These include individuals trained in CBT and family work, including many of the graduates of the programme, who contribute to the tutor network. Each service has designated tutors with whom the teams are linked at the beginning of the course. The CBT and family tutor network has grown considerably in recent years as many more graduates of the programme have been produced. These tutor groups meet monthly and concentrate on casework.

PROGRESS TO DATE

The programme has, from its inception in 1997, trained over 150 mental health professionals from a variety of professional backgrounds. Eight non-professionals, including service consumers, have also enlisted in the programme, and the content of many of the modules has been adjusted to focus on the user perspective. Independent evaluation from the University of Durham is ongoing, but the clear finding hitherto is the widespread support for the programme in each service throughout the West Midlands Region. The interviews with the Chief Executive of each mental health service revealed a strong and genuine understanding and commitment to the programme. The evaluation specifically measured changes in a consumer-focused value base, which tracked an overwhelming change in a positive direction and an increase in implementation.

The evaluation also accesses the experience of service consumers who are on the caseloads of course trainees. The confidential interviews have reported a major improvement in the collaborative approach to care and in the respect consumers feel that professionals have towards them.

Having an Impact on Practice: Some Guidelines for Effective Training Programmes

Over the past 5 years, through the organization of the two West Midlands programmes, we have become aware of the strategies that need to be employed if training is to have an impact on practice in early intervention services:

1. Training must not be viewed in isolation, but should be incorporated within a programme of service and organizational development.
2. In developing new services, the focus needs to be on the activities the teams will perform and the services they will deliver, not simply on structures. This requires a focus on team values, and skills and attitudes of staff.
3. Opportunities need to be created for people from different agencies who are involved with young people to meet together in order to gain an understanding of different organizational cultures and ways of working.
4. The training must be perceived as being sanctioned at the highest level, preferably at Department of Health or Government level.
5. Psychosocial interventions must be given a status as being 'core' rather than peripheral. As they do not traditionally have this status, it needs to be made explicit through writing their importance into business plans of organizations, into service agreements with purchasers, and into the job descriptions of staff.
6. Adequate supervisory systems must be put in place.
7. Management at all levels in organizations must be on board and in agreement with the training, and will themselves require training and support.
8. Service consumers and carers can play an important role in ensuring that psychosocial interventions are available to them.
9. Issues such as caseload size and workload must be addressed, at least in the initial period post-training, and also how crises are handled in services.
10. The implementation of programmes needs to be followed up closely over time. There is often a sense that new approaches to care are transitory, and staff go along with whatever

is 'flavour-of-the-month'. If PSI is to become integral to mental health services, the commitment to the implementation of the approach must continue over a number of years—at least 5, and more likely 7.

CONCLUSIONS

While the implementation of psychosocial approaches in early intervention will be dictated by local policies, personnel and resources, the West Midlands training programmes provide a possible example of how a strategic approach to the training of mental health professionals in consumer-based values and psychosocial intervention training can be undertaken. Undoubtedly, their success owes much to collaboration at the highest level between regional government, mental health services and the universities. The multidisciplinary ethos of the programmes has been crucial in promoting multidisciplinary respect and collaboration, and has succeeded, we believe, in promoting a genuine consumer-focused value base. Independent evaluation of both programmes clearly shows that not only are these interventions more widely practised, but this is corroborated by consumers who value the greater respect they are afforded, and the help they receive.

REFERENCES

Bailey, R., Burbach, F.R. & Lea, S.J. (2003). The ability of staff trained in family interventions to implement the approach in routine clinical practice. *Journal of Mental Health*, **12**, 131–141.

Birchwood, M., Fowler, D. & Jackson, C. (2000). *Early Intervention in Psychosis*. Chichester: John Wiley & Sons.

Chadwick, P., Birchwood, M. & Trower, P. (1996). *Cognitive Therapy for Hallucinations, Delusions and Paranoia*. Chicester: John Wiley & Sons.

Chadwick, P., Williams, C. & Mackenzie, J. (2003). Impact of case formulation in cognitive therapy for psychosis. *Behaviour Research and Therapy*, **41**, 671–680.

Department of Health (1995). *Report of a Clinical Standards Advisory Group on Schizophrenia* (Vol. 1). London: HMSO.

Department of Health (1998). *Modernising Mental Health Services: Safe, Sound and Supportive*. London: HMSO.

Department of Health (2000). *National Service Framework for Mental Health*. London: HMSO.

Department of Health (2002a). *Developing Services for Carers and Families of People with Mental Illness*. London: HMSO.

Department of Health (2002b). *Schizophrenia: Core Interventions in the Treatment and Management of Schizophrenia in Primary and Secondary Care*. London: National Institute for Clinical Excellence.

Dixon, L.B. & Lehman, A.F. (1995). Family interventions for schizophrenia. *Schizophrenia Bulletin*, **21**, 631–643.

Dixon, L., Lyles, A., Scott, J., Lehman, A., Postrado, L., Goldman, H. & McGlynn, E. (1999). Services to families of adults with schizophrenia: From treatment recommendations to dissemination. *Psychiatric Services*, **50**, 233–238.

Drayton, M., Birchwood, M. & Trower, P. (1998). Early attachment experience and recovery from psychosis. *British Journal of Clinical Psychology*, **37**, 269–284.

Durr, H. & Hahlweg, K. (1996). Familienbetreuung bei schizophrenen Patienten: Analyse des Therapieverlaufes. *Zeitschrift fur Klinische Psychologie*, **25**, 33–46.

Fadden, G. (1997). Implementation of family interventions in routine clinical practice following staff training programs: A major cause for concern. *Journal of Mental Health*, **6**, 599–612.

Fadden, G. (1998). Family Intervention. In C. Brooker & J. Repper (Eds), *Serious Mental Health Problems in the Community: Policy, Practice and Research*. London: Ballière Tindall Limited.

Fadden, G. & Birchwood, M. (2002). British models for expanding family psychoeducation in routine practice. In H.P. Lefley & D.L. Johnson (Eds), *Family Interventions in Mental Illness*. Westport, CT: Praeger.

Falloon, I.R.H., Boyd, J.L., McGill, C.W., Razani, J., Moss, M.B. & Gilderman, A.M. (1982). Family management in the prevention of exacerbations of schizophrenia: A controlled study. *New England Journal of Medicine*, **306**, 1437–1440.

Fowler, D., Garety, P. & Kuipers, E. (1995). *Cognitive Behaviour Therapy for Psychosis*. Chichester: John Wiley & Sons.

Freemantle, N., Grilli, R., Grimshaw, J.M. & Oxman, A. (1995). Implementing findings of medical research: The Cochrane Collaboration on Effective Professional Practice. *Quality in Healthcare*, **4**, 45–47.

Gillam, T., Croft, M., Fadden, G. & Corbett, K. (2003). *Child and adult interfaces project report*. MERIDEN Programme (unpublished report).

Goldstein, M.J. & Miklowitz, D.J. (1995). The effectiveness of psychoeducational family therapy in the treatment of schizophrenic disorders. *Journal of Marital and Family Therapy*, **21**, 361–376.

Grol, R. (1992). Implementing guidelines in general practice care. *Quality in Healthcare*, **1**, 184–191.

Jackson, C. & Iqbal, Z. (2000). Psychological adjustment to early psychosis. In M. Birchwood, D. Fowler & C. Jackson (Eds), *Early Intervention in Psychosis: A Guide to Concepts, Evidence and Interventions*. Chichester: John Wiley & Sons.

Jackson, H., McGorry, P., Edwards, J., Hulbert, C., Henry, L., Francey, S., Maude, D., Cocks, J., Power, P., Harrigan, S. & Dudgeon, P. (1998). Cognitively-oriented psychotherapy for early psychosis (COPE). Preliminary results. *British Journal of Psychiatry*, **172**, 93–100.

Johnson, D.L. (1994). Current issues in family research: Can the burden of mental illness be relieved? In H.P. Lefley & M. Wasow (Eds), *Helping Families Cope with Mental Illness*. Switzerland: Horwood Academic Publishers.

Kavanagh, D.J., Piatkowska, O., Clarke, D., O'Halloran, P., Manicavasagar, V., Rosen, A. & Tennant, C. (1993). Application of cognitive-behavioural family intervention for schizophrenia in multi-disciplinary teams: What can the matter be? *Australian Psychologist*, **28**, 181–188.

Kay, S.R., Fiszbein, A. & Opler, L.A. (1987). The positive and negative syndrome scale (PANSS) for schizophrenia. *Schizophrenia Bulletin*, **13**, 261–276.

Leff, J., Kuipers, L., Berkowitz, R., Eberlein-Vries, R. & Sturgeon, D. (1982). A controlled trial of social intervention in the families of schizophrenic patients. *British Journal of Psychiatry*, **141**, 121–134.

Lomas, J. (1991).Words without actions? The production, dissemination and impact of consensus recommendations. *Annual Review of Public Health*, **12**, 41.

Lehman, A.F., Steinwachs, D.M. & the Survey Co-Investigators of the PORT Project (1998). Patterns of usual care for schizophrenia: Initial results from the schizophrenia Patients Outcomes Research Team (PORT) Client Survey. *Schizophrenia Bulletin*, **24**, 11–20.

Magliano, L., Fadden, G., Madianos, M., Caldas de Almeida, J.M., Held, T., Guarneri, M., Marasco, C., Tosini, P. & Maj, M. (1998). Burden on the families of patients with schizophrenia: Results of the BIOMED 1 study. *Social Psychiatry and Psychiatric Epidemiology*, **33**, 405–412.

Mari, J.J., Adams, C.E. & Streiner, D. (1996). Family intervention for those with schizophrenia. In C. Adams, J. Mari De Jesus & P. White (Eds), *Schizophrenia Module of the Cochrane Database of Systematic Reviews, The Cochrane Library*. Oxford: The Cochrane Collaboration.

McGlashan, T.H., Levy, S.T. & Carpenter, W.T. Jr (1975). Integration and sealingover. Clinically distinct recovery styles from schizophrenia. *Archives of General Psychiatry*, **32**, 1269–1272.

Nelson, H. (1997). *Cognitive Behaviour Therapy in Schizophrenia—A Practice Manual*. Cheltenham: Stanley Thornes.

Newstead, L. & Kelly, M. (2003). Early intervention in psychosis: Who wins, who loses, who pays the price? *Journal of Psychiatric and Mental Health Nursing*, **10**, 83–88.

Palmer, C. & Fenner, J. (1999). *Getting the Message Across: Review of Research and Theory about Disseminating Information within the NHS*. London: Gaskell.

Penn, D.L. & Mueser, K.T. (1996). Research update on the psychosocial treatment of schizophrenia. *American Journal of Psychiatry*, **153**, 607–617.

Pilling, S., Bebbington, P., Kuipers, E., Garety, P., Geddes, J., Orbach, G. & Morgan, C. (2002). Psychological treatments in schizophrenia: I. Meta-analysis of family intervention and cognitive therapy. *Psychological Medicine*, **32**, 763–782.

Smith, G. & Velleman, R. (2002). Maintaining a family work service for psychosis service by recognising and addressing the barriers to implementation. *Journal of Mental Health*, **11**, 471–479.

Tait, L., Birchwood, M. & Trower, P. (2003). Predicting engagement with services for psychosis: Insight, symptoms and recovery style. *British Journal of Psychiatry*, **182**, 123–128.

Tarrier, N., Yusupoff, L., McCarthy, E., Kinney, C. & Wittkowski, A. (1998). Some reasons why patients suffering from chronic schizophrenia fail to continue in psychological treatment. *Behavioural and Cognitive Psychotherapy*, **26**, 177–181.

Thompson, K.N., McGorry, P.D. & Harrigan, S. M. (2003). Recovery style and outcome in first-episode psychosis. *Schizophrenia Research*, **62**, 31–36.

WHO (1992). *Schedules for Clinical Assessment in Neuropsychiatry*. Geneva: World Health Organization.

Index

activity scheduling 34,56
Addiction Severity Index 197
aggression
  in families 111
  reducing 12
akathesia 179
alogia 235
amphetamine 127
Antecedent and Coping Interview 49
antidepressants 12
antipsychotic medication 3, 7, 9, 95–6
  during prodrome 6
anxiety 34
  social 9, 10, 29
assertive community treatment (ACT) models of
  care 8
assertiveness training 29
assessment 26, 66–71
  cannabis and 143–6
  cognitive-behavioural therapy and 49
  family 105–6
  training 275
  see also engagement
attachment theory 85
Attenuated Psychotic Symptoms Group 24
Auditory Hallucination Subscale of the
  Psychotic Symptom Rating Scales 197

basic symptoms 32
Beck Depression Inventory (BDI) 210
  Short Form 197
Beck Hopelessness Scale (BHS) 185
behavioural strategies 34
Beliefs About Voices Questionnaire (BAVQ) 49
Benedetti, G. 81
benzodiazepines 7
biopsychosocial model 64
Bleuler, E. 216, 231, 232
borderline personality disorder 11
Brief Limited Intermittent Psychotic Symptoms
  Group (BLIPS) 24
Brief Psychiatric Rating Scale (BPRS) 159, 182,
  185, 209
  Expanded Version 196
Calgary Depression Scale (CDS) 221
Camberwell Family Interview 100
cannabis 126–7, 137–56

existing treatments 139–41
interventions 139–40
motivational interviewing 140
prevalence and correlates 137–9
psychosis and 140–1
relapse and 127, 163–4
see also Cannabis and Psychosis (CAP)
  intervention
Cannabis and Psychosis (CAP) intervention
  137, 141–52
challenges and lifestyle 151
commitment building 146–51
education resources 148
engagement and assessment/feedback 143–6
goal-setting 151
origins 141–2
phases 143–52
randomized-controlled trial 141
relapse prevention 151–2
setting 142
treatment group 142–3
Caregiver Burden Scale 113
Chestnut Lodge naturalistic study 84
childhood abuse 162–3
clinical recovery 247
clozapine 8, 10, 12, 194
  suicide and 179
cocaine 127
Cochrane plots 209
cognitive analytic therapy (CAT) 10, 11, 36, 85
cognitive-behavioural therapy (CBT) 7, 8, 13,
  15, 41–61
assessment 49
behavioural experiments 54
booster sessions 58–9
common elements 211
coping strategies and 54–6
core beliefs (schema) 56–7
definition 210–11
delusions and 51–4
distraction 55–6
emotional dysfunction and 209–28
engagement 47–8
formulating the case 50–1
hallucinations and 51–4
in implementation 266
modified 10

cognitive-behavioural therapy (CBT) (*cont.*)
  for negative symptoms 56, 235
  normalizing symptoms and education 49–50
  for prolonged recovery 194–5
  randomized-controlled trials 209-10, 211–16
  rational responses 55
  staying well 58
  for substance misuse 140, 141
  see also COPE therapy; SoCRATES study
cognitive dissonance 148
cognitive functioning, improving 11
cognitive imagery 57
cognitive interventions 169–70
cognitive restructuring 29, 32, 34
cognitive strategies 34
Cognitively Oriented Psychotherapy for Early
    Psychosis therapy *see* COPE therapy
coherence, sense of 89
collaborative empiricism 209, 211
Colombo technique 69
communication strategies 13
communication training 168
  family and 109–10
community care 4
comorbidity 9, 33–5, 112
compliance 10
  relapse and 167–8
concept mapping 181
conceptual meaning 85
concurrent syndromes 6
Conolly, John 1
continuity of care 89
COPE (Cognitively Oriented Psychotherapy for
    Early Psychosis) therapy 11, 42, 142
  adaptation 71–7
    concept 71–2
    coping enhancement 75–6
    identity 74–5
    instilling hope 73–4
    strategies for promoting 72–3
  aims 65
  assessment 66–71
    agenda for therapy 69–71
    psychological issues in recovery 66–8
    strategies 69
  in case management 76–7
  origins 64–5
  therapy overview 65–6
coping 10, 11, 109–10
  with alternative beliefs 253–4
  cognitive-behavioural therapy and 54–6
  denial as 265
  enhancement strategies 13, 31, 75–6
  maladaptive 29, 31
core beliefs (schema) 56–7
countertransference 86

crisis home 90
crisis intervention 11, 13
critical period 8, 65
cultural issues 111–12

'Dealing with Voices' handout 203–4
decisional grid 149–51
deficit, concept of 233
deficit state 230
deficit syndrome 229, 233–4
delusional thought
  cognitive-behavioural therapy and 51–4
  reality testing 31
  verbal challenge 30–1
dementia praecox 2
denial 13
  as coping style 265
depression 6, 9, 10, 23, 32–3, 178
developmental anomaly, emotional dysfunction
    and 218–20
diary use 29, 52
discourse planning 231
discrepancy 149
distraction 29, 31, 34
  cognitive-behavioural therapy and 55–6
duration of untreated psychosis (DUP) 6
dynamic psychotherapy 81–98
  antipsychotic medication 95–6
  clinical aspects 87–94
  dynamic understanding of acute psychosis
      86–7
  first meetings 87–9
  genogram 89
  historical background 81–6
  planning for near future 90–2
  problems 94–6
  recovery and post-psychotic depression 92–4
  suicidality 95
  systematic studies 82–3
  therapeutic attitude 94–5
Dysfunctional Attitudes Scale 29
dysfunctional thought record (DTR) 52
dysfunctional thoughts 29
dysphoria 179

early intervention 4–5
early psychosis as new paradigm 3–5
Early Psychosis Prevention and Intervention
    Centre (EPPIC) 64, 76, 77, 103–4, 137,
    141, 142, 158, 175, 178
early psychosis programs 102–4
Early Psychosis Treatment and Prevention
    Program (EPP) (Calgary, Canada) 102–3
education 11, 13, 30, 128–9
  family 168
ego 85

electroconvulsive therapy (ECT) 3
emotional dysfunction 216–23
  arising from developmental anomaly and
    trauma 218–20
  implications for cognitive behavioural
    therapy 220–3
  as intrinsic to psychosis 217
  as psychological reaction to psychosis 217–18
emotional recovery 251–2
emotional support 11
empathy 149
empty-chair techniques 76
engagement 26, 195–202
  barriers to 264–6
  cannabis and 143–6
  cognitive-behavioural therapy and 47–8
EPISODE II 169
exercise 29
Experience of Caregiving Inventory (ECI) 100,
  113
exposure techniques 34
expressed emotion (EE) 85, 100–1, 164, 168

Family and Friends Information Sessions 104
family conflict 111
family, early stages of psychosis and 99–135
  early psychosis programs 102–4
  family assessment 105–6
  first-episode families 101–2
  objective burden 100
  outcome 113–14
  patient rejection and 112–13
  special needs 111–13
  stage model 104–5
  subjective burden 100
family education 168
family groups 110–11
family interventions 11, 13, 101,
  106–14
family therapy 84–5
fight and flight response 28
first-episode psychosis (FEP)
  experience 64–5
  principles of treatment 6–8
Five Factor Model of personality 161
formulation
  cognitive-behavioural therapy and
    50–1
  of risk of relapse 165–70
four-column technique 76
Freud, Sigmund 2
Fromm-Reichmann, Frieda 2, 81

genogram, family 89
Global Scale of Delusions Severity
  196–7

goal-setting 29, 32, 151
group intervention 13
group psychotherapeutic intervention 117–35
  first-episode psychosis and 119–20
  psychodynamic group therapy 118–19
  psychoeducational group therapy 118
  Youth Education and Support (YES) group
    120–33
guided discovery 252

Hahlweg Rating Scale 269, 270
hallucinations
  cognitive-behavioural therapy and 51–4
  reality testing 31
  verbal challenge and 30–1
Health of the Nation Outcome Scale (HoNOS)
  181
hierarchy of needs 13
history of interventions 1–3
homelessness 8
hope 73–4, 249
hopelessness 178

identity 74–5, 124–6, 250
implementation 261–77
  barriers to engagement 264–6
  blocks to 262–6
  cognitive-behavioural therapy and 266
  planning, development and delivery 262
  psychosis as a biological disorder 263
  training 261–2, 266–7
    aims 272–3
    assessment 275
    course contents 273–5
    Meriden interventions training programme
      266, 267–8, 269–72
    progress to date 276–7
    RECOVER programme 266, 272
    staff 263–4
    support and supervision 275
insight 124, 178
InterSePT Study 179

Jackson, J. Hughlings 232

ketamine 127
knowledge deficits 50
Kraepelin, E. 2, 63, 230, 233
Krawiecka, Goldberg and Vaughn Scale,
  modified 49

Lambeth Early Onset (LEO) service 180, 186
language issues, 111–2
learning theory 85
life events, relapse and 164–5
LSD 127

mania 6
Maudsley Assessment of Delusions Schedule
    (MADS) 49, 197
meditation 29, 34
Meriden interventions training programme 266,
    267–8, 269–72
moral treatment 1
motivational interviewing 8, 34, 35, 45
    principles of 149
    for substance abuse 140, 141

narratives of possibility 248
necessity of psychological treatments 9–12
need-adapted treatment 85
needs, hierarchy of 13
negative symptoms 10, 32–3, 229–43
    cognitive-behavioural therapy and 56,
        235
    history 230–5
    treatment 235–8
negative syndrome 6
Neo-Freudians 2
Nordic Investigation of
        Psychotherapeutically-orientated treatment
        for new Schizophrenia (NIPS) 4

organic disease model for schizophrenia 2

passivity 251
peer pressure and substance use 126–8
persistent psychosis in young people 191–208
    clinical context 192
    cognitive-behavioural therapy for prolonged
        recovery 194–5
    psychological treatment 192–4
    randomized-controlled trials 193–4
    Treatment-Resistant Early Assessment Team
        (TREAT) 192
    see also systematic treatment of persistent
        psychosis (STOPP)
person schemas 72
Personal Assessment and Crisis Evaluation
    (PACE) (Melbourne) 23–36
    assessment/engagement 26
    case management 27–8
    collaborative approach 26
    comorbidity 33–5
    depression 32–3
    modules 28–35
    negative symptoms 32–3
    phases of therapy 26–7
    positive symptoms 30–2
    stress management 28–9, 33
    stress–vulnerability model of psychosis 25,
        28
    termination phase 26

treatment modules 26
treatment phase 26
Personal Questionnaire Rating Scale Technique
    (PQRST) 211, 216
personal therapy 86
personality trait, schizophrenia as 87
Pinel, P. 1
Positive and Negative Syndrome Schedule
    Scores (PANSS) 42, 44, 209, 273
positive psychosis 6
positive psychotic symptoms 10
positive symptoms 30–2
positive thought disorder 231
positive withdrawal 234
possible selves, concept of 74
post-psychotic depression (PPD) 92–4, 217–18,
    219
post-traumatic psychosis 252–3
post-traumatic stress disorder (PTSD) 9, 216,
    217, 219
predromal phase 5–6
prepsychotic phase 5–6
Present State Examination 49
Prevention and Early Intervention Program for
    Psychosis (PEPP) 133
prevention, secondary (early intervention) 4–5
problem list 48, 49
problem-solving strategies 29, 32
    family intervention and 109–10
prodromal risk, transition to psychosis,
    reduction in 12
protective withdrawal 33
psychoanalysis 2, 81–4
psychological recovery 247
psychodynamic group therapy 118–19
psychodynamic knowledge 13
psychoeducation 28, 29, 30, 33, 73, 101,
    107–9
    group therapy 118
Psychological General Well-being Scale 113
psychological intervention
    key principles 12–14
    optimal range 13–14
    sequence and phase-oriented delivery 14
psychosurgery 3
psychotherapy as phase-specific treatment 84
psychotic crisis reaction 89
Psychotic Symptom Rating Scales (PSYRATS)
    49, 211, 216
    Auditory Hallucination Subscale 197

quality of intervention 6
Quality of Life Scores 185

randomized-controlled trials
    cannabis and 141

cognitive-behavioural therapy and 209–10, 211–16
  persistent psychosis and 193–4
rational responses, cognitive-behavioural therapy and 55
reality testing, delusions and 31
RECOVER programme 266, 272
recovery 130–1, 247–54
  clinical 247
  coherent account of experience 249
  definition 247
  emotional 251–2
  hope 249
  living and coping with alternative beliefs 253–4
  medication 254–6
  narratives of possibility 248
  positive personal and social identity 250
  psychological 247
  psychosis as post-traumatic reaction 252–3
  relapse and 8–9
  responsibility for/active involvement in 250–1
  social 130–1, 247
  social identity 248
  spiritual beliefs 249–50
  supportive others 249
  themes 248–51
  vocational 11
  whole-person approach 256–7
recovery library 249
Recovery Plus Study 205
rehearsal techniques 29
relapse 157–74
  cannabis and 151–2, 163–4
  childhood abuse 162–3
  definition 160–1
  distal factors 161–2
  formulation of risk 165–70
  interpersonal stress 164–5
  life events 164–5
  proximal factors 163–5
  rates after first-episode psychosis 158–61
  recovery and 8–9
  risk factors 161–5
  substance abuse 127, 163–4
relapse prevention 12, 47, 166–70
  cognitive interventions 169–70
  compliance interventions 167–8
  early pharmacological intervention 167
  family education and communication training 168
  psychosocial 'package' approaches 168–9
relationships 128–9
  see also family
relaxation 29, 34
resistance 149

risperidone 25
Robson Self-Esteem Questionnaire 221
role-play 76

safety behaviours 217
Scale for the Assessment of Negative Symptoms 197
SCAN 273
scheduling and monitoring of mastery and pleasure activities 32
schema 56–7, 72
Searles, H. 81
Sechehaye, M. 81
self-efficacy 149
self-esteem 57
self-monitoring of symptoms 31
self-perception 148
self-stigmatization 49, 65
self-talk 29, 34
self-therapy 58
setting for meetings 87
sexual abuse 112
shared care 8, 9
sleep disturbance 23
social anxiety 9, 10, 29
social identity 248
social recovery 247
social skills 32, 130–1
SoCRATES study 42–7, 77
  acute psychotic symptoms 46
  detention 45–6
  developmental and familial issues 47
  disagreements regarding treatment/diagnosis 45–6
  drugs and alcohol 45
  keeping well 46–7
  location, length and timing of sessions 44–5
  rapid resolution of symptoms 46–7
  treatment approaches 42–4
  treatment modifications 44–7
Socratic dialogue 199
Socratic questioning 31
spiritual beliefs 249–50
staff training 263–4
Stauder's Lethal Catatonia 177
stigma 5, 10, 11, 13, 129–30
  self- 49, 65
Strauss 232
stress
  family 6, 8
  interpersonal 6, 164–5
  management 28–9, 33, 34
  monitoring 29
  relapse and 164–5
  vocational 6
stress-inoculation training 34

stress-reduction techniques 31
stress–vulnerability model of psychosis 25, 28,
    73–4, 77, 85, 108
substance abuse 6, 8, 9, 10, 13, 34
    cognitive-behavioural therapy 140, 141
    comorbid 8, 12
    motivational interviewing for 140, 141
    peer pressure and 126–8
    psychosis and 140–1
    relapse and 127, 163–4
    see also cannabis
Substance Use Disorder (SUD) 126
suicide 8, 9, 95
    in first-episode psychosis 178–9
    LifeSPAN model 179–86
    patterns 175–8
    prevention 12, 175–89
    zoning system of care 180, 186
Suicide Ideation Questionnaire (SIQ) 185
Sullivan, Harry Stack 2, 4
systematic treatment of persistent psychosis
        (STOPP) 142, 191, 195–202
    engagement in psychological therapy
        195–202
    implementation 202–4
    phases
        collaborative working relationships
            development 196–8
        exploring and coping with psychosis
            198–200
        finishing and moving on 201–2
        strengthening capacity to relate to others
            200–1
    rating scales 196–7
    see also COPE

tardive dyskinesia 7
therapeutic alliance, development of 9–10
thought broadcasting 29
thought stopping 34
time-line technique 75
time management 29
timing of intervention 6
training 261–2, 266–7
    aims 272–3
    assessment 275
    course contents 273–5

Meriden interventions training programme
        266, 267–8, 269–72
    progress to date 276–7
    RECOVER programme 266, 272
    staff 263–4
    support and supervision 275
Trait and State Risk Factor Group 24
transference 86
trauma 10
    emotional dysfunction and 218–20
treatment resistance 9, 10
Treatment-Resistant Early Assessment Team
        (TREAT) 192

Ugelstad, E. 4
ultra high risk (UHR) patients 23
    identification of 24
    negative symptoms 32
    positive symptoms 30
    symptoms described by 25, 26

verbal challenge, delusions and 30–1
vocational failure 8
vocational recovery 11
vulnerability–stress model see stress–
        vulnerability model

whole-person approach to recovery 256–7
Wing, J.K. 232
withdrawal 31, 255

York Retreat 1
Youth Education and Support (YES) group
        120–2
    early warning signs/early intervention 131–2
    evaluation 133
    identity 124–6
    introduction to group therapy 122–3
    peer pressure and substance use 126–8
    rationale and content of sessions 122–33
    recovery and social skills 130–1
    relationships/education 128–9
    review/celebration 132–3
    stigma and strategies 129–30
Youth Suicide Prevention Strategy 180

Zoning System of care 180, 186

CPSIA information can be obtained at www.ICGtesting.com
Printed in the USA
BVOW10s0417211015

423388BV00007B/28/P